TITANIC
— MINUTE BY MINUTE —

TITANIC

— MINUTE BY MINUTE —

JONATHAN MAYO

First published in 2016 by Short Books
Unit 316, Screenworks
22 Highbury Grove
London N5 2ER

10 9 8 7 6 5

A CIP catalogue record for this book is available from the British Library.

ISBN 978-1-78072-269-6

Printed and bound in Great Britain by CPI Group (UK) Ltd, Croydon, CR0 4YY

Image credits:

Cover Photo
Bow view of the White Star Line's Olympic class ship the *Olympic*, sister ship of the *Titanic*, in Thompson Graving Dock
HOYFM.HW.H1825 © National Museums Northern Ireland, Collection: Harland & Wolff, Ulster Folk & Transport Museum

Page 8 (Introduction)
The *Titanic* is pulled away by tugs from the White Star Dock at Southampton
Courtney #6 © National Museums Northern Ireland, Collection: Ulster Folk & Transport Museum

Pages 24-5, *Titanic* profile and boat deck plan by Two Associates

Page 26 (Sunday 14th April 1912)
The first-class reading and writing room on the *Titanic*
Picture ID: 20 1 31, © Fr. Browne S.J. Collection

Page 126 (Monday 15th April 1912)
Wireless operator Harold Bride at work in the *Titanic*'s radio room
Picture ID: 20 1 27, © Fr. Browne S.J. Collection

Page 244 (In the Lifeboats)
A lone *Titanic* officer walking along A-deck
Picture ID: 20 1 19, © Fr. Browne S.J. Collection

Page 264 (After 1912...)
Titanic survivors Charlotte Collyer and her daughter Marjorie
Library of Congress, Prints & Photographs Division, LC-DIG-ggbain-19397

The 'Minute by Minute' format is applied to this publication with the permission of TBI Media

TBI ✳
The Big Idea

For Hannah and Charlie

Contents

Noon, 10th April 1912. The Titanic is pulled away by tugs from the White Star Dock at Southampton.

Introduction

At 5.47am on 22nd January 1909, 24-year-old Jack Binns, the wireless telegraph operator on the White Star Line's passenger ship the *Republic*, was just turning in after working all night transmitting telegrams, when he heard the distant blast of a ship's foghorn. His liner, one of the finest in the White Star Line's fleet, had left New York the previous day bound for the Mediterranean, and was sailing in dense fog in busy shipping lanes 100 miles east of the coast of Massachusetts. The *Republic* sounded her foghorn in reply, and reversed her engines. However, the other ship, the liner *Florida*, New York bound with over 1000 immigrants on board, did not turn to starboard as the regulations stated but ploughed straight on.

The *Florida* hit the *Republic*'s side, making a huge hole in her hull, above and below the waterline. Seawater flooded her engine room. The crumpled bow of the *Florida* proceeded to scour the *Republic*'s main deck. Two sailors were killed instantly on the *Republic* and four on the *Florida*; half of Jack Binns' wireless hut was ripped away – but he survived.

Despite the damage, Binns was able to repair his apparatus and send out 'CQD' distress signals, staying at his post for

18 hours. Binns worked for the pioneering wireless company Marconi, and 'CQD', which stood for 'all stations: distress', was their version of 'SOS'. The White Star Line's passenger ship *Baltic* and about a dozen other vessels arrived in time to transfer the *Republic*'s passengers before she sank in 40 fathoms. The rescued passengers were then taken back to New York.

Jack Binns was hailed a hero and became a legend among the Marconi Company's young operators, earning the nickname 'CQD Binns'. He wrote up his story the day after the disaster for the *New York Times*; a tickertape parade was held in his honour, and a silent movie was made called *CQD or Saved by Wireless*. Binns would later successfully sue the film company Vitagraph, claiming the actor portraying him made him look ridiculous, 'smiling and smoking a cigarette, and winking and making grimaces'.

At the time of the sinking of the *Republic*, on slipway 3 in the Harland and Wolff shipyard in Belfast – the same yard that had built the *Republic* – the keel of the latest White Star Line ship, the *Titanic*, was being laid. The loss of the *Republic* did not give the *Titanic*'s designers pause for thought – far from being seen as a warning, the incident only served to reinforce their confidence in their ships. After all, the White Star Line's safety record was extremely good. Since 1902 they had carried 2,179,594 passengers with only two deaths – the men on the *Republic*.

The main conclusions drawn from the collision were that modern liners, even if seriously damaged, sink slowly, allowing plenty of time for passengers to be transferred to other ships. Also, that ships with wireless on board are able to summon help quickly. Both conclusions encouraged the idea among all shipbuilders and ship owners that lifeboats for every passenger were unnecessary. On that foggy January day off the coast of

Massachusetts, the *Republic* had enough lifeboats for only half her passengers.

At the beginning of the 20th century, it was widely accepted that accidents happened in the fledgling technologies of the motor car and the aeroplane; for example, on the *Titanic*, the Ryerson family was travelling home early because their son had been killed in a car accident, and author Helen Candee because her son had been injured in a plane crash. However, liners were considered part of a reliable and long-standing seafaring tradition, constantly updated with the latest technological innovations. What happened to the *Republic* didn't alter the public's confidence in ocean travel.

The sinking of the *Titanic* is so familiar to us that it's hard to imagine what a shock it must have been in April 1912. One simple, but telling, illustration of its impact is a homemade inscription on the outside wall of a house in the Norfolk Broads. Scratched neatly and deeply into the Victorian brick are the words: '14th April 1912. The *Titanic* has sunk with 1500 lives lost.' It was such shattering news, that the householder felt that they had to get out a nail, and mark the moment for posterity.

Edward Talbot, bishop of Winchester, preaching in Southampton a few days after the sinking, said it was 'a mighty lesson against our confidence and trust in the strength of machinery and money'.

The widespread shock very swiftly turned to a grim fascination with the details of the sinking. After some of the bodies of passengers and crew were brought ashore at Halifax, Nova Scotia, the local police had to burn the clothes to stop souvenir hunters stealing them. Within a month of the disaster, a film called *Saved from the Titanic* was released, starring Dorothy Gibson, one of the survivors, who wore the same dress she had on that night.

The reason this fascination with the *Titanic* has endured is very much to do with the length of time it took her to sink. If she had survived only 15 minutes, the event would have been remembered as a terrible maritime disaster, but there wouldn't have been the scope for all the *Titanic* films and none of the *Titanic* literature. Because she sank in two hours and 40 minutes, there was time for many terrible and poignant dramas to unfold, and for 710 people (a shamefully small number nonetheless) to survive to tell the world what had happened. Each subsequent generation has asked themselves, what would I have done? Would I have forced my way into a lifeboat? Would I have stayed with my husband if we couldn't both be saved? Would I have prayed – or got drunk?

There is fascination too in how, during those hours between collision and rescue, the world of 1912 was shaken up. The *Titanic* was constructed in a way that kept the upper, middle and working classes apart, and also separated the passengers from most of the crew. The collision with the iceberg meant that, in the lifeboats, New York millionaires were rowing alongside Lebanese immigrants; grimy firemen were comforted by genteel governesses; honeymoon couples were sitting next to grieving widows. The strict dress codes that dominated society in 1912 became irrelevant – women forgot their hats for the first time in their lives, and wore fur coats over nightclothes; men took to the boats wearing slippers and pyjamas.

There are so many accounts from survivors that it's possible to piece together a sequence of events, thanks to the clinical observations of passengers like Lawrence Beesley and Archibald Gracie. But a timeline poses a number of challenges when telling the story of a disaster such as the sinking of the *Titanic*. Not everyone carried a timepiece. The courageous Fred Barrett told the British inquiry, 'As a rule a stoker never carries a watch when he is at work.' Second Officer Charles Lightoller was in such a rush to help on deck that he left his wristwatch in his cabin. Most of the *Titanic*'s crew and passengers did carry watches – including many women, as it was fashionable in 1912 to wear wristwatches or have timepieces as brooches. When I have come across interesting events with little indication of when they took place, I have estimated the time.

The research of Samuel Halpern into the chronology of events was particularly useful.

Accounts from the same eyewitness were sometimes contradictory, for example 17-year-old Jack Thayer writing eight days after the disaster, asserted that before he and his friend Milton Long jumped from the ship, 'we did not give any messages for home, because neither of us thought we would get back'. In 1940 he wrote: 'we sent messages through each other to our families.' I've chosen to go with the accounts that were written closest to the sinking, therefore freshest in the survivor's mind.

The transcriptions of the US Senate Inquiry and British Board of Trade Inquiry were a goldmine of small details and gripping tales. Dialogue is taken from the transcripts of the inquiries as well as the many autobiographies, books, articles and interviews given by survivors.

Some accounts of the disaster were spiced up by American and British newspaper reporters, keen to outdo each other for stories of heroism and cowardice, but they rarely ring true.

All accounts of the sinking of the *Titanic* face the problem of the distortion of hindsight. I have tried to follow the advice of the survivor Lawrence Beesley, who as early as 1912 recognised how easily those fascinated by the *Titanic* can rush to judgement:

'So that if the reader will come and stand with the crowd on deck, he must first rid himself entirely of the knowledge that the *Titanic* has sunk... he must get rid of any foreknowledge of disaster to appreciate why people acted as they did.'

Description of the *Titanic*

In the summer of 1907 Bruce Ismay, the chairman and managing director of the White Star Line, together with Lord Pirrie, chairman of the world's biggest shipyard, Harland and Wolff, dreamed up the idea of three colossal ships, the *Olympic*, the *Titanic* and the *Gigantic* (later renamed the *Britannic*), that would outclass anything their rivals the Cunard Line possessed. In 1906 Cunard had launched two 'superliners', the *Lusitania* and the *Mauretania*, but the White Star Line's new *Olympic* class would be 100 feet longer and more luxurious.

Harland and Wolff was the largest shipbuilder in the world. Most shipyards just built the hull, but Harland and Wolff also built the engines, boilers and the other mechanical components. Over 15,000 workers were employed to build the *Olympic* and *Titanic*, side by side on slips 2 and 3, beneath a structure known as the Great Gantry that dominated the skyline of Belfast.

31st May 1911 was a momentous day – the *Olympic* was completed and officially handed over to the White Star Line, and the *Titanic*, already known as 'the *Olympic* perfected' was launched. One hundred thousand people lined the banks of the River Lagan and watched from especially built grandstands, or climbed rooftops and masts. The Giant Gantry had a large Union Flag and a Stars and Stripes hanging from it, as well as signal flags spelling out 'Success'. The superstructure atop the *Titanic* was newly painted in white, and the ship's hull was black, with dark red below the waterline.

At 12.05pm a red flag was raised on the *Titanic*'s stern, as a signal to shipping on the river to get well clear. At 12.10pm a rocket was fired, indicating five minutes to go. Underneath the hull a crew of painters hastily touched up marks left as the wooden supports were knocked away; workmen ran clear, some stopping to pick up their tools as their foremen shouted, 'Never mind the hammers! Hurry up!'

At 12.14pm a second rocket exploded – the signal to launch. There was no champagne bottle smashed against the hull – at Harland and Wolff, ships were just 'let go'. The valves of the hydraulic triggers holding the *Titanic* opened, and for a moment the great ship didn't move. Then the workers on her decks felt a tremor, and cheered as she began to slide over the 21 tons of tallow and soap that had been spread on the slipway to ease her journey to the water. Their cheers were joined by whistles and sirens from steamers on the river. After a journey lasting 62 seconds, the *Titanic* entered the water.

At this point the *Titanic* was an empty shell. Her first destination was the fitting-out jetty, where she would be brought to life. Harland and Wolff workers had a 300-page 'builders' specification book' that covered everything from descriptions of sofas and writing tables to the ventilation of the mail room on G-deck.

Over the next few months, scores of companies helped fit out the *Titanic*. Perry & Co. of Bond Street provided a 21-light candelabra for the grand staircase; Royal Crown Derby chinaware for the à la carte restaurant; Henry Wilson & Co. of Liverpool the kitchen equipment, and R. Waygood and Co. the passenger and goods lifts; lifebelts came from Fosbery of London; books and magazines for the libraries were supplied by the *Times*' book club. The fitting-out proceeded smoothly, with only the occasional hiccup. An unreliable fabric supplier prompted an internal memo from Harland and Wolff's interior decorating department: 'Their blankets and quilts arrived last week, before we really needed them. And now we have to wait to finish the settee for the restaurant reception room. Really!'

On 2nd April 1912, the *Titanic* successfully carried out her sea trials in Belfast Lough, which included manoeuvring at different speeds and an emergency stop. She rode high in the water, as her bunkers were not yet full of coal. With her tilted funnels and sleek lines (Harland and Wolff ships were influenced by yacht designs), all observers agreed that the *Titanic* looked magnificent. A thin gold line added to the hull's upper edge completed the White Star Line's service colours. The Board of Trade surveyor Francis Carruthers was happy to hand over a signed and dated certificate that the *Titanic* was 'good for one year from today, 2.4.12'. At 8pm the same day she sailed under the command of Captain Edward J. Smith to Southampton from where she would start her maiden voyage.

The *Titanic* was 882 feet 9 inches long and 92 feet wide; the top of the bridge was 105 feet above the bottom of the keel, and her hull was held together by over three million rivets whose weight alone was more than 1200 tons. The *Titanic* was exactly the same size as the *Olympic*; what made her the largest ship in the world was the fact that modifications to her hull made her 2% heavier – her gross weight was 46,328 tons.

The greatest amount of space on the ship was given over to her first-class passengers. Their accommodation was spread over five decks – A down to E, and access was by two grand staircases, several smaller staircases and three electric lifts. The *Oceanic*, launched in 1870, the first ship made for the White Star Line by the Harland and Wolff shipyard, did away with the tradition copied from the Royal Navy of placing the best cabins at the stern. From then on, all White Star first-class cabins were amidships, away from the noise of the propellers, where the heaving effect from the waves was least felt.

First-class passengers were provided with a dining saloon, an à la carte restaurant, a lounge, a lending library, a barber shop, a dark room, a squash court, a Turkish bath and the world's first on-board swimming pool with 'dressing boxes and fresh water showers'. (Not everything was perfection on board – shortly after leaving Belfast for Southampton, the *Titanic*'s masseuse, Maud Slocombe, spotted a half-eaten sandwich in the Turkish bath, left behind by a shipyard worker.)

The second-class accommodation was further forward in the middle three decks, and its passengers had their own dining saloon, smoking room and library.

The three middle decks aft, and the lowest deck forward and aft were for third-class accommodation. Their smoking room bar was towards the stern and their dining saloon two decks below the first-class dining saloon. Third-class passengers could exercise on the two open well decks and the poop deck at the stern; second and first class had promenade decks on B-deck and the boat deck.

The crew's quarters were on E-deck, separated from the passengers' accommodation and close to a wide corridor nicknamed 'Scotland Road', after a main street in Liverpool (the officers called it 'Park Lane'.)

The heart of the *Titanic* was her engine room, with 29 boilers heated by 159 furnaces – each filled by shovel. Nearly 600 tons of coal were needed to keep her running at 22 knots. The engines provided 55,000 horse power for three massive propellers, as well as electricity for anything from the ship's 10,000 lights to the kitchen mincing machines.

The Passengers

The *Titanic* had first-class passengers on board who made the transatlantic trip many times each year; she also carried immigrants with a one-way ticket, with all their possessions in bags and trunks, leaving the old world for the new. Some of those millionaires in first class had grandparents or great-grandparents who had travelled in similar poverty and with similar hopes, only a few decades before.

The migrants on board the *Titanic* included about 80 Lebanese and a dozen Armenians who had to bribe the governing Turkish authorities in order to escape; Swedes and Norwegians who first came by boat to Hull and then by train to Southampton, plus those who had a more straightforward passage – Germans, Irish and British. There were very few Eastern Europeans on the White Star Line ships, as the company thought them 'objectionable travellers'.

The third-class cabins on the *Titanic* were filled with a wide variety of tradespeople: blacksmiths, farm workers, boxers, bakers, carpenters, barmen and seamstresses.

Many had never seen the sea, let alone such a magnificent ship as the *Titanic*. For some, the voyage was their first holiday.

Second class was full of teachers, clergymen, missionaries, engineers and shopkeepers – as well as some of the servants of those travelling in first class.

The crew of the *Titanic* numbered almost 900, and was divided into three departments – Deck, Victualling and Engine. The Deck crew consisted of seven ship's officers, the surgeon and assistant surgeon, seven quartermasters, six look-outs, two mess stewards, two masters-of-arms, a boatswain, a lamp trimmer, a storekeeper, 29 able seamen and two window cleaners.

The Victualling Department had 431 in the catering crew

– including a roast cook, a vegetable cook and a 'Hebrew cook'; there were 290 stewards and stewardesses, a matron, five postal clerks and two telegraph operators – who because they worked for Marconi had an 'M' in gold on their caps rather than the White Star Line flag. The size of the Victualling Department reflected the importance the White Star Line gave to looking after the needs of their passengers. Telephones were installed in every first-class cabin, so there had to be plenty of staff on hand to respond to each request.

The *Titanic* relied on manual labour to move the required 600 tons of coal a day her engines needed. The Engine Department had 280 men – 13 leading firemen, 162 firemen (also known as stokers), 72 trimmers and 33 greasers. The greasers lubricated the engines, while trimmers shovelled coal out of the bunkers and delivered it at top speed in heavy barrows to the firemen who then shovelled it into the furnaces for seven minutes, cleared white-hot clinkers for seven minutes and then raked the ashes for a further seven minutes. The firemen rested every 21 minutes until a gong sounded and the cycle started again. They worked in four-hour shifts, twice a day.

The leading firemen monitored steam pressure, and banged the metal stokehold floor with a shovel when a furnace needed attention. Most of the Engine crew had a rag tied around their necks to collect sweat. They would suck on one end of the moist rag to stop them drinking large amounts of water, which would give them stomach cramps.

A resident of Southampton described the firemen's return after a voyage: 'They all came home like walking skeletons, and they had one glorious booze-up, which led to fighting – and then off they went again.'

Cast of Main Characters

Titanic Officers

Edward J. Smith – captain
Henry Wilde – chief officer
William Murdoch – first officer
Charles Lightoller – second officer

Herbert Pitman – third officer
Joseph Boxhall – fourth officer
Harold Lowe – fifth officer
James Moody – sixth officer

Titanic Deck Department

Arthur Bright – quartermaster
Frederick Fleet – lookout
Albert Haines – boatswain's mate
Robert Hichens – quartermaster
George Hogg – lookout
Archie Jewell – lookout
Thomas Jones – able seaman
Reginald Lee – lookout
William Lyons – able seaman
Alfred Olliver – quartermaster

Dr William O'Loughlin – surgeon
Frank Osman – able seaman
Albert Pearcy – steward
Walter Perkis – quartermaster
John Poingdestre – able seaman
George Rowe – quartermaster
Joseph Scarrott – able seaman
Dr John Simpson – assistant surgeon
George Symons – lookout
Walter Wynn – quartermaster

Titanic Victualling Department

Reginald Barker – assistant purser
George Beedem – bedroom steward
Harold Bride – wireless operator
Henry Etches – steward
Percy Fletcher – bugler
Violet Jessop – stewardess
Charles Joughin – chief baker
Thomas Kelland – library steward
Thomas McCawley – gymnasium steward
Herbert McElroy – chief purser
Evelyn Marsden – stewardess

Paul Maugé – à la carte restaurant maître d'
Jack Phillips – wireless operator
Frank Prentice – storekeeper
Frederick Ray – steward
Annie Robinson – stewardess
Pierre Rousseau – à la carte restaurant chef
Mary Sloan – stewardess
John Stewart – steward
Robert Wareham – steward
Joseph Wheat – steward
Frederick Wright – squash attendant

Titanic Engine Department

Frederick Barrett – fireman
George Beauchamp – fireman
Thomas Dillon – engine room trimmer
Alfred Evans – lookout
Herbert Harvey – engineer

Samuel Hemming – lamp trimmer
James Hesketh – junior second engineer
Walter Hurst – greaser
Jonathan Shepherd – junior assistant
    engineer

Titanic Mail Room Clerks

William Gwinn, John March, John Smith, James Williamson, Oscar Woody

Titanic Band

Theo Brailey – pianist
Roger Bricoux – cellist
Fred Clarke – bass violinist
Wallace Hartley – violinist and leader

Jock Hume – violinist
Georges Krins – violinist
Percy Taylor – pianist
John Wesley Woodward – cellist

Titanic First-Class Passengers

Thomas Andrews – managing director of Harland and Wolff
John Jacob Astor IV – millionaire

Madeleine Astor – wife of John Jacob Astor IV
Léontine 'Ninette' Aubart – mistress of Benjamin Guggenheim
Helen Beckwith – girlfriend of Karl Behr
Richard, Sallie and Helen Beckwith – businessman and his wife and daughter
Karl Behr – tennis player and boyfriend of Helen Beckwith
Helen and Dickenson Bishop – honeymoon couple
Margaret 'Molly' Brown – suffragette and wife of mine owner J.J. Brown
Major Archibald Butt – aide to President Taft
Helen Candee – author
William, Lucile and Billy Carter – Pennsylvania businessman and his family
Eleanor Cassebeer – returning to the US after visiting her son in Europe
Virginia Clark – returning home to Los Angeles
Thornton and Orian Davidson – businessman and his wife, the daughter of Charles and
    Clara Hays
Washington and Ruth Dodge – banker and his wife
Walter and Mahala Douglas – industrialist and his wife
Sir Cosmo Duff Gordon – sportsman
Lady Lucy Duff Gordon – clothes designer
Elizabeth Eustis and Martha Eustis Stephenson – sisters travelling home to Massachusetts
Edith Evans – travelling home to New York City
Margaret Fleming – secretary to Marian Thayer
Mary Fortune – travelling with her husband Mark and their daughters
Laura 'Franks' Francatelli – secretary to Lucy Duff Gordon
Marguerite Frölicher – travelling to New York to meet her fiancé
Dr Henry, Clara and Isaac Frauenthal – orthopaedic surgeon and his wife and brother
Dorothy Gibson – silent movie actress
Victor Giglio – Benjamin Guggenheim's secretary
Colonel Archibald Gracie – amateur historian
Margaret Graham – young American travelling with her mother Edith and governess
Benjamin Guggenheim – millionaire
Henry B. and Renée Harris – Broadway producer and his wife
Bruce Ismay – chairman and managing director of the White Star Line
Charles and Clara Hays – the president of the Grand Trunk Railroad and his wife
Milton Long – gentleman of leisure
Roberta Maioni – maid to the Countess of Rothes
Frank Millet – artist and close friend of Major Archibald Butt
Philipp Mock – travelling with his sister Emma Schabert
Alfred Nourney – the self-styled 'Baron von Drachstedt'
Major Arthur Peuchen – businessman and yachtsman
George Rheims – businessman
Edith Rosenbaum – fashion journalist writing under the name Edith Russell
George Rosenshine – ostrich feather importer
Lucy, Countess of Rothes – meeting Earl of Rothes in New York
Martin Rothschild – clothes manufacturer
Arthur and Emily Ryerson, with Suzette, Emily and John – lawyer and his wife and
    children
Emma Schabert – travelling with her brother Phillipp Mock
Frederick K. Seward – lawyer
Elizabeth Shutes – governess to Margaret Graham
William Sloper – stockbroker and friend of Dorothy Gibson
James Clinch Smith – friend of Archibald Gracie
William Stead – journalist
Isidor and Ida Straus – owner of Macy's and his wife

Elmer Taylor – businessman travelling with Fletcher Williams
Jack Thayer – son of John Thayer and Marian Thayer
John and Marian Thayer – vice-president of the Pennsylvania railroad and his wife
Maybelle Thorne – travelling with George Rosenshine
George, Eleanor and Harry Widener – banker and streetcar magnate, his wife and son
Charles Williams – travelling from Geneva
Fletcher Williams – businessman travelling with Elmer Taylor
Richard Williams – tennis player and son of Charles Williams
Hugh Woolner – businessman
Jay Yates – gambler

Titanic Second-Class Passengers
Lawrence Beesley – schoolteacher
Kate Buss – travelling to the US to marry her fiancé Samuel Willis
Reverend Ernest and Lillian Carter – Anglican vicar and his wife
Sidney Collett – theology student
Harvey, Charlotte and Marjorie Collyer – emigrating to a fruit farm in the US
William Harbeck – filmmaker
Benjamin, Esther and Eva Hart – emigrating to Winnipeg
Masabumi Hosono – railway official
Michel Navratil (Hoffman) – fleeing to the US with his sons Michel and Edmond
Douglas Norman – electrical engineer and pianist
Elizabeth Nye – travelling home to New York
Imanita Shelley and Lutie Parrish – mother and daughter
Leopold and Mathilde Weisz – stonemason and his wife emigrating to Quebec
Marion Wright – emigrating to the US to marry her fiancé Arthur
Henriette Yrois – model and lover of William Harbeck

Titanic Third-Class Passengers
Rhoda Abbott – returning to the US with sons Rossmore and Eugene
Olaus Abelseth – farmer returning to the US with his cousin Peter and brother-in-law
    Sigurd
Leah Aks – returning to the US with her baby son Frank
Daniel Buckley – farm labourer emigrating to the US
Jeremiah Burke – farm labourer emigrating to the US
Gurshon 'Gus' Cohen – printer emigrating to the US
Eugene Daly – uilleann piper emigrating to the US
Maggie Daly – emigrating to the US with her cousin Eugene
Frank, Emily and Frankie Goldsmith – toolmaker emigrating with his family to the US
The Goodwin family – emigrating to Niagara Falls
Joseph Hyman – picture framer emigrating to the US
Bertha Mulvihill – travelling with Maggie and Eugene Daly, emigrating to the U.S.
Sahid, Waika and Maria Nackid – emigrating to the U.S. from the Lebanon
Julius Sap – farm hand emigrating to the U.S.

Californian Crew
Stanley Lord – captain	James Gibson – apprentice officer
Herbert Stone – second officer	Cyril Evans – wireless operator
Charles Groves – third officer	Ernest Gill – assistant engineer

Carpathia Officers
Arthur Rostron – captain	James Bisset – second officer
H.V. Dean – first officer	Harold Cottam – wireless operator

Glossary

Aft/abaft – towards the after part, or stern, of the ship. The phrase applies all over the vessel, i.e. moving aft.

Afterbridge – a raised platform towards the stern used to supervise docking operations.

Amidships – in, or towards the middle of the ship.

Beam – the width of the vessel.

Bow – the forward end of a vessel, beginning where the hull arches inwards.

Bridge – the control centre for the ship.

Bulkhead – watertight divisions inside the hull.

Companionway – a stairway leading from one deck to another.

Cutter – a small rowing boat, similar to a lifeboat.

Davit – a small crane for loading cargo and launching lifeboats.

Falls – ropes attached to a davit.

Fathom – a measurement of depth. 1 fathom = 6 feet.

Fore – the front of the ship.

Gunwales – the upper edge of the side of a boat.

Head – the fore part of a vessel.

Helm – the steering wheel.

Hull – the body of the ship.

Keel – the central steel beam running from the bow to the stern around which a ship is built.

Knot – a unit of speed; 1 nautical mile per hour = 1.3 mph.

Log – an instrument for ascertaining the ship's speed and the distance run.

Poop deck – the raised aftermost deck of the vessel.

Port – the left-hand side of the vessel, when facing the bow.

Starboard – the right-hand side of the vessel, when facing the bow.

Stateroom – a de luxe cabin.

Stern – the after, or rear, end of a vessel.

Stokehold – the compartment on the ship where the boilers and furnaces are housed.

Well deck – open deck lower than the decks either side.

Watertight doors – mechanically operated doors giving access through watertight bulkheads

The *Titanic* – Profile View

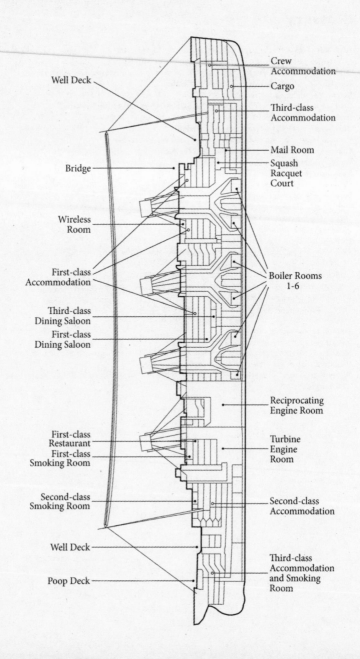

Crew Accommodation

Cargo

Third-class Accommodation

Mail Room

Squash Racquet Court

Well Deck

Bridge

Wireless Room

First-class Accommodation

Third-class Dining Saloon

First-class Dining Saloon

Boiler Rooms 1-6

Reciprocating Engine Room

First-class Restaurant

First-class Smoking Room

Turbine Engine Room

Second-class Smoking Room

Second-class Accommodation

Well Deck

Poop Deck

Third-class Accommodation and Smoking Room

The *Titanic* – Boat Deck

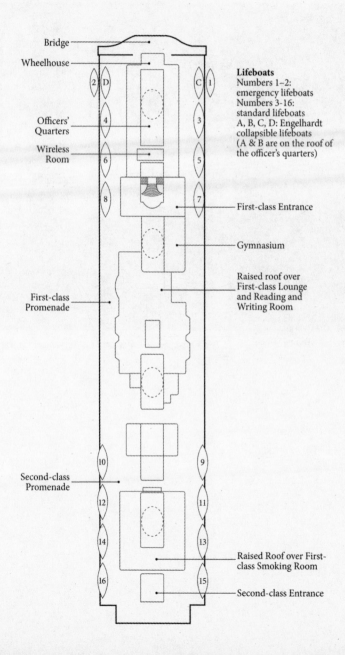

Bridge

Wheelhouse

2 D

C 1

Lifeboats
Numbers 1–2:
emergency lifeboats
Numbers 3-16:
standard lifeboats
A, B, C, D: Engelhardt
collapsible lifeboats
(A & B are on the roof of
the officer's quarters)

Officers'
Quarters

4

3

Wireless
Room

6

5

8

7

First-class Entrance

Gymnasium

Raised roof over
First-class Lounge
and Reading and
Writing Room

First-class
Promenade

Second-class
Promenade

10

9

12

11

14

13

Raised Roof over First-
class Smoking Room

16

15

Second-class Entrance

The first-class reading and writing room on the Titanic.

Sunday 14th April 1912

Midnight Titanic *Bridge Time – 8 Bells, Change of Watch*

In the middle of the North Atlantic, a small bottle is bobbing in the water. Inside it is a piece of paper with a message written in pencil:

13/4/1912

From *Titanic*

Goodbye all
Burke of Glanmire
Cork

The man who wrote the note is 19-year-old Irishman, Jeremiah Burke. He is currently many miles to the west of his floating bottle, in his third-class cabin on the world's most famous ship, the *Titanic*. Jeremiah is a farm labourer hoping to start a new life in America, joining his two older sisters Mary and Nellie who have settled in Boston. Mary sent Jeremiah the money to pay for his ticket.

The sharp bow of the *Titanic* is cutting through the cold water at about 22 knots, sending a plume of spray arcing outwards on either side. She is the largest mobile object on the planet.

The *Titanic*'s brass bell, hanging outside the windows of the bridge, rings out eight times, signalling the end of the four-hour watch. At the same time, the ship's clocks are being adjusted to allow for the change in time zone as she sails westward.

> *On the* Titanic *the bell strikes don't relate to the number of the hour; they are rung every half-hour across a four-hour watch, culminating in eight bells. The half-hour strikes are a tradition from the days of the 30-minute hourglass; but the* Titanic *also has the latest electric clock technology. On westbound voyages White Star Line vessels adjust their clocks at midnight by anything from 35 to 45 minutes, depending on the distance the ship is estimated to make by noon the next day. The* Titanic *has 48 clocks throughout the ship, which are slaved to a pair of master clocks secured in watertight cases in the chart room. This is the* Titanic's *Bridge Time.*

On the bridge, Fourth Officer Joseph Boxhall and Sixth Officer James Moody are taking over from Third Officer Herbert Pitman and Fifth Officer Harold Lowe. The bridge is completely dark. Any light will disrupt the men's night vision. The shutters in the wheelhouse are closed, shielding the faint light illuminating the compass. The officers talk about how the ship is running, and the so-called 'items of interest' – the weather, and the *Titanic*'s course and speed. When the eyes of the new watch have become accustomed to the dark, the others will turn in for the night.

The *Titanic*'s captain, the legendary Edward J. Smith, is in his quarters just behind the bridge.

> *Captain Edward Smith was described by the* Titanic's *second officer, Charles Lightoller, as 'tall, full whiskered and broad… with a pleasant, quiet voice and invariable smile'. He is affectionately*

known as 'E.J.'. His other nickname is 'the millionaire's captain' because of his popularity among the wealthy transatlantic passengers. Smith is famous for having been with the White Star Line for 30 years, captaining 17 of their ships and sailing two million miles. Smith is the commodore of their fleet on a salary of £1250 a year, with a bonus of £1000 on condition that the ships reach port in good order.

Interviewed by the New York Times in 1907, Captain Smith spoke about his career:

'When anyone asks me how to describe my experience of nearly 40 years at sea, I merely say "uneventful". Of course there have been winter gales, and storms and fog and the like, but in all my experience, I have never been in any accident of any sort worth speaking about.'

That was not entirely true. White Star Line ships under his command ran aground in 1889, 1890 and 1909. In 1901 the Majestic, and in 1906 the Baltic, both had serious on-board fires. Yet Smith remained well respected and trusted by the White Star Line.

The bridge is the centre of Captain Smith's world. Situated at the forward end of the Titanic's boat deck, it has two wings open to the elements, and engine order telegraphs which connect the bridge with the engine room, to allow the officers to communicate the desired speed. Within the bridge is a wheelhouse containing the main ship's wheel and a steering compass. On its rear wall are two clocks – one showing Greenwich Mean Time and the other the local ship's time – and an inclinometer showing how many degrees the ship is listing to port or starboard.

There is a senior officer on each watch whose responsibility is the navigation and safety of the ship. He is not permitted to leave the bridge during his watch and there is no seat for him to sit on – a senior officer has to remain alert.

29

In the semi-circular crow's nest 90 feet above the water and 26 feet above the bridge, lookouts Frederick Fleet and Reginald Lee are being replaced by Alfred Evans and George Hogg, who have climbed a ladder inside the steel foremast to reach them. The lookouts change every two hours. Above their heads is a brass warning bell, 17-inches in diameter. They also have a telephone that allows them to communicate directly with the bridge. They usually have a pair of binoculars, but these have gone missing.

> *Although some officers are dismissive about the need for binoculars, preferring the naked eye instead, it is White Star Line practice to have them in the crow's nest. The* Titanic's *lookouts were given a pair for the voyage from Belfast to Southampton that belonged to the second officer, David Blair. But Blair was left behind at Southampton the day before they sailed, following the arrival of Henry Wilde as the new chief officer. It seems likely that Blair simply forgot to tell anyone where the binoculars were kept before the* Titanic *sailed.*
>
> *George Bartlett, marine superintendent of the White Star Line with 30 years' experience at sea, told the British Board of Trade Inquiry into the loss of the* Titanic *that lookouts should use their eyes and immediately report anything they see to the bridge. The officers would then use binoculars to identify the hazard. However, in the aftermath of the disaster, Arctic explorer Admiral Robert Edwin Peary claimed, 'With a good clear night, one could have seen farther, much farther with a binocular. [But] many things are forgotten during a ship's rush to its maiden voyage.'*

In the *Titanic*'s wireless room on the boat deck, between the first and second funnels, Marconi operators Harold Bride and Jack Phillips are working late, hunched over their wireless telegraph trying to get it to work. An hour ago, Bride, the junior operator, had been fast asleep in their quarters next door, but he got up because Phillips needed help to fix the equipment. It looks as if a short has developed in the secondary wiring of a transformer.

At only 25, Jack Phillips is one of the most experienced wireless operators in the world. After working as a telegraphist in the post office in Godalming in Surrey, in 1906 he enrolled at the Marconi training school in Liverpool. After six months' study he started work on ships such as the Lusitania *and* Mauretania, *moving to the White Star Line in 1911. Harold Bride is his deputy and three years younger. He too started as a post office telegraphist, and completed his training at the British School of Telegraphy in July 1911. The* Titanic *is his fifth ship.*

The hero of the sinking of the Republic, *Jack Binns, turned down a job on the* Titanic *because he'd secured a job in New York as a journalist. He'd sailed on the liner* Minnesota *the week before. In 1909 he'd testified before Congress that a wireless telegraph should be mandatory on all ships. By 1912 only 400 out of 20,000 British registered ships have wireless.*

The Titanic's *wireless operators have three interconnecting rooms – on the port side is the dynamo room containing the main transmitting equipment; in the middle is the operating room which has two pieces of Marconi wireless apparatus, one for receiving and one for sending; and to starboard are the men's sleeping quarters. The five-kilowatt generator to power the apparatus is backed up by an independent storage battery, in case the* Titanic's *generators fail. The wireless has a range of 400 miles, although in freak conditions it can reach further – when the* Titanic *was in the Irish Sea, Jack Phillips exchanged messages with operators in Tenerife and Port Said.*

The Marconi Company recruits ambitious young men between 21 and 25, who are keen to avoid what the company's literature calls

31

'blind alley careers'. They transmit to each other in their own mock public-school language of 'old man' and 'I say, old boy'. The Jack Binns story proved just how exciting the job could be.

In the decks below the officers on the bridge and the lookouts and the wireless operators, the majority of the *Titanic*'s 1316 passengers are asleep in the cabins. The lights in the public areas were dimmed or turned off an hour ago. It is the end of the fourth of an eight-day voyage to New York, and both passengers and crew are beginning to get used to this mighty ship.

Second Officer Charles Lightoller wrote after the sinking that although he knew many types of ship 'from a battleship to a barge', it took him 14 days from when he joined the Titanic *in Belfast to be able to find his way from one part of the ship to the other by the shortest route.*

Even for those passengers used to sailing across the Atlantic, the Titanic *is impressive, and some couldn't wait to share their thoughts on the ship with friends and family, using White Star Line notepaper with 'On Board the R.M.S "Titanic"' on the top right-hand corner. The passengers' letters are now well on their way to their destinations. Some addressed to British homes have already been delivered.*

On Wednesday, six hours after departing from Southampton, the Titanic *arrived at Cherbourg to pick up passengers and mail. On Thursday she called at the Irish port of Queenstown (now called Cobh) and took on board more passengers and mail. A small number of mail sacks were brought ashore. The RMS* Titanic *is carrying 3423 sacks of mail to New York (RMS stands for Royal Mail Ship or Steamer). On board are five clerks who work in the*

Titanic's mail room – two British and three Americans. By the time she reached Queenstown they had sorted about 100,000 of the seven million items the Titanic is carrying.

One of those who had posted a letter from the ship is second-class passenger Harvey Collyer, who is heading to the US with his wife Charlotte and eight-year-old daughter Marjorie for a new life – fruit farming in Idaho. In the inside pocket of his jacket he is carrying all their life savings in bank notes – the proceeds of selling their grocer's shop in Bishopstoke in Hampshire; in the Titanic's hold are their possessions for their new home. Charlotte suffers from tuberculosis, and they are hoping the Idaho climate will alleviate her symptoms.

Harvey wrote to his parents just before the mail was collected for Queenstown:

My dear Mum and Dad,

It don't seem possible we are out on the briny writing to you. Well dears so far we are having a delightful trip the weather is beautiful and the ship magnificent. We can't describe the tables it's like a floating town. I can tell you we do swank, we shall miss it on the trains as we go third on them. There is hardly any motion she is so large we have not felt sick yet.

Lots of love, don't worry about us. Harvey, Lot & Madge.

By strange coincidence second-class passenger Marion Wright is also heading to a fruit farm in America – to marry its owner Arthur Woolcott, whom she met in Somerset a few years before. They plan to get married soon after she arrives.

Dearest Dad,

Just a few lines to post to you from Queenstown... It is lovely on the water, & except for the smell of new paint, everything is very comfortable on board. The food is splendid and so

*far I have had 3 meals... So far the vessel doesn't seem a bit
crowded, & there are dozens of tables empty in the dining
saloon... God be with you all & bring me safe home in a few
years' time to see you once again. Much love & many thanks
for all have given me,*

Your ever loving child,
Marion

On the first evening of the voyage on Wednesday 10th April,
Marion offered to share a steamer rug on deck with 36-year-old
Kate Buss from Sittingbourne in Kent, who is on her way to marry
her fiancé Samuel Willis, who emigrated to San Diego two years
ago. Kate is keen to travel in April to avoid a May wedding, which
she considers bad luck. As Kate and Marion chatted, they discovered they both had their wedding presents in the Titanic's hold.
Kate also wrote a letter from Queenstown, telling her brother how
much she liked the Titanic but 'the only thing I object to is new
paint so far...'

Marion Wright's observation that the ship isn't crowded is correct
– the Titanic is half full. She has the capacity to take 2603 passengers but is carrying only 1316. It would have been even fewer, but
there had been a coal strike that meant that other shipping lines
transferred their coal and many of their passengers to the Titanic.
However she is fully booked for her return voyage.

The American writer and artist Frank Millet loves the Titanic – he
wrote to a friend, 'It has everything but taxi cabs and theatres' – but
he is not so keen on some of his fellow first-class passengers:

*Queer lot of people on the ship. There are a number of obnox-
ious, ostentatious American women, the scourge of any place they
infest and worse on shipboard than anywhere... many of them
carry tiny dogs, and lead husbands around like pet lambs.*

Frank Millet is a renowned painter. Copies of his works are owned by many of the Titanic's *wealthier passengers. He has had a varied life – from drummer boy in the American Civil War to war correspondent in the Spanish–American War. He may have been referring to Helen Bishop and her husband Dickenson in his letter. They are on their honeymoon and bought a dog in Florence they named Freu Freu. There are 12 dogs on board, most in kennels on F-deck, looked after by the ship's butcher; some first-class passengers keep their dogs in their cabins – to which the stewards turn a blind eye. Helen Bishop has made a den in her cabin for Freu Freu, behind two suitcases.*

The Titanic *has a ship's cat called Jenny to catch the mice and rats. She gave birth to kittens just before they sailed from Southampton, and the whole family is being fed with scraps by the kitchen staff.*

'With no dusters or anything to work with, I wish the bally ship at the bottom of the sea.'

George Beedem is a bedroom steward who joined the Titanic *on 4th April, having previously served on the* Olympic. *He'd written a number of letters to his wife Lilly and their seven-year-old son Charles, but didn't have any stamps. Queenstown was his first chance to send them all.*

> *Tuesday*
> *My Dear Lill & Charlie*
>   *This is the last night and thank goodness we are off tomorrow… the last three days I've felt rotten & what with no dusters or anything to work with, I wish the bally ship at the bottom of the sea…*

During the midnight to 4am watch on 11th April, George wrote another letter to his family:

My dear little treasures

We have a decent crowd on board this time although not too many. There is a lot to come on at Queenstown I think, the more the merrier... I have just had a shave etc. & I shall be glad when 4 o/c comes... Now tata, glad you liked the pictures & I suppose those chocolate eggs have disappeared down that great big hole.

With fondest love to both of you.

Da Da

Lawrence Beesley is a 34-year-old teacher from Dulwich, south-east of London, on his way to Toronto to visit his brother. Beesley is a widower, and after several unhappy years, gave up a position at Dulwich College where he'd taught science. Among his pupils was the future crime writer Raymond Chandler. He wrote this letter to his young son soon after leaving Southampton:

My dear Kit,

We had an exciting experience just as we were passing the last wharf in Southampton Water. The New York was lying alongside the Oceanic... the suction of this monster ship as she approached, drew the New York outward and one by one her hawsers broke... only one in the bow held. Out came her stern toward our port side. Just in the nick of time a tug came up and they made fast a steel rope and checked the outward swing. The Titanic, meanwhile, went hard astern, & the New York's stern just cleared our bows... Anyhow it was exciting when the hawsers began popping one after the other, & the men ran in bunches to escape the flying ends of rope. Now we are running past the Isle of Wight. I hope not to have any more accidents.

The near collision Beesley describes was prevented just in time – the ships were only four feet apart when two tugs intervened. A number of people had got on board the New York *to watch the* Titanic *set sail and were terrified. The* Southampton Times *commented that they 'will doubtless retain for years vivid recollections of the first sailing of the* Titanic *from Southampton docks...'*

Because of their size, the Olympic-class ships are hard for even experienced pilots and captains to handle. On 20th September 1911, the Olympic *was setting off from Southampton on her fifth voyage. As she made a turn passing the east end of the Isle of Wight, guided not by Captain Edward Smith, but by a pilot, an elderly cruiser named HMS* Hawke *was unable to take avoiding action in time and the two ships collided. The* Hawke's *bow buried itself deep into the* Olympic's *hull. The fact that the* Olympic *remained afloat having been hit by a vessel designed to ram enemy ships was seen as further proof that modern liners, and the Olympic class in particular, were unsinkable.*

The Olympic *sailed back to Belfast, where the* Titanic *was being built. The* Titanic's *starboard propeller shaft and other components were transferred to her damaged sister ship, and as a result the* Titanic's *maiden voyage was postponed from 20th March to 10th April 1912.*

An Admiralty Court concluded that the Olympic *was to blame for the collision. 'We are not taking it lying down,' Captain Smith wrote to a friend. But the White Star Line lost the appeal.*

Some letters sent from Queenstown were more mundane. Mrs Ida Straus, the 63-year-old wife of Isidor Straus, one of the owners of Macy's department store in New York, wrote to Mrs Lilian Burbidge, the wife of the managing director of Harrod's, to thank her for the gift of roses and carnations delivered to her cabin. First-class passenger Joseph Loring wrote home with instructions about the installation of a new motor-horn on his Daimler.

The Titanic *has a band of eight musicians, chosen to play on the maiden voyage of this famous ship because they are among the best in their profession. Their bandleader, 33-year-old Wallace Hartley, wrote to his wife at their home in Dewsbury, just after they sailed:*

Just a line to say that we have got away all right. It has been a bit of a rush but I am just getting a little settled. This is a fine ship and there ought to be plenty of money around. We have a fine band and the boys seem very nice.

00.15am Titanic *Bridge Time*

The 'fine band' is in their second-class quarters on E-deck, having played their final pieces of the day in the first-class Palm Court. There are two cabins for the musicians, with bunk beds, a wardrobe and a chest of drawers, plus a storeroom for their instruments. The musicians divide into a piano trio playing in the first-class à la carte restaurant or in the Café Parisien, and a piano quintet playing in the first-class Lounge during afternoon tea and outside the D-deck dining saloon during luncheon and dinner.

The band has already made a good impression. A number of passengers mentioned them in the letters sent from Queenstown. Kate Buss, travelling to San Diego to marry her fiancé, is very much taken with John Wesley 'Wes' Woodward, whom she refers to every day in a journal as 'The Cello Man'. Kate wrote on 11th April: 'The Cello Man is a favourite of mine. Every time he finishes a piece he looks at me and we smile.' On the 13th: 'He is quite gentlemanly... we chatted, amongst other things, about the Olympic. He was on her when the accident happened.'

Wes Woodward had been playing draughts with the rest of the Olympic's band during a break between performances when the collision with HMS Hawke occurred. They were only 10 feet away, but as the Olympic barely shuddered, they carried on with their game.

Woodward plans to give up performing on ships at the end of the summer of 1912 and to return to Eastbourne where he's played with the Devonshire Park Orchestra for many years. With him on the Olympic and now on the Titanic is 21-year-old Jock Hume, a fine violinist – always up for some mischief.

On a previous trip Jock fooled a troublesome woman passenger into thinking he'd played a complicated classical piece when it was in fact a ragtime song slowed down. Just before he sailed, Jock's girlfriend Mary told him that she was expecting his baby.

Bandleader Wallace Hartley has played on ships for the past three years and has made more than 80 transatlantic crossings. He's worked his way up from second violin to be bandmaster on the Mauretania – in 1910, the world's fastest liner. Wallace is engaged, and like Wes Woodward, plans to retire from the sea and get concert work on land.

Three of the band have never played on a ship before – bass player Fred Clarke, pianist Percy Taylor and Belgian violinist Georges Krins, who'd been talked out of joining the army by his father who thought the life of a musician would be safer. The two remaining members are cellist Roger Bricoux and pianist Theo Brailey.

2.00am Titanic *Bridge Time* – 4 Bells

In the crow's nest, lookouts George Symons and Archie Jewell replace Alfred Evans and George Hogg.

'This first voyage is going to make history in ocean travel.'

3.00am Titanic *Bridge Time – 6 Bells*

In her first-class cabin on A-deck, Lady Lucy Duff Gordon is fast asleep. Across the corridor is her husband Sir Cosmo. Lucy loves her cabin with its electric heater and pink décor. Close to her bed are a warm coat and wrap, and her jewellery box. Since she first booked the tickets for the *Titanic* at the White Star Line's Paris office, she has felt uneasy about the trip. The booking agent had told her: 'This first voyage is going to make history in ocean travel.'

Lucy Duff Gordon's secretary Laura 'Franks' Francatelli is sleeping in her cabin four decks below on E-deck.

The Duff Gordons are an unlikely couple. He is an old Etonian baronet, an Olympic fencer and an expert at bridge; she is a divorced clothes designer who has made a name for herself selling daring underwear from a shop in Mayfair called Maison Lucile. Lucy Duff Gordon is the first person to use the word 'chic' to describe ladies' fashions, and by 1909 was making £40,000 a year and employing a thousand people. As well as the everyday jewellery she has in her cabin, Lucy Duff Gordon has in the purser's safe a $50,000 pearl necklace that she hasn't paid for, or insured. She has borrowed it from her jeweller's in Venice with the promise of buying it in the future. The necklace is probably only to impress her fellow passengers – potential clients of Maison Lucile.

It is rare for the Duff Gordons to travel together. Lucy once wrote to her mother that Cosmo was 'most extraordinarily dull to be with'.

The Olympic class ships' extravagant décor is designed to capture the wealthy transatlantic traveller. Each first-class large cabin (or stateroom) has a telephone, a heater, a table fan, bells to summon a steward, hot and cold running water and electric curling tongs; some even have their own promenade deck. The rooms are decorated in different styles: Georgian, Louis XVI and Queen Anne. The very wealthy can purchase a number of cabins with interconnecting doors, creating a large suite of their own. The Thayers, one of the richest families in Pennsylvania, have chosen to take advantage of this facility. John and Marian Thayer are in C-68 and their 17-year-old son Jack is next door in C-70. The Thayers have been on a European vacation, visiting Germany, Austria, Holland and England. John is vice-president of the Pennsylvania railroad, one of America's largest. They are a good-looking family; indeed, Marian has been described as 'one of the handsomest women in Philadelphia'. Jack's future has already been mapped out by his father. He will finish his studies in Philadelphia and then attend Princeton, where, after graduating, he'll again tour Europe, and then return to the States to start a career in banking.

The second-class cabins on the Titanic are as good as the first-class cabins on many other liners. The Harland and Wolff designers have ensured that they are as bright as possible – most have portholes and white enamel walls. Instead of beds, the cabins have berths attached to the walls, with a curtain for privacy. Linoleum, a recent invention, is on the floor. There are technological innovations too – first- and second-class cabins and lavatories have electric lights that come on when someone enters, and turn off when they leave.

The second- and third-class accommodation has all the internal workings of the ship showing, such as pipes and girders; in first class they are concealed behind wooden panelling or tapestries.

The Titanic's third-class passengers are sleeping in relative

41

comfort. Those emigrating to Canada from England in the Mount Temple, sailing just a few hundred miles from the Titanic, are in cabins that are used as cattle stalls on the return journey. On the Titanic, the cabins are small, but they have ventilation, electric lights, wash basins, and coverlets on the beds in the White Star Line colours of red and white. Most cabins are designed for two or four occupants, with some taking up to ten. Both second- and third-class accommodation decks have shared bathrooms; in third class there are only two baths for 710 passengers, in second there are plenty more.

The White Star Line has its own policy for sleeping arrangements. Single men and women are kept well apart. In third-class accommodation, single women and families are towards the stern, while single men and married couples are forward. Married couples and families have their own rooms.

When the third-class passengers arrived at the top of the ship's gangplank they were met by a team of doctors led by the Titanic's chief surgeon Dr William O'Loughlin. Each passenger's upper eyelid was rolled back to check for symptoms of trachoma. Anyone with the disease was turned back, as stipulated by US immigration laws.

US law also stipulates that there should be gates between third class and the other passengers to prevent the spread of disease.

One family who underwent the gangplank check is that of Frederick Goodwin, currently asleep in the stern accommodation. Frederick is travelling from Fulham to Niagara Falls with his wife Augusta and their six children: Lillian, 16, Charles, 14, William, 11, Jessie, 10, Harold, 9, and 18-month-old Sidney. Frederick's brother had written to tell him that a large power station was being built there, with good job opportunities. They'd booked on a smaller steamer sailing from Southampton but because of the coal strike they had been switched to the Titanic.

4.00*am* Titanic *Bridge Time – 8 Bells, Morning Watch Begins*

The midnight to 4am shift of firemen and trimmers are leaving the boiler rooms and heading to their dining saloon on E-deck for their favourite meal of the day, oodle – joints of beef, carrots and onions stewed for hours in large water-filled buckets.

On the bridge, Third Officer Herbert Pitman and Fifth Officer Harold Lowe replace Fourth Officer Joseph Boxhall and Sixth Officer James Moody. In the crow's nest, lookouts Frederick Fleet and Reginald Lee replace Archie Jewell and George Symons. Quartermasters Arthur Bright, Walter Wynn and Walter Perkis take over from Robert Hichens, Alfred Olliver and George Rowe.

Asleep in the first-class accommodation are two of the men responsible for the creation of the *Titanic* – Bruce Ismay, managing director and chairman of the White Star Line, and Thomas Andrews, managing director of the Harland and Wolff shipyard.

Forty-nine-year-old Ismay is occupying a magnificent suite of rooms on B-deck – B-52, B-54 and B-56. It was his father, Thomas Ismay, who in the 1870s bought and made the bankrupt White Star Line profitable. Thomas intimidated and bullied his son and his staff. If he saw a leaf on the carriage-drive leading up to his house on the outskirts of Liverpool, he would place a stone on it to mark it. If his ten gardeners failed to spot the leaf, there would be a display of his infamous temper.

Bruce Ismay took full control of the White Star Line following his father's death in 1899. He is tall, softly spoken, difficult to get to know, and, like his father, intolerant of any inefficiency. On the day of the launch of one of his ships, he can be seen running his fingers along the woodwork to check whether any dust has been missed by a steward. Ismay is always looking for improvements to his ships; he travelled on the Olympic's *maiden voyage and made a number of suggestions to her designers – from the need for cigar holders in the first-class lavatories, to sliding glass windows in the forward part of A-deck to protect passengers, who complained of being hit by spray from the ship's bow.*

Although the Titanic *has 'Liverpool' written across her stern (the city where she is registered), was built in Belfast and has a crew almost entirely from Southampton, she is not a British ship. In December 1902, the White Star Line was taken over by the International Mercantile Marine Company, a conglomerate financed by John Pierpoint Morgan, the brilliant but ruthless American financier, after he made an offer the company's shareholders couldn't refuse. He persuaded Bruce Ismay to stay on as its managing director and chairman, and to take on the presidency of International Mercantile Marine.*

Such is J.P. Morgan's wealth that he is in effect the United States' central banker, upholding the value of the dollar and steadying economic confidence in times of crisis. His acquisition of the White Star Line was a sign that economic power was transferring across the Atlantic – in 1861, the United States had three millionaires; by 1900 it had 3800.

J.P. Morgan's money has not bought him contentment; he was once described as 'the saddest of millionaires'. By 1912 he had amassed a vast art collection in his London and Paris homes but now wanted to send it to New York. In January the first shipments were sent by White Star Line across the Atlantic. The Titanic *was supposed to carry a significant amount of the collection, but a bureaucratic complication meant that shipments were suspended in March. Morgan intended to sail on the* Titanic's *maiden voyage, occupying the suite on B-deck that had been especially built for him, but at the last minute he decided to stay in Paris. Bruce Ismay is occupying his suite.*

What few people know about Ismay is that he is trying to withdraw from the shipping business. He plans to retire as president of International Mercantile Marine in 1913, but he wants it kept secret for the moment. In February he wrote to Charles Steele, the secretary of J.P. Morgan and Company: 'the 30th June, 1913, is a "FAR CRY", and much may happen between now and then...'

As well as being managing director, Thomas Andrews is chief designer at Harland and Wolff, and the nephew of its chairman Lord Pirrie. He is on board to spot any improvements that need to be made to his ship. His cabin, A-36, is littered with designs and charts.

At the age of 16 Andrews started a five-year apprenticeship in the shipyard, working with the painters, fitters, shipwrights and cabinet makers, ending with 18 months in the drawing office. In 1905 he was made chief of the Design Department and two years later managing director.

Andrews is well loved by the workers and ships' crews, and is not afraid of intervening to break up sectarian fights at the shipyard or beat up bullies.

He is also a devoted husband. On Friday 12th April, the third day of the voyage, as Andrews was going to dinner, he stopped to talk to stewardess Mary Sloan. The Titanic's chief surgeon, Dr William O'Loughlin, was calling 'Tommy!' to attract his attention, but all he wanted to talk about was Belfast, his and Mary's home town, and how his father and his wife Helen were poorly. Mary congratulated him on his beautiful new ship. Andrews replied, looking sad, that what he didn't like was that the Titanic was taking him 'further away from home every hour'.

Andrews built the Titanic to withstand running aground, colliding with an obstacle, or being hit by another ship. She has a double bottom – two sets of steel plates, seven feet apart to ensure that if the keel is holed, the ship won't flood. Fifteen bulkheads divide the Titanic into 16 watertight compartments; in a head-on collision she will float even if the first four compartments flood. If a ship rams the Titanic side on, she could float with any two central compartments flooded. The bulkheads have watertight doors that are closed by a switch on the bridge.

5.00am Titanic *Bridge Time – 2 Bells*

The Marconi wireless operators Jack Phillips and Harold Bride have finally fixed the *Titanic*'s transmitter. They start logging their wireless messages according to New York Time, rather than Greenwich Mean Time.

Asleep in his second-class cabin F-2 on F-deck towards the stern is Louis Hoffman and his two young sons, Lolo, aged three, and Louis, aged two. Hoffman has told other passengers that his wife has recently died. Since they've been on board he's hardly let the boys out of his sight.

But Louis Hoffman is in fact an alias. He is a 32-year-old Slovak called Michel Navratil, and he has abducted his sons, whose real names are Michel and Edmond, and is fleeing to America.

Michel Navratil married Marcelle Carretto in 1907 and they moved to Nice in the South of France. But it was a stormy relationship and in 1912 Michel moved out. The couple filed for separation on the grounds of incompatibility, and the court awarded custody to Marcelle's uncle, who also lived in Nice. In April the boys went to their father's house for the Easter holiday, but when Marcelle came to collect them, they were gone. Michel took the name Louis Hoffman from a neighbour who helped him, and fled to London, where he booked tickets for the Titanic. *He sent a letter from Queenstown to his mother in Hungary, suggesting that if his trip to America was unsuccessful, the boys could be taken in by his sister and her husband.*

In the pockets of Michel Navratil's grey overcoat, hanging up in the cabin, is evidence of their flight from Nice to London – a bill for Room 126 in the Charing Cross Hotel, a receipt from Thomas Cook and Co. from their bureau de change, a ticket for the *Titanic* and a loaded revolver.

> **One rarely heard stewards complain that they found years of bell-answering, slop-emptying, floor-washing, bed-making, tea-carrying or the trundling of baggage monotonous or distasteful. They never realised that the very monotony had eaten like a canker into their souls.**
>
> **Violet Jessop, Stewardess**

6.00am Titanic *Bridge Time – 4 Bells*

In the crow's nest, lookouts Alfred Evans and George Hogg arrive to take over from Frederick Fleet and Reginald Lee. Below them on the bridge, Second Officer Lightoller is talking to Chief Officer Wilde, whom he is about to replace as officer of the watch.

Violet Jessop's day is just beginning. The 24-year-old is getting ready in her cabin for her 17-hour shift as a stewardess in first class. Violet does not always enjoy her job. She's been at sea since 1908, first with the Royal Mail Line and then the White Star Line, her last ship being the *Olympic*. Violet's fellow stewards often annoy her with their lack of ambition, their obsession with getting tips from passengers.

There are many types of stewards on the Titanic – deck stewards, smoking room stewards, bath stewards, bedroom stewards, library stewards and saloon stewards. The latter serve meals in the dining saloons and are always male. Violet looks after approximately a dozen cabins, together with a male steward.

Her job is either extremely busy or very quiet. When it's busy she grabs food in the pantry and eats it there, standing up. It can be at its busiest – and noisiest – before a ship leaves port, with piles of luggage and endless requests for drinks and vases. Flowers are a particular bugbear, as some first-class passengers have more than a dozen boxes of flowers delivered to the ship as farewell gifts, and there are never enough vases on board. Once, when handed some flowers to give to a passenger by a friend come to see them off, Violet responded cheekily: 'Next time send her books. That is the most acceptable gift for a voyage, unless it is one's last voyage.' But Violet generally just smiles.

At sea, Violet is often lonely, but at least on the *Titanic* she has a room-mate, Elizabeth Leather, who transferred with her from the *Olympic*. The designer of both ships, Thomas Andrews, has incorporated some of the features suggested by the stewards to make their life easier, for example proper bathrooms. As a token of thanks, on *Olympic*'s maiden voyage the Victualling Department presented Andrews with a walking stick to help him cope with his varicose veins, brought on, Violet reckons, by too much walking and standing on ships' decks. He is 'the finest and kindliest of men'.

When Violet came aboard the *Titanic*, she was delighted to

find that Andrews had even incorporated some of her suggestions – her bunk was positioned in a way to give more privacy and there was a wardrobe to prevent her clothes from smelling if she had a roommate with 'a devotion to whisky and smoke'. Nevertheless, Violet and Elizabeth have made some further modifications of their own – managing to persuade some junior electricians to rig up some extra lights to illuminate the darker corners of the cabin. As she dresses, Violet is surrounded by pictures on the wall of her family and calendars with country scenes.

Violet looks forward to the time when she can return home to her mother's house and sit in her warm kitchen counting out her earnings, which are so desperately needed to pay the bills.

When she joined the *Titanic*, one of the first things that Violet did was scan the passenger lists to see what famous names might be on them. Would they be as described in the popular press? What would their particular idiosyncrasies be? By far the most famous names on the list are Colonel John Jacob Astor IV, one of the richest men in America, and his young wife Madeleine. The Astors have taken a suite of rooms, C-62 and C-64, at a cost of $4350 (about $100,000 today) and are travelling with a maid, a nurse, a manservant and a pet dog named Kitty.

The Astors are not in Violet Jessop's part of the ship, although she did see them embark at Cherbourg. Violet wrote later: 'Instead of the radiant woman of my imagination, one who had succeeded much opposition and marrying the man she wanted, I saw a quiet, pale, sad-faced, in fact dull young woman arrive listlessly on the arm of her husband...'

What Violet will probably not have known is that Madeleine Astor is four months pregnant, and that her severe morning sickness has curtailed their European tour.

John Jacob Astor is the great-grandson of the first John Jacob

Astor who emigrated to America in 1783 and made a fortune in the fur trade and real estate. By the 20th century, the family owned numerous properties and hotels in New York (including the Astoria Hotel that John Jacob built next door to his cousin's Waldorf Hotel, just to spite him). Such is John Jacob Astor's importance that when he went missing for 16 days while sailing in the Caribbean, real estate markets in New York were severely affected.

He is certainly idiosyncratic – he made himself a colonel during the Spanish–American War, wrote a science fiction novel, invented a bicycle brake and owns a vast collection of motor cars. He was once fined for speeding in Croydon.

So far on the voyage the couple have been keeping themselves to themselves, mainly because Madeleine's morning sickness has been so bad, but also for another reason. In 1909 Astor's first wife sued him for divorce and the following year he fell in love with the 18-year-old Madeleine Force whom he met while playing tennis at a country club. John Jacob was 45. The couple found it hard to find a minister prepared to marry them, but a $1000 fee helped persuade a Rhode Island clergyman to officiate. The ceremony in September 1911 was a private occasion as their relationship was considered a public scandal – their friends ostracised them.

Passenger lists are not just for the stewards. In every first-class and second-class cabin there is a printed list of the other passengers on board and their destination. At least three men are travelling under assumed names – first-class passenger Harry 'Kid' Homer is on the list as H. Haven; former Los Angeles car salesman Charles H. Romaine is down as C. Rolman; George 'Boy' Brereton is George Brayton. They are all travelling under aliases as they are professional gamblers known as 'boat men' – very common on liners and usually well known to the crew, but tolerated as long as their winnings aren't excessive. The Titanic's passenger list carries a warning against such men:

'...certain persons, believed to be Professional Gamblers, are in the habit of travelling to and fro in Atlantic Steamships... the Managers desire to invite [travellers'] assistance... in discouraging Games of Chance, as being likely to afford these individuals special opportunities for taking advantage of others...'

How curtailed that enjoyment would have been had the presentiment come to me telling how near it was to being my last plunge, and that before the dawn of another day I would be swimming for my life in mid-ocean... in a temperature of 28° Fahrenheit!

Colonel Archibald Gracie, first-class passenger

6.30am Titanic *Bridge Time – 5 Bells*

Some of the second-class passengers are being woken up by the sound of cockerels crowing, as they have done every morning of the voyage. Four are being imported to the United States by a first-class passenger and are kept close to the dog kennels. Every animal on board has its own ticket.

In the *Titanic*'s squash racquet court that spans F and G decks, the lowest area of first class, the ship's professional player Frederick Wright is playing a game with 54-year-old Colonel Archibald Gracie. Gracie is an amateur military historian, who has just written *The Truth About Chickamauga*, a book about an obscure American Civil War battle in which his father fought. Gracie is a regular transatlantic traveller, and his routine on board ship is to play squash every day. However, this is his first game on the voyage, as he's preferred to browse the books in *Titanic*'s well-stocked library, rather than take any exercise. Once he has played this half-hour game, the colonel plans a swim in the ship's heated saltwater pool.

Gracie tries to keep fit because he is a diabetic and his health is often poor. He recently had an operation, and a trip to Europe was a chance to recuperate, as well as to research his next book on the 1812 war between the United States and Britain. He is married with one surviving daughter; two died in infancy and a third died in a lift accident in 1903.

7.00am Titanic *Bridge Time – 6 Bells*

Bedroom steward Henry Etches is knocking on the door of cabin A-36, belonging to Thomas Andrews. Etches has a tray with Andrew's regular breakfast of tea and fruit. He knows Andrews well as they met several times when Etches was stewarding on the *Olympic*. Etches has also volunteered some suggestions about how the *Titanic* can be improved, which Andrews noted down. Sometimes Etches comes into the cabin to find Andrews has thrown a grimy blue surveyor's suit on the bed, as he's been down in the engine room.

In first and second class, stewards are delivering the *Atlantic Daily Bulletin*, a newspaper containing news summaries, stock exchange prices and racing results – all received from shore stations by the wireless operators Bride and Phillips.

In third class, Alfred Rush is getting ready for a big day – it is his 17th birthday. Alfred is travelling with Emily and Frank Goldsmith and their young son Frankie to Detroit, where Alfred's older brother lives. He plans to mark his birthday by wearing his first pair of long trousers.

> **She [Titanic] impressed on me her personality, as I stood at the bow alone and absorbed her spirit. She was a monarch of the seas as her bow cut into the**

waves, throwing tons of water to right and to left as though in lighthearted playful intent. Her indifference to mankind was significant in its utter self absorption.

Helen Candee, first-class passenger

7.20am Titanic *Bridge Time*

After some early showers, Sunday is dawning bright and clear. The crew who are due to start the forenoon watch are having breakfast.

About 7.30am Titanic *Bridge Time – 7 Bells*

There is a woman standing on the bow of the *Titanic*. She is enjoying the sensation of the breeze generated by the ship steaming at 22 knots. This is not the first time that Helen Candee has done this, but it is the first time that she's been there alone.

> *Fifty-three-year-old Helen Candee is the author of the international bestseller* How Women May Earn a Living *and the western* An Oklahoman Romance. *She's been forced to fend for herself after divorcing her abusive husband, and is travelling to the United States to be with her son who has been injured in a plane crash. Helen Candee likes to spend the late mornings on the* Titanic *reading on the A-deck promenade, taking up two chairs, 'one for myself and the other for callers – or self protection.'*
>
> *She has had a number of callers over the past few days – in particular a well-tailored Englishman named Hugh Woolner, seven years her junior. Woolner, a cousin of novelist Evelyn Waugh, is an ex-bankrupt travelling to America to visit his fiancée – a rich widow named Mary Dowson.*

8.00am Titanic *Bridge Time – 8 Bells, Forenoon Watch Begins*

Four hours after they left the bridge, officers Boxhall and Moody return to replace Pitman and Lowe, and quartermasters Hichens, Olliver and Rowe take over from Bright, Wynn and Perkis.

Breakfast is being served by stewards to the first-, second- and third-class passengers in their respective dining saloons.

In the first-class dining saloon on D-deck, passengers are seated on padded leather chairs – another innovation as most liners have saloon seats bolted to the floor – around tables for two, four or six, and eating from white bone china with the White Star Line logo.

In the second-class dining saloon, also on D-deck, there are large rectangular tables surrounded by swivel chairs, the idea being that their movement will help cancel out the movement of the ship.

In the third-class saloon on F-deck, passengers are eating their breakfast around long tables that seat 20 – sitting on wooden benches to discourage lice. There are hooks on the walls for jackets and scarves. This morning the passengers in third class have a choice of oatmeal porridge and milk, vegetable stew, fried tripe and onions, bread and butter, marmalade, Swedish bread, tea and coffee. For the poorer passengers, it is the best food they have ever had.

This is just a small selection of the food taken on board at Southampton for the Titanic's *five-day voyage:*

Fresh eggs 40,000	*Coffee 2200lb*
Fresh meat 75,000lb	*Tea 800lb*
Fresh fish 11,000lb	*Fresh milk 1500 gallons*

Poultry and game 25,000lb *Fresh butter 6000lb*
Sausages 2500lb *Potatoes 40 tons*
Flour 200 barrels *Lettuce 7000 heads*
 Tomatoes 2¾ tons

Titanic's *dining stewards have at their disposal 3000 tea cups,*
12,000 dinner plates, 2000 wine glasses, 1000 oyster forks, 100
grape scissors and 2000 egg spoons.

9.00am Titanic *Bridge Time – 2 Bells*

In the ship's gymnasium on the boat deck, 44-year-old Margaret
'Molly' Brown (soon to be known as 'the unsinkable Molly
Brown') is keeping fit by hitting a punch ball. It's been her
morning routine since she boarded the *Titanic* at Cherbourg.
Boxing is considered to be good for women as it firms up
the waist and upper body, and reduces the need for a corset.
Molly is being watched by the gymnasium steward Thomas
McCawley, to whom she has paid a fee of one shilling.

As well as punch balls, dumb-bells and rowing machines, the
gymnasium has innovative exercise machines such as a mechan-
ical horse to test equestrian skills and a mechanical camel to
improve abdominal and back muscles. The gymnasium is strictly
segregated; men and women have set hours when they can use
its facilities.

In 1893 Molly Brown's husband J.J. struck it rich when he discov-
ered gold in a Colorado mine named Little Jonny. The mine was
soon producing 135 tons of gold ore per day, making J.J. one
of the richest men in America. The Browns travelled the world
together, and Molly became a campaigner for women's rights, and
helped Judge Benjamin Lindsey establish the United States' first

juvenile court. Molly and J.J. are estranged due to his drinking and a temper made worse by a stroke.

> **Senator Smith: What is an iceberg made of?**
> **Fifth Officer Harold Lowe: Ice, I suppose.**
> **(Laughter)**
>
> **US Senate Inquiry, April 1912**

9.12am Titanic *Bridge Time*

In the wireless room, Jack Phillips is receiving a warning from the captain of the Cunard liner RMS *Caronia*: 'Captain – *Titanic*. West-bound steamers report bergs, growlers, and field ice in 42°N., from 49 to 51° W. April 12. Compliments. Barr.' Harold Bride takes the message to the bridge.

> *The definition of an iceberg is a block of ice higher than 16 feet above sea level, and between 98 and 164 feet thick. A 'growler' extends less than 3 feet above the sea and although transparent can appear green in colour. Icebergs begin life as tips of glaciers (the vast majority in Greenland) and about 10,000 break off each year, with 1000 surviving to plague Atlantic shipping lanes. They will have travelled as far as 1800 miles. As they drift into warmer water they melt and 'calve' smaller fragments, and their centre of buoyancy changes, resulting in rolling. Icebergs can roll several times a day.*
>
> *April is one of the worst months for icebergs in the Atlantic.*

10.00am Titanic *Bridge Time* – 4 Bells

Breakfast for the passengers is now over. Meanwhile, in the *Titanic*'s first- and second-class shared kitchen, and in the third-class kitchen, lunch is being prepared. For first-class passengers there will be a buffet including Norwegian ancho-vies, roast beef, veal and ham pie, bologna sausage and corned ox tongue. From the grill, mutton chops will be served with a choice of mashed, fried or baked potatoes. Finishing touches are being made to the custard pudding and apple meringue. Iced draught Munich lager will be available for 3d or 6d a tankard.

The second-class cooks are preparing pea soup, spaghetti au gratin, vegetable dumplings, corned beef, roast mutton, roast beef, sausage, ox tongue, pickles, salad, tapioca pudding, apple tart, fresh fruit, cheese and biscuits.

The third-class kitchen is preparing bouillon soup, roast beef and brown gravy, green beans, cabin biscuits, bread, prunes and rice.

On the bridge of the *Titanic*, First Officer William Murdoch takes over from Second Officer Charles Lightoller as officer of the watch. Lookouts Frederick Fleet and Reginald Lee replace Archie Jewell and George Symons.

About 10.15am Titanic *Bridge Time*

This is a popular time to take the air, exercise, play games such as quoits, or to socialise and flirt while walking the prom-enade decks. Second-class passenger Kate Buss, travelling to San Diego to marry her fiancé Samuel, often walks here. She wrote in her journal two days ago that she gets 'an occasional wink or blink at some apparently interested passer-by'.

Today, however, she is walking with Reverend Ernest Carter and his wife Lillian. He is the vicar at St Jude's Church in Whitechapel, East London, and she is the daughter of Thomas Hughes, the author of *Tom Brown's Schooldays*. Carter's parish is poor and predominantly Jewish – some Sundays the choir outnumber the congregation. The Carters are going to Kansas to visit friends. Kate enjoys their company.

Science teacher Lawrence Beesley is standing on the starboard boat deck between lifeboats 13 and 15. He's been there many times in the past few days, studying the motion of the *Titanic*. By gazing at two fixed points on the ship and then looking at the horizon, he's concluded that she has both a side-to-side roll and a long, slow heave up and down, and that this is probably due to the angle the ship is taking as she cuts across the Gulf Stream. Beesley attempts to calculate the average time it takes the *Titanic* to do one up and down motion. It's too cold to stay on deck for long.

> The boat deck is the top deck of the Titanic, and gets its name from the lifeboats stored there. In a letter to a friend, artist Francis Millet gave an idea of its size: '500 people don't make a show on the decks.' Passengers are discouraged from roaming the full length of the deck by an iron gate between first and second class that has a 'Not Allowed' sign. The forward part of the deck around lifeboats 1 and 3 on the starboard side and 2 and 4 on the port side is reserved for the use of the ship's officers.
>
> There are no lifeboats in the third-class promenade deck areas – the forward well deck, the aft well deck, and the poop deck at the very stern.

10.28am Titanic *Bridge Time*

The *Titanic* sends a message from Captain Smith in reply to *Caronia*'s ice warning: 'Thanks for message and information. Have had variable weather throughout – Smith.'

10.45am Titanic *Bridge Time*

In the first-class dining saloon, Captain Smith is conducting a well-attended Divine Service, using the White Star Line's own prayer book. Smith is following the Royal Navy rule that states that a service should be held every Sunday 'solemnly, orderly and reverently'. One of the hymns the congregation is singing is no. 418 in the White Star hymnal, 'Oh God, Our Help in Ages Past'.

> *Colonel Archibald Gracie wrote later:*
> *'What a remarkable coincidence that at the first and last ship's service on board* Titanic, *the hymn we sang began with these impressive lines:*
>
> > *O God, our help in ages past,*
> > *Our hope for years to come,*
> > *Our shelter from the stormy blast*
> > *And our eternal home.'*
>
> *The saloon is a grand room, 114 feet long and 92 feet wide (the full width of the hull), decorated in a Jacobean style and painted all white. It can seat 500 people and is the largest room ever built on a ship.*

Services are being held for second- and third-class passengers in their respective dining saloons.

11.00am Titanic *Bridge Time* – 6 Bells

This was the scheduled time for a boat drill, but it has been cancelled.

It has never been established why the boat drill was cancelled. It may have been because of high winds, or because a brief boat drill involving lifeboats 13 and 15 had already been carried out in Southampton. Boat drills are rare; trimmer George Cavell, a veteran of three White Star Line ships before the Titanic, *told the Board of Trade Inquiry into the sinking that he'd never been mustered for a boat drill at sea, only in New York harbour when there were no passengers on board.*

Although there has been no boat drill, on the morning of 11th April, just before the Titanic *arrived at Queenstown there was a full emergency test of the watertight doors in the engine and boiler rooms. Alarm bells rang for ten seconds and red lights flashed above the doors before they dropped into place. Assistant electrician Albert Ervine posted a reassuring letter to his mother from Queenstown that mentioned the successful drill: 'so you see it would be impossible for the ship to be sunk in collision with another...'*

11.20am Titanic *Bridge Time*

The crew about to form the afternoon watch are having lunch. However, the trimmers and firemen rarely touch it – it could lead to stomach cramps. George Garrett, fireman on the *Mauretania*, recalled: 'Men dared not risk a heavy meal prior to going down the stokehold to manoeuvre slice bars, wrestle molten clinkers out, inhale sulphur fumes and sweat non-stop.'

About 11.30am Titanic *Bridge Time – 7 Bells*

Thirteen-year-old Madeleine Mellenger is returning with her mother Elizabeth to their second-class cabin, having been to the Divine Service in the first-class dining saloon. Captain Smith is walking towards them with some of his officers, looking to young Madeleine just like King Edward VII, 'beard and all'. She asks the captain and his officers what they are doing, and is told that they are inspecting the *Titanic*'s watertight compartments and doors.

Colonel Archibald Gracie is in conversation with a couple he has got to know on the voyage – 67-year-old Isidor Straus and his wife Ida. The Strauses are very excited, as they are about to have the novel experience of communicating with their son and his wife who are sailing to Europe on the Hamburg Line ship *Amerika*. They will leave a handwritten message at the purser's office, which will be sent by a pneumatic tube to the *Titanic*'s wireless telegraph office, and then transmitted to the *Amerika*.

These Marconigrams were very lucrative for the company. They cost 12½ shillings for ten words, and nine pence per word thereafter.

Isidor Straus and Archibald Gracie have a common bond – Gracie's father fought for the Southern Confederacy, and Straus helped break the North's blockade to supply them. A decade after the end of the Civil War, Isidor and his brother Nathan started supplying goods for the New York department store Macy's. By the end of the century, they owned it. Isidor and Ida are returning from a visit to Jerusalem, and it is clear to anyone who meets them that they are devoted to each other. They told Lady Duff Gordon that in their long years of married life, they had never been separated for a single day or night. She's nicknamed them 'Darby and Joan'.

Travelling with the Strauses are Isidor's valet John Farthing and Ida's maid Ellen Bird, a shepherd's daughter from Norfolk whom they employed only a fortnight ago.

11.47am Titanic *Bridge Time*

Caronia relays to the *Titanic* a message from Captain Krol of the SS *Noordam* sailing from New York to Rotterdam: 'Captain SS *Titanic*. Congratulations on new command. Had moderate westerly winds, fair weather, no fog. Much ice reported in lat. 42°24' to 42°45'[N] and long. 49°50' to 50°20'[W]. Compliments. Krol.'

'hello Boy dining with you tonight in spirit heart with you always best love Girl'

Midday Titanic *Bridge Time – 8 Bells, Afternoon Watch Begins*

In accordance with company rules, the *Titanic*'s whistles are being tested at noon. The whistles, which the White Star Line claim are the largest ever made, are mounted on the first two of her four funnels. The engine order telegraphs connecting the bridge and the engine room are also tested.

> *There are whistles mounted on the third and fourth funnels, but they are dummies, and there purely for aesthetic purposes. Ships' whistles are used to indicate manoeuvres or to give warnings.*

On the bridge, officers Pitman and Lowe are taking over from Boxhall and Moody. Quartermasters Bright, Wynn and Perkis replace Hichens, Olliver and Rowe. Lookouts Evans and Hogg are replacing Fleet and Lee.

12.05pm Titanic *Bridge Time*

There is a small crowd outside the purser's room where a notice has been posted giving the distance the *Titanic* has travelled in the previous 24 hours. It is a ritual on the Atlantic crossing for passengers to place bets on the figure. The average speed calculated was 22.06 knots, and the ship had covered 546 miles.

12.30pm Titanic *Bridge Time – 1 Bell*

In the wireless room, the message from Mr and Mrs Straus is being sent to their son and his wife, travelling on the Hamburg Line ship, *Amerika*: 'Strauss [sic], *Amerika*. fine voyage fine ship feeling fine what news.'

Other messages sent from the *Titanic* on 14th April included:

'hello Boy dining with you tonight in spirit heart with you always best love
    Girl'

'reserve two rooms with bath and single arriving Wednesday
    Fortune.'

'hardly wait get back cable me awfully happy
    Mutzie'

'Rose greatly improved eats well sleeps well
    Dave'

'No seasickness all well notify all interested poker
    Business good
    Al'

The hero of the Republic, Jack Binns, was called as a witness at the US Senate Inquiry into the sinking of the Titanic and described the role of the wireless operator:

'Normally, the operator is under the command of the captain, whose orders he must at all times obey. There are no fixed regulations in this respect, and the operator, being in charge of an apparatus that no one else on board understands, is to a great extent thoroughly in charge of the working of it. Where a single operator is employed on the ship, he uses his own discretion as to the times when he is on duty. The general practice on the Atlantic Ocean is to remain on watch throughout the greater part of the day and take a rest at night.'

Second Officer Lightoller takes over on the bridge as officer of the watch to allow First Officer Murdoch a half-hour break for lunch. Although he has officially been demoted to second officer for this trip, Lightoller still has the two stripes of a first officer on his sleeve.

Charles Herbert Lightoller has packed a great deal into his 38 years. He went to sea aged 13 to serve his apprenticeship on sailing ships. The following year he was shipwrecked in a storm on an island in the South Indian Ocean, and rescued after eight days when a passing ship saw the smoke from a camp fire. When he was serving as third mate on the Knight of St Michael, her cargo of coal ignited. Lightoller fought the blaze and saved the ship. In 1898 he left the sea to take part in the Yukon gold rush, and when that proved fruitless he became a cowboy in Canada. Lightoller travelled home, first as a hobo on the railroads, then as a cattle wrangler on a cargo ship. He joined the White Star Line in 1900, serving under Captain Smith as first officer on the Majestic. One of his jobs as Second Officer on the Titanic is to make sure the navigation instruments are in good order, as well as the firearms and ammunition. Lightoller retains a love of sailing ships; he longs for 'the towering tiers of bellying canvas, the sound of water rushing past... in place of the monotonous clank and bang of machinery... I missed the feel of something living under my feet.'

The man he's relieving, First Officer William Murdoch, comes from a family of sailors, and he too served his apprenticeship on sailing ships. Murdoch is more at home on the Titanic than Lightoller, as he was first officer on her sister ship the Olympic. When he joined the White Star Line he worked first on the Australian run, before transferring to the North Atlantic liners.

12.45pm Titanic *Bridge Time*

Captain Smith shows Lightoller the *Caronia*'s ice warning. Lightoller makes a mental note of the meridians – 49° to 51° west longitude.

1.00pm Titanic *Bridge Time – 2 Bells*

In first class, 26-year-old Percy Fletcher puts a bugle to his lips and blasts out the tune of 'The Roast Beef of Old England', the traditional White Star Line signal that lunch is served. He then heads to second and third class to do the same.

About 1.30pm Titanic *Bridge Time – 3 Bells*

In the second-class dining saloon, teacher Lawrence Beesley is eating with some other passengers at the table of the assistant purser, Reginald Barker; they are talking about the *Titanic*'s latest daily run of 546 miles.

Barker says, 'They are not pushing her on this trip and I don't intend to make any fast running: I don't suppose we shall do any more than 546 now; it is not a bad day's run for the first trip.'

The group starts talking about their experiences of sailing on other liners, and they are unanimous that the *Titanic* is 'the most comfortable boat they have been on' and that the speed of other ships creates an uncomfortable vibration.

> The Titanic's engines are designed to produce a smooth ride for her passengers, and also to be economical. She has two reciprocating (or piston) steam engines that drive her port and starboard propellers, while the exhaust steam from these engines, instead of going up a funnel, powers a low-pressure turbine that in turn drives a central propeller.
>
> The Titanic *runs two knots slower than Cunard's* Lusitania *and* Mauretania, *with their four propellers powered entirely by steam turbines, but the* Titanic's *three-engine design causes significantly less vibration.*
>
> It has often been claimed that Bruce Ismay wanted the Titanic to win the Blue Riband from Cunard's Mauretania, which had held the record for the fastest westbound Atlantic crossing since 1909, and therefore insisted that Captain Smith sail her at maximum speed. But Ismay would have known that a record-breaking run was impossible, as the Titanic *could not match the* Mauretania's 24 knots. However, he was probably hoping to beat the Olympic's maiden voyage crossing time, and arrive in New York on Tuesday night rather than Wednesday morning.

Lawrence Beesley draws his table's attention to something he's noticed on deck – the ship has a slight list to port. He gets them all to look out of the saloon portholes on the port side where they can see both sea and sky; then he asks them to look out of the portholes on the starboard side where only sky can be seen.

The assistant purser, Reginald Barker, also on Beesley's table, has a theory – he explains it's probably due to the fact that coal for the boilers has been taken mostly from the starboard side.

> *Reginald Barker is correct about the cause of the list but ignorant of the reason why the starboard side is emptier. When the Titanic left Southampton on 10th April, there was a fire in a starboard coal bunker between boiler rooms 5 and 6. The crew finally managed to put the fire out yesterday by raking the 8000 tons of coal out of the bunker. This is producing a list to port.*
>
> *If the fire was still burning by the time they reached their destination, Captain Smith would have had to make a humiliating request to the New York City Fire Department to extinguish it.*
>
> *The fire wasn't reported to Maurice Clark, the assistant emigration officer at the Board of Trade who inspected the Titanic in Southampton on the morning of 10th April, so there was no reason why an assistant purser would know about it. The fire should have been either reported to or detected by Maurice Clark. If Clark had known about it, he would probably have delayed the Titanic's maiden voyage.*

1.49pm Titanic *Bridge Time*

The *Titanic* receives a message from the captain of the *Amerika*: 'Passed two large icebergs 41°27 min. N., 50°8 min. W., on the 14th April. – Knuth.'

Because the message is intended for the Hydrographic Office in Washington via the Cape Race wireless shore station, and doesn't have the prefix MSG (Master Service Gram) which would indicate it has to go straight to the captain, wireless operator Harold Bride decides it doesn't have to be taken to the bridge.

1.54pm Titanic *Bridge Time*

Harold Bride receives a message from the White Star liner the *Baltic*: 'Captain Smith, "Titanic". Have had moderate variable winds and clear fine weather since leaving. Greek steamer "Athenai" reports passing icebergs and large quantities of field ice today at lat. 41°51'N., long. 49°52'W. Last we spoke German oil-tank streamer "Deutschland", Stettin to Philadelphia, not under control, short of coal, lat. 40°42'N. long. 55°11'W. Wishes to be reported to New York and other steamers. Wish you and "Titanic" all success. – Commander.'

Harold Bride writes the message on a slip of paper, puts it into an envelope and takes it to the bridge.

'In this soft silence the titan was flying like an arrow on the trackless sea.'

2.00pm Titanic *Bridge Time – 4 Bells*

On the bridge, the officer of the watch is now Chief Officer Wilde. Archie Jewell and George Symons arrive in the crow's nest to take over from Alfred Evans and George Hogg.

Kate Buss is having a sleep in the steamer chair allocated to Reverend Ernest Carter – his wife Lillian insisted that Kate had a rest, as she looked so tired.

About 2.10pm Titanic *Bridge Time*

Captain Smith meets Bruce Ismay, who is on his way down to the dining saloon for a late lunch. Smith gives Ismay the ice warning from the *Baltic*. Ismay reads it, and then puts the piece of paper in his pocket.

2.30pm Titanic *Bridge Time – 5 Bells*

A wind has got up, and the air is now so cold that few people are venturing on the *Titanic*'s pine decks. First-class passenger Helen Candee described the scene a few weeks later:

'The acres of decks were cleared of loungers, even of those whose chairs were placed well behind the plate-glass weather screen... servants brought tea and toast and a general feeling of well-being brought content and in this soft silence the titan was flying like an arrow on the trackless sea.'

Many passengers commented later that the size and splendour of the Titanic *made them forget they were on a ship. For Dr Washington Dodge, walking on her decks was just as steady as walking along Market Street in his home city of San Francisco. Colonel Archibald Gracie described the* Titanic *as being like 'a summer palace on the sea-shore surrounded with every comfort – there was nothing to indicate that we were on the stormy Atlantic Ocean'. The sense of security the ship brought was to prove hazardous later that day.*

As a result of the uninviting outside temperature, the *Titanic*'s second-class library on C-deck is crowded this afternoon. It has well-stocked glass-cased shelves, comfortable armchairs and a good number of writing and card tables. On the wall is a chart of the North Atlantic, showing the *Titanic*'s progress. With his back to the shelves is the library steward Thomas Kelland, who normally has little to do but lend books, but today he is busy giving out US Customs Declaration forms for passengers to fill in. New York is now only two days away.

Lawrence Beesley is in the library talking to the Reverend Ernest Carter. Although the men differ theologically – Beesley is a Christian Scientist and Carter an Anglican – they agree that it's a pity that there is no Sunday evening service on board. Their church service that morning in the second-class dining saloon had been very brief. Carter asks Beesley if he knows Mr McElroy, the ship's purser, well enough to ask for permission to use the dining saloon for some hymn singing. Beesley agrees to ask him.

On the port and starboard sides of the library are glass-enclosed promenades, which have become play areas for children. Michel and Edmond, the two boys known to their fellow passengers as Lolo and Louis, are playing there. Their father, Michel Navratil, who has abducted them from their mother in Nice, is watching their games. Lawrence Beesley, looking at them through the library windows, is impressed by how attentive he is.

In the library are a couple who also have a secret. Twenty-two-year-old Henriette Yrois is playing the card game patience, watched by a man people (Lawrence Beesley included) assume to be her husband. He is in fact 45-year-old William Harbeck, a documentary filmmaker from Seattle. Henriette is a model he met in Paris a few weeks ago. Harbeck is married with two sons.

William Harbeck made a name for himself filming the aftermath of the 1906 San Francisco earthquake (including one famous shot taken from a burned-out cable car as it was pushed down Market Street) and had been to Paris to meet with Leon Gaumont, the pioneering French filmmaker. Harbeck is making a documentary about the Titanic's maiden voyage; he filmed her departure from

Southampton, and there is a plan for him to be taken off the ship by tug before they get into New York harbour so he can film her arrival.

In his luggage there are 110,000 feet of film.

Esther and Benjamin Hart and their seven-year-old daughter Eva are also in the *Titanic*'s second-class library. Esther is writing a letter home to her elderly parents in Essex, but finds the slight rolling of the ship makes it hard to keep her arm steady. Benjamin is a master builder whose business has been struggling, so he is taking his family to Winnipeg in the hope of setting up a new life there. Esther is already homesick.

'I am always shutting my eyes and I see everything as I left it. I hope you are all quite well. Let this be an all round letter as I can't write properly to all till I can set my foot on shore again...'

Esther has vowed that she won't fall asleep at night, but will instead rest during the day. Every night since Southampton she has sat fully dressed on a case or laid wide awake on their bunk convinced that something terrible will happen to the ship. She wants to be ready. But earlier, as the family was leaving the dining saloon after breakfast, Esther saw a notice saying there would be a service later that morning. For the first time she decided to stay up rather than go to bed.

The Harts had booked on the Philadelphia, *and when that sailing was cancelled due to the coal strike Esther, nervous about any voyage, was relieved. But Benjamin quickly bought tickets for the* Titanic *instead. When they arrived at the quayside at Southampton he said to his wife, 'There, old girl, there's a vessel for you! You're not afraid now.' But Esther was not reassured.*

Esther continues her letter:

'There has been no tempest, but God knows what it must be when there is one. This mighty expanse of water, no land in sight and the ship rolling from side to side is very wonderful...

'This morning Eva and I went to church and she was so pleased they sang "Oh Lord Our Help in Ages Past", that is her hymn she sang so nicely, so she sang out loud, she is very bonny. There is to be a concert on board tomorrow night in aid of the Sailors Home and she is going to sing, so am I... It is nice weather but awfully windy and cold. They say we may get into New York Tuesday night but we were really due early on Wednesday morning...'

The Titanic's *crew has got to hear about Esther's nocturnal vigil. At lunch an officer had joined their table.*

'Does that mean that now we are getting across the Atlantic you have got over your fears?' he asked Esther.

'Oh no. I'm going to bed now.'

'Ah, well, we shall be quite safe if you look after us again tonight,' he said kindly, patting her on the shoulder.

Esther decided to stay up a little longer and write a letter in the library.

She finishes it by saying:

'It's the longest week I ever spent in my life. I must close now, with all our fondest love to all of you,

'From your loving Ess'

Then her daughter comes over to add her own greeting:

'Heaps of love and kisses to all from Eva xxxxxxxxxxxxxxxx'

2.57pm Titanic *Bridge Time*

Harold Bride sends Captain Smith's reply to the ice warning from the fellow White Star liner *Baltic*. 'Thanks for your message and good wishes; had fine weather since leaving. – Smith.'

'Am going to take my very much needed rest on this trip, but I cannot get over my feeling of depression and premonition of trouble.'

4.00pm Titanic *Bridge Time – 8 Bells*

Officers Joseph Boxhall and James Moody replace Herbert Pitman and Harold Lowe on the bridge. Lookouts Fleet and Lee swap with Jewell and Symons in the crow's nest. Quartermasters Hichens, Olliver and Rowe take over from Bright, Wynn and Perkis.

The *Titanic*'s heating system is not working everywhere – in some first- and second-class public areas, people are wearing fur coats. It is so cold that Edith Rosenbaum has stayed in bed in her first-class cabin all day. She finally decides to get dressed and go on deck.

> *The 33-year-old journalist, who writes under the name Edith Russell, has been in Paris reporting on the latest fashions. She's paid for a cabin on E-deck, just to store the large number of trunks filled with clothes she has for her clients in America. When she tried to get insurance for the trip, she was told it was unnecessary as the* Titanic *was unsinkable.*

In fact, the White Star Line never described Titanic *as 'unsinkable.' During the ship's construction they described her watertight doors in their literature like this:*

'…in the event of an accident, or at any time that might be advisable, the captain can, by simply moving an electric switch, instantly close the doors throughout – practically making the vessel unsinkable.' The word 'practically' was soon forgotten.

Edith Rosenbaum is not enjoying the voyage. In a letter to her secretary in Paris, sent from Queenstown, she wrote:

> *It is a monster, and I can't say I like it, as I feel as if I were in a big hotel, instead of on a cozy ship; everyone is so stiff and formal. There are hundreds of help, bell boys, stewards, stewardesses and lifts. To say that it is wonderful, is unquestionable, but not the cozy ship-board feeling of former years… Am going to take my very much needed rest on this trip, but I cannot get over my feeling of depression and premonition of trouble.*
>
> *How I wish it were over!*
> *Yours sincerely, Edith*

It's not only passengers who feel uneasy. Even the Titanic's *chief officer Henry Wilde wrote to his sister in a letter sent from Queenstown: 'I still don't like this ship… I have a queer feeling about it.'*

About 4.30pm Titanic *Bridge Time – 1 Bell*

In first class, maids, valets and bedroom stewards are laying out clothes for their passengers to wear for what some are calling this evening's 'gala dinner'.

There are dress codes in first class, which not every traveller may be aware of. Shortly after the loss of the Titanic, *a book called* Etiquette *by society hostess Emily Post was published. She wrote: 'On the de luxe steamers, nearly everyone dresses for dinner; some actually in ball dresses, which is the worst possible taste, and, like all overdressing in public places, indicates they have no other place to show their finery. People of position never put on formal evening-dress on a steamer, not even in the à la carte restaurant... in the dining saloon they wear afternoon house dresses – without hats – for dinner. In the restaurant they wear semi-dinner dresses.'*

There is no laundry service on the Titanic. *The White Star Line believe passengers won't require newly washed clothes because her voyages will be so swift.*

5.00pm Titanic *Bridge Time – 2 Bells*

The *Titanic* reaches 'the corner', a location 42° north latitude and 47° west longitude where ships heading west take a more southerly route to avoid icebergs. Captain Smith orders the change of course to be made at 5.45pm.

In 1899, official Atlantic shipping lanes were agreed to keep east-bound and westbound ships at a safe distance, and to increase the chances that a ship in trouble could be helped by another following the same course. The Titanic *is following the 'southern track', a route used by ships in the Atlantic between 15th January and 23rd August to avoid drifting ice and fog.*

In the wireless room, Harold Bride is sitting at what is called the operating table – the table that holds the transmitting apparatus – working on his accounts, tallying up the cost of the telegrams sent yesterday. He is still wearing his telephone headset, to listen to any incoming messages.

5.05pm Titanic *Bridge Time*

Renée Harris, the wife of Broadway producer Henry B. Harris, is walking down the grand staircase from B-deck to C-deck. She is taking a break from a poker game in the stateroom of first-class passenger Charlotte Cardez. Renée is feeling rather pleased with herself as she's ahead by $90, but she needs a short break and is heading to her cabin.

Renée fails to spot a cream cake that has been dropped on the stairway – she slips and falls, breaking her right arm. A steward runs to find Dr O'Loughlin, the ship's surgeon.

5.45pm Titanic *Bridge Time*

Quartermaster George Rowe is at the helm, and alters the *Titanic*'s course to S85°W, N71°W. The *Titanic* has travelled 129 miles since noon, at an average speed of 22.3 knots. She is now lined up almost exactly with the entrance to New York harbour.

> *On a big boat like that a man working inside doesn't go on deck very often. Sometimes you don't get a peep at the water for days at a time. It's just like working in a big hotel. But I knew that it was mighty cold outside, and I knew what the reason was, too... it's because there's icebergs around.*
>
> **Walter Nichols, assistant saloon steward**

6.00pm Titanic *Bridge Time – 4 Bells, Second Dog Watch Begins*

Two ladies are on deck braving the cold. Marian Thayer and her friend Emily Ryerson are watching the pink sunset while seated on steamer chairs in the first-class section of A-deck.

Contrary to legend, the Titanic *does not have any deckchairs to rearrange; instead it has heavier adjustable wooden steamer chairs. One of the first-class steamer chairs went ashore at Queenstown with photographer Thomas Barker who had asked a crew member if he could have one for a souvenir. Barker placed it in his garden until the sinking, then he gave it to his housekeeper.*

Emily Ryerson is hurrying home to New York after a shopping trip to Paris with her attorney husband Arthur was cut short by the news of the death of their eldest son in a motor car accident. This is the first day of the voyage that Emily has left her stateroom. Travelling with Emily and Arthur are their surviving children, Suzette, Emily and John.

Bruce Ismay, tall and looking impeccable in a dark-blue suit, walks over to them. When he had heard the reason for the Ryersons' hastily arranged journey home, he offered them an extra stateroom and a steward to make their passage easier. Ismay knows Marian Thayer from previous voyages on White Star ships. She is 39, attractive, wealthy, and a fashion icon for the Philadelphia papers.

'I hope you are comfortable, and are all right,' Ismay says to Emily Ryerson. They chat for a while, but the conversation is awkward. An introvert, Bruce Ismay is not good at small talk.

'We are in amongst icebergs,' Ismay says, and produces the ice warning from the *Baltic* that Captain Smith gave him before lunch.

'The ship hasn't been going fast but we may fire up extra boilers this afternoon or evening.'

Although Ismay doesn't let the ladies hold the wireless message, Emily Ryerson can see a mention of another vessel that seems to be in trouble.

'That's the *Deutschland* wanting a tow – "not under control".'

'What are you going to do about that?' Emily Ryerson asks him.

'We have no time to worry about the *Deutschland*, we want to get in [to New York] and surprise everybody.'

Arthur Ryerson and John Thayer arrive to join their wives, and Bruce Ismay says his farewells and walks inside. The Ryersons and the Thayers follow him, discussing what they will do if the *Titanic* arrives on Tuesday night rather than Wednesday morning.

> *Later, when asked to recall the conversation, Ismay could remember only Marian Thayer being there. He quickly acquired a fascination with her during the* Titanic's *short voyage.*

With sunset approaching, oil lamps are being put in the *Titanic*'s two emergency lifeboats by trimmer Samuel Hemming. This is a task that is done every day at this time. The emergency lifeboats, nos. 1 and 2 of the ship's total of 16 wooden lifeboats, are used if a man falls overboard.

> *The name 'lamp trimmer' comes from the days of oil lamps, which needed almost constant attention – either their wicks had to be trimmed or their reservoirs had to be topped up.*

On the bridge, it's another change of watch. Officers Herbert Pitman and Harold Lowe have arrived to take over from Joseph Boxhall and James Moody. Quartermaster Bright takes over from George Rowe at the ship's wheel. Fleet and Lee climb down the ladder inside the foremast, leaving Evans and Hogg in charge of the crow's nest.

6.15pm Titanic *Bridge Time*

Journalist Edith Rosenbaum is wrapped up against the cold, standing at the rear of the boat deck, watching the wake stirred up by the ship's three enormous propellers. She wrote later: 'The foam whirled in a great crusade, made blood-red by the rays of a glorious setting sun. It looked like a crimson carpet stretching from the ship to the horizon.'

Edith then heads to A-deck and her stateroom, to dress for dinner. She intends to wear a white satin evening gown with velvet slippers.

6.30pm Titanic *Bridge Time – 1 Bell*

Dr O'Loughlin, the ship's surgeon, and Dr Henry Frauenthal are leaving Renée Harris's cabin. O'Loughlin recruited first-class passenger Frauenthal, an orthopaedic surgeon, to help him set her fractured arm.

Wearing a sling, Renée turns to her husband Henry and says, 'Help me get dressed. I'm going up for dinner. I'm hungry.'

Henry looks at her in surprise.

6.45pm Titanic *Bridge Time*

Bedroom steward Henry Etches is laying out clothes for the *Titanic*'s chief designer, Thomas Andrews. Most people get ready for dinner earlier, but Etches knows that Mr Andrews is always late dressing.

6.52pm Titanic *Bridge Time*

The sun has disappeared over the horizon, in front of the *Titanic*'s bow.

7.00pm Titanic *Bridge Time* – 2 Bells

In first class, Percy Fletcher once more blasts out the tune of 'The Roast Beef of Old England' on his bugle. Dinner is served.

The ship's last three primary boilers, which had been heating up for a number of hours, are being connected to the engines. The *Titanic* is now being powered by all 29 of her boilers. Her speed increases to 22.5 knots.

First Officer Murdoch arrives on the bridge to allow Second Officer Lightoller to go for dinner in the officers' mess towards the rear of the boat deck.

In the crow's nest, lookout George Hogg notices that the wind has dropped. The temperature has dropped to 43° Fahrenheit.

7.10pm Titanic *Bridge Time*

Bruce Ismay is sitting in the first-class smoking room. It is a beautiful room with a tiled floor, carved mahogany-panelled walls and elaborately etched mirrors. Captain Smith approaches and asks for the ice warning from the *Baltic* he gave him earlier in the day, as he wants to put it on the board of the chart room to alert his officers. Without any comment, Ismay gives him the message.

> Ismay said later that he had placed it in his jacket absent-mindedly. 'If the information I had received had aroused any apprehension in my mind – which it did not – I should not have ventured to make any suggestion to a commander of Captain Smith's experience and responsibility, for the navigation of the ship rested solely with him.' The British inquiry into the disaster concluded that 'it was irregular

for the Master [Smith] to part with the document, and improper for Mr Ismay to retain it, but the incident had no connection or influence upon the manner in which the vessel was navigated by the Master'.

7.15pm Titanic *Bridge Time*

First Officer Murdoch is talking to lamp trimmer Samuel Hemming. 'When you go forward, see the fore-scuttle hatch is closed as we are in the vicinity of ice, and there is a glow coming from it, and I want everything dark before the bridge.' Murdoch doesn't want anything disturbing his or the lookouts' night vision.

7.22pm Titanic *Bridge Time*

Harold Bride is in the wireless room still absorbed in his accounts. A message comes in from the Leyland Line ship the *Californian*, heading to Boston from London under the command of Captain Stanley Lord: 'Three large bergs five miles to southward of us, regards, Lord.'

Bride doesn't write the message down or acknowledge it.

> **It was a rare gathering of beautiful women and splendid men. There was that atmosphere of fellowship and delightful sociability which made the Sabbath dinner on board ship a delightful occasion.**
>
> **May Futrelle, first-class passenger**

7.30pm Titanic *Bridge Time – 3 Bells*

Second Officer Charles Lightoller has finished his dinner and returned to the *Titanic*'s bridge. First Officer Murdoch tells him that the temperature has dropped a further 4°, to 39° Fahrenheit – a drop of 10° in two hours.

Lightoller goes onto the bridge wing with Third Officer Herbert Pitman to take a set of star sights to calculate the ship's position.

It seems likely that Pitman miscalculates by one minute when he translates these measurements to the Titanic's chronometer time. This will have serious consequences for the rescue attempts later that night and indeed for the attempts decades later to find the Titanic at the bottom of the ocean.

The *Titanic*'s first-class à la carte restaurant is almost full. Those dining are paying an extra tariff – the food served here is not included in the price of their ticket, unlike in the dining saloons. It helps to keep it exclusive.

The restaurant is panelled with French walnut with gilded mouldings and a dark rose-coloured Axminster carpet. The White Star Line chose London-based restaurateur Gaspare Gatti to run it – his staff are drawn from the capital's finest kitchens.

At one table is a 'boat man' or professional gambler, who sits, 'with a cold-blooded smile on his face', as one passenger later recalled. At another table, 46-year-old ostrich feather dealer George Rosenshine is dining with his 38-year-old mistress Maybelle Thorne; they are travelling as Mr and Mrs G. Thorne.

Margaret 'Molly' Brown is in the restaurant with her friend Emma Bucknell. They watch Captain Smith arrive for a large private dinner party hosted by George and Eleanor Widener. Emma whispers, 'Shouldn't he be on the bridge? I've heard rumours of ice and such.'

'Nonsense, he often dines with first-class passengers,' Molly replies.

Captain Smith pauses at the table of Broadway producer Henry B. Harris to compliment his wife Renée on being up and about so soon after breaking her arm.

'I'd suffer just as much in our room as I would here, and I wouldn't have these gay surroundings,' Renée jokes.

The Wideners have invited a select number of people to dine with them and Captain Smith. Their large table, partially hidden in an alcove in the forward starboard quarter of the restaurant, is the centre of attention. Lady Duff Gordon, sitting nearby, can hear a great deal of laughter and chatter from the party. Around the Wideners' table are some of the wealthiest people on the East Coast.

George Widener is a banker and streetcar magnate, and he and his wife Eleanor are returning from a shopping trip in Paris to buy their daughter's trousseau for her imminent wedding. Their daughter has stayed behind in France, but their 27-year-old son Harry is with them. Harry is a keen and renowned collector of rare books; with him on the Titanic *is his latest purchase – a rare 1598 edition of Francis Bacon's essays that he bought in London for £260.*

The other guests around the table are John and Marian Thayer; William 'Billy' Carter and his wife Lucile, who are returning from hunting in England; and, sitting next to Marian Thayer, Major Archibald Butt, an aide-de-camp to former US President Theodore Roosevelt and now to his successor, President William Howard Taft. Marian and the major have never met before but are getting along famously. They agree to meet on Monday so that Marian can show him a method of 'controlling his nerves' that she learned from a Swiss doctor.

> *Butt is returning from a holiday in Europe that President Taft had suggested his 'dear Archie' should take. Marian wrote later to President Taft that Major Butt 'did not know how he was going to stand in the rushing life he was returning to, and we were going to work so hard over it, the rest of the time on board'.*
>
> *Butt is indispensible to President Taft – he plays golf with him (often losing deliberately); he is his chief of protocol and soothes the president when he is upset by children shouting 'Hello, Fatty' at him.*
>
> *Not dining at the Wideners' table is the man who Major Butt always introduces as 'Millet, my artist friend who lives with me'. Francis Millet, the artist who a few days before had written a letter complaining about 'obnoxious, ostentatious American women' with their tiny dogs and compliant husbands, is dining in the first-class saloon two decks below. Millet has a wife in Massachusetts but he shares a house in Washington with Butt, staffed by house-boys from the Philippines.*

'Now that's the way a lady should look!'

In the first-class dining saloon the atmosphere and style easily match that of the restaurant. The ladies are showing off their Parisian gowns, jewellery and the latest hairstyle – a hair-piece called the 'transformation'. Businessman Elmer Taylor recalled, 'It was a brilliant assembly – contentment and happiness prevailed. Conversations were perhaps animated by a social cocktail or two...'

On the dining-saloon tables are souvenir menus. There is a wide choice for dinner: various hors d'oeuvre, oysters, consommé Olga, cream of barley, salmon, mousseline sauce, cucumber, filet mignons Lili, sauté of chicken Lyonnais, vegetable marrow farcie, lamb, mint sauce, roast duckling, apple sauce, sirloin of beef, chateau potatoes, peas, creamed carrots, boiled rice, parmentier and boiled new potatoes, punch Romaine, roast squab and cress, cold asparagus vinaigrette, pâté de foie gras, celery, Waldorf pudding, peaches in Chartreuse jelly, chocolate and vanilla éclairs and French ice cream.

Thirty-six-year-old Eleanor Cassebeer arrives at the purser's table in the dining saloon wearing a white lace dress and ermine stole. The ship's designer Thomas Andrews exclaims, 'Now that's the way a lady should look!'

Twenty-two-year-old Marguerite Frölicher is looking rather pale at the table she's sharing with her mother and father. The voyage so far has been smooth, but Marguerite has been seasick almost continually since they left Queenstown on 11th April. ('If only the darn ship would sink!' she'd said to her father.) Dressed in a warm woollen suit, this is the first time she's been out of her stateroom for days. Marguerite desperately wants to be well by the time they reach New York, as she is meeting her fiancé Robert there – but she is starting to feel nauseous again. The *Titanic*'s doctors offer only two cures for seasickness – beef tea or smelling salts.

John and Marian Thayer's son Jack is in the reception room outside the dining saloon, close to the piano, waiting for the musicians to start playing. He hasn't been invited to dine at the Wideners' table upstairs in the à la carte restaurant. Jack has spent much of the day walking around the ship with his parents talking with acquaintances such as Thomas Andrews and Bruce Ismay.

A young man sitting by himself with his back to Jack gets up and asks if he can use the box of matches on Jack's table. Jack passes them to him and the man introduces himself as Milton Long, the son of Judge Charles M. Long of Springfield, Massachusetts. He says he's returning home after skiing in St Moritz.

Bruce Ismay has left the smoking room and is now in the restaurant, two decks above Jack and Milton, eating with Dr William O'Loughlin, as he often does when they sail together. They have a table in the middle of the room. O'Loughlin, looking very smart in his crisp white uniform, has worked at sea since the 1870s.

On the next table, Lucy Duff Gordon is dining with her husband Cosmo. On their table, much to her delight, is a vase of beautiful fresh daffodils. The *Titanic*'s ability to provide such luxuries in the middle of the Atlantic prompted her to say to Cosmo earlier in the voyage, 'Why, you would think that we were at the Ritz!'

Lucy Duff Gordon hasn't dressed formally for dinner – she's wearing warm clothes since the temperature dropped after lunch. Even shutting the portholes in her cabin and leaving her electric heater on made no difference.

The second-class dining saloon on D-deck is full of the smells of dinner: baked haddock, curried chicken and rice, roast turkey with savoury cranberry sauce, peas, turnips, boiled and roast potatoes.

Esther Hart, who has vowed not to go to bed at night on

the ship, and her husband Benjamin are eating their evening meal. Their daughter Eva is asleep in their cabin, cuddling her favourite doll.

Third-class passengers on F-deck are enjoying rabbit pie, baked potatoes, bread and butter, rhubarb-and-ginger jam, Swedish bread and tea.

About 7.37pm Titanic *Bridge Time*

In the second-class dining saloon, Kate Buss, the Englishwoman travelling to San Diego to marry her fiancé, is being teased by her dinner companions. Earlier that evening the pianist in the ship's band, Theo Brailey, had asked Kate if she would 'take round the subscription' [collect the tips] the next day as she liked their music so much. Kate is trying to persuade a young Scot named Douglas Norman to do it for her; he agrees saying, 'Meet me on the upper deck at six in the morning. I will talk it over.'

In the *Titanic*'s wireless room, Harold Bride hears the *Californian* send a message to another Leyland Line ship, the *Antillian*. It's the same message sent to him 20 minutes ago: 'Three large bergs five miles to southward of us, regards, Lord.'

This time Bride jots it down and taps out a message to the *Californian*, thanking them. He then heads off to the bridge to give it to the officer of the watch, Charles Lightoller.

8.00pm Titanic *Bridge Time – 8 Bells*

There's a change of watch. Officers Joseph Boxhall and James Moody replace Herbert Pitman and Harold Lowe. Boxhall comes into the chart room and Pitman hands over the set of star sights he and Lightoller took earlier in order to calculate the ship's position.

'Here's a bunch of sights for you, old man. Go ahead.'

Pitman heads to his cabin for a sleep, as he's back on duty at midnight.

Quartermaster Hichens is on standby, ready to convey any messages from the bridge. He looks at the thermometer. It reads 31.5° Fahrenheit.

It's noticeably colder in the crow's nest for lookouts Jewell and Symons, who have started their watch, replacing Evans and Hogg.

> **Nothing on board was more popular than the orchestra. Everyone asked of it some favourite hit.**
>
> **Helen Candee, first-class passenger**

8.15pm Titanic *Bridge Time*

In the reception room outside the first-class dining saloon, not far from Jack Thayer and Milton Long, Colonel Archibald Gracie is enjoying coffee with his old friend James Clinch Smith, and the architect Edward Kent. They are enjoying the music played by the ship's band and commenting on the number of attractive women on the *Titanic*. Gracie doesn't plan to stay long as he wants an early night – he's going to exercise in the gym in the morning. His bedroom steward Charles Cullen has promised to wake him.

Some passengers are asking Wallace Hartley and his band to play a favourite piece of music by Dvorak or Puccini. One young girl asks for a dance tune, and as the band plays, she sways to the music.

Each first-class passenger was given a copy of the White Star Line Music Book containing 352 tunes. They call out a number, and the band, who have rehearsed them all, play it. This is the origin of a song being known as 'a number'.

Earlier that evening the musicians played a piece from Offenbach's The Tales of Hoffman. *Many years later, Lucy, Countess of Rothes was dining out with friends when she suddenly had 'the awful feeling of intense cold and horror'. She realised it had been the last piece of music that she'd heard the* Titanic's *band play.*

There is music in the third-class dining room too – an impromptu party is taking place, with passenger Eugene Daly providing the music with his uilleann (elbow) pipes. Even the sight of a rat scurrying across the deck doesn't spoil the mood – some young boys try to catch it.

Eugene Daly's uilleann pipes have provided a musical soundtrack for much of the third-class passengers' voyage thus far – he often plays them on the aft well deck, one of the promenade areas for third class.

Twenty-nine-year-old Daly boarded the Titanic *at Queenstown, and as the ship sailed away from Ireland, he played a sad farewell on his pipes – 'Erin's Lament'.*

Eugene's father, a policeman, was killed when he was 12, and since then, Eugene has been the main breadwinner for the family. He is travelling to New York in the hope of finding work and has timed the journey to coincide with a pipes competition that is part of a Gaelic Festival in Queens. Eugene is travelling with his cousin Maggie Daly.

8.20pm Titanic *Bridge Time*

As it's too cold for an evening stroll on deck, many second-class passengers are heading to their dining saloon for some hymn singing organised by the Whitechapel vicar, Reverend Ernest Carter.

In the reception room outside the first-class dining saloon, Jack Thayer is still talking with Milton Long. They have covered a wide range of subjects – the differences between cricket and baseball, stamp collecting, the fact that Milton was forbidden from doing the Cresta Run by his parents as they feared their only child's safety.

About 8.30pm Titanic *Bridge Time – 1 Bell*

The hymn singing in the second-class dining saloon is about to start. About one hundred people have turned up and are sitting at the tables with their fixed swivel chairs.

Harold Bride is getting into his bunk in the cabin next to the wireless room. He can hear Jack Phillips hard at work next door, and can tell just by his tapping of the transmitting key that he's establishing contact with the shore station at Cape Race in Newfoundland. Bride's shift is due to start at 2am, but he's promised he will get up earlier, as Phillips had been very busy the previous night.

8.45pm Titanic *Bridge Time*

Dinner over, Dr William O'Loughlin is making his rounds, visiting any first-class passengers who have been taken ill.

In his cabin in the officers' quarters close to the bridge, Fifth Officer Harold Lowe is fast asleep. He went to bed only a few minutes ago, but he has no trouble sleeping. He explained once, 'We do not have any too much sleep and therefore when we sleep, we die.'

Like his fellow officers Wilde, Murdoch and Lightoller, 29-year-old Harold Lowe learned his trade in sailing ships rather than steamers. He is a tough character – at the age of 12, when his father's punt capsized, he swam half a mile to shore in his boots. At 14 he ran away to sea to be a cabin boy on a schooner, after his father tried to get him to take up an apprenticeship with a Liverpool businessman. Lowe joined the White Star Line just over a year before setting sail on the Titanic. He feels like an outsider on the Titanic, as all the other officers have already served together. Lowe can speak fluent Welsh, but his English has no trace of a Welsh accent.

'This is a knock-out'. We seem to be miles above the water, and there are certainly miles of promenade deck. The lobbies are so long that they appear to come to a point in the distance. Just finished dinner. They call us up to dress by bugle! It reminded me of some Russian villages where they call the cattle home from the fields by a horn made from the bark of a tree. Such a dinner!!! My gracious!!!

Arthur Gee, first-class passenger

8.55pm Titanic *Bridge Time*

Captain Smith has left the Wideners' dinner party and is on the bridge talking to Second Officer Charles Lightoller about the icy conditions.

'There's not much wind,' Smith says.

'No, it is a flat calm as a matter of fact.'

'A flat calm,' Smith repeats.

Lightoller says that he wishes there was some wind, as it would create waves that would make 'a dog's bone of foam' on the base of bergs, making them easier to spot.

'If it becomes at all doubtful let me know at once – I will be just inside,' the captain says. He heads for his quarters, just behind the bridge.

Lightoller tells Sixth Officer James Moody to use the telephone to call the crow's nest and instruct Jewell and Symons to keep a sharp lookout for small ice – particularly growlers. He then tells quartermaster Robert Hichens to get the ship's carpenter to check on the fresh water supply – stored in tanks below the waterline – as it might freeze.

> *A steamship's carpenter performs many tasks that were the responsibility of his predecessors in the age of sail. Fresh water used to be stored in wooden barrels, and so it was the carpenter's job to check that they were well sealed.*

James Moody calls the crow's nest on the telephone. George Symons answers, and holds the receiver so Archie Jewell can also hear.

'Keep a sharp lookout for small ice until daylight, and pass the word along.'

Moody hangs up, but he hasn't mentioned growlers. Lightoller overhears and gets him to call the lookouts again with the correct instruction.

About 9.00pm Titanic *Bridge Time* – 2 Bells

On the bridge, Lightoller is scanning the darkness, occasionally using the binoculars that are always to hand. What Lightoller doesn't know is that the *Titanic* has been sailing past icebergs for almost an hour.

Lookouts Symons and Jewell are well wrapped up against the cold. The *Titanic*'s speed causes a breeze to whip around the crow's nest.

'By the smell of it, there's ice about. As a rule you can smell the ice before you get to it,' Jewell says.

A passenger can also smell the ice. Governess Elizabeth Shutes, in her first-class cabin on C-deck, thinks the air has a strange odour, and it reminds her of the time she visited an ice cave on the Eiger Glacier in Switzerland.

9.15pm Titanic *Bridge Time*

The hymn singing in the oak-panelled second-class dining saloon is going well. The young Scotsman Douglas Norman is playing the saloon's Steinway upright piano. Marion Wright, whom he's befriended on the voyage, is singing solo verses from the hymns 'There Is a Green Hill Far Away' and 'Lead, Kindly Light'. It's an informal gathering – people call out the hymn they'd like sung and Reverend Carter speaks briefly about its author and tells the story of how it was written. Lawrence Beesley, who has helped organise the evening, notices that the hymn 'Eternal Father, Strong to Save', with its lines 'for those in peril on the sea' is being sung in hushed tones.

Theology student Sidney Collett, on his way to join his family in America, is admiring Marion's singing.

Just before the Titanic *left Southampton, Collett was standing at the rail looking down to the quayside at his uncle and aunt, who had come to see him off. His aunt was beckoning vigorously to him, pointing at a girl standing nearby. It was Marion Wright, a friend of the family. Since then, Collett has taken Marion and her new friend Kate Buss under his wing. However, Marion and Kate are not keen on Collett's evangelical fervour. In the letter in which Kate expressed her admiration for 'The Cello Man' in the ship's band, she complained that Collett 'tries to teach us all religion'.*

Thirty-seven-year-old Mathilde Weisz is enjoying the hymn singing. Her husband Leopold is walking up on deck because, unlike his wife, he is Jewish. He is the same age as her and originally from Bromsgrove. A stonemason, he has found plenty of work in Quebec, and has returned to fetch Mathilde. He is wrapped up against the cold in a black Astrakhan coat that has $15,000 worth of gold coins sewn into its lining – all their life savings.

In the first-class reception room, Wallace Hartley is drawing the band's performance to a close. They now have to set up in the C-deck entrance foyer to entertain second-class passengers for half an hour.

Lucy Duff Gordon is sitting with her secretary Laura 'Franks' Francatelli by the electric heater in her stateroom on A-deck and discussing the evening.

Ice is forming on the glass of the portholes of empty cabins.

9.30pm Titanic *Bridge Time – 3 Bells*

Among the groups of passengers enjoying the luxury of the oak-panelled first-class lounge on A-deck, with its many alcoves for private conversations and card games, is 22-year-old American actress Dorothy Gibson. She is playing bridge with her mother Pauline, Frederick K. Seward whom she knows from her church in New York, and 28-year-old William Sloper, a stockbroker from Connecticut. Dorothy had seen Sloper writing a letter on the other side of the room and asked him to join them at bridge and make a fourth. Although Sloper admitted to being a poor player, he agreed to join them once he'd finished his letter. For the maiden voyage, the chief steward has relaxed the White Star Line's Sunday ban on card games.

Dorothy Gibson made her name, first as a model and then as a silent movie star for the New Jersey-based studio Éclair. In October 1911 she met 41-year-old movie mogul Jules Bruletour and they began an affair. They are both married.

In the last couple of years Dorothy has starred in a number of melodramas such as Love Finds a Way *and* The Kodak Contest. *She's paid $175 a week (about $4000 today). In March 1912, desperate for a holiday, Dorothy and her mother sailed for Europe, but after three weeks the studio summoned her home, as she was needed to star in a new series of films. Despite the interruption, Dorothy sailed from Cherbourg for New York on the* Titanic, *feeling 'like a new woman'.*

It's now so cold that Second Officer Lightoller asks the standby quartermaster Robert Hichens to find the deck engineer and get him to bring up the key for the heaters in the officers' quarters, the wheelhouse and the chart room.

9.40pm Titanic *Bridge Time*

For those not keen to retire to their cabins just yet, the open fire in the first-class reading and writing room on A-deck is proving popular. Fifty-two-year-old Martha Eustis Stephenson and her 54-year-old sister Elizabeth are enjoying its warmth. Martha is reading Ernest Shackleton's book *The Heart of the Antarctic*, with its fine selection of pictures of glaciers and icebergs.

9.45pm Titanic *Bridge Time*

Quartermaster Robert Hichens, who is running messages from the bridge, tells First Officer Murdoch that he's due on the bridge in 15 minutes.

The Hart family are in their second-class cabin. Seven-year-old Eva is fast asleep in her bunk, and her father Benjamin is reading in the bunk above. Esther is keeping her anxious vigil, sitting on a suitcase fully dressed, all the time waiting and listening, knowing that something bad is going to happen.

9.52pm Titanic *Bridge Time*

Stewardess Violet Jessop is on deck, getting some air and having a few moments alone with her thoughts. Her 16-hour shift is over and time on her own is rare. She shivers from the cold. It was, she wrote later, 'a night for bed, warmth and cozy thoughts of home and firesides'. As she steps indoors, Violet thinks of the men high in the crow's nest on this cold night and feels sorry for them. She can see that the first-class corridors are mostly deserted, apart from a few stewards yawning 'with one eye on the companion clock', and passengers heading with friends to their staterooms for a final drink and a smoke.

The freighter SS *Mesaba* is sending a message to all ships heading west: 'Saw much heavy pack ice, and a great number large icebergs. Also field ice. Weather good. Clear.' The message is picked up by Jack Phillips in the *Titanic*'s wireless room, but he simply puts the message under a paperweight. He is frantically busy, getting through a backlog of passengers' messages to send to America now they are in range of the wireless shore station at Cape Race in Newfoundland, 400 miles away. Harold Bride is asleep in the cabin next door.

On the afterbridge at the stern, quartermaster George Rowe is feeling the cold. He can see what's nicknamed 'whiskers round the light' – minute splinters of ice caught in the glow of the deck lights.

He calls up the bridge and speaks to his fellow quartermaster Robert Hichens to give him the log reading. It shows that *Titanic* has travelled 45 nautical miles since the last reading at 8pm, at an average speed of 22.5 knots.

One of the key tasks of the quartermaster on the afterbridge is to measure the ship's speed and the distance run every two hours, using a log-line that trails in the ship's wake.

The Titanic *is sailing at speed and at night into an area where Captain Smith has been warned there is ice. The Antarctic explorer Ernest Shackleton said in 1912 that it was his policy to slow his ship to 3 to 4 knots when there was a danger of ice.*

10.00pm Titanic *Bridge Time – 4 Bells*

The lights in the third-class public rooms are being turned off. The impromptu uilleann pipes party winds up.

The *Titanic*'s chief designer Thomas Andrews is back in state-room A-36 working at his desk. There are charts and drawings rolled up by the side of his bed, as well as on the table.

First Officer Murdoch is taking over from Charles Lightoller as officer of the watch, while Frederick Fleet and Reginald Lee have finished their climb to the crow's nest, relieving Archie

Jewell and George Symons. Murdoch and Lightoller are standing, looking ahead, chatting as Murdoch's eyes get used to the dark. They talk about how well the ship is running, and the 'items of interest': the weather, how clear the night is – they can see stars right down to the horizon – ice reports and the *Titanic*'s course and speed.

Robert Hichens is now at the helm in the wheelhouse.

> *Lookout Frederick Fleet is a 25-year-old former Barnado's boy, who has been at sea since he was 16. Before joining the* Titanic *he spent four years as a lookout on the White Star Line's* Oceanic. *During that time he's never spotted an iceberg.*
>   *Icebergs are generally easy to see at night if there are waves breaking at their base. Tonight it is very calm.*

Seventeen-year-old Jack Thayer is braving the cold and walking around the first-class section of the boat deck. The wind is whistling through the stays supporting the funnels, which are churning out black smoke. Thayer is struck by how smooth the sea is under the starry night; he described it later as 'innocent looking... it was the kind of night that made one glad to be alive'.

> *The* Titanic's *rear funnel is a dummy funnel whose purpose is to provide ventilation for the engine room. When the ship called at Queenstown, one of the firemen climbed up the ladder inside it. His soot-covered face shocked the passengers, and was taken by some as a bad omen.*

In the second-class dining saloon, the congregation is singing 'Stand up, Stand up for Jesus' (without any accompaniment from pianist Douglas Norman as he doesn't have the sheet music), while the stewards lay out coffee and biscuits. The Reverend Carter can see that it's time to end the hymn singing; he thanks the purser for permission to use the room and says how much everyone is looking forward to their arrival in New York.

'It is the first time that there have been hymns sung on this boat on a Sunday evening, but we trust and pray it won't be the last,' he adds.

10.10pm Titanic *Bridge Time*

Despite her broken arm, Renée Harris and her husband Henry are in their C-deck stateroom playing Double Canfield – their favourite card game. Renée is wrapped up in a bathrobe and a blanket as the room is so cold.

Before he turns in for the night, Charles Lightoller is doing the rounds of the ship, to see that all is well. He is heading for the stern afterbridge to check that quartermaster George Rowe is at his post. His route takes in the E-deck passage that runs almost the entire length of the *Titanic* and is nicknamed Scotland Road. Before Lightoller can get to bed, he must walk well over a mile.

10.21pm Titanic *Bridge Time*

On the bridge of the Leyland Line cargo ship, the *Californian*, her third officer, 24-year-old Charles Groves, spots white patches in the water ahead. He thinks it's a school of porpoises crossing their bows. The *Californian*'s captain, Stanley Lord, sees them too, but he knows they aren't porpoises – they're ice. Standing at the engine order telegraph, he rings 'Full Speed Astern'.

The Californian *is a cargo vessel, although she can take 47 passengers. On this voyage, she has none. Lord is 34 years old and has been a captain with the Leyland Line for five years. He is autocratic, and his officers are intimidated by him.*

10.24pm Titanic *Bridge Time*

The *Californian* comes to a stop, surrounded by light field ice. Captain Lord tells Groves to take in the log-line at the stern – but it's already been cut by the ice.

Lord decides that the *Californian* should stay put for the night. Although it is his first encounter with Atlantic ice, he knows it is too dangerous to proceed.

The *Californian* is on the edge of an ice field 28 miles long. The *Titanic* is less than an hour away and heading right for it.

11.00pm Titanic *Bridge Time – 6 Bells*

On the bridge of the stationary *Californian*, Charles Groves can hear two sounds: ice bumping against the side of the hull, and an Irish voice coming up from a stokehold ventilator in the engine room, singing the song 'Annie Laurie'.

Her brow is like the snaw-drift,
Her neck is like the swan,
Her face it is the fairest,
That 'er the sun shone on.

That 'er the sun shone on
And dark blue is her e'e,
And for bonnie Annie Laurie
I'd lay me down and die...

On the *Titanic*, the music from the band in the Palm Court has ended, and the first-class passengers are saying goodnight to each other as the musicians put their instruments in their cases.

The lights are now off in the third-class public rooms and all the dining saloons. However, in the second-class smoking room there are about 40 men talking, some playing cards

11.10pm Titanic *Bridge Time*

On the *Californian*, Charles Groves sees what he thinks could be the lights of a large steamer coming over the horizon from the east. But it's hard to tell what it is on such a clear night, as the stars are so low on the horizon.

One deck below, Captain Lord is looking at the same lights through the chart room porthole, and reckons it's a ship about the same size as the *Californian*. Lord heads to the wireless room to ask the 20-year-old operator Cyril Evans if he knows of any other ships nearby.

'Only the *Titanic*...'

Lord tells Evans to warn the *Titanic* that they have stopped and are surrounded by ice. Lord is convinced that the light he can see is not from the largest and most famous ship in the world but from another vessel.

11.15pm Titanic *Bridge Time*

Lawrence Beesley is sitting up in bed in his cabin on D-deck. At Southampton he was delighted to discover that he had a two-berth cabin all to himself, and that it was well positioned – only a matter of feet from the dining saloon and a stairway. Beesley notices that the engines are making his mattress vibrate more than usual, and assumes that the *Titanic* has picked up speed.

As he reads, Beesley can hear through the ventilation grill the sound of stewards talking as they go about their work.

Theology student Sidney Collett is getting ready for bed. He's not as fortunate as Lawrence Beesley and is sharing his cabin with two other second-class passengers. He says his prayers out loud. Collett finishes, and the room is so quiet 'you could hear a pin drop'. One of his cabin mates thanks him for the prayers.

Violet Jessop is in the top bunk of her cabin and fellow stewardess Elizabeth Leather is in the bunk below. Violet is reading the magazines *Tatler* and *Sketch* that Thomas Kelland, the library steward, kindly dropped off for her.

As instructed by his captain, the wireless operator on the *Californian*, Cyril Evans, is sending a message to the *Titanic*: 'Say old man we are surrounded by ice and stopped.' Because the *Californian* is so close, the message comes through Jack Phillips' headset at a deafening level.

'Shut up, shut up, I am busy working Cape Race!' Phillips taps back in irritation.

This time it's Evans' turn to be deafened. Passengers' messages to the United States are Phillips' priority.

Phillips has just received a warning that there is an ice field only 45 minutes away from the *Titanic*. But because Cyril Evans failed to use the MSG code governing priority messages – a message with MSG had to go straight to the captain – Phillips ignores it. He also probably believes that the bridge, alerted to the threat of ice earlier in the day, will be taking appropriate measures. Captain Lord didn't ask Evans to get confirmation that the *Titanic* received the vital message.

11.25pm Titanic *Bridge Time*

On the bridge of the *Californian*, Charles Groves is now fairly sure that the lights that are moving past his starboard side about 10 or 12 miles away belong to a passenger steamer. Captain Lord had told him he wanted to be informed if any ship was sighted, so Groves heads to the chart room to wake him.

'What?'

11.30pm Titanic *Bridge Time – 7 Bells*

Library steward Thomas Kelland comes into the large first-class reading and writing room on A-deck and calls, 'Lights out, it's 11.30!'

Journalist Edith Rosenbaum, still dressed in her evening gown and velvet slippers, takes a couple of books from the shelves and walks towards her cabin forward on A-deck.

Thomas Kelland then approaches actress Dorothy Gibson's bridge party, consisting of her mother, Frederick Seward and William Sloper, the stockbroker whom Dorothy's just met. The steward politely asks them to finish their game so he can turn out the lights.

Arthur Gee is loving his voyage on the *Titanic*. Staff even found a first-class cabin with a porthole for him yesterday when he requested one. Right now, though, Gee is not happy. He can hear firemen at the end of their shift making a terrible racket as they walk down Scotland Road, on the other side of the ship. Gee presses his bell to summon his bedroom steward, Alfred Theissinger, to ask them to be quiet.

The wireless operator on the *Californian*, Cyril Evans, takes off his headset. After the 'Shut up, shut up, I am busy working Cape Race!' rebuke from the *Titanic*, he had listened for a while, but now he's going to bed.

Evans turns off his equipment, puts on his pyjamas, gets into his bunk and starts reading a magazine. The *Californian* now has no wireless connection with the outside world.

Meanwhile, on the bridge, Evans' shipmate Charles Groves, is using a Morse lamp to signal the single word 'What?' to the mysterious ship in an effort to get it to identify itself. (A Morse lamp is a hand-held lantern with a shutter that opens and closes to transmit Morse code.) Captain Lord suggested that he should try and make contact.

There is no response from the ship.

About 11.35pm Titanic *Bridge Time*

In the *Titanic*'s first-class accommodation on C-deck, Jack Thayer calls 'goodnight!' to his parents in the adjoining state-room. He's half opened a porthole to get some fresh air in his cabin, and a breeze is whistling in. The ship's engines are throbbing below him. 'It was,' he wrote later, 'a fine night for sleeping.'

His mother, Marian, rings the bell for their steward; she needs their porthole opened.

At the top of the stairs that take them down to their first-class cabins, Dorothy Gibson tells the group that she'd like to take a brisk walk around the boat deck. Her mother and Frederick K. Seward decline, but William Sloper runs quickly to his cabin to get a hat and overcoat.

11.39pm Titanic *Bridge Time*

To lookout Frederick Fleet it didn't seem to be very large at first – a black object high above the water, even darker than the darkness.

Fleet rings the brass bell above him three times and then reaches across Reginald Lee to grab the telephone and call the bridge. Sixth Officer James Moody answers in the wheelhouse.

'Yes. What do you see?'
  'Iceberg dead ahead!'
  'Thank you.'

'Iceberg dead ahead!' Moody shouts to the officer of the watch, William Murdoch. Murdoch looks forward into the night, then runs to the engine order telegraph shouting, 'Hard a starboard!'

He swings the twin handles of the telegraph, signalling to the engine room to 'Stop'.

In the wheelhouse behind him, quartermaster Robert Hichens rapidly turns the ship's wheel four revolutions anti-clockwise.
  'Hard a-starboard. The helm is hard over!' Moody calls in confirmation.

In the crow's nest, Frederick Fleet puts down the telephone. Next to him Reginald Lee can see the bow is already slowly turning to port. The iceberg is rapidly getting closer.

In the engine room the red 'Stop' signal appears on the illuminated boiler room telegraphs. 'Shut the doors!' leading fireman

Frederick Barrett shouts in boiler room 6, instructing that the furnaces should be closed.

The iceberg's peak is now just below the height of the crow's nest.

Fleet and Lee think the *Titanic* has turned in time.

11.40pm Titanic *Bridge Time*

Forty-six thousand tons of metal and wood collide with 500,000 tons of ice.

An underwater spur from the iceberg dents and punctures the *Titanic*, making a series of gashes no more than an inch high, along 250 feet of her starboard hull.

On the bridge they can hear the iceberg grinding.

In boiler room 6, fireman Frederick Barrett sees seawater explode through a split that's opened up two feet above the floor.

In her cabin on E-deck Kate Buss hears a sound like a skate on ice.

In an engine room bunker, stoker George Cavell falls over and coal topples on top of him.

Tons of sliced-off ice falls onto the forward well deck.

Margaret Brown is thrown to the floor of her first-class cabin.

Twenty-one-year-old Gretchen Longley is showered in ice as she sleeps under the open porthole of her starboard D-deck cabin.

In his second-class cabin towards the bow, Harvey Collyer staggers but doesn't fall. To his wife Charlotte it's as if the ship has been 'taken by a giant hand and shaken once; twice...'

Bedroom steward Alfred Theissinger hears a sound like a rowing boat being dragged over gravel.

In a galley a pan of new rolls falls from the top of an oven and scatters on the floor, much to the annoyance of night baker Walter Belford.

Jack Thayer, about to get into bed, sways slightly.

As the iceberg passes the bridge Murdoch shouts, 'Hard a port!'

   He wants to swing the ship around the berg. The grinding noise stops. He turns the lever to shut the *Titanic*'s watertight doors.

In the engine room, red warning lights are flashing above the watertight doors – they will drop down in 10 seconds. Fireman Frederick Barrett and assistant second engineer James Hesketh run for the door between boiler rooms 6 and 5. They dive under it just in time.

Captain Smith runs out of his quarters.

   'Mr Murdoch, what was that?'

   'An iceberg, sir.'

   'Close the watertight doors.'

   'The watertight doors are closed, sir.'

In cabin C-89 on the starboard side of the ship, Virginia Clark looks through her porthole and sees instead of the night sky a 'huge white mass, just like a mountain'. She runs into her bathroom and stands on the bath to look out of its porthole, but sees nothing but darkness. 'Which shows,' she wrote later, 'the rapidity with which the ship must have passed the huge white thing after it was hit.'

Ice is pushing against the windows of the Café Parisien aft on B-deck.

Stewardess Violet Jessop, reading in her bunk, hears a low crunching, ripping noise, then the sound of doors opening and people running.

Standing under the afterbridge at the stern, quartermaster George Rowe feels a slight jar, then looks to starboard and sees an iceberg, looking like a large sailing ship, drift slowly past. It's so close he thinks it's going to hit the afterbridge.

Everyone in the first-class smoking room on A-deck has jumped up and is trying to get through the revolving doors to the verandah and out onto the promenade deck to see what's happened.

Esther Hart's worst nightmare has come true. She leaps up from the suitcase she's been sitting on, fully dressed for just such an emergency, and shakes her husband.

'Daddy, get up at once! We have hit something I am sure – and it's serious.'

'Oh woman – again?' Ben says sleepily. 'I really don't know what I shall do with you.'

'Ben, something *has* happened! Go up on deck and find out what it is.'

Able seaman Joseph Scarrott rushes up to the forward well deck and sees the piles of ice by the starboard rail. Looking aft and to starboard he can see the iceberg moving away, about a ship's length distant. 'It looks like the Rock of Gibraltar,' he thinks.

Second Officer Charles Lightoller leaps out of bed in his pyjamas and hurries out onto the port side of the boat deck. He leans over the rail. Nothing. He runs round to the starboard side. Nothing. Freezing cold, he heads back to bed. If he's needed, his colleagues will know where to find him.

Lawrence Beesley, lying in his bunk reading, feels what seems to be a heave of the engines and his mattress lift slightly – but no noise. He carries on reading.

On the starboard bridge wing, Captain Smith and officers Murdoch and Boxhall are looking aft to see if they can see the iceberg. Boxhall's eyes aren't yet used to the dark and can't see much. Murdoch asks for a note of the time to be put in the log-book. It is 20 minutes to 12.

The *Titanic* is 400 miles from land.

At the subsequent inquiries, lookout Reginald Lee claimed that there was haze that night – 'we had our work cut out to pierce through it just after we started.' Frederick Fleet disputed the existence of haze and the British inquiry concluded Lee was just searching for an excuse for not having spotted the iceberg sooner.

But, in an exchange during the US Senate Inquiry, Fleet revealed himself to be a lookout of dubious quality:

> *Senator Smith: How large an object was this when you first*
> *saw it?*
> *Fleet: It was not very large when I first saw it.*
> *Senator Smith: How large was it?*
> *Fleet: I have no idea of distances or spaces.*

On the *Californian*, Third Officer Groves sees the lights on the mystery ship go out.

The lights seem to disappear because the *Titanic*'s manoeuvre to evade the iceberg means she is now facing the *Californian* head on and is therefore showing less of her hull.

The *Titanic*'s engines have stopped. As Lawrence Beesley wrote later, 'The dancing motion and vibration ceased suddenly after being part of our existence for four days, and that was the first hint that anything out of the ordinary had happened.'

The ship's hull has been damaged along a 250-foot section. Six watertight compartments have been breached – something never seen before in maritime history.

> *If the* Titanic *had hit the iceberg head on she would have survived;*
> *six years later, in the First World War, the* Olympic *proved how well*
> *built the class was by successfully ramming and sinking a German*
> *U-boat.*

'Sounds as if something has happened...'

11.41pm Titanic *Bridge Time*

Helen Candee has been calling for her steward a number of

times and is standing outside her room waiting. He finally appears.

'What has happened?' she asks.

'Nothing has happened, ma'am.'

'Then why are the engines not running? I don't hear them.'

'I tell you nothing has happened. You better go to your room and go to bed.'

'Steward, I'm an old traveller and am not afraid, but I know something has happened. But I'll go to my room to make things easier for you.'

Stewardess Violet Jessop is lying still in her bunk, listening to the sounds of the ship and trying not to panic. She once became hysterical during a storm at sea and was mocked by the ship's crew, so she's vowed never to show fear again. She leans over the side of the bunk; Elizabeth looks up and says calmly, 'Sounds as if something has happened...'

Violet stifles a laugh at the understatement.

Jack Thayer puts on a heavy overcoat and a pair of slippers and looks around the door that connects his cabin with his parents'.

'I'm going up on deck to see the fun!'

His father says he'll join him.

11.42pm Titanic *Bridge Time*

Convinced that the *Titanic* has dropped a propeller blade, Lawrence Beesley slips on a pair of shoes, puts a dressing gown over his pyjamas and goes out into the corridor. A steward is leaning against the D-deck staircase looking unconcerned.

'Why have we stopped?'

'I don't know, sir. But I don't suppose it is anything much.'

111

'Well, I'm going on deck to see what it is.'

The steward smiles indulgently. 'All right, sir, but it is mighty cold up there.'

Beesley strides up the stairs feeling rather foolish – no one else is about. After three flights he reaches the boat deck and opens the vestibule door. Beesley can feel the cold cutting through his dressing gown.

Throughout the *Titanic*, the ship's stewards are providing reassurance:

'I don't believe there is any trouble...'

'We've probably struck a Newfoundland shipping boat...'

'Something might be wrong with the machinery...'

'Everything will be all right...'

'It is nothing serious. You can go back to bed...'

About 11.43pm Titanic *Bridge Time*

On the bridge, Captain Smith is ringing the engine order telegraphs to 'Slow Ahead'. The *Titanic* starts to move again.

Fourth Officer Joseph Boxhall is making his own inspection of the ship. He's been down across the forward well deck and is now making his way through the lower passenger areas in the bow. He's found nothing untoward so far.

Lying in his bunk near the bow, lamp trimmer Samuel Hemming can hear a loud hissing sound. He leaves his cabin to investigate and bumps into storekeeper Frank Prentice – they decide to follow the noise together.

On the *Californian*, Captain Lord comes onto the bridge. He can see that the ship in the distance has stopped.

'That doesn't look like a passenger steamer,' he says to Third Officer Groves.

'It is, sir. When she stopped, her lights seemed to go out, and I suppose they have been put out for the night.'

'Well, the only passenger steamer near us is the *Titanic*.'

Groves had served as an officer with P&O in the Far East where it was common for ships to dim their lights around midnight to encourage passengers to go to bed. He left P&O a few months before, as 'he couldn't stand the passengers'.

On the *Titanic*'s E-deck, Kate Buss has put on her dressing gown and slippers and has left her cabin to find her friend Marion Wright. Marion has had the same idea and they meet in a corridor; they decide to go up on deck and find out what's wrong.

About 11.45pm Titanic *Bridge Time*

First-class passenger Emma Bucknell looks out of her cabin door and glances left towards the porthole at the end of the short corridor. The porthole is broken and there is ice and glass on the floor.

She calls to a passing steward, who reassures her that 'there is no danger as a result of the collision'. Although his voice is calm, Emma can see from his face that he's scared.

Edith Rosenbaum is at the forward end of A-deck looking down into the well deck. With her, and frowning at the ice scattered on the pine decking, is fellow journalist William Stead. Artist Francis Millet walks down the companionway behind her from the boat deck.

'What do they say is the trouble?' asks Stead.

'Iceberg,' Millet says.

'Well, I guess it's nothing serious. I'll go back to my cabin and read. Cheerio, all!'

Sixty-four-year-old William Stead is a journalist and campaigner for many disparate causes – the adoption of babies, public libraries, British naval supremacy ('two keels to one!'), and housing for the poor. He became infamous in 1885 when he wrote an article describing how easily he was able to purchase the services of a 13-year-old prostitute. Stead served a short prison term for abduction, but his stunt led to the passing of the Criminal Law Amendment Act of 1885, which raised the age of consent for girls from 13 to 16.

Stead spends much of the voyage writing, but at meal times enjoys holding forth in the first-class dining saloon about the great men he has interviewed. He is often 'cut' by the more conservative passengers because of his radical, pacifist views.

Stead is travelling on the Titanic *to take part in a peace conference on 21st April at New York's Carnegie Hall, at the invitation of President Taft.*

In 1886, he published an article entitled 'How the Mail Steamer Went Down in Mid-Atlantic, by a Survivor', the story of a mid-ocean collision in which too few lifeboats led to many deaths. Stead added this comment as editor: 'This is exactly what might take place and will take place if liners are sent to sea short of boats.'

Twenty-one-year-old Irishman Daniel Buckley jumps out of his bunk in third class and into water. He can see it seeping in under the door. He says to the three other men sleeping in the cabin, 'Get up! Something's wrong – water's coming in!'

'Get back to bed – you're not in Ireland now!' one says, and they all laugh.

Buckley gets dressed as quickly as he can. Because their cabin is so cramped, he leaves to give them more room to dress – although none of them shows signs of moving.

Two crew members walk past him shouting, 'All up on deck, unless you want to get drowned!'

Buckley is a farm labourer, heading to the United States in search of work. He boarded at Queenstown together with three men and three women from Kingwilliamstown (now Ballydesmond) in County Cork.

On A-deck towards the stern, Lawrence Beesley is comparing notes with Douglas Norman, the young Scotsman who'd played the piano at the hymn singing earlier in the evening. Norman also rushed up on deck from his cabin when the engines stopped, and is convinced he's seen the iceberg and wishes he'd brought his camera.

Looking over the starboard rail and forwards towards the bridge, they can't see anything wrong, so they decide to head down to B-deck.

Towards the bow, lamp trimmer Samuel Hemming and store-keeper Frank Prentice have found the source of the loud hissing noise. Air is coming out of a vent pipe with great force, which means that the forepeak tank is filling with water, and the water is pushing the air out.

Chief Officer Henry Wilde arrives, also trying to trace the noise.

'What is it, Hemming?'

'The air is escaping from the forepeak tank, sir. She must be making water there, but the storeroom is quite dry.'

'All right,' Wilde says, and walks on.

Hemming and Prentice return to their bunks.

Quartermaster Robert Hichens is at the ship's helm in the wheelhouse. Captain Smith comes in and looks at the ship's inclinometer. It already shows a 5° list to starboard.

Captain Smith rings 'Stop' on the engine order telegraph.

The *Titanic*'s engines stop for the last time. Her three propellers spin slowly to a halt.

11.46pm Titanic *Bridge Time*

The chairman of the White Star Line, Bruce Ismay, arrives on the bridge – his first visit of the voyage. He is wearing a coat over his pyjamas and slippers.

'What's happened?

'We have struck ice,' Smith tells him.

'Do you think the ship is seriously damaged?'

'I am afraid so.'

There is a tarpaulin stretched over the hatch to hold 1, and it is ballooning up from a rush of air underneath it. Boatswain's mate Albert Haines stares at the tarpaulin in amazement as it can be caused by only one thing – water filling the hold at a rapid rate. Haines decides to go to the bridge to tell them this disturbing news.

> The Titanic's hold has a varied cargo, including: 78 cases of gloves, 225 cases of mussels, 19 cases of orchids, 107 cases of books, 63 cases of champagne, 12 cases of feathers, 860 rolls of linoleum and one box of golf balls.

Fireman Frederick Barrett has climbed an escape ladder and is looking down into boiler room 6 from which he'd escaped minutes ago. There is already eight feet of water in there.

'I expect the iceberg has scratched off some of her new paint, and the captain doesn't like to go on until she is painted up again!'

11.47pm Titanic *Bridge Time*

Lawrence Beesley, in his pyjamas and dressing gown, is standing with Douglas Norman in the second-class smoking room on B-deck, talking to a group of men playing cards. They felt the ship heave and have seen an iceberg drift past the windows and away into the night. Beesley is amazed that none of them made an effort to find out what, if anything, was wrong – they had just got on with their game.

'How big was it?' he asks.

'About 100 feet...'

'About 60 feet...' another says.

Then a man who says he is a motor engineer adds, 'Well, I am accustomed to estimating distances, and I put it at between 80 and 90 feet.'

One man has a theory as to why they've stopped.

'I expect the iceberg has scratched off some of her new paint, and the captain doesn't like to go on until she is painted up again!'

Another says to a man behind him, 'Just run along the deck and see if any ice has come aboard; I would like some for this,' and he points to the whisky glass on the table next to him.

They all laugh.

11.50pm Titanic *Bridge Time*

Fourth Officer Joseph Boxhall, having finished his tour below decks, reports to Captain Smith that he can see no sign of any damage there. Smith sends him to find the ship's carpenter, John Hutchinson.

The *Titanic* in fact has 4000 tons of water in her first five watertight compartments.

The five mail clerks are trying to save the hundreds of sacks stored in the orlop deck (the lowest deck) by carrying them up the stairs to the sorting room above. But the water is creeping up the staircase.

Helen Candee is walking through the first-class lounge with one of her admirers – the smooth-talking English businessman Hugh Woolner. A young Brazilian boy, whom Helen has seen a few times walking with his elderly father, dashes up to her, and with a mischievous look shows her some ice in his cupped hands.

'Take some! Take some! It's what we struck! I picked it up from the lower deck!'

Helen reluctantly takes a piece.

'As a souvenir!' the boy laughs, and then runs to find his father.

In their stateroom on A-deck, Dr Washington Dodge and his wife Ruth can hear running footsteps on the boat deck above; he decides to get up and investigate.

In the second-class accommodation, 56-year-old Mary Hewlett, can also hear running feet. The young people down her corridor often make a noise this time of night, but this sounds different.

The *Titanic*'s chief designer Thomas Andrews is rushing down the grand staircase. A group of first-class ladies ask him what's the matter.

'Be easy, it will be all right,' he says before hurrying on.

In a third-class cabin aft, 39-year-old Rhoda Abbott is tucking in her two sons Rossmore, 16, and Eugene, 13. The boys had been keen to go up on deck to find out the source of the scraping sound that had woken them all up, but Rhoda had told them to stay in the cabin. She found a steward who said that all was well and that they should go back to sleep.

Rhoda, a member of the Salvation Army, is recently divorced from Stanton Abbott, a former US middleweight boxing champion. After enduring many years of violence from Stanton, Rhoda left their home in Rhode Island and returned to her native England in 1911 on the Olympic, *to live with her widowed mother in St Albans. But after only six months Rossmore and Eugene were so homesick that Rhoda decided to return to the States.*

The *Titanic* has come to a stop, and she is now facing north-northwest.

Steam is no longer heading to her engines, so pressure in her massive boilers is rising dangerously. The safety valves attached to each boiler activate, sending the steam to exhaust pipes at the forward and aft end of each of the four funnels. These eight pipes are now making an extraordinarily loud noise.

About 11.52pm Titanic *Bridge Time*

The pumps in boiler room 5, aft of room 6, are working well. Although the coal bunker closest to the gash is filling with water, the stokehold for room 5 is dry.

Not everyone feels reassured by the stewards' calming words – many passengers are after more information. Colonel Archibald Gracie is patrolling the boat deck, trying to find any evidence of the collision that he's sure has occurred. He walks towards the officers' quarters but finds no one he can ask. The colonel turns around and comes to the iron gate between first and second class with its 'Not Allowed' sign, half expecting to be challenged as he vaults over it. The only other people on the boat deck are a couple contentedly arm in arm.

Meanwhile, Eugene Daly, the uilleann piper, comes out of his cabin in third class wearing his lifebelt. He is immediately teased by other passengers as he's the only person wearing one. Embarrassed, Daly returns to his cabin, puts a coat over the lifebelt to be less conspicuous, and in its pockets places his rosary beads, money and a watch.

Fourth Officer Joseph Boxhall, sent to find the ship's carpenter John Hutchinson, bumps into him already on his way to the bridge. Hutchinson tells him the ship 'is making water fast'. Boxhall heads to the mail room where he can see that the water is already about two feet from the top of the sorting room.

In the first-class accommodation on D-deck, a man is unable to open the door to his cabin – it's jammed. A friend of Jack Thayer's, 21-year-old Richard Williams, breaks down the door, much to the disgust of a steward, who threatens to have him arrested when they get to New York, for 'defacing the beautiful ship'.

The jammed D-deck cabin room door is above the flooding compartments, and may well be an early sign of the *Titanic*'s structure shifting following the collision.

11.54pm Titanic *Bridge Time*

There are six feet of water in the ship's squash court on G-deck, just behind the mail room.

With the engines stopped and no need to shovel coal into the furnaces, the firemen and trimmers have been told to leave their posts, and they are heading up onto E-deck.

Then the electric lights suddenly go out in the stokeholds, making the fight against the flooding in boiler room 6 almost impossible. There's a shout for oil lamps.

'But if she does go down, I'm sure we can cheat the drink for about 48 hours.'

11.55pm Titanic *Bridge Time*

Captain Smith, although he doesn't yet know the full extent of the damage, orders all hands to turn out to get the lifeboats ready.

Although boiler room 6 is flooding, there are still men in there trying to extinguish the fires in the furnaces on the port side where the water is shallower – as a result of the *Titanic*'s 5° list to starboard. 'That will do!' someone shouts in boiler room 6, much to the relief of fireman George Beauchamp – the water is rising fast. He climbs the ladder that takes him up to Scotland Road, hoping for the chance of a lifeboat.

First-class passenger Norman Chambers is one of those exploring the ship, convinced that something is amiss. He looks down from F-deck into the G-deck trunk room – it's full of water almost up to the ceiling. He'd come back to his cabin on E-deck to get warm clothing, when he'd spotted two mail clerks, wet up to their knees, having brought up some bags of registered mail to safety. Norman had asked the clerks to show him the flooding.

As Chambers and the mail clerks stare down at the trunk room, they all joke about the soaked baggage and the letters floating on the surface. Chambers has no sense that the ship is in any danger.

Violet Jessop is at the top of a flight of stairs on her way up from E-deck when she bumps into Jock Hume, the Scottish violinist in the ship's band. Violet and Jock have sailed together before on the *Olympic*.

She'd seen him earlier in the evening when he'd joked about finishing the band's set with a 'real tune, a Scotch tune'.

Now he looks pale, and clutching his violin, says to Violet, 'Just going to give them a tune to cheer things up a bit...'

In first class, Margaret Brown is putting on seven pairs of woollen stockings, a black velvet two-piece suit and a sable stole. She opens the safe in her room, takes out $500 in cash and puts it in a wallet around her neck. She puts on her lifebelt, and takes a blanket from the bed. Then for luck she pockets a small turquoise statue she bought in Egypt.

In her first-class D-deck cabin, 62-year-old Kornelia Andrews puts on a fur coat, and picks up three hat pins – but forgets to bring a hat.

In her cabin, journalist Edith Rosenbaum, in evening dress, fur coat, fur scarf and a knitted woollen cap, is reluctantly locking her steamer trunks. A fellow passenger had knocked on her door and told her that she should put on a lifebelt. She pauses at the door, puts a lifebelt under her arm and looks longingly at her warm, comfortable stateroom with its pink light, pink quilt and warm heater.

As she walks along the carpeted corridor on her way to the first-class lounge on A-deck, she sees her bedroom steward Robert Wareham. He is running.

'Thank God you're here, miss.'

'Well, Wareham, let me tell you what I think about your ridiculous British regulations. Imagine getting people...' She breaks off, realising he is worried.

'What's the matter, Wareham? Is there any danger?'

The steward begins to help Edith get into her lifebelt.

'Danger, miss? It's a rule of the Board of Trade that even in the threat of danger lifebelts will be donned by all passengers. Not that I think that this ship can sink. She's an unsinkable ship. Everybody knows that.'

Pause.

'But if she does go down, I'm sure we can cheat the drink for about 48 hours.'

Edith thinks of her trunkloads of Paris fashions.

'If the *Titanic* sinks, will they transfer the luggage?'

'No one thinks at a time like this. We can only hope – and pray.'

Edith remembers that she has left her lucky mascot in her cabin – a pig that plays the song 'La Maxixe' if you twist its tail. She asks Wareham to collect it and bring it up to her in the lounge.

The pig was a gift from her mother after Edith narrowly survived a car accident in France in which the driver was killed. Her mother discovered that a pig was considered a symbol of luck in France so

> *gave it to her, saying, 'Look here, you crazy thing, I'm giving you a mascot. Promise me you'll have it with you always.'*

Sitting in her second-class cabin with her husband Harvey and daughter Marjorie, Charlotte Collyer can hear the sound of hundreds of hurried footsteps 'like rats scurrying through an empty room'. Charlotte looks at her face in the mirror opposite, and can see that she's gone very pale.

Her husband Harvey stammers, 'We had better go on deck and see what's wrong.'

Despite the noise from the exhausts on the funnels, work in the wireless room continues. Harold Bride comes in from the sleeping quarters next door.

'How are you getting on?'

Jack Phillips says that he's just finished receiving a large batch of messages for passengers from the shore base at Cape Race.

11.56pm Titanic *Bridge Time*

On board the stationary *Californian*, 26-year-old assistant engineer Ernest Gill comes up on deck for some air. Looking over the starboard rail, he can see the lights of a 'very large steamer about 10 miles away'. Gill watches her for a minute and then goes below.

About 11.58pm Titanic *Bridge Time*

First-class passenger Isaac Frauenthal has gone in search of Captain Smith or any officer who can tell him what has really happened. He reaches the boat deck and can see that millionaire John Jacob Astor has had the same idea and is talking to the captain.

'Captain, my wife is not in good health. She has gone to bed, and I don't want to get her up unless it is absolutely necessary. What is the situation?'

'Colonel Astor, you had better get your wife up at once. I fear that we may have to take to the boats.'

Astor thanks the captain and walks away. Frauenthal now knows they are in danger.

Thomas Andrews' bedroom steward, Henry Etches, half-dressed, is poking his head around the door of the large E-deck cabin he shares with 20 other first-class stewards. He sees a group of third-class passengers coming his way and he starts walking towards them. One is carrying a large piece of ice.

'Will you believe me now?' he shouts, mistaking Etches for another steward, and throwing the ice on the deck. Stunned, Etches goes back to finish dressing.

Wireless operator Harold Bride at work in the Titanic's radio room.

Monday 15th April 1912

'We had something else to think of.'

Midnight Titanic *Bridge Time*

Fourth Officer Boxhall has returned to the bridge and tells Captain Smith that the mail room is taking in water.

'All right,' is all Smith says. He leaves the bridge to look at the flooding for himself.

For the first time on the voyage, the *Titanic*'s clocks are not being adjusted to allow for the change in time zones as she sails west.

> At the US Senate Inquiry into the sinking, there was this exchange with Third Officer Herbert Pitman:
>
> > Senator Smith: When were the ship's clocks set; do you know?
> > Pitman: They are set at midnight every night.
> > Senator Smith: And were they set at midnight Sunday night?
> > Pitman: No. We had something else to think of.

The *Titanic* is now flooded with 7000 tons of water.

On the *Californian*, Ernest Gill is waking up his shipmate William Thomas.

'Are we in the ice?' Thomas asks.

'Yes, but it must be clear off to the starboard – I saw a big vessel going along full speed. She looked as if she might be a big German.'

About 00.02am Titanic *Bridge Time*

After his trip to the upper decks, schoolteacher Lawrence Beesley is back down in his cabin, reading on the sofa.

Lucy Duff Gordon's secretary Laura 'Franks' Francatelli is standing outside her cabin on E-deck in her dressing gown, so she can see if anyone else is concerned. A man rushes past saying, 'The hold, luggage and mail room have gone!'

She's already seen a number of the *Titanic*'s officers walk past to check on any damage, so this news is the evidence she's been waiting for. Laura goes into her cabin to collect some things and alert her employers four decks above.

Lucy Duff Gordon is just learning of the danger. Her husband Sir Cosmo, looking grave, is telling her that he met Colonel Astor on deck who told him they had hit an iceberg and may have to get into lifeboats. He was going to tell his wife Madeleine to get dressed. Astor suggested to Sir Cosmo that he did the same.

Lucy immediately starts getting some warm clothes.

Up on the boat deck, in the officers' quarters, Fourth Officer Joseph Boxhall knocks on Second Officer Charles Lightoller's cabin door and says quietly, 'We've hit an iceberg.'

'I know you've hit something.'

'The water is up to F-deck in the mail room,' Boxhall says, and leaves Lightoller to get dressed. Boxhall knocks on Third

Officer Herbert Pitman's cabin next door.

The Collyer family have reached the second-class promenade on A-deck, where they find officers shouting, 'There is no danger! No danger whatever!'

Their reassurance seems unnecessary, as there is no sign of panic. A few passengers are looking over the rail into the sea.

The electric lights come back on in the stokeholds, where oil lamps had been brought in to provide light for those trying to stop the flooding.

Having been stranded in the crow's nest since the collision, lookouts Frederick Fleet and Reginald Lee are now coming down the ladder inside the steel foremast and onto C-deck as George Hogg and Alfred Evans have relieved them. Fleet and Lee are met by the sight of greasers and firemen who have been forced to come up to C-deck from E-deck, because their quarters are flooding.

Those third-class passengers whose accommodation is close to the bow don't need to be told to leave their cabins, as they are flooding. Some are making their way aft along Scotland Road with their luggage and lifebelts. Some of the suitcases are wet.

00.05am Titanic *Bridge Time*

The *Titanic* is about 2° down at the head.

On E-deck, Laura Francatelli steps out of her cabin wearing a hastily flung together outfit of nightclothes, sweater and a long woollen motoring coat. To her horror, she can see water creeping up the corridor.

The ship's band is tuning up at the entrance of the enclosed promenade deck on A-deck – getting ready to play to the passengers who've come up from their cabins to find out what's going on. Fourth Officer Joseph Boxhall walks past them, trying to see the state of the flooding in the mail room. The watertight doors are closed, so he's having to take a longer route. He hears the band play 'Alexander's Ragtime Band'.

> *It seems likely that the band was requested to play by the chief purser, McElroy, or by the captain. But the musicians didn't have to play; they are listed as second-class passengers and are employed not by the White Star Line but by a Liverpool-based agency called C.W. & F.N. Black, who supply musicians to the major shipping lines.*

Martha Eustis Stephenson and her sister Elizabeth are getting dressed in their D-deck stateroom on the port side of the *Titanic*. They had both been fast asleep when they were woken by the jarring of the ship and a ripping sound. Although a steward has reassured them that 'it was nothing at all', it reminded Martha of the time her house shook during the catastrophic 1906 San Francisco earthquake.

Martha and Elizabeth aren't hurrying, but are dressing as if for breakfast in the dining saloon. They are taking with them letters of credit, some money and their watches. Elizabeth puts on a fur coat and slips her glasses and a clean handkerchief into a pocket.

John Thayer, whom they know well as they are neighbours in Pennsylvania, knocks on their door and tells Martha and Elizabeth they should come up to see the ice on deck. The sisters leave the lights on, and their electric heater, so the room will be warm on their return.

John Jacob Astor and his wife Madeleine are on A-deck with

a group of fellow first-class passengers; Madeleine is wearing a glamorous black broadtail coat and a diamond necklace, and is carrying a muff. Astor runs up for another conversation with Captain Smith, and the group watch, trying to make out what Smith is telling him. Astor comes back and tells them they all need to put on their lifebelts.

Dr Washington Dodge is also on A-deck, looking down at the third-class passengers playing football with the ice in the forward well deck. He judges there are 'several cartloads'. Some first-class passengers call down to the third-class passengers in the well deck, asking for a bit of ice. Several snowballs are thrown up.

'Do you think there is any danger, sir?'

Dodge turns to find two firemen who have come up from the engine room. They would never normally be allowed on A-deck.

'If there was any danger it would be due to the vessel having sprung a leak, and you ought to know more about it than I.'

'Well, sir...' one says anxiously, 'the water was pouring into the stokehold when we came up, sir...'

Dodge walks back to his stateroom, where his wife and young son are waiting for news.

'Imagine, wouldn't something like this happen when his nanny isn't with us?' Ruth Dodge says.

Elmer Taylor knocks on the door of his business partner, Fletcher Williams, the managing director of the British Mono-Service Company, a manufacturer of hotel paper cups. Taylor was the cup's inventor.

Williams is the picture of nonchalance. He is sitting up in bed in his dressing gown, smoking a huge cigar and sipping a highball.

'Well, Williams, we have struck an iceberg and I have brought you a piece of it to put in your highball, so here goes,' Taylor says.

'Is there any cause for alarm?' Williams asks.

Taylor reassures him the ship is unsinkable.

Edith Rosenbaum has decided not to join the people on the boat deck. She is sitting in an armchair in the first-class lounge on the deck below, watching white uniformed bakers take loaves to the lifeboats. Her bedroom steward Robert Wareham brings her lucky pig.

'I hope we get out of this all right. I have a wife and five little kiddies at home,' Wareham says.

00.08am Titanic *Bridge Time*

On the *Californian*, which is still stationary due to an ice field, 24-year-old Second Officer Herbert Stone has arrived on the bridge to relieve Third Officer Groves. Stone looks at the ship in the distance through binoculars. He can see one masthead light and a red side-light and two or three less distinct lights. Groves brings his colleague up to date.

'She's been stopped since 11.40. She is a passenger steamer. At about the moment she stopped she put her lights out. I called her on the Morse lamp, but got no answer.'

In the later inquiries, Herbert Stone said that Groves described the ship only as a steamer, not a passenger steamer. Stone claimed he believed it to be a tramp steamer (a cargo ship with no fixed schedule) about five miles away. Stone has little self-confidence, and is afraid of Captain Lord.

On the *Titanic*, Second Officer Charles Lightoller is getting men to take the covers off the eight lifeboats on the port side of the boat deck (nos. 2, 4, 6, 8, 10, 12, 14, 16). They have to release the grips holding the boats to the deck, and get the ropes, known as falls, ready for lowering. Some crew members are working by the lifeboat cranes, known as davits, fixing in the cranks that operate them.

Lightoller had been in such a hurry when the news of the collision was broken to him by Fourth Officer Boxhall, that he'd not bothered to take off his pyjamas, but just put trousers, a sweater and a white muffler on top of them.

Lightoller, who has survived a shipwreck, and many subsequent adventures, is in his element. He is telling the men what to do by gestures; no one can hear him give an order, as the steam coming out of the eight exhausts on the funnels is deafening. In Lightoller's words they were loud enough to have drowned out the sound 'of a thousand railway engines thundering through a culvert'.

On the opposite side of the ship, First Officer Murdoch is supervising the preparation of her eight starboard lifeboats (nos. 1, 3, 5, 7, 9, 11, 13, 15). Chief Officer Wilde is overseeing both sides of the ship.

The Board of Trade is the government department responsible for determining how many lifeboats ships carry. Those over 10,000 tons have to carry at least 16 lifeboats, and if the boats 'under the davits do not furnish sufficient accommodation for all persons on board, then additional wooden, metal, collapsible, or other boats of approved design (whether placed on davits or otherwise) or approved life-rafts shall be carried'. But if a ship has watertight compartments – as the Titanic does – then the number of lifeboats can be reduced. The Board of Trade stipulated that the Titanic needed enough lifeboats for 825 people. In the end, the White Star Line decided upon 14 standard wooden lifeboats with a capacity of

65 people each, two wooden emergency lifeboats with a capacity of 40 each, and four Engelhardt collapsible boats with a capacity of 47 each. So, in total, the Titanic has enough lifeboats for 1178 people. On her maiden voyage, she is carrying 2224 people.

Titanic's original design included a new type of davit that allowed lifeboats to be double-banked, giving spaces for 1700. But late in the day, the White Star Line decided double-banked lifeboats would take up too much deck space.

In 1911, the periodical Engineering explained the predicament for ship owners:

'Nowadays the success of a line of passenger-carrying steamers depends largely upon its popularity among the travelling public... passenger lines must provide vessels not only safe... but also ships which are attractive and offer special facilities for the pleasurable occupation of the long hours of enforced leisure. For these and other reasons, saving in deck-space is a distinct advantage...'

The Titanic is not alone in having too few lifeboats. Cunard's Carmania has lifeboats for only 29% of her passengers and crew. If the Hamburg Line's Amerika sank, 2000 passengers and crew would discover there was no place in a lifeboat for them.

Captain Smith and most of the officers know that there are not enough lifeboats for everybody. Their priority from now on will be to prevent panic developing among the passengers, which could lead to the boats being swamped.

00.10am Titanic *Bridge Time*

Out of his cabin, dressed in a Norfolk jacket and trousers, Lawrence Beesley is on the port side of the boat deck, watching an officer climb onto lifeboat 16 and start to take off its cover, just in case they need to be lowered. There are plenty of passengers on deck, but no one is paying the officer much attention.

Beesley turns to go down to his cabin once again and then stops. Always observant, he is sure he can detect a slight dropping of the deck towards the bows. Beesley heads for the stairs, and as he descends he has a strange sensation of being off-balance. The steps look normal, but he feels as if he's putting his feet in the wrong place.

When he reaches the corridor outside his cabin, a man standing at the far end, fastening his tie, says to him, 'Anything fresh?'

'Not much. She is a little down at the bows, but I don't think it is anything serious.'

'Come and look at this man – he won't get up!'

Beesley follows him into a cabin, where on a top bunk a man is in bed with his head turned away from the door.

'Why won't he get up? Is he asleep?'

'No, he...'

The man snaps, 'You won't catch me leaving a warm bed to go up on that cold deck at midnight. I know better than that.'

After some good-humoured banter to persuade the man to get up and get dressed, Beesley goes back to his cabin. He picks up his book once more and sits on the sofa to read. He's now feeling more uneasy – he keeps the door open.

Belfastman Dr John Simpson, the *Titanic*'s assistant surgeon, who looks after second- and third-class passengers, is in his cabin giving stewardesses Mary Sloan and Evelyn Marsden some whisky and water to steady their nerves. He has just told them the mail room is flooded. Evelyn is crying, which irritates Simpson; he turns to Mary.

'Are you afraid?'

'No, sir'

'Spoken like a true Ulster girl.'

The two stewardesses help him on with his greatcoat, and then Simpson hurries away to see if anyone has been hurt. He had become a ship's doctor as the strain of his Belfast practice had been too much for him.

First-class passenger Major Arthur Peuchen is standing towards the front of A-deck with fellow Canadian Charles M. Hays, the president of the Grand Trunk Railroad.

'Why, she is listing; she should not do that – the water is perfectly calm, and the boat has stopped,' Peuchen, a keen yachtsman, says.

'You cannot sink this boat. No matter what we have struck, she is good for eight or ten hours.'

Peuchen is not so sure.

He watches as about a hundred firemen make their way up from A-deck to the boat deck.

Helen Candee and Hugh Woolner are at the top of the stairs on the port side of the boat deck and can't get down to A-deck because of the number of firemen coming up. Covered in soot and framed by the white stairway, to Helen they look like cut-out black paper silhouettes.

She watches them each touch their cap as they pass Captain Smith and stand beside the lifeboats. 'Each one knew what the passengers did not know, and these men had each been given a chance to fend for himself,' she wrote later.

Then suddenly an order is given and the firemen start to file off the deck. They must return below; women and children will fill the lifeboats first. Peuchen is impressed by how obedient the men are, putting up no resistance. Helen Candee can see the anguish on their faces 'though their bravery was supreme'.

At the stern end of the B-deck promenade, the two friends heading to the States to get married, Marion Wright and Kate Buss, together with the young Scot, Douglas Norman, are standing by the rail overlooking the aft well deck. They are watching third-class passengers emerge, many of them carrying bags and suitcases. A man nearby makes a mocking remark about how protective they are being of their property. Kate snaps back, 'Those trunks may contain all they have in the world!'

Before an argument develops, Douglas Norman suggests to Kate and Marion that they all go below to get warmer clothing.

Stewardess Annie Robinson on E-deck overhears Thomas Andrews say to Captain Smith as they walk back from the mail room and the squash court, 'Well, three have gone already, Captain.'

> *Andrews is talking about the three watertight compartments – 1, 2 and 3. Neither man yet believes that the* Titanic *is likely to sink; she is designed to float with four compartments flooded.*

On the afterbridge at the stern, quartermaster George Rowe is waiting to be relieved – his watch ended ten minutes ago. His replacement, Arthur Bright, is fast asleep.

Third Officer Groves goes into the *Californian*'s wireless room – it's in total darkness. Operator Cyril Evans is still in bed. Groves had hoped for a chat and a chance to have a go at the equipment, as he's teaching himself wireless telegraphy. Groves turns on the light and sees Evans asleep in his bunk with a magazine still in his hands. Groves wants to know what other vessels are in range.

'What ships have you got, Sparks?'

'Only the *Titanic*,' Evans replies sleepily. 'You know, the new boat on its maiden voyage.' After a 16-hour shift, he is in no mood for a conversation.

Groves picks up the wireless headphones. Silence. He doesn't realise that for the wireless to work, its clockwork magnetic detector has to be wound up, and it had run down when Evans went to bed. Disappointed, Groves places the headphones on the table, says goodnight to Evans, who has already fallen back to sleep, and turns out the light as he leaves.

Less than ten miles away, the largest ship in the world is sinking into the icy water.

On the *Californian*'s bridge, a young apprentice officer called James Gibson is standing in the cold with Second Officer Herbert Stone. He looks at the lights of the ship in the distance; he can see a red port light and a glare of lights on her afterdeck. Gibson also concludes that the ship is a tramp steamer.

00.12am Titanic *Bridge Time*

On the *Titanic*'s bridge, Captain Smith is giving the order to 'swing out the boats and have the passengers called up with life preservers on'. The White Star Line chairman Bruce Ismay is watching. He heads out of the bridge and onto the starboard boat deck.

Colonel Archibald Gracie sees Ismay walking along the deck and thinks he looks preoccupied, so decides not to speak to him. The colonel reckons that Ismay is putting on a brave face.

Everywhere I found extraordinary calmness. To satisfy my pride, I assumed an indifference to facts all too obvious. People... were standing in groups on the companion square, chatting in the restrained, well-bred manner of the day.

Violet Jessop, stewardess

About 00.14am Titanic *Bridge Time*

In his cabin close to the bridge, Fifth Officer Harold Lowe is getting out of bed to find out why he's been woken up by the noise of running feet. Opening the door of the officers' quarters, he can see passengers walking about with lifebelts on. Lowe runs back into his cabin and starts getting dressed. He can feel that the ship is down slightly at the head. Whatever has happened to the *Titanic*, he has slept right through it.

Lowe puts his Browning automatic revolver in his pocket.

Cranking handles are turning, and the lifeboats' davit arms are swinging out away from the ship. There is a drop of about 70 feet from the lifeboats to the sea. Because of the flooding forward, this distance is already shorter for the lifeboats towards the bow than for those towards the stern.

In first-class cabin B-49, Helen Bishop has decided to leave her pet dog Freu Freu behind; she knows that there would be 'little sympathy for a woman carrying a dog in her arms'. But Freu Freu is hanging onto Helen's dress and ripping it. As well as her dog, Helen Bishop decides to leave three gold purses worth $1500 and jewellery worth $18,000.

00.15am Titanic *Bridge Time*

Captain Smith comes into the wireless room on the boat deck, just as Jack Phillips is about to go to bed.

'We've struck an iceberg and I'm having an inspection made to tell what it has done to us. You better get ready to send out a call for assistance. But don't send it until I tell you.'

This is the first that the two young Marconi operators have heard about the collision; they've been too busy with passengers' telegrams to notice anything else. Harold Bride is still in his pyjamas and dressing gown.

Marguerite Frölicher is on A-deck with her parents. She has been seasick for most of the voyage; her evening meal in the saloon hasn't helped her feel much better. It's so unusual to see her outside her cabin that a Swiss banker friend of the family comes up and says, 'Ah, Miss Frölicher – it takes an iceberg to get you on deck!'

Laura 'Franks' Francatelli bursts into Lucy Duff Gordon's cabin. She is almost hysterical. She has heard that the crew are preparing the lifeboats and she's seen water in her corridor. Lucy immediately starts getting dressed, pulling a squirrel fur coat over her nightdress and kimono and tying a scarf around her head. She ignores Cosmo's attempts to reassure her. A steward comes to the door.

'Sorry to alarm you, madam, but the captain's orders are that all passengers are to put on lifebelts.'

He is calm and jovial, laughing as he helps the three of them into their lifebelts.

In a stateroom on C-deck, bedroom steward Charles Cullen is helping Colonel Archibald Gracie with his lifebelt. Cullen bumped into him in the corridor and insisted he put one on. Gracie leaves the stateroom with a spare lifebelt in case someone else needs it.

Having arranged bread for all of the lifeboats, the ship's chief baker Charles Joughin is having a drink in his cabin on E-deck.

'All passengers on deck with life jackets!' a steward shouts as he opens the cabin belonging to Rhoda Abbott and her two teenage sons Rossmore and Eugene. They start dressing, but in no great haste. Rhoda decides to put on her Salvation Army uniform; the boys overcoats, sweaters and boots.

About 00.19am Titanic *Bridge Time*

The telephone on the bridge is ringing. It's the lookouts George Hogg and Alfred Evans up in the crow's nest. They can see people running around on deck with lifebelts, and they want to know what's going on and if they are still needed.

No one answers the telephone.

'Do you mind if I stick with you?' On A-deck, Milton Long, who befriended Jack Thayer earlier in the evening, bumps into him, his parents and his mother's maid Margaret Fleming coming up the stairs from their rooms on C-deck.

'No, come ahead, keep with us,' Jack replies.

They all have lifebelts under their overcoats, as does Long. Having already been up on the cold boat deck, Jack is well prepared. He is wearing a green tweed suit, a shirt and two vests – one of them made from mohair.

Milton Long has experience of a drama at sea. On 30th June the year before, during a trip around the world, he had been sailing between Seattle and Alaska on the SS Spokane *when she hit a rock and sank rapidly. Although Milton barely got his feet wet, two of the passengers were drowned.*

In cabin C-104, Major Arthur Peuchen is contemplating what to do about the contents of a tin box on the table. In it are $200,000 in bonds and $100,000 worth of stocks. He takes off his dinner jacket and puts on warmer clothing and a lifebelt as he thinks about it. Peuchen decides to leave the box, and after taking one last look around his cabin, he slams the door behind him and heads for the C-deck stairway and the boat deck.

In the third-class accommodation forward, water in the corridors has alerted many of the passengers, but in the accommodation aft, well away from the flooding, stewards are having to turn on cabin lights and shout to wake people. 'Everybody up! Get your lifebelts on and get everybody on deck!'

On A-deck, Marguerite Frölicher is feeling ill again.
'You can't be sick at a time like this!' her father fumes.
'I don't care! I'm going back to my cabin!' she says, storming off. Marguerite's parents follow her.

00.20am Titanic *Bridge Time*

The Thayers, Margaret Fleming and Milton Long are in the lounge on A-deck, which is full of people and quite noisy. No one is paying much attention to the band playing.

Marguerite Frölicher and her parents have got as far as B-deck. Her father asks a stewardess if there is any danger.
'Yes, sir, there is. Take your lifejackets and go up to the boat deck.'

The *Titanic*'s designer Thomas Andrews is walking with Henry Etches, his bedroom steward, down the pantry staircase from B-deck to C-deck.

142

'Be sure and make the passengers open their doors, and to tell them the lifebelts are on top of the wardrobes and on top of the racks. Assist them in every way you can to get them on.'

'All passengers on deck with lifebelts on!'

Sitting in his cabin reading, Lawrence Beesley can hear through his open door the shout from C-deck above him. He puts two books in the outside pockets of his Norfolk jacket, picks up his lifebelt and dressing gown and walks up the stairs, tying the lifebelt as he goes. No one is running or seems at all agitated. But then he sees two ladies coming down the stairs. One grabs Beesley by the arm.

'I have no lifebelt; will you come down to my cabin and help me find it?'

Beesley leads them both down the stairs to the second-class section of F-deck, feeling his arm being gripped tightly all the time. There they find a steward who takes the ladies to their cabin and finds them lifebelts.

In their first-class cabin, Martha and Elizabeth Eustis are putting on their lifebelts, carefully reading the labels 'inside front' and 'inside back' before putting them over their heads and heavy coats.

The Titanic *carries 3560 lifebelts made by Fosbery of London. They are the latest overhead type, made of cork and with a canvas covering, and have been approved by the Board of Trade. In the words of the* Titanic's *chief baker Charles Joughin: 'These were a new patent, better than the old ones. You slipped it over your head, and it was like a breastplate and a backplate, and you tied two straps.'*

Major Arthur Peuchen is back in his cabin, reconsidering whether he should bring the tin box containing his stocks and bonds. He hesitates, then picks up a lucky badge and three oranges, and leaves.

As he works, Second Officer Lightoller can see that the *Titanic* is already noticeably down at the head. All the lifeboats have now been swung out, ready for passengers and a crew. Lightoller heads towards the bridge to find the captain.

00.22am Titanic *Bridge Time*

Thomas Andrews is running up the grand staircase three steps at a time; he knows that his precious ship is doomed. He has now seen with his own eyes that the second, third, fourth and fifth compartments are breached. Although the forepeak store-room is undamaged, the tank below it, with its capacity of 190 tons, is flooded. He has designed the *Titanic* to survive four ruptured compartments, but not five.

The first two watertight bulkheads extend only as high as D-deck; the next eight to E-deck. With five compartments breached, the weight of water will pull the *Titanic* down until the water cascades over the bulkheads into the sixth compartment, filling it and then pouring over the bulkhead into the seventh, and so on until the ship sinks.

> The bulkheads had originally been planned to reach as high as B-deck, but it was decided to reduce their height for reasons of cost.

'Hadn't we better get the women and children into the boats, sir?'

Second Officer Lightoller shouts with both hands cupped

around Captain Smith's ear, over the noise of the exhausts on the funnels.

'Yes, and lower away,' Smith shouts back. He orders Lightoller to lower the boats from the boat deck to A-deck one level below, where access to the lifeboats will be easier.

In the ship's gymnasium on the boat deck, John Jacob Astor and his young wife Madeleine are sitting on its two mechanical horses with their lifebelts on. He has another lifebelt on his lap and is cutting it open with a penknife to show Madeleine what it's made of. In his overcoat pocket he has $4000 in notes.

Two rows of the *Titanic*'s portholes are now under water.

'Well, if you value your life, put your belt on.'

About 00.25am Titanic *Bridge Time*

A steward appears in the first-class lounge.

'Women and children will kindly proceed to the boat deck. Women and children *only*!'

Thomas Andrews is telling the captain that, based on what he's seen and been told, their ship will stay afloat for an hour, perhaps an hour and a half – but no more.

It is clear that the *Titanic* is too badly damaged to sink slowly like the White Star Line's *Republic*, which went down 18 hours after a collision, allowing time for her wireless operator Jack Binns to summon help.

The wooden bulkhead that separates the seamen's quarters

on E-deck and the third-class passengers' accommodation collapses. Seawater floods in. Able seaman John Poingdestre, down there to collect a pair of boots, finds himself waist-deep in freezing water. He wades out as quickly as he can.

Poingdestre can't believe his misfortune. Only a month before he had been serving aboard the P&O ship the Oceana *when she collided with another ship in the English Channel and sank off Eastbourne. Nine men drowned.*

Bedroom steward Henry Etches looks after eight cabins on B-deck, as well as Thomas Andrews' cabin on A-deck. He is currently in B-84 with one of the *Titanic*'s richest passengers, millionaire Benjamin Guggenheim. Andrews has just told Etches to assist passengers in every way and that is what Etches is endeavouring to do. He's been into cabins, reaching up to the top of wardrobes to get spare lifebelts, tying them around passengers and banging on doors to get people out and up on deck.

Etches gets the three lifebelts on top of Benjamin Guggenheim's wardrobe, gives one to his English secretary Victor Giglio, and tries to get one on Guggenheim.

'That hurts my back,' Guggenheim protests. Etches removes the lifebelt, adjusts it, puts it on Guggenheim and then gives him and Giglio a sweater each.

'Put on some clothes and I will return in a few minutes,' Etches says patiently.

Benjamin Guggenheim is travelling with Victor Giglio, his chauffeur René Pernot and his mistress, the cabaret singer Léontine 'Ninette' Aubart. Since they came aboard at Cherbourg, 46-year-old Guggenheim and 24-year-old Aubart have kept a respectable distance from each other – he has a wife and three daughters in New York.

Although born into the wealthy mine-owning Guggenheim dynasty, in his twenties Benjamin lived a tough life running a large silver mine in Colorado; in the evenings he would play cards and drink with the miners, armed with a revolver in his belt. He left the family business in 1901, having fallen out with his older brothers, who thought Benjamin too much of a playboy.

Guggenheim is not the only passenger with a cabaret singer girl-friend on board. American hockey star Quigg Baxter has installed Belgian Berthe Mayne in a cabin on C-deck. Berthe's stage name is Madame de Villiers, after a former lover who joined the French Foreign Legion.

Following the order from Captain Smith, Second Officer Lightoller shouts for lifeboat 4 to be lowered from the boat deck to A-deck, as it should be easier for the women and children to be loaded in from there.

On the boat deck a steward relays the news to Marian Thayer, who retorts impatiently, 'Tell us where to go and we will follow. You ordered us up here and now you are taking us back!'

Stewardess Annie Robinson is coming up from E-deck where she's been to see the flooded mail room; Thomas Andrews spots her. 'Put your lifebelt on and walk about and let the passengers see you.'

'It looks rather mean,' Annie replies.

'Well, if you value your life, put your belt on.'

Captain Smith opens the door to the wireless room, but doesn't bother to go in.

'Send the call for assistance' he says.

'What should I send, sir?' Phillips asks.

'The regular international call for help. Just that.'

Smith leaves, and Phillips starts tapping out the Marconi Company's emergency code 'CQD'.

Helen Candee and her admirer Hugh Woolner can hear the sound of sparks in the wires overhead; it's the messages being sent by Bride and Phillips. It sounds like sheets being ripped.

Colonel Archibald Gracie is heading down to his cabin when he meets the ship's squash attendant Frederick Wright on his way up.

'Hadn't we better cancel that appointment for tomorrow morning?' Gracie jokes.

'Yes' is all he says in reply. Frederick Wright looks pale; he knows that the water has already risen high enough to flood the court on G-deck.

The Thayer family, Marian's secretary Margaret Fleming and Jack's new friend Milton Long are on the freezing boat deck trying to find out where they are supposed to be.

Lucy Duff Gordon is taking a last look at her cabin. It looks so pretty and so much like a bedroom on land that any thought they are in danger seems ridiculous. Then suddenly a vase of flowers falls off the washstand. She and her secretary Laura Francatelli look at each other.

The *Titanic*'s band is playing as crowds of passengers mill around waiting for instructions.

For Lawrence Beesley, towards the stern of the starboard side of the boat deck, the fact that the *Titanic* feels so steady and still 'like a large rock in the middle of the ocean', is extremely reassuring. And yet, the noise of the steam blowing off from the boilers – 'like 20 locomotives all at once' – is disconcerting, and it makes any conversation difficult. Should he go down and get some warmer clothing? he wonders. Beesley looks through the window at the top of the staircase and can see so many people coming up, he decides against it.

He then watches the crew getting lifeboats 9, 11, 13 and 15 ready – taking out the masts and sails to make more space, arranging the oars and the ropes for the pulleys to lower them to the sea.

On the port side of the boat deck, Major Arthur Peuchen, with his three oranges and lucky badge in his pocket, is standing in lifeboat 2 with members of the crew helping to get it ready, using a knife to hack away the ropes holding the mast.

Some stewards on the boat deck are pinning steamer rugs around passengers' waists to keep them warm.

Second Officer Lightoller and Captain Smith have both forgotten that the *Titanic*, unlike her sister ship the *Olympic*, has a glass-enclosed forward A-deck, so it is impossible for passengers to board there until stewards have found the handles needed to lower the windows. So lifeboat 4 is being winched back up to the boat deck. Disgruntled passengers are following it via the stairways. The crew has also pointed out to Lightoller that the *Titanic*'s sounding spar – a pole used to help 'sound' the depth of the water as she enters port – is sticking out right under lifeboat 4. Lightoller has sent able seaman Sam Parks and storekeeper Jack Foley to find an axe to hack it off, while he loads other boats.

On the boat deck, Lawrence Beesley spots an officer striding from the first-class end. He looks underdressed to Beesley – a white muffler around his neck is the only concession to the bitter cold. It's Charles Lightoller, who shouts, 'All women and children get down to the deck below and all men stand back from the boats!'

Beesley watches as the men step away.

00.27am Titanic *Bridge Time*

In the wireless room, Phillips is sending 'CQD MGY' distress signals giving their coordinates (MGY is the code for *Titanic*) as 41°44'N, 50°24'W. They're picked up by *La Provence* on the Le Havre to New York route, the cargo ship *Mount Temple* and the wireless shore station at Cape Race. The *Californian*, the nearest ship to them, has her wireless set switched off for the night.

On the boat deck, able seaman John Poingdestre, trousers soaking from his adventure below decks to get his boots, hears Captain Smith say, 'Start putting the women and children in the boats.'

Poingdestre heads towards the port side and his appointed lifeboat – no. 12.

Fourth Officer Boxhall is on the bridge looking at a bright light on the *Titanic*'s port bow. Second Officer Lightoller and a number of passengers have seen it too. Colonel Archibald Gracie on A-deck says with great confidence to a group of unaccompanied ladies he's taken under his wing that it is a ship about five miles away coming to their rescue. John Jacob Astor overhears and asks Gracie to show the ship to him.

Lightoller tries to reassure passengers by pointing to the

ship's lights, and saying that launching the lifeboats is 'just a precaution'.

> The light is from the Californian, which has been stationary and facing north since she stopped in the ice. She is now slowly swinging to starboard, revealing her lights for the first time.

The Thayers and their friends have got cold standing outside and are now in the crowded hallway at the top of the grand staircase on A-deck. The stewards start calling out, 'All women to the port side! All women to the port side!' Jack and his father say farewell to Marian and Margaret Fleming who then both walk up to the boat deck. Milton, John and Jack head to the starboard side of the ship. No lifeboats have yet been launched from the *Titanic*.

'Is it really serious?' Fourth Officer Boxhall asks Captain Smith on the bridge.

'Mr Andrews tells me he gives her from an hour to an hour and a half,' Smith replies.

With all her first-class passengers now dressed, equipped with lifebelts and on deck, Violet Jessop is back in her cabin with her room-mate Elizabeth Leather. Violet is tidying up and folding her nightgown when she realises they're being watched. It's a steward called Stanley – he steps forward and clutches her arm.

'My God! Don't you realise that this ship will sink, that she has struck an iceberg, and that you have to follow the rest upstairs as quickly as possible?'

Violet says nothing. She opens her wardrobe and starts looking for a coat – then hesitates. It's spring; she hadn't thought of bringing a warm coat for icebergs.

Elizabeth meanwhile starts slowly putting on a mackintosh.

Stanley impatiently grabs the first coat he sees.

'No, Stan, that won't do. That's no rig for a shipwreck, all fussed up and gay!' Violet tries to keep the mood light-hearted, afraid she might burst into tears.

'What about a hat?' Stan says, opening a hat box.

'What, that thing with sweet peas round it? No, Stan, you would not wish me to go up in that...'

With Elizabeth now wearing her mackintosh, Violet picks up a scarf and ushers them both out of the door, which she then locks. Stan walks away, back along the corridor.

'So long, Stan, come up soon yourself, won't you?' Violet calls.

He is standing, arms clasped behind him, at his usual post. Violet thinks Stan looks suddenly very tired.

About 00.28am Titanic *Bridge Time*

Gurshon 'Gus' Cohen is heading to get his lifebelt from his berth in the forward third-class passenger accommodation. He stops in his tracks – the corridor is full of water. He's seen the ice in the well deck, and people praying, but now for the first time he realises that it's 'time to act'. He decides to go to the boat deck and see if he can get in a lifeboat.

> *Cohen is travelling to the United States, where he hopes to earn a better living as a printer than he can in the East End of London. Once he is established, his plan is to send for his fiancée Hettie. A family friend lent him the money for the voyage. Cohen had originally booked to sail on the* Teutonic, *but his strict Orthodox father forbade him to travel on a Jewish holiday, so he switched to the* Titanic.

Martha Eustis Stephenson and her sister Elizabeth take each other's hand so they're not separated, and follow Marian Thayer

and Margaret Fleming towards the boat deck. When they get
to the top of a narrow metal stairway, they see Captain Smith
waiting there, impatient to get down and looking worried.

Two cabins along from Benjamin Guggenheim's, steward
Henry Etches is banging on a door with both hands.

'What is it?' an American man calls out.

'Tell me what the trouble is,' a woman joins in.

'It's necessary that you should open the door, and I'll explain
everything, but please put the lifebelts on or bring them into
the corridor,' Etches says.

'I want to know what's the matter,' the woman repeats.

'Kindly open the door!' Etches says again.

He bangs a few more times but finally leaves the occupants
of B-78 to their fate.

> *The officers implored people to get on board, but they
> seemed to fear hanging out over the water at a height
> of 75 feet...*
>
> *Dickinson Bishop, first-class passenger*

> *Well, we put all the women in that was there, and
> children. Up to that time there was not many people;
> we could not get them up; they were rather afraid to
> go in the boat; they did not think there was anything
> wrong.'*
>
> *Archie Jewell, lookout*

> *We had not enough women to put into the boats. I
> cannot understand why we didn't take more men.*
>
> *Major Arthur Peuchen, first-class passenger*

153

00.30am Titanic *Bridge Time*

In the wireless room the mood has lightened. For the last five minutes, Jack Phillips and Harold Bride have been cracking jokes as Phillips taps out the call for assistance. Captain Smith comes back to make sure his order is being carried out.

'What are you sending?'

'"CQD", sir,' Phillips, at the transmitting key, replies.

'Send "SOS",' Bride interjects, 'it's the new call, and it may be your last chance to send it!'

This makes Phillips and Captain Smith laugh.

Third-class steward John Hart is standing on E-deck awaiting instructions. He has made sure that the 59 passengers he is responsible for are awake and have been told they need to put on lifebelts. Some don't think it is necessary, as they don't believe the *Titanic* is seriously damaged, so he's left spare ones on the floor along Scotland Road in case they change their minds. Then he hears a call, 'Pass your women and children up to the boat deck!'

Two policies are operating on the Titanic *that will have significant consequences. On the starboard side, First Officer Murdoch is allowing women and children first, while on the port side, Second Officer Lightoller is allowing women and children only. If there are no more women around the lifeboat or no more women prepared to board, then Lightoller launches it with empty seats. Murdoch tends to allow men to take those places. Furthermore, the officers in charge of the lifeboats don't believe that it is safe to lower a full lifeboat; they're afraid the davits won't hold. Lightoller told the British inquiry: 'It is more important to get a boat into the water than it is to actually fill her at the boat deck, because it is no use filling her if you are going to lose those people before you get her* down.' Third Officer Herbert Pitman testified to the British inquiry that although lifeboat 5 wasn't full, 'it took as many as it would take off the davits'. Yet, after the sinking, lifeboats identical to the Titanic's were tested by the Board of Trade, and it was shown they could safely carry 130 suspended from the davits.

There seems to be no general policy regarding the evacuation of third-class passengers. The Titanic's officers know that there are insufficient lifeboats. To avoid creating panic on the boat deck, they keep the third-class women and children below until 12.30am. Low, waist-high gates between the well decks and the boat deck, as stipulated by US Immigration to keep third-class passengers separate from first and second class, are being manned by stewards to keep men back. However some third-class men are getting past or finding their own way up to the boat deck by a different route.

It is possible that some of the Titanic's floor to ceiling gates – so-called Bostwick gates, installed to separate passengers and crew – are shut, but that others are open; some are manned by crew members keeping passengers from passing through until told otherwise, and others are not.

There are a number of other factors which hold back the third-class passengers: some obediently wait to be told what to do out of social deference – but orders do not always come as few of the third-class stewards show the initiative of John Hart; there are no signs in the lower decks showing passengers how to get to the upper decks; many of the third-class passengers are migrants who don't speak English; some routes are blocked by watertight doors closed by the crew trying to contain the flooding.

Questioned during the British Board of Trade Inquiry, John Hart was irritated by lawyer W.D. Harbinson's accusation that the initial reassurances given by himself and other stewards that the ship wasn't badly damaged led to third-class passengers refusing to go up on deck. Hart admitted that the instructions he was given were 'to keep

> *them quiet, it is quite obvious…' but he then defended his record: 'if*
> *you will pay attention you will find some people were taken to the*
> *boat deck.' This drew the response: 'Please do not be impertinent.'*

First Officer William Murdoch and lookout Archie Jewell are finding it hard to fill up starboard lifeboat 7. Standing nearby are actress Dorothy Gibson and the rest of her bridge party from earlier in the evening. She's saying loudly over and over, 'I'll never ride in my little grey car again. I'll never ride in my little grey car again.' Her companions William Sloper and Frederick Seward help Dorothy and her mother into the lifeboat. 'Keep a stiff upper lip,' Sloper tells her.

Dorothy grabs his hand. 'We won't go unless you do.'

'What do you say?' Sloper asks Seward.

'What's the difference, we may as well go along with them.'

The four find places in the boat. Sloper recalled later, 'for about ten minutes we looked up into the faces of the passengers looking down at us, trying to make up their minds to get in.'

> *Dorothy Gibson's little grey car is a gift from her lover, movie studio*
> *boss Jules Brulatour.*

First-class passenger Sallie Beckwith is standing on the starboard side of the boat deck with her husband Richard and their daughter Helen. They are returning home from a Grand Tour of Europe, which was both a vacation and a way of keeping their daughter away from a former classmate of hers named Karl Behr, a 26-year-old lawyer and former US Davis Cup tennis player.

Helen and Karl have fallen in love, but her parents disapprove of the match. The Beckwiths joined the *Titanic* at Southampton, but were dismayed when Karl embarked later that day at Cherbourg. He claimed it was a coincidence and that he had been on a long-planned business trip to France.

Now Karl is with them on the boat deck and neither he nor the Beckwiths feel it necessary to get into one of the lifeboats, despite Bruce Ismay, the chairman of White Star, insisting that the women in the party should. He tries again, virtually ordering them, and this time Sallie Beckwith agrees to get into lifeboat 5 with her daughter. She asks Ismay quietly if Karl and her husband and another couple, Edwin and Gertrude Kimball, could also get in the boat.

'Of course, madam. All passengers, men and women, go in these boats.'

The *Titanic*'s urgent message: 'CQD here, position 41°44'N, 50°24W'. We require assistance', is picked up by the cargo ship the *Ypiranga*.

In the third-class accommodation, a Lebanese family – 20-year-old Sahid Nackid, his 19-year-old wife Waika and their one-year-old daughter Maria, are fast asleep. They are emigrating from the Lebanon to Waterbury, Connecticut, where they will live with Sahid's mother, Josephine.

00.32am Titanic *Bridge Time*

The *Californian*'s assistant engineer, Ernest Gill, can't sleep and he's desperate for a cigarette, but smoking is forbidden between decks. He makes his way to the upper deck.

About 00.35am Titanic *Bridge Time*

A current is making the *Titanic* drift very slowly south-south-west. She is now 3° down at the head.

Violet Jessop is walking back to her room for a coat, passing brightly lit rooms in which she can see scattered possessions, jewels on dressing tables, and in one, a pair of silver slippers that look as if they've been kicked off in a hurry. She decides not to go all the way to her cabin for a coat and instead picks up a silk eiderdown from a first-class bedroom.

'Come along, ladies!' Third Officer Pitman shouts above the noise of the releasing steam, as he stands in a half-empty lifeboat 5 – one of First Officer Murdoch's boats.

Two large seamen help Marguerite Frölicher and her mother Margaretha in – there is little time for Marguerite to think about feeling seasick. Marguerite's father Maximilian starts to get in – after all there are spaces. The seamen stop him.

'Ladies first, sir.'

Maximilian Frölicher steps back onto the deck. He has tears in his eyes as he says, '*Auf weidersehen.*'

The *Titanic*'s chief designer Thomas Andrews is shouting something to passenger Eleanor Cassebeer, but she can't hear him. He motions to her to get into lifeboat 5.

'Why don't you get in as well?' Eleanor says to him.

'No, women and children first.'

Eleanor Cassebeer later claimed that Thomas Andrews told her earlier in the voyage that Titanic *wasn't finished. 'He said that the only reason they allowed her to go when they did was that the sailing day had already been fixed; they simply had to start.' Eleanor took as evidence of this the fact that in her stateroom there was an empty frame which should have contained a notice about the location of the lifebelts.*

Lucy Duff Gordon, her secretary Laura 'Franks' Francatelli and her husband Sir Cosmo are in the gymnasium on the boat deck. It is a warm, brightly lit refuge, and it is quieter than being on deck. They also found the wisecracks of some of the younger male American passengers in unbearably poor taste. Looking out of the windows, they can see that the starboard side of the deck is very much less crowded than the port.

In her cabin one deck below are all of Lucy Duff Gordon's jewels and pearls.

On the port side of the boat deck, Major Arthur Peuchen is now working on lifeboat 4, making more space for passengers by removing its mast and sail.

Bedroom steward Henry Etches is on the opposite side of the boat deck, getting lifeboat 5 ready for launch. On the well-lit deck, he can see Benjamin Guggenheim and his secretary Victor Giglio. They have taken off the lifebelts and sweaters Etches gave them, and instead are in evening dress.

'What's that for?' Etches asks bluntly.

'We've dressed up in our best, and we are prepared to go down like gentlemen,' Guggenheim says. He asks Etches for a favour: 'If anything should happen to me, tell my wife in New York that I've done my best in doing my duty.'

Etches agrees to pass the message on.

00.36am Titanic *Bridge Time*

Fourth Officer Joseph Boxhall comes into the wireless room with a corrected position for the *Titanic*. Phillips is busy transmitting a message to the cargo ship the *Asian*, which is towing the disabled tanker the *Deutschland* into the port of Halifax, Nova Scotia. Boxhall can't make himself heard over the noise of the exhausts, so he writes the position for Phillips and Bride on a piece of paper: '41°46'N, 50°14'W'

'Require immediate assistance. We have collision with iceberg. Sinking. Can hear nothing from noise of steam.'

00.37am Titanic *Bridge Time*

About 60 miles away, the small Cunard liner the *Carpathia* is on her regular run to Gibraltar, with 743 passengers on board, having left New York at noon on Thursday 11th April. In the ship's Marconi wireless room above the second-class smoking room, Liverpudlian operator Harold Cottam is getting ready to turn in for the night. He has taken off his jacket and is undoing his boot laces, but still has his headphones on, just in case he picks up any messages. Cottam has been hard at work since 7am; as is usual with all but the largest liners, he has no relief operator.

As an afterthought, Cottam decides to call up the *Titanic* to tell her that he has a number of messages for her that came via the Cape Cod shore station.

'I say, old man, do you know there is a batch of messages coming through for you from MCC?'

Suddenly a message breaks in. It's from the *Titanic*.

'Come at once. We have struck a berg. It's a CQD, old man. Position 41°46'N, 50°14'W'.

'Should I report this to the captain?' Cottam asks.

'Yes. Come quick.'

Cottam runs to the *Carpathia*'s bridge.

On the *Titanic*, 34-year-old Joseph Hyman is standing on A-deck, surrounded by people putting on lifebelts. He hasn't got one. Although there were several back in his shared third-class cabin, he never thought about bringing one up with him, but he isn't too worried. Originally from Manchester and a picture framer by trade, he's travelling alone to Springfield, Massachusetts to visit his brother. Earlier, Joseph had followed some others up to the boat deck and asked an officer if there was any danger, and was told, 'No, no, just keep calm.'

Many third-class passengers who had to flee the rising water with their belongings have now made their way up to the forward well deck. Some, like Joseph Hyman, have been able to climb the stairway to B-deck and then up two levels to the boat deck. It is a different story aft. Steward John Hart is trying to persuade third-class passengers to come up to the aft well deck, but many are reluctant, preferring to wait in the third-class smoking room and the general room.

00.38am Titanic *Bridge Time*

Another message is being sent from the *Titanic*. Phillips is finding it hard to work, even with headphones, because of the sound of the exhausts.

'MGY (*Titanic*) sends CQD, here is corrected position 41°46'N, 50°14'W. Require immediate assistance. We have collision with iceberg. Sinking. Can hear nothing from noise of steam.'

The message is picked up by the wireless operator on the *Ypiranga*.

00.39am Titanic *Bridge Time*

On the *Carpathia*, Captain Arthur Rostron is in his cabin, in bed, about to drop off to sleep. Wireless operator Harold Cottam and First Officer H.V. Dean see a light under the door, so burst in without knocking.

'What the hell?' Rostron exclaims and demands to know the

reason for the intrusion. Cottam tells him about the message from the *Titanic*. Rostron asks Cottam twice if he's sure the *Titanic* is in distress – Cottam assures him she is. All three men run to the bridge where Captain Rostron writes out the *Carpathia*'s position for Cottam to send to the *Titanic*.

Rostron then starts shouting orders:

'Stop her. Send for the chief engineer! Send for the chief officer! Call all the officers! Call all hands on deck and get ready to swing out the boats!'

Carpathia's second officer James Bisset, dozing in his bunk behind the bridge, hears the captain's orders and leaps out of bed. By the time he gets to the bridge, Captain Rostron is in the chart room, calculating the *Titanic*'s position.

00.40am Titanic *Bridge Time*

Jack Thayer is watching a scene that is a mixture of order and confusion. To the side of the boat deck, firemen covered in grime, stewards and other members of the crew are lined up awaiting orders. Groups of passengers are standing around, staying out of the way of the crew getting the lifeboats ready. 'It seemed we were always waiting for orders, but no orders ever came,' Jack wrote later.

> *The size of the boat deck and the noise of the exhausts make it hard to coordinate the launching of the lifeboats. Furthermore the crew have had no proper boat drill, they are unfamiliar with the davits, and many are unsure to which boat they have been assigned.*

Lawrence Beesley watches as Kate Buss's 'Cello Man' Wes Woodward runs down an almost deserted starboard A-deck, dragging his cello behind him – its spike scraping along the deck. Woodward is heading to the boat deck to join the rest of the band who have set up there.

Lifeboat 7 on the starboard side is the first to be launched. First Officer Murdoch has put lookout George Hogg in charge. The boat has 27 people on board including honeymoon couple Helen and Dickenson Bishop, actress Dorothy Gibson and her mother, as well as Frederick Seward and William Sloper.

Helen Bishop claimed in a newspaper interview that one of Titanic's officers said that brides and grooms should get into the boats first, although she never mentioned this in her testimony to the US Senate Inquiry into the disaster.

Also in lifeboat 7 is a man who calls himself Baron Alfred von Drachstedt; he has brought with him from his cabin his pipe, some food and a bottle of whisky.

Baron von Drachstedt had tried to befriend Helen Candee earlier in the voyage. The source of his wealth is a mystery. She felt that he had 'a certain sleekness that lessened the value of his good looks', and she avoided him from then on. She was right to be suspicious – the baron's real name is Alfred Nourney, but his deception is harmless; he wants only to impress.

Alfred Nourney is in fact a 20-year-old car salesman from Cologne, who has spent $2320 on clothes and jewellery for the voyage. He bought a second-class ticket in Paris for the Titanic, but unhappy with his cabin when he embarked at Cherbourg, paid the bursar a $38 surcharge to be moved to first class. Delighted with his new accommodation, he wrote a postcard to his mother in Germany:

Dear Mother, I'm so happy being in first class! I already know

163

> *some nice people! A diamond king! Mr Astor, one of the richest*
> *Americans, is on board! A thousand kisses, Alfred.*

> *Also in lifeboat 7 is 36-year-old American James McGough, who*
> *claimed later that he had his back to the boat but was pushed in*
> *by an officer who said, 'Here, you are a big fellow – get in the*
> *boat.' This may or may not have been true. Edward Beane, in life-*
> *boat 13, said in an interview with his local newspaper the* Syracuse
> Herald *that the boat was only half-full and that he had had to jump*
> *into the sea and swim for a long time to reach it. In fact, the boat*
> *was completely full when it was launched; he'd simply stepped in*
> *off the deck, another man to benefit from First Officer Murdoch's*
> *policy of women and children first.*

From the *Titanic*'s bridge they can still see the lights of a ship
on the horizon. Captain Smith tells Fourth Officer Boxhall to
signal to the ship using the Morse lamp.

'Tell him to "come at once, we are sinking".'

Through binoculars, Boxhall is convinced he can see two
masthead lights.

00.42am Titanic *Bridge Time*

The *Titanic* is communicating with the liner *Frankfort*.

'CQD. Come to our help, we are on ice.'

'OK, stdbi.' ['standby']

Jack Phillips tells Harold Bride to find the captain and inform
him that the *Frankfort* has picked up their 'CQD'.

'Lower away! Lower away! Lower away! Lower away!'

Bruce Ismay is in a state of agitation, keen to get lifeboat 5
down and away from the ship.

Fifth Officer Harold Lowe is at the davits, holding onto the cranking handles, about to lower the lifeboat, and has had enough of this interfering passenger.

'If you get the hell out of my way, I'll be able to do something! You want me to lower away quickly? You'll have me drown the whole lot of them! You ******!'

Chastened, Ismay moves forward to lifeboat 3 directly in front. Lowe has no idea that he's just sworn at the chairman and managing director of the White Star Line. Many of the crew, watching amazed, certainly do.

Harold Lowe discovered he had insulted Bruce Ismay when a steward told him later, 'Do you know what you said to Mr Ismay?'

'I don't know Mr Ismay.'

'Well, you used very, very strong language with him.'

'Did I?'

'Yes, you did.'

'I cannot help it if I did.'

On 24th April, the fifth day of the US Senate Inquiry, Lowe was asked about his heated exchange with Bruce Ismay. Ismay, who was present, said that he had no objection to Lowe repeating the word he used, although 'it was not very parliamentary'. He suggested the word be written down and given to the inquiry's chairman, Senator William Smith. This Lowe did.

'You uttered this to Mr Ismay?' Senator Smith asked.

'It was in the heat of the moment...' Lowe replied.

In his cabin on the *Carpathia*, Captain Rostron is briefing his officers, the chief purser, the chief steward, and the ship's doctor, in a clear and steady voice.

'The *Titanic* has struck a berg and is in distress 58 miles from here on the bearing N.52°W. We will make our utmost speed in going to her rescue. Call out an extra watch in the engine room and raise every ounce of steam possible. We may reach her in four hours. We may have to pick up 2000 or more people.'

00.43am Titanic *Bridge Time*

The wireless operator on the *Carpathia*, Harold Cottam, relays their position to Jack Phillips on the *Titanic*, telling him that they are steaming at full speed towards them.

Marconi operator Harold Bride finds Captain Smith on the boat deck, and tells him that the *Frankfort* has received their distress call. Smith asks him to find out her latitude and longitude.

The *Frankfort* is too far away from the *Titanic* to be able to assist – the *Carpathia* is closer.

00.45am Titanic *Bridge Time*

First Officer William Murdoch tells Third Officer Herbert Pitman to keep lifeboat 5 close to the ship. Then he shakes Pitman's hand and says, 'Goodbye and good luck.'

Pitman realises for the first time that Murdoch thinks the ship is doomed.

Dr Henry Frauenthal, who had treated Renée Harris's broken arm, recklessly leaps into lifeboat 5, along with his brother Isaac, his boots crashing into Annie Stengel's ribs, much to the fury of her husband watching from the deck.

Henry Etches, the steward who had been so diligent in getting Benjamin Guggenheim and other passengers into lifebelts, is already in lifeboat 5, his appointed boat. He waves a farewell to Guggenheim. A stout American gentleman leans into the lifeboat to kiss his wife goodbye.

'I can't leave you,' she says. Etches turns politely away.

The crew start to lower the lifeboat.

When Etches looks back, the stout man is now in the boat beside his wife.

'Throw that man out of the boat!' someone shouts.

It's too late. Lifeboat 5 is on its way down the side of the ship.

Then the launch goes wrong.

One davit crew is lowering faster than the other, and lifeboat 5 is rearing up dangerously. The passengers shout in alarm. The crews turn the cranking handles the other way to bring the lifeboat back up to the boat deck.

Marguerite Frölicher screams to her father, 'Come, otherwise I'm getting back out!'

Other women and children are screaming too. Then an officer (possibly Murdoch) relents and says, 'Let the men in. Make haste.'

Marguerite Frölicher's father and some other men gratefully get on board.

> **With a gasping sigh one word escaped the lips of the crowd: 'Rockets!' Anybody knows what rockets at sea mean.**
>
> **Lawrence Beesley, second-class passenger**

00.47am Titanic *Bridge Time*

Fourth Officer Boxhall has brought out the 12 distress rockets kept on the bridge, as the Morse lamp has failed to provoke a definite response from the ship on the horizon.

There is a crowd of stewards on the bridge and boat deck, all looking at the lights of the distant ship. Boxhall said later, 'Some said that she had shown a light in reply, but I never saw it...'

Boxhall places the first rocket in the socket on the starboard wing of the bridge.

He pulls the lanyard, and the rocket fires into the air and explodes, shooting out white stars 600 feet above the *Titanic*.

At the stern of the boat deck there is a gasp from the people around Lawrence Beesley as the rocket explodes in the air. It illuminates the four giant funnels, the masts, the dark water, and the faces of the passengers – some fully dressed, some in their nightclothes.

Beesley can see on some of those faces the realisation that they are all in great danger.

Others remain optimistic. Helen Candee watches the rocket fall as she stands on the boat deck with Hugh Woolner.

'The rocket must be for the *Olympic*, a sister ship of the line. It must be her lights that I can see over the port quarter,' she says.

'That's cheerful news,' is his only comment.

By the davits for lifeboat 3, Fifth Officer Lowe looks up and sees the face of the man working next to him lit up by the rocket's flash. It's the agitated passenger he swore at when lowering lifeboat 5, Bruce Ismay.

Alone on the bridge of the *Californian*, Second Officer Stone is pacing up and down to keep warm. Above the mystery steamer he sees a white flash in the sky. At first he thinks it's a shooting star – then he realises it's a rocket.

Out on deck, the *Californian*'s assistant engineer Ernest Gill sees it too.

00.48am Titanic *Bridge Time*

In the *Titanic*'s wireless room, Jack Phillips is still trying to communicate with the *Frankfort*.

'Are you coming to our assistance?'

'What is the matter with you?'

Phillips taps back impatiently: 'You are a fool. Keep out and do not interfere with our communication.'

> Harold Bride explained to the US Senate Inquiry why he and Phillips lost patience with the Frankfort's wireless operator:
>
> 'Any operator hearing a CQD, giving a ship's position, when on the job would immediately, without inquiring further into the matter, go to his captain and inform him. It would be a waste of time asking anything about it. The less time spent in talking, the more time can be spent in getting to the ship.'

Jack Phillips, in uniform, points out to Harold Bride that he still has his pyjamas and dressing gown on, and sends him to get dressed. Bride comes back with Phillips' overcoat, which he drapes over his shoulders as he taps away.

On the afterbridge at the stern, a white object in the water catches quartermaster George Rowe's eye. Bewildered, he phones through to Joseph Boxhall on the bridge.

'Do you know that a lifeboat has been lowered?'

Boxhall replies that they do, and asks Rowe to bring up the 12 distress rockets kept in the afterbridge. Such is the size of the *Titanic* and the activity on the bridge that Rowe has been forgotten.

About 00.49am Titanic *Bridge Time*

The wireless operator on the *Carpathia*, Harold Cottam, can hear the *Olympic* calling the *Titanic*. But on the *Titanic*, Phillips can't hear *Olympic*'s faint message because of the noise of the steam.

Harold Bride is with Captain Smith in the wheelhouse and tells him that the *Carpathia* is on her way. Bride heads back to the wireless room to find out which other ships they are in communication with.

> **We were in semi-darkness on the boat deck, and owing to the immense length and breadth of the vessel… we only knew what was going on about us within a radius of possibly 40 feet.**
>
> **Dr Washington Dodge, first-class passenger**

00.50am Titanic *Bridge Time*

Captain Smith and officers Wilde and Murdoch are in the latter's cabin behind the bridge, watching Charles Lightoller opening a locker. Lightoller takes out some Webley revolvers and ammunition, still in their protective grease, and gives them to Wilde.

As they leave Wilde gives a gun back to Lightoller.

'Here you are – you may need it.'

As he returns to the lifeboats along the port side of the boat deck, Lightoller passes the owner of Macy's department store, Isidor Straus, and his wife Ida.

'Can I take you along to the boats?' he asks Ida.

'I think I'll stay here for the present.'

'Why don't you go along with him, dear?' Isidor says.

'No, not yet.'

On E-deck, in the third-class quarters forward, a steady stream of passengers is still heading aft. Twenty-five-year-old steward Albert Pearcy is sending them towards the first-class saloon on the deck above, from where they should be directed to the boat deck. He is one of a long line of stewards posted on the route. Earlier he had helped third-class passengers with their lifebelts. Pearcy doesn't normally have anything to do with passengers; his job is to work in the third-class pantry.

Albert Pearcy is an experienced steward; by the time he joined the Titanic *from the* Oceanic, *he'd been with the White Star Line for five years. But he has been on the* Titanic *for less than a fortnight, and like many of her crew, finds it hard to find his way around the enormous ship. Giving evidence to the British Board of Trade Inquiry in May 1912, there was the following exchange between Albert and the attorney general Sir Rufus Isaacs:*

Isaacs: Were you off-duty when the collision occurred that Sunday night?

Pearcy: Yes.

Isaacs: Were you standing with others outside the pantry?

Albert: Yes.

Isaacs: Is that on E-deck?

Pearcy: Yes, I think that is E-deck. I am not quite sure.

Isaacs: He said E-deck, but I am not sure he is right.

Pearcy: I am not sure I am right. I know it is just outside the pantry.

Isaacs: I am going to ask a question that will clear that up. Was it on the same deck as the third-class stewards had their quarters?

171

Pearcy: Yes.
Isaacs: On the same deck as the third-class dining saloon?
Pearcy: Yes.
Isaacs: Then it is F-deck.

Steward John Hart has found it hard to persuade some third-class women and their children to go up to the boat deck, but he's managed to assemble a group of 30. The route to the lifeboats is a complicated one, because of the American immigration rules stating third-class passengers must be separated from first class. Hart's group are seeing parts of the ship they have never seen before. They emerge from the first-class grand staircase out onto the boat deck, then walk towards lifeboat 8; Hart can see it is ready for lowering.

The *Titanic*'s engineers are determined to fight the rising water, and now that some of the watertight doors have been unlocked from the bridge, they have brought portable suction pipes forward through boiler rooms 1, 2, 3 and 4.

Above them on F-deck, steward Joseph Wheat has been to get some personal items from his cabin near the Turkish baths, and to check the rooms of the bath attendants are empty. Wheat turns to go up the stairs and stops in his tracks. There is a trickle of water coming down the stairs from E-deck; it's just deep enough to cover the heels of his boots.

This means that water is now flooding the decks above boiler rooms 4 and 5, where the engineers are battling to reduce the flooding. It is only a matter of time before it finds a way down to them.

00.52am Titanic *Bridge Time*

Hovering now by lifeboat 8 are Isidor and Ida Straus. Ida helps her maid Ellen Bird to get on board, and then steps onto the gunwales herself as if to join her. Suddenly Ida has a change of heart. She takes off her fur coat and gives it to Ellen. 'I won't be needing it,' she says, and climbs out and clings to her husband.

'We have been together all these years. Where you go, I go.'

Helen Candee is watching the crowds on the boat deck, some in evening dress, some in their nightclothes. 'Each one walked with his life-clutching pack to await the coming horrors. It was a fancy-dress ball in Dante's Hell.'

> *John Hart: Those that were willing to go to the boat deck were shown the way. Some were not willing to go to the boat deck, and stayed behind. Some of them went to the boat deck, and found it rather cold, and saw the boats being lowered away, and thought themselves more secure on the ship, and consequently returned to their cabin.*
>
> *Solicitor-General Simon: You say they thought themselves more secure on the ship? Did you hear any of them say so?*
>
> *Hart: Yes, I heard two or three say they preferred to remain on the ship than be tossed about on the water like a cockleshell.*
>
> *Steward John Hart's testimony to the*
> *British Board of Trade Inquiry*

About 00.53am Titanic *Bridge Time*

Quartermaster George Rowe is carrying a heavy tin box full

of distress rockets across the boat deck towards the bridge. He can hear the ship's band playing.

Colonel Archibald Gracie has gone down to his first-class stateroom on C-deck to get some blankets to use in the lifeboats, only to find the door locked. A passing steward he doesn't recognise says, 'It's to prevent looting.'

Together they go to the cabin stewards' quarters where spare blankets are stored.

Some of the third-class women and children that John Hart brought to lifeboat 8 are clambering out and dashing inside to the top of the first-class staircase in order to keep warm. Hart walks aft as quickly as he can to find some more women and children – but he's finding it hard to make it through a crowd of third-class men in the stern well deck waiting to get up to the boat deck.

00.55am Titanic *Bridge Time*

Fourth Officer Boxhall and quartermaster George Rowe are sending up the distress rockets about every five minutes. Each time they set off a rocket, they have to clear everyone away from lifeboat 1, which is almost ready to go, as the launch socket is so close to its bows.

On the *Californian*, assistant engineer Ernest Gill watches the rockets and says to himself, 'That must be a vessel in distress.'

He knows it's not his job to notify the bridge or the lookouts, and besides, he's convinced they must have seen them.

So far, lifeboats 7 and 5 have been launched. Lifeboats 3 and

1 are about to be lowered. All these are on the starboard side and under the supervision of officers Murdoch and Lowe. On the port side, Charles Lightoller is about to launch his first lifeboat, no. 8.

The launching of lifeboats is erratic all night; for example, 40 minutes pass after the launching of first lifeboat before any of the eight boats at the stern are released. This is due to the fact that the Titanic *has a lack of experienced seamen. The crews on liners in 1912 consist mostly of stewards, firemen and engineers. Out of the 862 crew, only about 50 are able seamen, and only a small proportion of those are competent at launching a lifeboat. As the night progresses and more seamen are put in the lifeboats to crew them, the number of competent sailors dwindles swiftly.*

The sight of the rockets has frightened Lucy Duff Gordon. She initially decided that she wouldn't leave her husband, despite sailors grabbing her by the arm and trying to force her into a boat. Sir Cosmo asks First Officer Murdoch if they can all get into the boat. 'Yes, I wish you would,' Murdoch replies. Lucy, then Laura 'Franks' Francatelli, then Sir Cosmo, clamber into lifeboat 1.

Down in boiler room 5, the battle against the rising water continues. Leading fireman Fred Barrett lifts a manhole so the engineers can get access to the valves for the pumps. The room is full of steam, as water has been hosed onto the fires to douse them, and visibility is only a few feet. About 20 men had been used to deal with the fires in boiler room 5 – they are now on their way out to the upper decks.

Junior assistant engineer Jonathan Shepherd runs across the boiler room to help his superior Herbert Harvey, but in the thick steam doesn't see the open manhole cover and falls into it, breaking his leg. Fred Barrett and Harvey carry him into no. 5's pump room.

00.57am Titanic *Bridge Time*

The noise from the eight exhausts on the *Titanic*'s funnels suddenly stops. Second Officer Lightoller wrote later that 'there was a death-like silence a thousand times more exaggerated, fore and aft the ship. It was almost startling to hear one's voice again'.

The sound of the ship's band can now more easily be heard around the boat deck.

Lifeboat 3 is being lowered down the starboard side of the *Titanic*. Officers Lowe and Murdoch watch its slow, careful descent, as does Dr Washington Dodge, whose wife and son are on board. He wonders if he's done the right thing – has he merely placed them in greater danger by putting them in a lifeboat in the middle of the Atlantic? He's heard some officers say that the *Titanic* will stay afloat for another eight or ten hours.

Lifeboat 3 has only 50 people on board – leaving space for at least 15 more. At the US Senate Inquiry, Fifth Officer Harold Lowe said that he couldn't get enough people to fill it. Asked if he 'arbitrarily selected' women from the deck, he replied, 'You say "select". There was no such thing as selecting. It was simply the first woman, either first class, second class, third class, or sixty-seventh class; it was all the same – women and children were first.'

'If they are sending the boats away, they might just as well put some people in them.'

1.00am Titanic *Bridge Time*

The first-class smoking room is empty except for four men sitting around a table – American businessman Clarence Moore, who's been to England to purchase 50 pairs of fox hounds, Major Archibald Butt, President Taft's aide, and Butt's close friend, painter Francis Millet. They seem to be indifferent to the drama taking place all around them.

Lifeboat 8 has just reached the water – it's one of Second Officer Lightoller's on the port side. The boat is briefly illuminated by the flare of matches, as two dining-room stewards light cigarettes, much to the irritation of 55-year-old Mrs Ella White. Her annoyance increases when another steward starts fumbling with an oar.

'Why don't you put it in the oarlock?' she says.

'Do you put it in that hole?'

'Certainly!'

'I have never had an oar in my hand before... but I think I can row.'

Lucy, the Countess of Rothes, on her way to meet her husband in Canada, has control of the tiller. Seaman Thomas Jones, who's been put in charge of the boat by Lightoller is only too pleased to give her the task.

'I saw the way she was carrying herself, and I heard the quiet determined way she spoke to the others, and I knew she was more of a man than we had on board,' he said later.

Travelling with the countess, and soon to take an oar, is her maid, 20-year-old Roberta Maioni. In the pocket of her kimono is a White Star Line badge given to her by a young steward she's become fond of. Her employer has no keepsake or anything of value with her – when she had walked past Herbert McElroy, chief purser, back on C-deck, he had called out, 'Hurry, little lady, there is not much time. I'm glad you didn't ask me for your jewels as some ladies have!'

Hugh Woolner is continuing his dutiful care of Helen Candee. He and another admirer, Edward Austin Kent, are walking towards lifeboat 6. Suddenly Captain Smith shouts at them, 'Hey, you two, come away from that boat! No men are allowed near the lifeboats!'

They drop back and Helen Candee gets in alone, tumbling when she steps on two oars lying lengthwise in the boat, breaking her ankle.

Lifeboat 1, on the starboard side of the *Titanic*, close to the bridge, is hanging from its davits, waiting to be lowered. It is a cutter used for emergencies, such as someone falling overboard, and can hold only 40 people. There are currently three passengers sitting in it – Sir Cosmo Duff Gordon, his wife Lucy and her secretary Laura 'Franks' Francatelli, plus lookout George Symons, who's been helping launch lifeboats 5 and 3.

American businessmen Charles Stengel, who earlier put his wife into a lifeboat, and saw her injured by Dr Frauenthal's boots, gets the nod from Murdoch and jumps up onto the high guard-rail of the boat deck, but then slips and tumbles into lifeboat 1.

'That's the funniest sight I have seen tonight', Murdoch laughs.

Stengel grins back, reassured by the officer's laughter. 'Perhaps it's not so dangerous as I imagined...' he thinks.

Murdoch is keen to get lifeboat 1 launched as he needs to start work on the four stern lifeboats as quickly as possible. The Titanic *is by now developing a list to port, which threatens to make launching starboard lifeboats harder – they risk scraping their way down the rivets on the ship's hull.*

1.05am Titanic *Bridge Time*

The *Titanic* is about 4° down at the head.

Lifeboat 1 is being lowered down the starboard side of the ship with 12 people on board. Six are firemen who've escaped the engine room. Greaser Walter Hurst, who has just come up to the well deck from the boiler rooms, watches the lifeboat.

'If they are sending the boats away, they might just as well put some people in them,' he thinks.

Then one of the falls supporting the lifeboat catches, and the cutter starts slowly tipping up as it drops.

'Cut it with a knife!' Murdoch calls down. No one has one, not even the crew, so Murdoch grabs a heavy metal bar and drops it down, shouting, 'Mind your heads!'

The impact of the bar shakes the cutter and frees the trapped fall.

'Pull away as quickly as possible, at least 200 yards!' Murdoch yells down.

As the lifeboat reaches the water and pulls away, Lucy Duff Gordon looks up and sees quartermaster Rowe setting off the distress rockets.

Lady Lucy wrote later: 'I shall never forget how black and deep the water looked below us, and how I hated leaving the big, homely ship for this frail little boat.'

Murdoch now heads aft to help with the launching of the remaining starboard lifeboats.

About 1.08am Titanic *Bridge Time*

Having been moved from lifeboat to lifeboat on the starboard side, Milton Long and Jack and John Thayer are on the port side of the boat deck where they are talking to first-class dining saloon steward George Dodd. To their surprise, Dodd tells them that Mrs Thayer is still on board and not safely in a life-boat as they had thought.

Wireless operator Harold Bride is making frequent trips to the boat deck and the bridge to update Captain Smith on the *Carpathia*'s progress and speed.

Meanwhile, Charles Lightoller is preparing to lower lifeboat 6 on the port side. It is only the second boat of his to get away. Lightoller can hear the sound of the ship's band playing. He wrote later: 'I don't like jazz music as a rule, but I was glad to hear it that night. I think it helped us all.'

1.10am Titanic *Bridge Time*

Lifeboat 6 is being lowered on the port side. As the seawater has spread more evenly across the width of the ship, the list to starboard has reduced, but those in the boat are still having to push it away from the *Titanic*'s hull. Molly Brown is one of the women on board. Second Officer Lightoller saw her start to walk away from the boat; then she was suddenly aware of 'a shadow, and a few seconds later I was taken hold of'. 'You are going, too!' Lightoller shouted.

Molly looks up from the lifeboat and sees Captain Smith

looking down 'like a solicitous father'. He calls out to them to 'row to the light in the distance', and to make sure 'all the boats keep together'. Then she looks down, and sees an open cabin porthole and water pouring into it.

There are about 28 people on board Molly Brown's lifeboat – two of whom are from the *Titanic*'s crew – Robert Hichens, the quartermaster who'd been at the helm when the ship struck the iceberg, and Frederick Fleet, the lookout who'd spotted it. It can hold 65.

The boat is about level with C-deck when Hichens shouts up to Lightoller that two men are not enough to handle the boat. Lightoller leans over and has a look, then turns to the men around him. 'Any seamen there?'

After a pause, Major Arthur Peuchen steps forward. 'I'm not a seaman but I'm a yachtsman, if I can be of any use to you.'

Lightoller points to the lifeboat's falls hanging from the davit head about ten feet away from the side of the ship.

'If you're seaman enough to get out on those falls, and get down into the boat, you may go ahead.'

Peuchen leaps across the gap, grabs hold of the falls and slowly lowers himself down into lifeboat 6.

Lifeboat 6 is the sixth lifeboat launched in the space of 20 minutes from the *Titanic*. They all contain only first-class passengers and crew members. Major Arthur Peuchen is one of the few men that Charles Lightoller allows in the lifeboats.

Lightoller said later that his plan was to get the half-full boats to come back to the gangway doors on the lower decks to collect more women and children. The boats would then be transferred to the other ship whose lights he could see in the distance. Lightoller said that he sent boatswain Alfred Nichols and six hands to open

> the port lower deck gangway door 'but neither he nor his men
> were ever seen again'.

There is suddenly a rush of water between the boilers in boiler
room 5. The bulkhead between rooms 5 and 6 has collapsed.
Engineer Herbert Harvey shouts at Fred Barrett to flee, and
Barrett runs for the escape ladder. He never looks back.

Harvey's assistant Jonathan Shepherd, unable to move
because of the leg he broke in the open manhole, drowns in
the rising water.

> **We were told that everything was all right, and we did
> not think there was a danger. But the ship did not go
> on, then some of us began to think that they were not
> telling us the truth and that we might be sinking.**
>
> **Mariana Assaf, third-class passenger**

About 1.12am Titanic *Bridge Time*

The homeward bound *Olympic* has been hearing her sister
ship's distress calls very faintly, and has been trying to call
her. Finally Jack Phillips replies to the *Olympic* and gives their
position.

The *Olympic* is 505 miles away.

Officers Lowe and Moody are standing by lifeboats 14 and
16.

'I've just sent boats away without a single officer in any of
them, so there best be an officer in one of these two,' Lowe
says, suggesting that one space should be kept either for him
or Moody.

'You go. I'll find another boat,' Moody replies.

Lowe gets into lifeboat 14, Moody starts loading lifeboat 16.

Harold Lowe would always be grateful to James Moody for his self-less decision. Moody, as the more junior officer, had every right to take a place in one of those lifeboats.

The *Carpathia* is steaming as fast as she can to the *Titanic*'s rescue. Captain Rostron has given an extremely detailed list of instructions to each of his officers and heads of department.

For the US Senate Inquiry into the sinking, Captain Rostron wrote out a list of the instructions he gave. Because the Carpathia *was on the 'Mediterranean run' she had more than one doctor to reflect the diversity of her passengers.*

• English doctor, with assistants, to remain in first-class dining room.

• Italian doctor, with assistants, to remain in second-class dining room.

• Hungarian doctor, with assistants, to remain in third-class dining room.

• Each doctor to have supplies of restoratives, stimulants, and everything to hand for immediate needs of probable wounded or sick.

• Purser, with assistant purser and chief steward, to receive the passengers, etc., at different gangways, controlling our own stewards in assisting Titanic *passengers to the dining rooms, etc.; also to get Christian and surnames of all survivors as soon as possible to send by wireless.*

• Inspector, steerage stewards, and master at arms to control our own steerage passengers and keep them out of the third-class dining hall, and also to keep them out of the way and off the deck to prevent confusion.

• Chief steward: That all hands would be called and to have coffee, etc., ready to serve out to all our crew.

• Have coffee, tea, soup, etc., in each saloon, blankets in saloons, at the gangways, and some for the boats.

• To see all rescued cared for and immediate wants attended to.

• *My cabin and all officials' cabins to be given up. Smoke rooms, library, etc., dining rooms, would be utilized to accommodate the survivors.*

• *All spare berths in steerage to be utilized for* Titanic's *passengers, and get all our own steerage passengers grouped together.*

• *Stewards to be placed in each alleyway to reassure our own passengers, should they inquire about noise in getting our boats out, etc., or the working of engines.*

• *To all I strictly enjoined the necessity for order, discipline and quietness and to avoid all confusion.*

• *Chief and first officers: All the hands to be called; get coffee, etc. Prepare and swing out all boats.*

• *All gangway doors to be opened.*

• *Electric sprays in each gangway and over side.*

• *A block with line rove hooked in each gangway.*

• *A chair sling at each gangway, for getting up sick or wounded.*

• *Boatswains' chairs. Pilot ladders and canvas ash bags to be at each gangway, the canvas ash bags for children [to get babies and children aboard].*

• *Cargo falls with both ends clear; bowlines in the ends, and bights secured along ship's sides, for boat ropes or to help the people up.*

• *Heaving lines distributed along the ship's side, and gaskets handy near gangways for lashing people in chairs, etc.*

• *Forward derricks, topped and rigged, and steam on winches; also told off officers for different stations and for certain eventualities.*

• *Ordered company's rockets to be fired at 2:45 a. m. and every quarter of an hour after to reassure* Titanic.

The Carpathia's *second officer, James Bisset, said later that once all these instructions had been handed out, 'we were all wide-awake.'*

'Those poor devils, they haven't a chance.'

About 1.15am Titanic *Bridge Time*

Stewardess Mary Sloan can see Captain Smith looks agitated. Later she wrote to her sister: 'Passengers wouldn't have noticed but I did. I knew then we were soon going.'

First-class passengers Jacques and May Futrelle are looking down from the boat deck at the third-class passengers in the stern well deck. To May they look 'quite unexcited'.

'Those poor devils,' Jacques says, 'they haven't a chance.'

Having put Helen Candee into lifeboat 6, Hugh Woolner is trying to persuade Ida Straus she should go too.

'I've always stayed with my husband; so why should I leave him now?'

Hugh Woolner and other passengers then try to persuade Isidor to leave the ship – if he goes, his wife will follow.

'I'm sure nobody would object to an old gentleman like you getting in. There seems to be room in this boat,' Woolner says.

'I will not go before the other men,' Straus replies. The couple then go to sit in two steamer chairs in the glass-enclosed part on A-deck.

Martin Rothschild, a New York clothes manufacturer, comes out of his stateroom on C-deck and bumps into dining saloon steward Frederick Ray. Ray is wearing an overcoat he's rescued from his cabin down on E-deck. He only just made it, as the forward part of E-deck is now under water. The two men know each other, as Ray waited on Rothschild on the *Olympic*. Ray asks where his wife is, and Rothschild says that she is safely in a lifeboat.

'This seems rather serious,' Ray says.

'I do not think there is any occasion for it,' Rothschild replies. Ray doesn't mention he's just seen E-deck flooding.

The two men walk together up to A-deck where they go their separate ways. Ray heads towards his assigned lifeboat, no. 9.

Piles of bread that haven't made it into the lifeboats litter the boat deck.

On the stationary *Californian*, no more than ten miles away, Second Officer Herbert Stone watches five rockets through his binoculars. He's not convinced they are coming from the distant steamer, as he can't see any initial flash on her deck, and the rockets seem to explode a good way beyond her.

He calls down the voice tube to the chart room where Captain Lord is sleeping – fully dressed.

'Are they company signals?' Lord asks.

'I don't know, but they appear to me to be all white.'

'Well, go on Morsing.'

'Yes, sir.'

'And when you get an answer, let me know by Gibson [the apprentice officer].'

'Yes, sir.'

Lying on the settee, Captain Lord can hear the sound of the Morse lamp clicking overhead. He drifts off to sleep.

Company signals are never white rockets, but coloured flares used between ships for identification purposes. Board of Trade regulations are clear, that if there is any doubt about any company signals they must be treated as distress signals. The international code for distress signals in 1912 states that at night 'rockets or shells, throwing stars of any colour or description, used one at a time at short intervals' should be used.

1.16am Titanic *Bridge Time*

In lifeboat 1, lookout George Symons sees water up to the second row of portholes under the *Titanic*'s nameplate.

'We spent two hours discussing the carpet for the first-class cabins and 15 minutes discussing lifeboats.'

About 1.20am Titanic *Bridge Time*

Lifeboat 7, the first to be launched, has now been in the water for 40 minutes. Some of its occupants are concerned that as the *Titanic* sinks, they will be sucked under. Helen Bishop, on honeymoon with husband Dickenson, who's sitting next to her in the lifeboat, is attempting to reassure her fellow passengers by telling them that an Egyptian fortune-teller predicted she would survive a shipwreck, and an earthquake, but meet her death in a motor car accident.

'We have to be rescued in order for the rest of my prophecy to be true,' she says.

In the engine room, water is seeping up through the steel plates on boiler room 4's stokehold floor. Engineer John Hesketh shouts to the firemen around him, 'We've done all we can, men – get out now!'

Most of the trimmers, greasers and firemen leave the stokeholds and engine rooms.

The fires in boiler room 2 are still burning in order to supply power to the *Titanic*'s emergency dynamos.

Water is now flowing ever further down Scotland Road and

down flights of stairs on either side. It is pouring through the open port side gangway door into the sea.

At the foot of the steps that lead to B-deck on the aft well deck, where many third-class passengers are congregating, the à la carte restaurant chef, Pierre Rousseau, and his maître d', Paul Maugé, are attempting to persuade stewards to let them pass. The stewards try to turn them away, thinking they are third-class passengers, but then Paul Maugé gives them their names, and they are allowed up.

There is an increasing urgency to get women away on lifeboats. Stewardess Mary Sloan is hesitating about getting into lifeboat 16. Thomas Andrews sees her.

'Why are you still here?'

'All my friends are staying behind. It would be mean to go...'

'It would be mean for you *not* to go. You must get in!'

On the starboard boat deck, journalist Edith Rosenbaum, wearing a fur coat and velvet slippers, and clutching her lucky toy pig, notices the White Star Line chairman Bruce Ismay looking at her.

'What are you doing on the ship? I thought all women had already left! If there are any other women around, come over to this staircase at once!' he calls.

Edith walks towards Ismay, who's standing at the top of the metal stairs that lead down to A-deck. Ismay takes her firmly by the arm and escorts her down to two crew members, who grab her.

'Don't push me!' she shouts, as they try to get her into a lifeboat.

'If you don't want to go, stay!' a sailor snarls back, and lets her go.

Edith searches for her velvet slippers that have come off in the struggle, and remains on the ship.

Bruce Ismay would have been well aware that there were not enough lifeboats to take all the Titanic's *passengers. He had been at a meeting at Harland and Wolff in early 1910 when the shipyard's managing director, Alexander Carlisle, proposed equipping the* Olympic, *the* Titanic *and the proposed third ship, the* Gigantic, *with 48 lifeboats, giving a total capacity of 2886. Ismay declared that 48 was too many and that they should settle on 16, as per Board of Trade regulations. The ships' décor was then discussed. Alexander Carlisle said later, 'We spent two hours discussing the carpet for the first-class cabins and 15 minutes discussing lifeboats.'*

> **It was not the launching of the boats that took the time. We got the whole boat out and in the water in less than ten minutes. It was getting the people together that took the time.**
>
> **Fifth Officer Harold Lowe, British Board of Trade Inquiry**

> **Mr Lowe was very young and boyish-looking; but somehow, he compelled people to obey him. He rushed among the passengers and ordered the women into the boat. Many of them following him in a dazed kind of way, but others stayed by their men.**
>
> **Charlotte Collyer, second-class passenger**

John and Jack Thayer have been reunited with Marian and her maid. Together with Milton Long, they are making their way down from the boat deck to the front of A-deck, where they've been told lifeboats are being loaded. Jack and Milton are trying to keep up with them as they make their way through the extremely crowded first-class lounge, but people keep pushing in front of them. Then Jack loses sight of his parents altogether.

1.22am Titanic *Bridge Time*

The *Olympic* receives a message from the *Titanic*: 'Captain says get your boats ready. Going down fast at the head. What is your position?'

A *Titanic* steward is standing smoking a cigarette with his hands in his pockets, surrounded by first-class passengers. Violet Jessop stares in disapproval.

Every time one of his port lifeboats is lowered, Second Officer Lightoller walks to the top of an emergency staircase that leads down to C-deck and looks down at the water level to judge how long the ship has got. He wrote later, 'That cold, green water, crawling its ghostly way up that staircase, was a sight that stamped itself indelibly on my memory. Step by step, it made its way up, covering the electric lights, one after the other, which for a time, shone under the surface with a horribly weird effect.'

1.23am Titanic *Bridge Time*

On the starboard boat deck, beside lifeboat 14, Dr John Simpson, the ship's assistant surgeon, passes Fifth Officer Harold Lowe a torch, and says, 'Here's something that will be useful to you.'

Standing close by are Harvey and Charlotte Collyer and their 8-year-old daughter Marjorie, who is wrapped up in a White

Star Line blanket from their cabin. Charlotte is wearing her husband's overcoat, in a pocket is the letter to her parents she wrote in the library that afternoon. Everything that they've packed for their new life fruit farming in Idaho is now underwater in the hold. Earlier, Charlotte had watched lifeboats 7 and 5 launch under the supervision of First Officer Murdoch, and she was impressed by his coolness and bravery. But it's Harold Lowe she's admiring now, as he loads lifeboat 14. Despite his youth he has a clear knack for getting people to do what he wants, and takes no nonsense.

Lowe needs to be tough – there is a rising mood of panic around the boats – among both passengers and crew. Sailors are yelling at men to keep away from the boats.

A sailor snatches Marjorie from her parents and propels her into the lifeboat.

'Now you too!' another man shouts at Charlotte. 'You're a woman. Take a seat in the boat or it'll be too late!'

One sailor grabs her by the arm and another puts both arms around her waist and together they drag her towards the lifeboat.

'Go, Lottie! For God's sake be brave and go! I'll get a seat in another boat!' Charlotte hears her husband call, just before she's thrown over the bulwark and into the boat. Charlotte stumbles and hits her head on an oarlock. She staggers to her feet in time to see Harvey walk away into a crowd of men. In the inside pocket of his jacket, he still has all their life savings in bank notes.

Charlotte has had no time to say goodbye to her husband, neither has Esther Hart, who is also in the lifeboat with her daughter Eva. Benjamin Hart told Lowe as the boat was loaded, 'I'm not going in. For God's sake look after my wife and child.' He told Eva to 'hold mummy's hand and be a good girl', then turned and left. Esther knows she will never see Benjamin again.

Fireman Thomas Threlfall has just come up on deck, having been released from the engine room minutes ago; he sees his chance and hurdles the rail into lifeboat 14. Officer Lowe, who has decided he will take charge of the lifeboat, also jumps aboard, shouting to the men at the davits, 'Lower away!'

A young man of about 16, who has been standing at the rail with his eyes fixed on Lowe, hoping desperately to be given permission to escape the sinking ship, jumps into the boat close to Charlotte Collyer. She and some of the other women instinctively hide him under their skirts and coats as he crawls under a seat. Lowe pulls out his Browning automatic and drags him from his hiding place. He points the gun right in the young man's face.

'I give you just ten seconds to get back on to that ship before I blow your brains out!'

He begs to be able to stay. Eight-year old Marjorie Collyer takes Lowe's hand.

'Oh, Mr Man, don't shoot. Please don't shoot the poor man!'

Lowe smiles at Marjorie, then lowers his gun and says gently to the teenager, 'For God's sake, be a man. We've got women and children to save. We must stop at the decks lower down and take on women and children.'

The young man turns and clambers out of the lifeboat, and over the rail. Charlotte Collyer watches him lie down on the deck, hiding his face. All the women in lifeboat 14 are sobbing.

'Lower away!' Lowe shouts again.

A male passenger suddenly jumps over the rail, landing on top of a small child in the lifeboat. Lowe, incensed, grabs him by the collar and pushes him back onto the *Titanic*. He's surrounded by a group of men on deck who beat him.

The lifeboat is being lowered at speed. To deter any further last-minute boarders, Lowe fires his pistol into the water – his blood is up.

'If any man jumps into the boat, I will shoot him like a dog!'

The lifeboat hits the sea with such force that its occupants are showered in spray and are forced to cling onto the gunwales to stop falling overboard.

> *At the British Board of Trade Inquiry, Harold Lowe explained that he allowed lifeboats that weren't full to be lowered because he was (like Lightoller) 'working on the idea that the gangway doors were going to be opened and take people from there'. Asked where he'd heard that the gangway doors were going to be open, Lowe replied that he'd overheard that the boatswain and a group of men had been sent down to sort it, and that he told those in charge of the lifeboats to stay within hailing distance of the ship, so they could return if necessary. Pressed on whether he'd taken any steps to open the gangway doors or to get passengers to the gangway doors, Lowe replied testily, 'Haven't I told you that the order had been given to open the gangway doors by someone else?'*

Under the supervision of Sixth Officer James Moody, lifeboat 16 is being lowered at the very rear of the port side of the boat deck. Moody has done a good job; the boat has 56 passengers, many of them women and children from third class, and is the fullest boat so far. Stewardess Mary Sloan, who saw Captain Smith looking so concerned a few minutes ago, is on board, as is her colleague Violet Jessop. Draped in the silk eiderdown she'd taken from a first-class cabin, Violet is cradling a baby that a steward thrust in her arms, saying, 'Look after this, will you?' just before the lifeboat was lowered.

One reason the lifeboat is fuller than the others is Moody's policy of allowing some men on board, something Second

Officer Lightoller would have disapproved of. One man is wearing white pyjamas, which in the gloom, one passenger thinks, make him look like a snowman.

1.25am Titanic *Bridge Time*

The *Titanic*'s designer, Thomas Andrews, and the chief deck steward are throwing steamer chairs and any other wooden objects they can find into the water, to help anyone who might jump overboard.

Thirty-four-year-old trimmer Thomas Dillon has been released from the engine room and is on the stern well deck among a number of third-class passengers – mostly men but also a few women. Dillon hears a voice call down from the boat deck, 'Any more women there?'

Dillon and some other crew members chase the remaining women up the ladders and usher them towards the lifeboats.

1.26am Titanic *Bridge Time*

The electric lights on the *Titanic*'s decks are dim but still working, thanks to the efforts of the engineers below decks.

Out of wireless range, the White Star liner *Baltic* sends a message to the Cunard liner *Caronia* to pass on to the *Titanic*: 'We are making for you, keep in touch with us.'

Jack Phillips notices that the wireless signal is getting weaker as his equipment slowly loses power.

> The Baltic *was the ship that helped rescue the* Republic's *passengers when she collided with the* Florida *in 1909, the incident that made wireless operator Jack Binns a hero.*

1.27am Titanic *Bridge Time*

American mail room clerk John Starr March's silver pocket watch stops.

> *All five mail clerks worked tirelessly, dragging the mail bags to an upper deck, despite being urged by steward Alfred Theissinger to escape: 'They shook their heads and continued at their work.' Either this was the moment John Starr March drowned or the moment his watch became waterlogged as he worked. The watch was found on his body.*

1.28am Titanic *Bridge Time*

The *Frankfort* sends a message to the *Titanic*:
  'Our captain will go for your course.'
  'OK; tks, tks.' ['thanks, thanks.']

Alfred Theissinger, who has been helping with lifeboat 15's falls, is hoping he would be allowed into the lifeboat.
  'There is no chance for you. I'm sorry,' an officer tells him.

The piper Eugene Daly is helping his cousin Maggie and their friend Bertha Mulvihill (who's travelling back to America to surprise her fiancé) into lifeboat 15, which has now been lowered to A-deck. There are still women and children waiting to board, but for Eugene 'life is sweet... and I wanted to save myself' – so he gets in the boat. An officer calls him back – Eugene ignores him, so members of the crew haul him out.

Twenty-five year old Imanita Shelley and her mother Lutie Parrish are sitting in steamer chairs watching the loading of lifeboat 12. Imanita isn't feeling very well. A sailor comes up to her. 'Young lady, for God's sake get into this lifeboat! They are getting ready to launch; it is the last one on board... you mustn't take any chances!' Seeing Lutie's reluctance, Ida Straus, still standing on deck with her husband Isidor, encourages her to go with the sailor. One of the crew has his own method of persuasion – he grabs Lutie Parrish and throws her across the widening gap between the ship and the lifeboat. Imanita jumps in after her

> *The ladies have had a most unsatisfactory voyage. At Southampton they had been given a second-class cabin in a lower deck that was unheated and so small that they referred to it as 'a cell'. After 11 complaints to the chief purser saying that Imanita was ill as a result of their accommodation and threatening to go to the captain, they were found a better cabin.*
>
> *Imanita Shelley gave a sworn affidavit to the US Senate Inquiry that was taken up, not with an account of the sinking, but mostly with complaints about their cabins. The second 'though large and roomy, was not furnished in the comfortable manner as the same accommodation procured on the Cunard and other lines...' In the first cabin it was 'impossible to open a regulation steamer trunk in said cabin. It was impossible for a third person to enter said cabin unless both occupants first of all crawled into their bunks'.*

1.30am Titanic *Bridge Time*

The low gates separating the third-class stern well deck and the boat deck are shut and guarded by stewards. But some men have spotted a way to get past by clambering up the two well deck cranes and over a railing.

Daniel Buckley, who jumped out of bed in his third-class cabin to discover water seeping under the door shortly after the collision, had been helping lower lifeboats on the boat deck, until a crew member said to him, 'Take a chance yourself.' Buckley can see a large number of men, mostly crew, surrounding lifeboat 13, which is swinging from the davits and half full with women. The men get in and Buckley follows suit. He is wearing a lifebelt given to him by a first-class passenger who had one spare.

Officers Murdoch and Moody spot them and order them out. They refuse. The officers then draw their revolvers and fire into the air. Daniel Buckley starts crying, and cowers low in the boat; a woman throws her shawl over him, and says, 'Lay down, lad, you're somebody's child.'

The other men reluctantly clamber out. Buckley remains hidden, but for the moment, lifeboat 13 isn't going anywhere.

The Lebanese family emigrating to Connecticut, Sahid and Waika Nackid and their one-year-old daughter Maria, have woken up and made their way to the boat deck, in nightclothes and coats. They slept through the collision and the initial calls for people to come up on deck.

Jack Thayer watches a first-class passenger come out of the A-deck lounge with a bottle of Gordon's gin, and down it in one. 'If I ever get out of this alive, there is one man I will never see again,' Jack thinks.

On lifeboat 12, Lutie Parrish looks up and sees Ida Straus smiling at her and waving. Lutie smiles back, amazed at how calm Mrs Straus is, 'not trying to get away and doing all to help the rest of us escape in comfort'.

Just as the lifeboat is about to hit the water, a young man described by those in the boat as 'a crazed Italian' and 'a foreigner of some kind' suddenly jumps from A-deck and lands on Lutie Parrish, bruising her right leg and side, and crushing her foot.

'She looks very queer out of the water – her lights look queer.'

About 1.34am Titanic *Bridge Time*

The *Titanic* is about 5° down at the head.

At the same time as lifeboat 12 is dropping down the *Titanic*'s hull, almost directly opposite on the starboard side, lifeboat 9 is ready to go. All night theology student Sidney Collett has been looking after the two ladies in his charge – family friend Marion Wright and their new acquaintance Kate Buss. Kate has her papers for US Immigration, but in her rush to put on a lifebelt, she has forgotten to bring her money. All her jewellery is still in the purser's office. The young Scot, Douglas Norman, who was Kate's table companion and accompanied Marion on the piano at the hymn singing yesterday, is also with them. He hangs back as Kate and Marion step into the boat. Sidney Collett follows them.

'Well, what of you, where are you going?' First Officer Murdoch says to Collett, revolver in hand.

'I have these young ladies in my charge and feel it my duty to take care of them.'

'Get in,' Murdoch says.

Kate Buss angrily insists that Douglas Norman should be allowed in the lifeboat too. Murdoch refuses. Norman hasn't bothered to put on a lifebelt as he is convinced that with the Marconi operators on board, help will come before the *Titanic* sinks.

Sidney Collett is the last to board lifeboat 9 just before it's lowered. It has 56 passengers, including Benjamin Guggenheim's mistress, the singer Léontine 'Ninette' Aubart. Guggenheim remains on the ship.

Lifeboat 2 is just aft of the bridge's port wing. Chief Officer Wilde is supervising its loading. What he hasn't noticed is that a group of crew members have crept aboard behind his back. But from the bridge Captain Smith has seen them, and asks for a megaphone.

'How many of the crew are in that boat? Get out of there, every man of you!'

The men jump out of lifeboat 2, and their place is taken by the women and children Wilde has found.

Standing by lifeboat 2, first-class passenger Mahala Douglas turns to her husband Walter, and asks him to come with her. A number of other first-class male passengers are watching.

'No, I must be a gentleman,' he says, and turns away.

Mahala calls after him, to give him some hope: 'Try and get off with Mr Moore and Mr Butt. They will surely make it!'

Sitting in lifeboat 11 as it's about to be lowered, stewardess Annie Martin can see the ship's band playing at the top of the staircase on A-deck, where there is a Steinway upright piano. Some are smoking and keeping time by stamping their feet. They all have lifejackets by their sides.

The passengers would give different accounts of what the musicians played. One heard them playing 'lively airs', another 'selections from opera and the latest popular melodies from Europe and America'. Jack Thayer heard 'The Star Spangled Banner'.

A few feet away from Annie Martin, Edith Rosenbaum is contemplating getting into lifeboat 11. There are now only two standard lifeboats left on the starboard side. But Edith is wearing a narrow skirt, and can't see how she is going to be able to jump the considerable gap between A-deck and the lifeboats. She was, as she put it, 'a prisoner of her own skirt'.

The crew on the starboard side are by now as impatient as those on the port side with the women who remain. A sailor grabs Edith's toy pig and throws it into lifeboat 11. Edith freezes, not knowing what to do.

'May I help?' asks fellow first-class passenger Philipp Mock, whose sister Emma is already in the boat. He suggests that if he crouches slightly and she puts her foot on his knee with her arm around his neck, he can get her onto the rail. This Edith does, but when she reaches the rail, she suddenly finds herself flying through the air and landing in a heap in the bottom of the boat, where she recovers her battered pig. Philipp Mock jumps in too.

Things are now running more smoothly for First Officer Murdoch. Lifeboat 11 is full – it has 70 passengers on board. It starts its descent from A-deck. Edith Rosenbaum looks up at the passengers leaning over the rails.

As lifeboat 11 hits the water, first-class passenger Alice Silvey, who has just said goodbye to her husband William, can see a number of people she believes to be foreign being pushed back from the rail to stop them jumping into other boats.

On the stationary *Californian*, Second Officer Herbert Stone and Apprentice Officer James Gibson are still fascinated by the rockets being fired above the mystery ship. Gibson has a better pair of binoculars than Stone, and he can see a white detonating flash on deck, the rocket flying into the sky and then the explosion and the fall of white stars.

Stone borrows Gibson's binoculars and looks into the night for a few minutes. He hands them back saying, 'Have a look at her now. She looks very queer out of the water – her lights look queer. A ship is not going to fire rockets at sea for nothing.'

Gibson looks and can see that the ship appears to be listing, her red port light has disappeared, and she has 'a big side out of the water'.

Despite the odd appearance of the lights, neither man has the confidence to disturb Captain Lord.

'I think I'll stick to the big ship, Billy, and take a chance.'

1.35am Titanic *Bridge Time*

Colonel Archibald Gracie is helping Second Officer Lightoller load lifeboat 4 through the lowered windows of A-deck. A stack of wooden steamer chairs has been turned into makeshift stairs to help people up to the level of the windows. The sounding spar that would have obstructed the lifeboat's progress to the water has been successfully cut away.

> *Archibald Gracie later described Lightoller at work: 'One of his feet was planted in the lifeboat, and the other was on the rail of deck A, while we, through the wood frames of the lowered glass windows on this deck, passed women, children and babies in rapid succession without any confusion whatsoever.'*

Gracie helps John Jacob Astor lift his pregnant wife onto the rail. They pass her to Lightoller, who helps Madeleine get seated in the boat. Astor leans out over the rail to speak confidentially to Lightoller, but Gracie overhears.

'Could I enter the boat to protect my wife, in view of her delicate condition?'

'No, sir, no men are allowed in these boats until women are loaded first.'

'Could you tell me the number of this boat to help me find my wife, should I be rescued?'

'Number 4,' Lightoller replies, not knowing who the Astors are, and assuming that the husband wants the number so he can make a complaint to the White Star Line about his behaviour.

'Goodbye!' Astor calls to his wife.

Martha Stephenson Eustis is finding it hard to squeeze through the open A-deck window into lifeboat 4, wearing a fur coat and lifebelt and carrying a steamer rug. She throws the rug back onto the deck.

Emily Ryerson steps forward with her son John and daughters Suzette and Emily. She and her husband Arthur are hurrying home to New York, following the death of their eldest son in a motor car accident. Charles Lightoller bars their way.

'That boy can't go.'

'Of course the boy goes with his mother! He is only 13!' Arthur Ryerson says angrily. Lightoller doesn't argue, perhaps because he knows he's running out of time and the lifeboat is far from full. He lets Emily and John on board, but adds testily, 'No more boys!'

By telling John Jacob Astor that men can't board 'until women are loaded first', Lightoller is modifying his earlier policy of women and children only. He faces the humiliation of his ship sinking without all her lifeboats launched, unless he can speed up the loading process.

George Widener, who was hosting a dinner party in the splendour of the first-class restaurant only six hours ago, is standing with his book-collecting son Harry, watching lifeboat 4 load. William Carter, one of his dinner party guests, says to Harry that he should try for a lifeboat.

'I think I'll stick to the big ship, Billy, and take a chance.'

In Harry's pocket is the precious 1598 collection of Francis Bacon's essays which he has just bought in London.

Steward John Stewart walks inside the first-class smoking room on A-deck to see if there are any passengers who need his help. He sees the *Titanic*'s designer, Thomas Andrews, standing alone, arms folded, in front of the fireplace, staring at the painting above it, 'The Approach to Plymouth Harbour' by Norman Wilkinson.

'Aren't you even going to try for it, Mr Andrews?'

Andrews says nothing. His lifebelt is on a card table next to him. Stewart leaves him to his thoughts.

Steward John Hart has taken a second group of about 25 women and children up from third class to the boat deck. It's taken longer to get up than he wanted, and now he can see only one lifeboat left on the starboard side – number 15.

Eighteen-year-old printer Gurshon 'Gus' Cohen has made his way up from third-class by himself, following a similar route to Hart, after crew members barred his way from the stern well deck. To his dismay, Cohen can see the situation is hopeless – there is no way he's going to get in a lifeboat. Cohen has at least found a lifebelt – it took him half an hour of patient searching around the boat deck to find one. He looks over the slanting rail into the sea.

> *One of our friends, a man by the name of Johan Lundahl who had been home to the old country on a visit and was going back to the United States, said to us, 'Goodbye friends; I'm too old to fight the Atlantic.' he went to the [third-class] smoking room and there on a chair*

> **was awaiting his last call. So did an English lady – she
> sat down by the piano and, with her child on her knee,
> played the piano until the Atlantic grave called them
> both.**
>
> **August Wennerström, third-class passenger**

1.36am Titanic *Bridge Time*

A message from the *Olympic*'s captain, yet to fully compre-
hend the situation, arrives in the *Titanic*'s wireless room:

'Are you steering southerly to meet us? Haddock.'

Jack Phillips replies, 'We are putting the women off in small
boats.'

The *Frankfort* sends a message:

'Are there any ships around you already?'

Phillips ignores it.

The *Frankfort* sends again.

'What's up, old man?'

Phillips has had enough.

'You fool, stand by and keep out.'

> *W. Zippel is the wireless operator on the* Frankfort, *and is probably
> not being as foolish as Phillips thinks. The* Titanic's *wireless signal
> is weak by now, and Zippel and operators on the other ships are
> picking up only some of her wireless signals, hence their confusion
> as to the state of the sinking ship.*

Steward Frederick Ray has been helping people get into lifeboats
9 and 11 at the rear of the boat deck. He's now assisting with
lifeboat 13, which has been brought level with A-deck. Daniel
Buckley is still hiding in the bottom of the boat under a woman's
shawl. The lifeboat is barely half full so there's a call for men

to get in (despite the fact that men had been ordered out at gunpoint earlier). Ray sees Dr Washington Dodge hanging back. He knows Dodge as he waited at table for him and his wife on the *Olympic* – in fact, the reason the family are on the *Titanic* is because he suggested they try her out on her maiden voyage.

Ray goes over to Dodge and asks him where his wife and son are; Dodge tells him they were put in a lifeboat a short while ago.

'You had better get in here, then,' Ray says, and pushes him into lifeboat 13, and then gets in himself.

A woman on A-deck who is being helped into the lifeboat starts to panic. 'Don't put me in that boat! I don't want to go in that boat! I've never been in an open boat in my life!'

Ray, standing in the rear of the lifeboat, has been patient all night, but has now had enough.

'You have got to go, and you may as well keep quiet!'

Still crying, the woman gets in.

A crew member on the deck then throws Ray a rolled-up blanket. He opens it up, discovers it's a baby boy and calls to the women in the lifeboat, 'Who'll take this babby?'

The boy's mother Sylvia Caldwell is already in the boat, and so the baby is passed to her. Albert Caldwell, his father, then gets in.

Standing by lifeboat 15, First Officer Murdoch asks steward John Hart, who's about to walk off to find more third-class passengers, 'What are you?'

'One of the crew. I've just brought these people up.'

'Go ahead, get into the boat with them.'

Hart joins the 25 third-class women and children he's brought onto the boat deck in the lifeboat. Looking back onto the deck, he can see a number of first-class women passengers standing with their husbands.

> **The other [third-class] passengers started arguing. One said that it was dangerous and the other said that it was not; one said white and the other said black. Instead of arguing with those people, I instantly went to the highest spot. I said to myself that if the ship had to sink, I should be one of the last. That was my first idea, which was the best.**
>
> **Bert Pickard, third-class passenger**

About 1.40am Titanic *Bridge Time*

Lifeboat 9 is pulling away from the side of the *Titanic*. Bert Pickard found it easy to get up from third class through second class and then onto the boat deck. But now he's in a lifeboat he's not sure he's made the right decision.

'I would rather be on the ship,' he says to a member of the crew next to him.

'Don't you see we are sinking?' the man laughs.

A shout of 'Everybody!' is heard in the stern well deck where many third-class passengers are standing, some waiting to get to the boats, some just waiting for someone in authority to tell them what to do. The gates are opened and many rush up to the boat deck. Twenty-six-year-old Norwegian fisherman and farmer Olaus Abelseth, his cousin Peter and brother-in-law Sigurd arrive in time to see the last three lifeboats on the port side of the *Titanic* being filled with women and children. The men are travelling to South Dakota where Olaus has a farm.

It is possible that about this time, some floor to ceiling Bostwick gates below decks are still locked to keep third-class passengers from swamping the remaining lifeboats on the boat deck, where officers are struggling to keep order.

By now the *Titanic* has a dangerous list to port. On the boat deck Chief Officer Wilde shouts, 'Everyone to the starboard side to straighten her up!'

Second Officer Lightoller hears and shouts the message to the crew and passengers around him.

From the boat deck, schoolteacher Lawrence Beesley has been watching the lifeboats launch for an hour. On his arm is a dressing gown he brought from his cabin. Only two lifeboats remain on the starboard side (other than the collapsibles).

A shout comes from below, 'Any more ladies?'

Beesley looks over the starboard rail and sees lifeboat 13 swinging level with A-deck. On board are crew members, including stokers and stewards, and about 25 women and children.

Fireman Fred Barrett is one of those on board. He witnessed the first flood of water when the iceberg hit, and was involved in drawing the fires in the boilers, and helping engineer Jonathan Shepherd when he broke his leg – now, wet through, he has a place in a lifeboat.

In all, there are about 60 people in lifeboat 13, so it's not at capacity.

'Any more ladies?'

Lawrence Beesley keeps watching. Then one of the lifeboat's crew looks up and sees him.

'Any ladies on your deck?'

'No.'

'Then you'd better jump!'

Beesley climbs onto the rail, throws his dressing gown into the lifeboat, then jumps ten feet into the stern.

Chef Pierre Rousseau and his maître d' Paul Maugé are also on the boat deck looking at lifeboat 13. Maugé jumps down into the lifeboat and then turns and shouts to Rousseau, '*Sautez! Sautez!*' ['Jump! Jump!']

One of the crew on A-deck grabs Maugé by the back of his coat and tries to pull him out, shouting, 'Shut up!'

There is a shout from the boat deck: 'Let no more in that boat; the falls will break!'

So the lifeboat's crew shout, 'Lower away!' and the davit cranks turn and lifeboat 13 descends. Maugé shakes himself free and looks up at Rousseau, who's still standing up on the boat deck.

'*Sautez! Sautez!*'

But Rousseau doesn't jump. Maugé said later, 'The chef was too fat, I must say – too big, you know?'

Since he boarded at Southampton, schoolteacher Lawrence Beesley has been fascinated with almost every detail of the *Titanic*. Although the ship is sinking and he's being lowered in a lifeboat in the middle of the Atlantic to an unknown fate, his keenness to observe every detail is undiminished. Beesley watches the two sailors on the boat deck lowering his lifeboat receiving instructions from the crew in the boat. 'Lower aft! Lower stern! Lower together!'

Beesley gazes at the illuminated cabins and saloons as they drop past by them in a series of jerks.

On the *Californian*, Second Officer Herbert Stone says to Apprentice Officer James Gibson as they watch an eighth rocket explode, 'A ship is not going to fire rockets at sea for nothing.'

'There must be something wrong with her,' Gibson replies.

Then as they watch, the ship seems to disappear to the southwest.

1.41am Titanic *Bridge Time*

Lifeboat 15, next to 13 in the starboard davits, starts its descent – the 13th to be launched. It has 70 passengers – the majority third-class passengers plus some of the ship's crew.

Below them, the people in lifeboat 13 are far from safe. Its bow is being lowered right over the condenser exhaust that's pumping seawater out of the side of the ship from the boiler rooms. The stream of water is three feet across and will easily swamp the boat. Washington Dodge, Paul Maugé and others start yelling to the men on the davits above to stop – but still they drop closer. The passengers frantically try to grab the lifeboat's oars, so they can push themselves away from the water jet, but they have been lashed together with twine and about ten people are sitting on top of them.

They get one oar free, and fireman Frederick Barrett pushes the lifeboat away from the hull and the exhaust's spewing water, allowing the boat to drop to the sea. 'During the few moments occupied by these occurrences I felt for the only time a sense of impending danger,' Washington Dodge wrote later.

Twenty-two-year-old Bridget Bradley leaps up from her seat in the lifeboat, convinced that it's sinking, and tries scrambling up the falls to get back on deck. Daniel Buckley, a friend of Bridget's from the same town in Cork, watches from under his shawl as she's pulled back down by others in the boat.

The water from the condenser exhaust is still posing problems for them. The boat is being pinned against the ship's hull and pushed aft by the water from the exhaust, right into the space where lifeboat 15 will hit the sea. The pin mechanism designed to release lifeboat 13 from the falls and allow it to move refuses to release. The people in the boat look up and see the white bottom of 15, and shout, 'Stop lowering! Stop lowering!'

But no one at the davits on the boat deck can hear them. The passengers in lifeboat 15 look down, see the danger, and then join in the yelling. But still 15 keeps on dropping – now only ten feet away from 13.

In the bows of lifeboat 13, Lawrence Beesley and a stoker stand up and reach out to push the approaching boat away.

'Stop lowering! Stop lowering!'

Then Barrett starts hacking at the stern falls of lifeboat 13 with a knife. Beesley and the stoker are now touching the wooden bottom of 15.

'One! Two!' Barrett shouts as each stern rope is cut. Lifeboat 13 swings clear from the *Titanic*, and 15 safely drops to the water.

On the boat deck, close to the bridge, Jack Thayer and Milton Long are discussing whether to fight their way into collapsible C, one of the *Titanic*'s four canvas Engelhardt collapsible lifeboats (identified by letters A, B, C and D). But such is the chaos and increasing panic, they think that the lifeboat will never reach the water the right way up.

1.42*am* Titanic *Bridge Time*

Captain Smith is standing between the bridge and lifeboat 2, watching it being loaded with passengers. He can see that it's lacking a seaman with any experience. Smith finds Fourth Officer Boxhall on the bridge, and orders him to 'get into that boat and go away [from the ship]'.

With lifeboat 1 now in the water, the preparations to launch collapsible C from its davits are well under way. Suddenly two men jump into collapsible C. Jack Thayer, watching with Milton Long, thinks they may be stewards. Purser Herbert McElroy, standing by the collapsible, pulls out his revolver and fires twice into the air, yelling, 'Get out of this! Clear out of this!'

The men are dragged away.

Third-class steward Albert Pearcy, along with other stewards, has come up on to the boat deck, their job of directing third-class passengers to safety now over. Albert sees two babies lying on the deck with no sign of their parents. He scoops them up and walks towards First Officer Murdoch who is supervising the loading of collapsible C.

The Lebanese family, the Nackids, are spotted by a crew member. Sahid is holding baby Maria, and his wife Waika is standing shivering, wearing only a nightdress. The crew member beckons them over and offers Waika a seat in the boat. Sahid helps her get in and then gives her the baby. He's about to get in too when he's pushed away. Maria starts to cry and reaches out for her father, but even though there are spaces, Sahid isn't allowed in.

Standing watching the loading of collapsible C are another third-class family – Rhoda Abbott returning to the United States with her two homesick teenage sons Rossmore and Eugene. Rhoda stands out from the other passengers as she's wearing her Salvation Army uniform.

Amy Stanley, Emily Goldsmith and May Howard, three women who have become friends of Rhoda's, as they have neighbouring cabins in third class, get into the lifeboat. Now it's Rhoda's turn. But she knows from watching the loading of other boats, that 16-year-old Rossmore won't be allowed in with her. With a heavy heart, Amy Stanley watches from the boat as Rhoda and the two boys walk away.

The *Titanic* replies once more to *Olympic*: 'Tell captain we are putting the passengers off in small boats.'

Then Jack Phillips sends out a general 'CQD' distress call and the message, 'engine room getting flooded.'

> **Senator Fletcher: Were there any ladies on the deck when you left?**
> **Edward Buley: No, sir... they went around and called to see if there were any, and they threw them in the boat at the finish, because they didn't like the idea of coming in.**
> **Fletcher: Pushed them in, you mean?**
> **Buley: Threw them in.**
>
> **Able seaman Edward Buley's testimony to the US Senate Inquiry**

1.43am Titanic *Bridge Time*

Lifeboat 10 is being loaded on the port side of the boat deck; Chief Officer Wilde is supervising.

'Keep the men back!' he's shouting to the stewards. Lifeboat 10 is the last of the group of eight lifeboats on the stern of the *Titanic*. Able seaman Frank Evans notices a three-foot gap between the lifeboat and the side of the boat deck rail. This is because the *Titanic* now has a list of 10° to port.

Evans is in the bow of the lifeboat, catching the lighter women and children thrown in by the ship's chief baker, Charles Joughin.

> Charles Joughin had been down on A-deck with three or four other crew members, and had to literally drag women who had been sitting on the deck up to the boats.

A young Frenchwoman tries to jump across the gap but slips

and falls. She just manages to grip the edge of the lifeboat with her hands, her feet just touching the railing on A-deck below. Crew members haul her up onto the boat deck. The woman jumps again, this time successfully.

'Room for two more!' an officer shouts. One man jumps the gap, followed by the only Japanese person on board, government railway official Masabumi Hosono.

> *A second-class passenger, Hosono had been sent below decks, as the crew assumed he was third class. He made his way up to the upper decks, debating whether to die an honourable death that 'wouldn't disgrace the Japanese people', but discovered his desire to live was stronger. He wrote later: 'I myself was deep in desolate thought that I would not be able to see my beloved wife and children anymore, since there was no alternative for me than to share the same destiny as the* Titanic. *But the example of the first man making a jump led me to take this last chance.'*

'I believe she's gone, Hardy.'

1.45am Titanic *Bridge Time*

The *Titanic* is 6° down at the head.

Lifeboat 2 enters the water with only 26 people on board. Steward James Johnson gets out a razor to swiftly cut the falls.

Guessing that no one in the boat would have a knife, he'd borrowed it from a seaman called McAuliffe who'd said, 'Remember me at Southampton and give it back to me!' In his pocket, Johnson also has three oranges he grabbed from a dining saloon – just in case.

Apart from Johnson, the only crew members that Fourth

Officer Joseph Boxhall has on board are a kitchen hand and a sailor called Frank Osman, who at least knows how to row. With Boxhall taking the other oar and trying to steer, they pull away from the *Titanic* until they are about 100 yards distant.

With lifeboat 2 afloat, Second Officer Lightoller takes another look down the emergency stairway to see how far the water has risen. He reckons his ship will sink very soon. Lifeboats 4 and 10 are still on the davits – but there is no way that Lightoller will let her go down with lifeboats still aboard.

The fact that Smith, Wilde, and Lightoller on the port side are allowing a lifeboat to be launched with only 26 people on board, more than two hours after the collision, is possibly also evidence that the ship's officers want the boats away before they are overwhelmed by the large number of passengers they know are on the lower decks, possibly being held back.

Looking from lifeboat 15, assistant steward Walter Nichols can see that the *Titanic*'s three giant propellers are now half out of the water.

First Officer Murdoch is walking along the deck with steward John Hardy, who has been helping him with the starboard lifeboats. Murdoch says quietly, 'I believe she's gone, Hardy.'

The *Olympic* wireless operator asks what weather the *Titanic* has.

About 1.46am Titanic *Bridge Time*

Charles Lightoller is hurrying back to launch lifeboat 4; there 'wasn't a moment to lose', he recalled. He bumps into the chief purser, Herbert McElroy, assistant purser, R.L. Barker, and surgeons William O'Loughlin and John Simpson.

Simpson looks at Lightoller, wearing no jacket, overcoat or lifebelt, but perspiring nonetheless.

'Hello, Lights, are you warm?'

They talk for a while and then shake hands. 'Frankly, I didn't feel like saying goodbye,' Lightoller wrote later, 'although I knew we shouldn't have the ship under us much longer.'

1.47am Titanic *Bridge Time*

The *Baltic* to the *Titanic*: 'Are there any boats around you already?'

Out on the water in lifeboat 14, Fifth Officer Harold Lowe is coming to terms with a lifeboat full of women and children, many of whom are crying. It's a situation that a life at sea hasn't prepared him for. He tries a variety of ways to console them.

'Don't cry, please don't cry... You'll have something else to do than cry; some of you will have to handle the oars... A good song to sing would be "Throw Out the Lifeline"... I think the best thing for you women to do is to take a nap.'

> *As far as I know Mr Phillips did not go to much trouble with her [Olympic] as we now realised the awful state of affairs, the ship listing so heavily to port and forward. The Captain also came in and told us she was sinking fast and would not last longer than half an hour.*
>
> *Harold Bride, wireless operator*

1.49am Titanic *Bridge Time*

The *Olympic*'s captain sends a message to the *Titanic*: 'Commander, Titanic. Am lighting up all possible boilers as fast as I can, Haddock.'

Desperate to find out what is happening, Jack Phillips is outside the wireless room. He sees that the well deck is awash and that the water is almost up to the boat deck.

The remaining men from the *Titanic*'s engine room, who have been working below decks keeping the pumps and the electric lights going, are coming up on the boat deck and the stern well deck. The engine room telegraphs on the bridge were 'rung off' a while ago. This was the signal that they were released from their posts and could make their way to the lifeboats. But the men can see that it may be too late; the last boats are being launched. Second Officer Lightoller, who has served with some on previous ships, exchanges a few words with them. 'It was surely a bleak and hopeless spectacle that met their eyes. Empty falls hanging loosely from every davit head, and not a solitary hope for any one of them,' he wrote later.

> *The journal* Scientific American *printed a tribute on 27th April 1912 to the engineers' bravery. 'They, above everyone else on that ship, must have known that she had received her death wound and that the hour of her sinking might be delayed, but not by any possibility averted... Those men standing on the double bottom of the ship may possibly have seen the submerged edge of the iceberg come ripping through the sides of the ship...'*

'Go on, lads, drink up. She's going down!'

1.50am Titanic *Bridge Time*

Quartermaster George Rowe fires his last distress rocket.

Baker Charles Joughin is standing by lifeboat 10. He's spent the last 20 minutes helping load it with reluctant women and children. Joughin waits for permission to get in – he knows that it would set a bad example if he didn't ask, even though this is the boat he is officially assigned to. Permission doesn't come; instead, two sailors and a steward are told to get on board.

'Lower away!'

As lifeboat 10 drops towards the cold water, Joughin turns and heads to his cabin in search of a drink.

A number of crewmen have had the same idea and are getting drunk in the bar of the first-class smoking room, where free whisky is being handed out by a steward.

'Go on, lads, drink up. She's going down!'

Trimmer Thomas Dillon, glass in hand, is contemplating finding a first-class cabin, shutting the door and waiting for the end.

Close to the bridge, lifeboat 4 has only 20 feet to find the water. Emily Ryerson, with her children Suzette, Emily and John around her, watches water pour into the square portholes on C-deck, flooding around the beds and furniture of the still brightly lit staterooms. Her husband Arthur stands watching by the rail as the lifeboat descends; he's promised his wife that he'll stay with John Thayer and that 'we will be all right'. Also standing with him are George and Harry Widener. Eleanor Widener is with Emily on board lifeboat 4.

Marian Thayer is also in the lifeboat with her maid Margaret Fleming. But neither her husband John nor her son Jack are at the rail to see her off – both are on the starboard side of the ship, but not together. Each assumes the other has managed to escape on a lifeboat.

Lightoller's command of 'No more boys!' on lifeboat 4 has been successfully evaded. Ten-year-old Billy Carter Jr is on the lifeboat with his mother, with a girl's hat firmly placed low over his head, just in case Lightoller thinks him too old.

Jack Phillips returns to the wireless room and tells Harold Bride that they should put their lifebelts on, and that 'the forward well deck is awash and they are putting women and children in the boats and clearing off'.

A large number of greasers, firemen, engineers and trimmers are standing by the electric crane on the starboard side of the boat deck. Two greasers are watching lifeboat 4 directly below them row aft, parallel with the hull. Thomas Ranger and Frederick Scott have no wish to hang around and let their fate be decided for them. They climb onto the empty davits that once held lifeboat 16 – the rear-most set on the port side of the ship – their bulky lifebelts making such a tricky manoeuvre even more difficult. At the end of a davit they swing onto the falls and ease their way down. Halfway to the lifeboat below, Scott loses his grip and tumbles into the water. Ranger continues down the falls until lifeboat 4 is only a couple of feet below him. With perfect timing he drops in, bone dry. Scott is pulled out of the water.

Gus Cohen has had the same idea. He has managed to climb along the metal arm of a davit; he's glad he's wearing gloves

– they have helped his grip. Cohen jumps for the falls, and desperately clutches at a rope that cuts through the gloves, burning his hands and cutting his forehead as he slips towards the dark water.

About 1.52am Titanic *Bridge Time*

In lifeboat 14, Fifth Officer Harold Lowe's attempts to calm his passengers aren't working.

'For God's sake, stop crying. If I had not the responsibility of looking after you I would put a bullet through my brain,' he tells them.

One hundred yards away from the *Titanic*, Fourth Officer Joseph Boxhall, in charge of lifeboat 2, hears a whistle from the boat deck, followed by Captain Smith shouting through a megaphone, 'Come round to the starboard side!'

Smith has now decided that the half-filled lifeboats should come back to collect people from the gangway doors.

Boxhall guides lifeboat 2 slowly around the stern of the ship.

Quartermaster Robert Hichens, at the tiller of lifeboat 6, also hears the whistle and the call.

'Stop rowing!' he says, so that he can hear the instructions.

'No, we are not going back to that boat,' he says, 'It is our lives now, not theirs.' It is the first order from an officer Hichens has ever disobeyed. In fact, Hichens insists that they pull away further from the *Titanic*. Many of the women who have husbands and sons on the ship protest, but there is little they can do, as Hichens controls the tiller and therefore the direction of the boat.

Charles Joughin is in his E-deck cabin having another half tumbler of spirits. The cabin in fact belongs to the confectioner and second baker, but as in his two previous ships, the *Teutonic* and the *Olympic*, Joughin has commandeered it, since it's better than the one assigned to him as the chief baker.

Joughin is not too drunk to notice that water is spreading over the floor of the cabin.

It's time to leave.

Then two men appear and tell him that they're going to close the watertight door just forward of his room. They pick up the large spanner by the door that's needed to close it. Joughin doesn't wait to see if they are successful, but heads up on deck.

> *When I first saw and realised that every lifeboat had left the ship, the sensation felt was not an agreeable one.*
>
> **Colonel Archibald Gracie, first-class passenger**

1.55am Titanic *Bridge Time*

Broadway producer Henry B. Harris and his wife Renée are walking across the *Titanic*'s bridge from starboard to port. Renée earlier broke her arm; one sleeve of her fur coat hangs limp.

Captain Smith, standing with Archibald Butt and Isaac Freuenthal, says to Renée, 'Why aren't you in a boat? How can your husband save himself and you too, with a broken arm?'

'I don't want to leave him!'

'You get into that boat – it is the last one. And lose no time – give your husband a chance!'

In lifeboat 2, Fourth Officer Joseph Boxhall and Frank Osman are managing to row slowly around the *Titanic*'s stern. They gaze in amazement at the ship's three massive propellers out of the water. Heavy steamer chairs and bits of wood are raining down around them. Their mission is to collect people from the starboard gangway doors, but Boxhall is worried that the lifeboat may get sucked towards the ship, and that passengers may swamp and capsize the boat. He decides they should pull away to a safer distance. There are 26 people in lifeboat 2.

Jack Phillips is tapping out a message: 'Women and children in boats, cannot last much longer.'

Harold Bride has got his lifebelt from under his bunk, and has put on a pair of boots and an extra jacket. He slips a lifebelt around Phillips as he works and wonders if he should get him his boots as well.

Bride is full of admiration for his colleague. 'How poor Phillips worked through it I just don't know. He was a brave man. I learned to love him that night,' he wrote later.

'Are there any sailors here? Are there any sailors here?' calls an officer looking for help with the Engelhardt collapsible boats, as he half runs along the port boat deck. Olaus Abelseth has sailed since he was six years old, and he looks at his cousin and his brother-in-law, neither of whom are sailors. They know what that look means and say to Olaus in Norwegian, 'No, let's stay together.'

So Olaus says nothing, and the officer goes past.

Olaus watches an old couple nearby. He hears Isidor Straus say to his wife, 'Go into the lifeboat and get saved.' Isidor puts his hand on her shoulder and says again, 'Please get into the lifeboat and get saved.'

'No, let me stay with you,' Ida replies.

221

1.57am Titanic *Bridge Time*

Captain Smith is in the wireless room, talking to Jack Phillips and Harold Bride. Outside they can hear the sound of people running.

'Men, you have done your full duty. You can do no more. Abandon your cabin. Now, it is every man for himself. You look out for yourselves. I release you. That's the way of it at this kind of time. Every man for himself.'

The captain leaves, and Harold Bride follows him. The boat deck forward is slowly disappearing under water.

On the poop deck at the stern, trimmer Thomas Dillon and 14 other drunk members of the crew are passing round a single cigarette. Dillon has been talked out of his solitary mission to die in the luxury of a first-class cabin.

On the *Carpathia*, now sailing at about 17 knots, well above her usual 14, wireless operator Harold Cottam hears the transmission from the *Titanic*: 'Engine room full up to boilers.'

Second Officer Lightoller has organised a number of crewmen to lock arms and form a semi-circle around collapsible D, which is being fitted into the davits recently used by lifeboat 2. Only women and children will be allowed through.

There is panic in the air and on the faces around him. Already Lightoller has had to brandish his revolver to get some 'Dagoes', as he calls them, out of the lifeboat (the gun isn't in fact loaded). He doesn't want anyone rushing the boat.

Henry B. Harris brings his wife Renée through the semi-circle formed by the crew.

'You can't come on board, sir.'

'I know, I'll stay,' he sighs.

Henry picks up his wife and puts her into the arms of a seaman. When Renée is safely in the lifeboat he throws in a blanket for her. All his wife's pearls and jewellery are in his pockets.

A man in a grey overcoat is kneeling on the deck, hugging his two young sons close to him, who are both wrapped up against the stabbing cold. This is the man who is recorded on the White Star Line passenger list as Louis Hoffman – but is, in fact, Michel Navratil, fleeing to America with his two sons Michel and Edmond, abducted from his wife's home in Nice.

Michel Navratil steps forward and passes two-year-old Edmond to Lightoller, who is standing by the boat deck rail. Then Navratil crouches down to whisper in young Michel's ear: 'My child, when your mother comes for you, as she surely will, tell her that I loved her dearly and still do. Tell her that I expected her to follow us, so that we might all live happily together in the peace and freedom of the New World.'

Michel Navratil then raises his hand in salute and walks away through the crowd.

> **Senator Smith: Who, if anyone, told you to enter the lifeboat?**
> **Bruce Ismay: No one, sir.**
> **Smith: Why did you enter it?**
> **Ismay: Because there was room in the boat. She was being lowered away. I felt the ship was going down, and I got into the boat.**
>
> **Bruce Ismay's testimony to the US Senate Inquiry**

2.00am Titanic *Bridge Time*

In the *Titanic*'s wireless room, Jack Phillips is tapping out: 'SOS SOS SOS SOS.'

A woman who has fainted is brought into the wireless cabin. Bride finds her a chair and a glass of water. Her husband wants them to leave quickly.

Collapsible C is swinging from its davits ready to be lowered. The sea is now less than 20 feet below the sloping boat deck. Quartermaster George Rowe is in charge. Emily Goldsmith is sitting in it with her nine-year-old son Frankie. Before they got in, her husband Frank hugged and kissed her and then leaned down to his son and said, 'So long, Frankie: I'll see you later.' They are planning to start a new life in Detroit, and are travelling with Tom Theobold, a friend from their home town of Strood in Kent, as well as Alfred Rush, who is celebrating his 17th birthday today. Alfred is small for his age and could pass for a child but, proudly wearing long trousers for the first time, he tells crew loading the lifeboat, 'I am staying here with the MEN!'

Alfred, Frank and Tom watch the boat slowly drop as the davit cranks are turned.

Emily Goldsmith has in her pocket Tom Theobold's wedding ring, which he gave her to give to his wife, 'if I don't see you in New York'.

Also in collapsible C are five crew members, and about 35 third-class passengers, many of them Lebanese women. Picture framer Joseph Hyman has also managed to get on board. Hidden in the bottom of the boat are four Chinese men, all third-class passengers.

The chairman of the White Star Line now makes a critical decision. As collapsible C starts to pass the rail of the boat deck, he steps in it. He's followed by first-class passenger William

'Billy' Carter, whose wife, daughter and son (wearing a girl's hat) are safely in lifeboat 4. William Carter is leaving behind two dogs in the kennels and a 25 horsepower Renault motor car in the hold.

Sahid Nackid sees his chance to join his wife and baby in collapsible C. He jumps in, landing flat on his face. He keeps down, afraid of retribution, and women around him cover him with their skirts.

The *Titanic*'s list to port is such that the lifeboat scrapes its way down the hull, catching on the large rivets as it goes.

Under questioning at the British Board of Trade Inquiry into the sinking, Bruce Ismay was asked, why, if he'd been helping women and children get into lifeboats for well over an hour, did he choose to get into collapsible C rather than search for more women and children on other decks. Ismay replied that he presumed that there were people below sending passengers up: 'I knew that every-body could not be up,' he admitted. In his next answer Ismay said, 'Everyone that was on that deck got into the boat.' It seems that, knowing there were others who still needed saving, the temptation of a seat in a lifeboat that wasn't full was simply too great. 'He was caught', H.G. Wells wrote later 'by the snare of the moment.'

Ismay stated to both the US and the British inquiries that no one ordered him into the boat, and yet August Weikman, the ship's barber, in a sworn affidavit said that Ismay had been ordered into the lifeboat by an officer. Ismay later confessed to his sister-in-law that Chief Officer Wilde had ordered him into the boat.

It's been suggested that Ismay was a masochist at heart, resigned to playing the villain, punishing himself for the sinking by allowing the world to believe that he stepped into the lifeboat without permission from the crew.

From the boat deck, Jack Thayer and Milton Long watch collapsible C's precarious progress to the water, shouting out advice to the crew manning the davits.

Twenty-two-year-old fireman George Kemish, exhausted and filthy after many battles in the boiler rooms, drawing fires and rescuing colleagues, is walking through the first-class smoking room – something he would never have dreamed of doing a few hours before. He walks past a short man with a white beard and dark moustache, sitting by himself reading, with the air of someone prepared to stay there until the very end.

The man is journalist William Stead, travelling on the Titanic *to take part in a peace conference at Carnegie Hall. He is a man with a deep belief in spiritualism and the afterlife.*

Jack Thayer and Milton Long are arguing about what to do next. From their position by a set of empty davits on the forward starboard boat deck, it looks as if every lifeboat is gone. Jack's convinced that his father is safely in one of those lifeboats.

In fact, John Thayer is only yards away from Jack, among the crowds on the boat deck. According to Colonel Archibald Gracie, John is looking 'pale and determined' as he talks to George Widener.

Jack's mother Marian and her maid Margaret Fleming are safely in lifeboat 4, which is pulling away from the *Titanic*.

The *Titanic* now has such a list to port that Jack is convinced that the ship is going to flip over as she sinks. He and Milton Long have to act soon. The davit falls are trailing in the water so Jack says he's going to jump out and slide down them, then swim out to the lifeboats whose white hulls they can just see in the darkness. He says he can do it as he's a strong swimmer. Three times he starts to climb onto the rail and each time Long holds him back.

The wireless operator on the cargo ship the *Ypiranga* picks up a faint signal from the *Titanic*: 'Stdbi – stdbi – stdbi.' ['Standby – standby – standby']

> **At times we were thoughtful and quiet, but the noise around us did not stop.**
>
> **Jack Thayer, first-class passenger**

2.05am Titanic *Bridge Time*

The *Titanic* is about 7° down at the head.

On the ice-locked *Californian*, Apprentice Officer Gibson has been sent to wake up Captain Lord, who is stretched out on the chart room settee. He tells the captain that the ship they've been watching is disappearing to the southwest and had fired eight rockets altogether.

'Were they all white rockets?'

'Yes, sir.'

'What time is it?'

'Two oh five, by the wheelhouse clock, sir.'

Captain Lord nods, turns out the light and once again goes back to sleep.

Captain Smith, holding a megaphone, walks past about a dozen men trying to free collapsible A. Steward Edward Brown hears him say, 'Well, boys, do your best for the women and children, and look after yourselves.'

Brown can also hear the ship's band still playing behind him, at the top of the grand staircase.

Standing watching the battle to free collapsible A are Rhoda Abbott and her sons Rossmore and Eugene. They know that if they can all jump in, they have a chance of survival.

Jack Thayer and Milton Long have moved further up the sloping boat deck towards the stern and stepped inside, finding the top of a stairway. There are crowds of people in there, with the aim, it seems to Jack, of just keeping away from the ship's rail.

Jack thinks about all the good times he's had in his life and all the future ones he would now be denied. He thinks about his mother and father, and his sisters and brothers back home. 'I pitied myself. It seemed so unnecessary. But we still had a chance...'

Collapsible C is pulling away from the side of the *Titanic*. Bruce Ismay has one of the oars. He has his back to his sinking ship.

Collapsible D is about to be lowered. Lightoller wants to get it away before the *Titanic* sinks beneath them. Chief Officer Wilde calls out to him from the bridge wing: 'You go with her, Lightoller.'

'Not damn likely!' he shouts, and he steps out of the boat to make room for someone else.

Archibald Gracie leads two women, Edith Evans and Caroline Brown, whose sister Malvina is safely on lifeboat 2, towards the crew standing by collapsible D. As they start to lower the lifeboat, Edith says to Caroline, 'You go first. You have children waiting at home.'

Caroline Brown gets on board. Seaman William Lucas calls out to Edith Evans: 'There is another boat going to be put down for you.'

Collapsible D can hold 40 people, but it is taking only 24 to safety.

John Jacob Astor, George Widener and John Thayer watch as collapsible D is lowered into the water.

Charles Lightoller heads towards the roof of the officers' quarters, where the remaining collapsibles are stowed.

Colonel Archibald Gracie and his friend James Clinch Smith are now running towards the *Titanic*'s stern, away from the advancing water. They can see no way they will be able to get on board one of the remaining collapsible lifeboats. Suddenly their way is blocked by third-class passengers rushing up onto the boat deck, who then turn and head for the stern, but are impeded by the low iron gate between first and second class with its 'Not Allowed' sign – which Gracie had jumped over two hours ago.

This may be the moment when some of the Bostwick gates below decks are opened, possibly by force, allowing the remaining third-class passengers to make their way to the higher decks.

Charles Lightoller is trying to free collapsible B on the roof of the officers' quarters. It's a struggle, as it's dark up there and the lifeboat weighs two tons. A seaman alongside him calls, 'All ready, sir!'

Lightoller recognises the voice of lamp trimmer Samuel Hemming.

'Hello, is that you, Hemming?'

'Yes, sir.'

'Why haven't you gone?'

'Oh, plenty of time yet, sir.'

About 2.08am Titanic *Bridge Time*

Hugh Woolner, who had been one of Helen Candee's admirers, is standing on the sloping and deserted A-deck with a young Swede named Mauritz Björnström-Steffansson. Lifeboat 4 had been the last boat to take passengers from that area. The sea is lapping over the edge of the deck.

'This is getting rather a tight corner,' Woolner says to Björnström-Steffansson. Then collapsible D drops into the water in front of them.

'There's nobody in the bows – let's make a jump for it!' Woolner yells. The two men leap into the boat – Björnström-Steffansson having to haul Woolner in from the water after he bounces off the side.

Frederick Hoyt, a New York stockbroker and an experienced yachtsman, whose wife is in collapsible D, has worked out how he can join her. He takes off his overcoat and dives into the water not far from the lifeboat. Woolner and Björnström-Steffansson fish him out of the water. Soon Hoyt, dripping wet, is sitting next to steward John Hardy, pulling on an oar.

2.10am Titanic *Bridge Time*

The *Titanic* is 8° down at the head.

The bulkhead between boiler rooms 5 and 4 bursts and the sea floods in.

The *Virginian* hears a faint 'V V' from Jack Phillips, still at his transmitting key.

The deck lights on the *Titanic* are starting to glow red – a sign that they are about to fail.

2.11am Titanic *Bridge Time*

The *Titanic* is about 9° down at the head. She is starting to sink faster.

The *Titanic*'s designer, Thomas Andrews, is throwing more steamer chairs overboard to help those in the water.

The ship's chief baker, Charles Joughin, is in the first-class lounge pantry to take 'a drink of water' when he hears a sound 'as if part of the ship had buckled... it was like as if the iron was parting'. The *Titanic* is starting to break up.

Then Joughin hears the sound of running feet on the deck overhead.

2.12am Titanic *Bridge Time*

Jack Phillips is still sending out the distress signal: 'CQD MGY CQD MGY CQD MGY'

2.13am Titanic *Bridge Time*

The *Virginian*, 150 miles away and heading east, hears the interrupted signal: 'CQ...'

The two operators leave the wireless room. Jack Phillips runs towards the rising stern; Harold Bride towards the bows and the collapsible lifeboat he'd seen Lightoller trying to launch earlier. Phillips can hear the ship's band still playing 'a ragtime tune, I don't know what'.

Those in the lifeboats can hear the music drifting across the water.

2.14am Titanic *Bridge Time*

The *Titanic* is about 10° down at the head.

Charles Lightoller, Harold Bride, Samuel Hemming and other crew members tip collapsible B off the roof of the officers' quarters and into the water that's now covering the boat deck. Hemming and Lightoller then run to the starboard side of the ship to see if there is anything more they can do.

'Everything I touched seemed to be women's hair.'

2.15am Titanic *Bridge Time*

The *Titanic* is about 11° down at the head.

As the *Titanic*'s bow dips further, the water that's been creeping aft up Scotland Road surges forward. Water starts pouring out of portholes above sea level.

Now on the poop deck, Charles Joughin, fortified by alcohol, is getting ready for the end. He tightens his belt and transfers the contents of his front pocket to a back pocket. Joughin looks at his watch; under the dim electric deck lights, he sees it says 2.15. He then puts it in his back pocket as well.

As the water pushes steadily up the deck, hundreds of people are rushing ahead of it, keeping as close to the centre of the ship as possible.

Jack Thayer and Milton Long shake hands and wish each other 'goodbye and good luck'. They are determined to get clear of the ship before she sinks completely – they don't want to get caught in the suction.

The *Titanic* suddenly starts to slide further. The two men must act now. They don't bother exchanging any messages for their families, as neither believes they will survive. Long sits on the boat deck rail, his brown boots dangling over the edge, while Thayer takes off his overcoat. Then Long twists round so he is facing the ship, and lowers himself until he is hanging onto the rail by his fingers. He looks up at Thayer.

'You're coming, boy, aren't you?'

'Go ahead, I'll be with you in a minute,' Thayer replies.

Long lets go and slides 30 feet down the side of the ship, facing the hull.

Thayer quickly straddles the rail and looks down into the oily water below, but can't see Milton.

He jumps.

The freezing cold water shocks Thayer as he tumbles and spins under water, his lungs aching. Disorientated, he swims in a direction he hopes is away from the sinking liner.

Charles Lightoller, standing on top the wheelhouse, looks at the mass of people heading for the stern, knowing full well they are merely prolonging the agony. There is no safety in a crowd. A few try to scramble up to join him on the roof. Lightoller turns and jumps into the water.

They were heroes if you like. I must say everything that has been said about them is perfectly true. They were

> **not asked to play but did it absolutely on their own initiative.**
>
> **Sarah Stap, stewardess**

> **They kept it up to the very end. Only the engulfing ocean had power to drown them into silence. The band was playing 'Nearer, My God, to Thee'. I could hear it distinctly. The end was very close.**
>
> **Charlotte Collyer, second-class passenger**

2.16am Titanic *Bridge Time*

An officer is brandishing a gun, threatening to shoot on the spot any man who gets into collapsible A. A group of women, including Rhoda Abbott, who's with her teenage sons, are standing close by, desperate to get in. Then piper Eugene Daly sees two men rush the boat and the officer shoots them dead.

Daly and steward Edward Brown are part of the group of men trying to launch collapsible A, having successfully got it onto the deck by sliding it down from the roof of the officers' quarters on two planks. The *Titanic*'s severe list to port is making it extremely hard to push the boat uphill into position under the davits, although they have managed, by slackening the falls, to attach them to the lifeboat.

Daly hears another gunshot and sees the officer lying on the deck.

Although no one was named by those who saw an officer shoot two men and then kill himself, it seems that it was most likely First Officer William Murdoch.

The *Titanic* plunges again, and water floods up the deck.

Suddenly collapsible A is afloat, still attached to the falls. Edward Brown jumps into the boat and starts hacking at the falls at the stern and shouts to a seaman in the bows to do the same. People are panicking and hanging onto the ropes around the edge of the lifeboat, some trying to scramble in. A steward named Whiteley gets tangled in the falls and tumbles into the water, breaking his leg. It's so cold he feels no pain. Just as Brown succeeds in cutting the ropes, he's washed away and sucked down in a whirlpool. He's been at sea 12 years – but can't swim.

Rhoda Abbott manages to grab her sons' hands as they are all swept into the water and down into the same whirlpool as steward Brown.

Colonel Archibald Gracie and James Clinch Smith are trying to clamber on top of the officers' quarters. Gracie is weighed down by a long overcoat, a Norfolk jacket and a lifebelt over both. They are suddenly hit by a wave as the ship surges forward – Gracie is propelled onto the roof of the officers' quarters; Clinch Smith is swept away.

Lightoller has come up for air, and he can see the lookouts' crow's nest ahead of him, now only just above the water. He's struggling to stay afloat and thinks it must be the weight of his Webley revolver that's dragging him down. He pulls the gun out of his pocket and lets it sink – but still he's being dragged under. Lightoller realises with horror that he's above a large air intake that leads 100 feet down into the engine room – and seawater is being sucked into it. Pulled under water, and with the ship falling beneath him, Lightoller gets pinned against a wire grating above the shaft as the water surges down around him. He is drowning. He thinks of lines from Psalm 91: 'He shall give his angels charge over thee...' Suddenly a vast bubble of hot air explodes from the depths of the *Titanic*, and Lightoller is pushed to the surface.

Edward Brown's lifebelt brings him up. He is gasping and surrounded by hundreds of people in the water, many without lifebelts, who start to grab hold of him, tearing at his clothing. Brown splashes his way as best he can towards a dark floating object, as he fights people off, but his boots are heavy. The dark object is collapsible A, half submerged with about 16 people hanging onto it.

Rhoda Abbott too has reached the surface – but her sons are nowhere to be seen. She desperately calls out their names: 'Eugene! Rossmore! Eugene! Rossmore!'

Piper Eugene Daly is in the water too. It is the stuff of nightmares. 'Everything I touched seemed to be women's hair. Children crying, women screaming, and their hair in my face. My God, if only I could forget those hands and faces that I touched!'

Further aft, first-class passengers George Rheims and his brother-in-law Joseph Loring are standing on the sloping deck close to the gymnasium, stripped down to their underwear. They've pledged to look after each other's families should they live. As the *Titanic* lurches again they are knocked off their feet. Loring says he wants to head to the stern, but Rheims says that's certain death and he should follow him into the water instead.

'I can't swim well enough,' his brother-in-law replies. Rheims jumps overboard.

First-class passenger Richard Williams is pitched into the sea with his father Charles. Richard finds himself face to face with a bulldog released from the *Titanic*'s kennels.

Trimmer Thomas Dillon, on the poop deck, can hear the sound of a violinist from the ship's band playing the hymn 'Nearer My God, to Thee'.

2.17am Titanic *Bridge Time*

The *Titanic* is 30° down at the head.

Olaus Abelseth and his cousin and brother-in-law are at the rear of the steeply sloping boat deck, hanging onto some davit ropes; around them people are sliding down the deck. They can hear the ship popping and cracking and the sound of explosions deep inside her.

'Can you swim?' Olaus shouts at them. They shake their heads.

'We had better jump off, or the suction will take us down!' Olaus's brother-in-law Sigurd shouts back.

'No! We won't jump yet. We haven't got much hope anyhow, so we might as well stay as long as we can.'

'We must jump off!'

'No! Not yet!'

Harold Bride sees Captain Smith jump from the bridge into the water.

Jack Thayer surfaces, facing the *Titanic*. He has been pushed about 40 yards clear of the ship towards the stern. He is already weak from the cold but his lifebelt is keeping his head above the water. For a reason he will never be able to explain he doesn't swim away, but watches transfixed as the *Titanic* continues her slide. Jack can see the remaining hundreds scramble up the decks towards the crowded stern. It is a stampede. More roars and explosions come from the belly of the ship.

The wave moving up the *Titanic* hits the dome above the grand staircase, where two hours ago Jack said goodbye to his mother. The dome collapses and thousands of gallons of seawater pour down the stairs.

Away from the ship, Harold Bride is underwater, his lifebelt pushing him up to the surface, but right under collapsible B. He fights to push it away. When Bride comes up gasping for air, he's surrounded by hundreds of people.

First Officer Lightoller is also floating among the swimmers and the drowning, 'an utter nightmare of sight and sound.' He swims towards collapsible B.

Richard Williams sees his father Charles in the water only about 12 feet away from him – they start swimming towards each other.

The *Titanic*'s lights go out, return for a moment, and then go out again.

On the *Californian*, Second Officer Stone sees the lights disappear.

Archibald Gracie is under water, hanging onto the railing on top of the officers' quarters as the ship slides down.

As the stern rises up, the eight stays holding the funnels are under tremendous strain. The port stays on the forward funnel snap, and with a roar it topples to starboard, crushing scores of swimmers struggling in the water.

Richard Williams watches as the funnel, still belching smoke, comes down on top of his father, just a few feet away from him, creating an enormous wave.

The funnel misses collapsible B by inches and its wave pushes it clear of the ship. Lightoller clings on.

As Eugene Daly treads water, he looks over his shoulder and sees people getting sucked down into the second funnel like flies.

Then the *Titanic* splits in two, between the second and third funnels.

The third funnel begins to topple forward, and in a spray of sparks, falls into the sea close to Jack Thayer, crushing scores of people on what's left of the deck and in the water. He's sucked under once more as the massive funnel sinks.

The *Titanic*'s stern settles back into the water and her fourth funnel topples backwards. Lookout George Symons, watching from lifeboat 1, thinks that by a miracle the stern section is going to float.

But the stern section hasn't fully separated from the submerged bow section, which is now under water, and is being slowly pulled down, its exposed decks flooding at great speed. The stern is lifting skywards again, twisting it as it does so.

2.18am Titanic *Bridge Time*

Jack Thayer surfaces by the side of an upturned collapsible life-boat; he clings onto its side. He can see four or five men lying on top of the boat and he asks them to help him up, which they do. Dripping and cold, Thayer sits on his haunches and watches the stern section of the once mighty ship rising up into the night sky. He can see hundreds of people clinging on in clusters 'like swarming bees', and many falling off.

Then the stern section pauses, like 'a sinister finger' pointing up to the sky, and hangs there.

To Harold Bride she looks like a duck about to go down for a dive. He is struck by how beautiful the ship looks.

Then the *Titanic* starts her final plunge. The stern is being dragged down further, still twisting to port, 'as if to hide from our sight the awful spectacle', in Jack Thayer's words.

2.19am Titanic *Bridge Time*

The *Titanic* has twisted so much that Charles Joughin is now able to crouch on the outside of the ship, holding onto a railing on the starboard side of the poop deck. As the *Titanic* twists he sees hundreds of people in the well deck below him thrown to the side of the ship. Their bodies are hurled together in a pile.

Jack Thayer's upturned lifeboat is now being sucked towards the *Titanic*, as what is left of the ship pivots and dives. Thayer can see her keel and three propellers dripping high above him. With only one oar, the men on the collapsible try to paddle away from the stern section – it looks as if it might fall back and crush them.

Still hanging onto the davit ropes as the *Titanic* slides down, Olaus Abelseth, his cousin and brother-in-law are only a matter of feet away from the sea. His brother-in-law Sigurd, who can't swim, takes Olaus's hand and the three men jump.

In collapsible C, Emily Goldsmith hides her nine-year-old son Frankie's face with her hands so that he can't see the ship. Frank, his father, is on board.

2.20am Titanic *Bridge Time*

Charles Joughin steps off the *Titanic* into the Atlantic, barely getting his hair wet.

The stern section of the *Titanic* slips under the sea, her limp Blue Ensign disappearing last of all.

In the water, Harold Bride waits to be sucked under.

Archibald Gracie has surfaced, expecting the water to turn scalding hot any moment as the *Titanic*'s boilers explode.

Nothing.

'She's gone,' say the men on Lightoller's lifeboat.

In lifeboat 5, Third Officer Herbert Pitman looks at his watch, and mutters, 'It is 2.20am.'

There is a pale, almost motionless vapour over the water.

Olaus Abelseth is under water with a rope coiled around him. He lets go of his brother-in-law Sigurd's hand to get himself free, thinking, 'I'm a goner.'

For a moment there is silence.

Then the calls for help begin. 'The agonising screams of death from over a thousand throats,' in Archibald Gracie's words.
'Help! Help!
'Boat ahoy! Boat ahoy!
'My God! My God!

A man in the water near trimmer Thomas Dillon is calling for his mother.

To Georges Rheims the cries are 'supernatural'.

To Jack Thayer it is 'one long continuous wailing chant'.

Olaus Abelseth is fighting for his life. A man without a lifebelt is holding onto his neck, trying to stay afloat.
'Get off! Get off!' Olaus splutters, but the man won't let go. Olaus kicks and swims away. He looks around. He can't see either Sigurd or cousin Peter.

The *Titanic* is plunging 12,000 feet to the ocean floor. Her streamlined bow is speeding to the bottom; her stern is sinking more slowly, breaking up as it does so. Crystal goblets, mail bags, coal, wedding presents, Steinway pianos, children's marbles, cases of books, pearl necklaces, the Renault motor car, possessions for new lives in America, are all tumbling through the dark water.

It will take ten minutes for all the remains of the *Titanic* to hit the seabed.

2.22am Titanic *Bridge Time*

Jack Thayer's water-soaked watch stops.

A lone Titanic officer *walking along A-deck.*

In the Lifeboats

It was hard to judge time in the lifeboats. Fifth Officer Harold Lowe told the British Board of Trade Inquiry: 'I have not the remotest idea of time from the time she went down until we boarded the *Carpathia*. All I know is that when we boarded the *Carpathia* in the morning, it was six o'clock.'

What follows is a snapshot, in number order rather than in chronological order, of what happened in each of the *Titanic*'s lifeboats after she sank at 2.20am on 15th April 1912.

Lifeboat 1 – Launched 1.05am

Lucy Duff Gordon, also known as fashion designer 'Lucile', is attempting to keep spirits up on board their boat, despite the fact that she is feeling seasick and has repeatedly vomited on her mauve silk kimono. Her audience is very small – lifeboat 1 has only five passengers and seven members of the *Titanic*'s crew. Lucy Duff Gordon teases her secretary Laura 'Franks' Francatelli about the strange assortment of clothes she's wearing.

'Just fancy, you actually left your beautiful nightdress behind you!'

They both laugh. Then a voice pipes up in the darkness.

'Never mind, madam, you were lucky to come away with your lives. Don't you bother about anything you've had to leave behind you.'

Another voice says, 'You people needn't bother about losing your things – you can afford to buy new ones when you get ashore. What about us poor fellows? We've lost all our kit and our pay stops from the moment the ship went down.'

Sir Cosmo Duff Gordon chips in, 'Yes, that's hard luck if you like, but don't worry, you'll get another ship. At any rate I'll give you a fiver each towards getting a new kit.'

It is an offer Sir Cosmo will regret.

Lifeboat 2 – Launched 1.45am

A slight breeze has got up and the 26 people on board can hear the eerie sound of water lapping against the base of the icebergs around them. They can't see much in the darkness beyond their boat. Mrs Walter Douglas, whose husband refused to enter the lifeboat ('No, I must be a gentleman', he said), is at the tiller.

Fourth Officer Joseph Boxhall is in charge of the lifeboat and has brought a box of green flares from the bridge with him so other lifeboats will be able to see where they are. He lights the first one, and suddenly there are screams from survivors still struggling in the water, thinking they are about to be rescued.

'Shall we go back?' Boxhall asks. Nobody in the lifeboat wants to.

Lifeboat 3 – Launched 00.55am

There are about 50 people in lifeboat 3 – the vast majority of them first-class passengers. The Spedden family is especially lucky; Frederic Spedden, looking immaculate in a suit, has survived, as has his wife Margaretta, his six-year-old son Douglas, and their maids Elizabeth Burns and Helen Wilson.

The lifeboat is slowly making its way through a field of vast icebergs. There is a hint of light in the sky.

'Oh, Muddie, look at the beautiful North Pole with no Santa Claus on it!' Douglas Spedden says to his mother.

Sitting huddled close to each other to keep warm are Clara Hays and her daughter Orian Davidson. Both women left their husbands aboard the *Titanic*. Orian Davidson is wearing a straw hat. They can see another lifeboat close by, and the women call out desperately:

'Mr Charles Hays, are you there?'

'Mr Thornton Davidson, are you there?'

'No!' is the shout that comes across the water.

Lifeboat 4 – Launched 1.50am

Under the command of quartermaster Walter Perkis, lifeboat 4 went to look for survivors, rescuing about eight men – including trimmer Thomas Dillon, who had contemplated going down with the ship in the luxury of a first-class cabin. Dillon is now lying unconscious at the bottom of the lifeboat with two dead men on top of him, one of whom is able seaman William Lyons. Lyons was dragged into the stern of the boat, and then lay down and lost consciousness.

Lifeboat 4 holds the wives of the most prominent first-class passengers – pregnant Madeleine Astor; Eleanor Widener, who hosted the dinner party in the à la carte restaurant yesterday; Emily Ryerson with her children, travelling home because of the death of her elder son; and, sitting at an oar since they launched, Marian Thayer, who doesn't yet know her son Jack is still alive.

The skies above the lifeboats are full of shooting stars.

Lifeboat 5 – Launched 00.43am

Karl Behr is rubbing Helen Beckwith's wet stockinged feet to keep them warm. Behr, an American lawyer and Davis Cup player, had followed Helen and her parents across Europe for six weeks, keeping his distance as the family disapproved of the relationship; they met 'by coincidence' on the *Titanic*.

As Behr rubs Helen's feet, someone nudges him. Behr looks up and sees that the man next to him is holding a nickel-plated revolver. He leans over and whispers into Behr's ear, 'Should the worst come to the worst, you can use the revolver for your wife, after my wife and I have finished with it.'

'Thank you,' is all the young man can think to say.

A variety of methods are being used to keep warm in the life-boats. Washington Dodge's wife Ruth in lifeboat 3 is wearing a pair of stockings that a crew member gave her, saying, 'I assure you, ma'am they are perfectly clean. I just put them on this morning.' Here in lifeboat 5, young Marguerite Frölicher is inevitably feeling seasick, but she's been revived by a swig of brandy from a fellow passenger's flask.

Third Officer Harold Pitman, in charge of the boat, has wrapped a sail around a woman from first class who was particularly suffering from the cold. Pitman is frustrated, as shortly after the *Titanic* sank, he wanted to go back and look for survivors.

'Now, men, we will pull towards the wreck! We may be able to pick up a few more,' he said.

'Appeal to the officer not to go back!' a woman begged steward Henry Etches. 'Why should we lose all of our lives in a useless attempt to save others from the ship?' Most agreed they shouldn't turn back, so Pitman relented.

Lifeboat 6 - Launched 1.10am

Standing at the tiller of lifeboat 6 is the man who a few hours ago was at the helm of the largest ship in the world. Robert Hichens is looking across a boat that is almost entirely filled with first-class passengers, and they are unimpressed by his behaviour. Before the *Titanic* sank, they begged Hichens to return to rescue those in the water, but he told them that they would be sucked under by the sinking steamer.

That suction never materialised, and now many of the passengers are asking again to return. They are a formidable bunch – Margaret 'Molly' Brown, Major Arthur Peuchen and Helen Candee all tell him to turn round.

Hichens replies with a graphic description of the 'frantic drowning victims' grabbing hold of the sides of the lifeboat and tipping it over. He adds that there is no need to go back as there is only 'a load of stiffs there'.

Peuchen, who had dramatically slid down the falls into the boat at the last minute, would like to wrestle control of the tiller from Hichens, but there are too many people in the way.

Lifeboat 7 - Launched 00.40am

To keep warm, Helen Bishop is hugging her husband Dickenson. She is trying to think of happy things – like their wedding day in Michigan last November when she walked down the aisle and was enveloped by the smell of the orange blossoms attached to her veil.

Helen prays that the prediction of the Egyptian fortune-teller will come true and that she will survive a shipwreck. She chooses not to think about the rest of the prophecy: an earth-quake, and her death in a motor car accident.

Lookouts Archie Jewell and George Hogg are on the boat, and Hogg has been doing his best to keep everyone's spirits up. There are only 28 people in the lifeboat and he pointed out that there was plenty of room for survivors if they rowed back, but no one wanted to risk it.

Actress Dorothy Gibson is sitting with her mother Pauline. Dorothy is wearing an evening dress, a long sweater, a short coat and an overcoat belonging to William Sloper, the passenger she had befriended on the ship. Dorothy rewarded the gift of the overcoat with a kiss. She aches from head to foot with the cold.

They all have wet feet, as the plug in the rainwater drainage hole at the bottom of the boat is missing. The women's lingerie and men's scarves they've used to replace it have only partly worked.

Lifeboat 8 – Launched 1.00am

Lucy, the Countess of Rothes is still at the tiller of the life-boat. Seaman Thomas Jones, who was put in charge by Second Officer Lightoller, is delighted at her seamanship. They are pulling towards the lights of a steamer on the horizon, as instructed by Captain Smith, who said, 'Row for the light, and land the passengers and return to the ship.' But they don't seem to be getting any closer to it. Earlier the countess suggested they all sang to keep their spirits up, and they started with 'Pull for the Shore'.

The atmosphere is now tense. The women are irritated that the other crew members from the *Titanic* are incapable of rowing. Thomas Jones offered the men advice until one snapped back, 'If you don't stop talking through that hole in your face, there will be one less in the boat.'

At one point Jones had made them turn round and look for survivors, but the women grew panicky, so he changed his mind, saying, 'Ladies, remember if any of us are saved, I wanted to go back. I would rather drown with them than leave them.'

Lifeboat 9 – Launched 1.34am

Lifeboat 9 is drifting with the current. Only occasionally are those on the oars doing any rowing.

Kate Buss, on her way to marry her fiancé in California, is lamenting the loss of all her possessions. All she has with her is a small handbag with no money in it, a bankbook and her needlework.

There is a Frenchwoman on board the lifeboat who has been making lots of agitated noises, and many people have tried to calm her down. Kate has had enough.

'Will you please be quiet!' she shouts at the woman (probably Benjamin Guggenheim's mistress, the singer Léontine 'Ninette' Aubart). Kate's outburst works: she does stay quiet.

Lifeboat 10 – Launched 1.50am

Mary Fortune is sitting with her daughters Ethel, Alice and Mabel. Mary knows that her son Charles and husband Mark are very likely to be dead. She is remembering what a soothsayer said to her in January, on the terrace of a hotel in Cairo. 'You are in danger every time you travel on the sea, for I see you adrift on the ocean in an open boat. You will lose everything but your life. You will be saved, but others will be lost.'

Lifeboat 11 – Launched 1.35am

Second-class passenger Marie Jerwan is one of 70 people in the lifeboat; it is full to capacity. She's listening to one of the *Titanic*'s crew tell of the only other accident he's witnessed 'in his 45 years as a sailor', when the *Olympic* collided with the cruiser HMS *Hawke* in the Solent. 'I thought I'd be more safe in the *Titanic*, as it had been so highly praised. I hardly expected to have an accident more terrible still and owe my safety to divine protection.'

Every now and then, one of the crew sets light to the end of a rope to let other lifeboats nearby see where they are.

Emma Schabert is in the lifeboat with her brother Philipp, who is rowing. Emma looks into the water without any fear – she knows that if she drowns it won't take long to die.

Lying at the bottom of the lifeboat is Belgian Julius Sap, a third-class passenger who was pulled out of the water by his hair. A woman is holding his hand and sometimes talks to him, and although he can't understand what she is saying, he knows she's doing it so he doesn't slip into unconsciousness. Sap is grateful to be lying here, as earlier some men had tried to have him thrown out of the boat and someone else had fired a shot to stop others getting in.

Edith Rosenbaum is entertaining the children in the boat by twisting the tail of her lucky pig, to make it play the song 'La Maxixe'.

Elizabeth Nye is holding a sleeping baby boy wrapped in a shawl, who was handed to her as she waited for the lifeboat to be lowered. Elizabeth's daughter Maisie died at about the same age as the boy in her arms. After the death of her husband 11 months ago, Elizabeth took a leave of absence from the Salvation Army in New York, where she worked in the uniform department, to spend time with her parents in Kent. She wonders if the baby's mother made it into a lifeboat.

Lifeboat 12 – Launched 1.30am

Gurshon 'Gus' Cohen is at one of the oars. He is struggling to row as his hands have rope burns and he injured his forehead while climbing out along a davit to escape the ship. Cohen is one of about a dozen people who have been pulled out of the water by lifeboat 12. Able seaman John Poingdestre is in charge. The rescues have been hard, as Poingdestre only has two men who can row.

Lifeboat 13 – Launched 1.40am

Lawrence Beesley is not downhearted. Being in a lifeboat is providing him with plenty of new things to observe and experience – for example, the sight of the Northern Lights (which had initially brought some cheer to the boat as they thought it was the dawn); and a lesson from stoker Frederick Barrett about how they will recognise a ship coming to their rescue: 'a single light on the horizon, the masthead light, followed by a second one, on the deck. If they remained in vertical alignment and the distance between them increased as the lights drew nearer, it would be a steamer.'

Beesley also systematically searched the lifeboat for food and water, but found only a zinc air tank for keeping the boat afloat if she capsizes. Even a voice in the dark saying, 'This is no joke; we may knock about here days before we are picked up – if at all' did not dismay him. It's the cold 'on us like a garment that wraps close around' that is the main discomfort.

Washington Dodge is at one oar. The man next to him says, 'Doctor, are your wife and baby safe?'

Dodge tells him that he put them in one of the first boats to be launched. Then he recognises the man is his table steward Frederick Ray.

'I had to idea you were here!'

'Why, I was right behind you as we left the steamer, and called you to get in.'

Earlier, Frederick Ray, always the considerate steward looking after his passengers, took out the six clean handkerchiefs he'd collected from his cabin at the last minute, and handed them out to the people in the lifeboat, suggesting they tie a knot in each corner and use them as caps to keep warm.

Leah Aks is praying that her ten-month-old baby Frank is safe. He was taken from her and put in lifeboat 11, but when Leah rushed to join him, the crew restrained her, thinking that she was trying to jump in an already full boat.

Lifeboat 14 – Launched 1.25am

Since the *Titanic* sank, lifeboat 14 has been rowing through chairs, cushions, rugs, benches, tables and a mass of black coffee beans.

Fifth Officer Harold Lowe is in charge of the boat. He is determined to ensure the lifeboats don't drift too far.

'Let all the boats keep as near together as possible. That's our only chance of being picked up. If we separate, we are lost.'

Esther Hart and her daughter Eva are huddled together. Eva has a White Star blanket pulled tightly around her for security and warmth; the sheepskin coat she has on is not enough. Esther is sure that her husband Benjamin is dead and that their dream of a new life in America is over. Officer Lowe has given her the job of bailing the water out of the boat. Her hand touches something under her seat. Esther looks closer – it's a man lying in about 15 inches of water who must have smuggled himself aboard without Lowe knowing.

Lifeboat 15 - Launched 1.41am

Bertha Mulvihill is transfixed by a small iceberg that keeps hitting the side of the lifeboat. Even when they row away, a short while later it drifts into them, each time right where she's sitting. Bertha is with Maggie Daly and they're both wondering if her cousin Eugene has survived.

The iceberg hits the wooden gunwale again. To Bertha it's something evil that's taunting her. She realises that her obsession with the iceberg has helped her forget that she's cold, hungry and has what feels like two broken ribs.

The sky is getting brighter. Bertha looks to the horizon and sees what looks like a light.

'Could that be a vessel coming for us?' she asks a sailor near her. He agrees it could be, but someone else says that it's only a light from a lifeboat.

The lights are coming nearer and becoming stronger. There is a streak of black smoke. It's clearly a steamship.

Lifeboat 16 - Launched 1.23am

Lifeboat 6, with quartermaster Robert Hichens at the tiller, is inches away from lifeboat 16, which has Master-at-Arms Joseph Bailey in charge. Bailey's boat has plenty of crew members from the *Titanic*, so someone in lifeboat 6 calls out, 'Surely you can spare us one man, if you have so many.'

Bailey agrees and sends a fireman over to row. He is still covered in soot and wearing only a thin jumper. Molly Brown takes pity on him and wraps her sable stole around his legs.

The lifeboats are now banging against each other in the darkness. Major Arthur Peuchen suggests they put some lifebelts between the hulls to act as fenders. Robert Hichens and Fred Fleet take theirs off and then lash the boats together. Helen Candee offers Hichens a half-wet blanket.

Everyone is getting colder now no one is rowing. Molly Brown, Peuchen and others tell Hichens the boats should separate, but he is enjoying his first sit-down in about three hours and refuses to move. Molly Brown tells a fellow passenger to cut the ropes anyway, and Hichens gets up to stop them.

'If you take one more step towards me, I'll throw you overboard!' Molly yells.

Hichens starts shouting insults down the boat at Molly Brown. The fireman, wondering what sort of boat he's joined, says to Hichens, 'Oi, don't you know you're talking to a lady?'

'I know who I am speaking to, and I am commanding this boat!' the quartermaster snaps back.

But Molly Brown gets her way, and lifeboats 16 and 6 are cut free from each other.

Collapsible A – Floated off

There's a foot of water in collapsible A – no one can manage to get the sides to stay up. It was swept from the deck of the *Titanic* before it could be fastened to the davits. Only the kapok fibre stuffing in the fenders and in the base of the collapsible is keeping it afloat. There are about 30 people on board and they are all standing to keep out of the icy water in the boat. One of them is Rhoda Abbott, who in vain called for her sons Rossmore and Eugene as she struggled in the water. Just as Rhoda was about to give up, a strong arm grabbed her and pulled her into the collapsible. She's standing, shivering in her sodden Salvation Army uniform.

Nearby, steward Edward Brown's feet have swollen so much from the cold, his boots have split. George Rheims is standing in his underwear, shaking uncontrollably.

Richard Williams who saw his father Charles crushed by one of *Titanic*'s funnels, asks the man standing next to him if he could use his hat to bail out water. The man refuses.

Another man asks Williams, 'Can I put my arm around your neck?'

'Sure,' Williams replies.

Olaus Abelseth is trying to keep a man alive. He recognises him as a fellow third-class passenger whom he met a few days ago. He can't remember his name but he knows he has a wife and child back home in New Jersey.

Abelseth swam for about 15 minutes after the *Titanic* sank, until he saw the dark shape of a collapsible boat. No one helped him get on, but no one stopped him either. He was only told, 'Don't capsize the boat.'

Olaus props the semi-conscious man up against a seat and takes his hand. 'We can see a ship now. Brace up,' Olaus says, and shakes him.

'Who are you? Let me be...'

Olaus tries to keep holding the man up, but he's getting tired and cold.

Collapsible B – Floated off

'Our Father, which art in Heaven,
   Hallowed be Thy name.

Thy Kingdom come,
Thy will be done, on Earth as it is in Heaven...'

The sound of 30 men reciting the Lord's Prayer carries over the North Atlantic. One crew member said, 'Don't you think we ought to pray? What religion are you all?' Each man called out their denomination – there were Catholics, Baptists, and Presbyterians, so it was decided that a prayer that united them all should be said.

The collapsible itself has capsized. The men are trying to cling on, but its smooth hull offers little to grip onto. Piper Eugene Daly is half in and half out of the water, his overcoat offering some sort of protection from the cold. Steward Thomas Whiteley is on board but feeling a bit ashamed. He was sitting on top of a wardrobe when he spotted collapsible B. Originally there were four of them on the wardrobe, but one by one they tumbled off. Whiteley then swam to the collapsible, but Second Officer Charles Lightoller refused to let him clamber on.

'It's 31 lives against yours. You can't come aboard – there's no room.'

Whiteley pleaded, but Lightoller was unmoved. Whiteley, hanging onto the side, prayed that someone might die, allowing him some room. He didn't have to wait long before someone lost consciousness and slid off the boat.

Now that Whiteley is aboard, he's ashamed about his prayer.

Charles Lightoller suggests to Harold Bride that he encourages them all by reciting the names of the ships that he and Phillips called to the *Titanic*'s assistance. Bride, who was recovered from the sea but whose feet have been crushed and badly frostbitten, recites, 'the *Baltic*, the *Olympic*, the *Carpathia*...'. He tells them that the *Carpathia* should be with them by 4am. As Bride is unable to stand, Jack Thayer is trying to hold him up and keep him out of the water.

Archibald Gracie is also on board. Soon after the *Titanic* sank he spotted collapsible B with men at the bow and stern using bits of wood as paddles, and he swam towards it. But another man on top of their precarious vessel was not welcome. As Gracie himself said, 'I met with a doubtful reception... no extending hand was held out to me.' He grabbed someone's arm and got his right leg up onto the hull. Soon, another dozen clambered on, and each time the boat sank lower into the water.

Now no one else is allowed on. The men with the paddles are steering the boat away from any remaining swimmers. Those who get too close are hit over the head with the bits of wood. Some are told: 'Hold on to what you have, old boy. One more of you would sink us all!'

This is met with silence, except for one man who says, 'All right, boys; good luck and God bless you...'

Archibald Gracie keeps his head turned away.

Collapsible C – Launched at 2.00am

Bruce Ismay is at one of collapsible C's oars. The White Star Line chairman didn't look round when his ship sank. It is small comfort that, because the passengers are mostly from third class, and mainly Lebanese, hardly anyone in the lifeboat knows who he is. Ismay is too shaken to speak to anyone.

Amy Stanley, on her way to Connecticut to become a nanny, makes a few people laugh when she says, 'At least we'll escape vaccination.' Third-class passengers were due to be vaccinated on board the *Titanic* on Monday.

Collapsible D – Launched at 2.05am

Hugh Woolner, with a cap on his head and a lifebelt tightly wrapped around a long overcoat, has been looking after three year-old Michel Navratil for most of the night. Both Michel and his younger brother Edmond have been crying since they left their father on the *Titanic*.

Towing collapsible D is lifeboat 14, and Fifth Officer Harold Lowe has her sail up – it's the only lifeboat that has. Lowe saw collapsible D low in the water about an hour ago and decided 'to pick her up and make sure of her'. The number of people in Lowe's lifeboat has increased by about 15 since launching, as he has already rescued the occupants of collapsible A, just as it was about to sink.

Woolner is standing in the bow of collapsible D looking at a very welcome sight. About 500 yards ahead of them is the *Carpathia*, come to a stop in the water. He can see a number of the *Titanic*'s lifeboats already alongside her and passengers lining her decks; someone starts taking photographs as the tiny convoy approaches.

They are now so close Lowe decides to take lifeboat 14's sail down. They will row the last few yards of their perilous voyage.

The *Carpathia*'s passengers discovered that their Mediterranean journey had become a rescue mission in different ways. Some heard the sound of the lifeboats being made ready overhead; some turned on the taps and found there was no hot water because the engines needed all the power they could get; others saw stewards carrying piles of blankets; most noticed that the engines were louder and that it had got much colder.

When the *Carpathia* reached the *Titanic*'s location at 4am, having negotiated her way through numerous icebergs, the ship was ready to take on hundreds of survivors. The chief steward had assembled his department and told them 'every man to his post and let him do his duty like a true Englishman'.

On the bridge there was amazement and concern – there was no sign of the *Titanic*. Then they saw the outline of a boat in the water and a flickering light. It was Fourth Officer Joseph Boxhall's lifeboat 2.

Boxhall was taken to the bridge to speak to Captain Rostron, who asked him, 'Where is the *Titanic*?'

'Gone! She sank at 2.20am.'

There was a moment of stunned silence.

'Were many people left on board when she sank?'

'Hundreds and hundreds! Perhaps a thousand – perhaps more!' Boxhall replied, his voice breaking with emotion. 'My God, sir, they've gone down with her...'

> *Unweighted and in most cases buoyed by lifejackets, the bodies of the* **Titanic's** *dead – the celebrities, the lesser-known, and the humble unknown to fame – were flotsam in the wide Atlantic for weeks, and some, it was believed, for months after the disaster. The mail steamers gave the region of the floating dead a wide berth; the Atlantic tracks were haunted, and even to this day [1955] shipmasters steer clear of the place where the* **Titanic** *sank.'*
>
> **James Bisset, the Carpathia's second officer**

About 1600 people went down with the *Titanic*, but only 18 were pulled out of the water. Most people didn't drown but were kept afloat by their lifebelts. The sea was two degrees below freezing point Celsius (28° Fahrenheit), which meant that some would have suffered instant cardiac arrest as they hit the water from the shock of the cold.

The people in the lifeboats need not have worried about being swamped. Those in the water could barely swim, as their limbs were numb. Pain would have made any rational thought impossible. Most people died of hypothermia within 15 to 30 minutes.

To search for bodies, the White Star Line chartered a cable-laying vessel called the *Mackay-Bennett,* which carried undertakers, tons of ice and hundreds of coffins. The crew were volunteers.

When they reached the site of the collision, the white lifebelts looked like a mass of seagulls on the water. The *Mackay-Bennett* recovered 306 bodies. The appearance of each one, their clothing and possessions were all noted in an inventory. Disfigured corpses were buried at sea; dead *Titanic* crew packed in ice and placed under a tarpaulin; second- and third-class corpses were sewn into canvas bags; first-class corpses put in coffins.

Collapsible A was left to drift by Fifth Officer Lowe, with three dead men aboard, their lifebelts placed over their faces. It was found a month later, 200 miles away, by the White Star liner *Oceanic*. A passenger described what he saw: 'Two sailors, their hair bleached by exposure to sun and salt, and a third figure, wearing evening dress, flat on the benches.'

When the *Carpathia* was half a mile from Manhattan, Captain Rostron ordered that the *Titanic*'s 13 remaining lifeboats be released, in order to deprive reporters of the chance to photograph them, and the public of the chance for a ghoulish souvenir.

Titanic survivors Charlotte Collyer and her daughter Marjorie, June 1912.
Charlotte has their White Star Line blanket.

After April 1912...

1514 people died when the *Titanic* sank: 818 passengers, 696 crew.

710 people survived: 498 passengers, 212 crew.

20% of men survived.
74.3% of women survived.
52.3% of children survived.

62% of first-class passengers survived; 41% of second-class; 25% of third-class.

68% of the Deck Department survived; 19% of the Victualling Department; 22% of the Engine Department.

Rhoda, Rossmore and Eugene Abbott

Sixteen-year-old Rossmore Abbott was buried at sea on 24th April; 14-year-old Eugene's body, if recovered, was never identified.

Their mother Rhoda, a lifelong member of the Salvation

Army, remarried in 1914 and lived in Florida for many years before moving to London. She died in 1946 at the age of 73. Rhoda Abbott was the only female passenger pulled from the water who survived.

Olaus Abelseth

The Norwegian farmer from third class told his story to the US Senate Inquiry, having spent time in hospital recovering. He farmed for 30 years in South Dakota, and had four children with Norwegian-born Anna Grinde. Anna lived to 101 and Olaus to 94. His brother-in-law Sigurd Moen and his cousin Peter Søholt both drowned.

Leah Aks

Leah saw another woman holding baby Frank on the *Carpathia*, who, when challenged, claimed he was hers. Captain Rostron asked each of them to prove she was the mother. Leah described a birthmark on Frank's chest and he was returned to her. The following year, a grateful Leah gave birth to Sarah Carpathia Aks – although the nuns filling out the birth certificate accidently wrote down Sarah Titanic Aks.

Thomas Andrews

The managing director of Harland and Wolff's body, if recovered, was never identified. As details of his actions during the *Titanic*'s final hours emerged, helping others to board lifeboats and put on their lifebelts, Andrews was elevated to the status of national hero. His greatest legacy was perhaps the *Olympic*, which served the White Star Line successfully for 24 years, retiring in February 1935. Her sister ship, the *Britannic*, was converted into a hospital ship in the First World War, and sank after hitting a German mine on 21st November 1916.

John Jacob Astor IV

John Jacob Astor was the first body taken off the Mackay-Bennett. The inventory read:

'Male – Estimated age 50 – Light hair and moustache

'Clothing – Blue serge suit; blue handkerchief with "A.V."; belt with gold buckle; brown boots with red rubber soles; brown flannel shirt; "J.J.A." on back of collar.

'Effects – Gold watch; cuff links, gold with diamond; diamond ring with three stones; £225 in English notes; $2440 in notes; £5 in gold; 7s. in silver; 5 ten franc pieces; gold pencil; pocketbook.'

Madeleine Astor

John Jacob's will stipulated that 18-year-old Madeleine could only benefit from a trust fund and live in their Fifth Avenue Mansion if she remained a widow for the rest of her life. The bulk of his fortune went not to their unborn child but to Vincent – his son from his first marriage. On 14th August, Madeleine gave birth to a boy she named John Jacob Astor VI (a cousin was John Jacob Astor V).

In 1915 she renounced her claim to the Astor fortune when she married William K. Dick and they went on to have two sons. After they divorced in 1933, she married prizefighter Enzo Fiermonte, whom she met on a transatlantic voyage.

Léontine 'Ninette' Aubart

On the *Carpathia*, Benjamin Guggenheim's mistress telegraphed a friend in Paris: *'Moi sauvee mais Ben perdu'* (I'm saved but

Ben lost). On 1st May Léontine submitted a personal injury claim to the White Star Line of $25,000, plus a list of the items she lost on the *Titanic*, including their value in francs.

TRUNKS:
1 trunk 'Innovation' for hats
1 trunk 'Innovation' for dresses
1 trunk 'Innovation' for lingerie
1 trunk 'Vuitton'
1 toilet-bag with silver fittings 3500 Frs.

24 dresses and wraps 25,000 Frs.
7 hats and 2 with aigrettes 2400 Frs.

SHOES:
6 pairs black
6 pairs evening
6 pairs satin with jewelled buckles
6 pairs (without description) 1800 Frs.

LINGERIE:
24 chemises
6 chemisettes
12 sets of knickers
24 night costumes of silk lace, corsets, corset-covers, handkerchiefs and neck-wear 6000 Frs.

Gloves and opera glasses 400 Frs.

JEWELLERY:
1 gold bag with sapphires 4000 Frs .
1 purse, gold with emeralds 2000 Frs.
1 money and powder purse, gold with sapphires 4000 Frs.

1 bracelet 3000 Frs.
1 tiara of brilliants 9000 Frs.
Total: 61,100 Frs ($12,220)

Léontine Aubart died in October 1964, aged 77.

Assistant Purser Reginald Barker
His body, if recovered, was never identified.

Frederick Barrett
On 25th May 1912, a few weeks after the sinking, fireman Frederick Barrett was serving on the *Olympic*. As part of the Senate Inquiry, Senator William Smith went to her engine room to talk with Barrett to get an impression of how conditions had been in the *Titanic*'s boiler rooms at the time of the collision.

George Beauchamp
The fireman told the British inquiry the story of his battle with the rising water in boiler room 6. He continued to work at sea and then towards the end of his life became a docker in Southampton. He died in April 1965, aged 77.

George Beedem
The bedroom steward's body, if recovered, was never identified.

Lawrence Beesley
For the rest of his life schoolteacher Lawrence Beesley had a fear

of the sea. He only ever had one seaside holiday, and insisted on turning his deckchair away from the water the whole time. Beesley was hired as a special advisor for the 1958 film *A Night to Remember*, and in an unthinking act of cruelty, was put into a caravan at Pinewood Studios and asked to record what the cries of the drowning sounded like.

Lawrence Beesley's son Kit married the author of *101 Dalmatians*, Dodie Smith.

Karl Behr, Helen Beckwith

Despite the reservations of Helen's parents, Karl's pursuit of her across Europe was rewarded – they were married a year after the sinking. The couple went on to have four children.

Karl died in 1949, and Helen later married one of Karl's tennis partners. She died in 1965.

Helen's parents, Richard and Sallie Beckwith, also survived the sinking.

In 1987 a leather satchel belonging to Richard Beckwith was recovered from the *Titanic* wreck site. It contained jewellery belonging to Charlotte Cardeza and other first-class passengers on B-deck, and a silver box with DG on it – belonging to the Duff Gordons. It seems likely that sometime after Charlotte Cardeza left the ship in lifeboat 3 at 12.55am, someone with a key to the cabins made their way through the first-class accommodation, looting as they went. The bag was probably abandoned by the thief on the boat deck or in the water.

Helen and Dickenson Bishop

Helen Bishop was told on her honeymoon that she would survive a shipwreck and an earthquake, before being killed in an automobile accident. In 1913 the Bishops settled in California, where their house was rocked by an earthquake. On 4th November that year she was in a car being driven by a friend when it hit a tree; Helen was thrown in the air and landed head first on a cement road. Surgeons fixed a silver plate over the damaged part of her skull.

Although Helen made a good recovery, relations with Dickenson deteriorated, and in January 1916 they were granted a divorce. Two months later, Helen tripped on a rug in a friend's sitting room, and hit her head on the floor. She suffered a massive brain haemorrhage and died on the morning of 15th March 1916, the day that Dickenson married for a second time.

Fourth Officer Joseph Boxhall

Joseph Boxhall retired from the sea in 1940, and later worked as an advisor on the film *A Night to Remember*. He died in 1967 and had asked for his ashes to be scattered at the location where he had calculated the *Titanic* sank: 41°46'N, 50°14'W. Sadly, the discovery of the wreck in 1985 showed he was 13 miles out.

Theo Brailey

The pianist's body, if recovered, was never identified. His parents Ronald and Amy were initially told that their son had survived. They attended a *Titanic* Band Memorial Concert at the Albert Hall in May 1912 to raise money for the band members' families. The conductors included Sir Edward Elgar, Sir Thomas Beecham and Sir Henry Wood. One of the orchestras that night was the London Symphony Orchestra which had been booked on the *Titanic* for a tour of the United States and Canada, but due to a fortunate rescheduling of venues had to depart a week earlier.

Harold Bride

Although exhausted and suffering from severe frostbite and injured feet, Bride helped the *Carpathia*'s wireless operator Harold Cottam send messages from the *Titanic*'s survivors to friends and family. The men were so busy they even ignored a request from President Taft for news of his aide Archibald Butt.

The day before they were due to arrive at New York, Bride received a message from American Marconi's chief engineer: 'Stop. Say nothing. Hold your story for dollars in four figures. Mr Marconi agreeing. Will meet you at the dock.'

After most of the passengers had disembarked, Guglielmo Marconi and journalist Jim Speers arrived in the wireless room of the *Carpathia* – Bride was still tapping out messages. 'That's hardly worth sending now, boy,' Marconi said.

Bride dictated his story to Speers, and the following day it appeared in the *New York Times*, the same paper that ran Jack Binns' story about the sinking of the *Republic*. Bride was paid $1000 for the story – more than three years' wages, and double what Binns was paid. Bride gave evidence a few days later to the Senate Committee in a wheelchair.

Harold Bride married in 1919 and the couple had three children. He disliked the continuing interest in the *Titanic*, and moved from England to a remote part of Scotland in the 1920s.

Arthur Bright

Like all of the *Titanic*'s quartermasters, Arthur Bright survived the sinking. He died in Southampton in October 1955.

Margaret 'Molly' Brown

Reporters gave her the nickname 'unsinkable' after she declared on arriving in New York: 'The ship can sink, but I can't; I'm unsinkable!' Margaret gave interviews wearing the same outfit she wore in the lifeboat.

In May 1912, as chair of the Survivors' Committee, she presented a silver cup to Captain Rostron of the *Carpathia* and a medal to each of her crew. Molly died in October 1932.

She was immortalised in the 1964 Broadway musical and film *The Unsinkable Molly Brown*.

Daniel Buckley

Twenty-one year-old-Buckley, who was protected by the women in lifeboat 13, served in the US Army in the First World War. He wrote many letters to his mother in County Cork; in one he asked her not to send him any more socks as he already had 15 pairs.

Daniel Buckley was killed a month before the end of the war.

Jeremiah Burke

Jeremiah Burke's body, if recovered, was never identified. His message in a bottle was found on a beach in County Cork in the summer of 1913. It was taken to the police, who passed it on to his family. The message has been framed and hangs on the wall of the house of his descendant John Burke.

Kate Buss

Kate reached San Diego and married Samuel Willis on 11th May 1912. She had travelled in April to avoid an 'unlucky'

May wedding. They had a daughter, Sybil. Kate died in Oregon in July 1972 at the age of 92.

Major Archibald Butt

Archibald Butt died in the sinking. President Taft wept at the news of the death of his favourite aide. His body, if recovered, was never identified.

Helen Candee

Helen's visit to the bow on the morning of the sinking is said to have inspired the Kate Winslet and Leonardo DiCaprio 'I'm flying!' scene in James Cameron's movie *Titanic*. Helen wrote after the sinking that after those moments on the bow, the ship seemed 'full of ghosts not aware that they were already dead'.

She continued to write and campaign for women's rights, and died in August 1949.

Reverend Ernest and Lillian Carter

The Carters' church in Whitechapel held a service of thanksgiving on 15th April, after early reports suggested that everyone on the *Titanic* had survived.

Ernest Carter's obituary in the *Times* said: 'He brought a merry enthusiasm which made it impossible for any gloom to settle down on any cause, however desperate, with which he was concerned... They were childless and their life was always lived for others.'

William, Lucile and Billy Carter

Lucile Carter divorced her husband William in 1914. Her

divorce suit said that after he told her and the children to get dressed, she didn't see him until the *Carpathia*. 'All he said was that he had had a jolly good breakfast and he never thought that we would make it.'

Their son Billy lived into his late eighties.

Eleanor Cassebeer

Newspapers made up a number of quotes purporting to come from first-class passenger Eleanor, saying the officers were drunk, that First Officer Murdoch wasn't on the bridge at the time of the collision, and that 'a spirit of recklessness was predominant'. She declared in response, 'I am a staunch admirer in American and British manhood.'

Virginia Clark

Virginia Clark was rescued in lifeboat 4. Her husband Walter perished in the disaster. She died in December 1958.

Fred Clarke

Only three of the band members' bodies were found. Fred Clarke was discovered on 24th April. He was easy to indentify as he was carrying a business card with his home address at Tunstall Street, Liverpool.

Gurshon 'Gus' Cohen

The 18-year-old printer was photographed on the *Carpathia* fast asleep in a steamer chair. He cut the picture out and sent it to his family, with the caption 'This is me'.

Cohen acquired the nickname 'The Cat' for escaping death

so many times. He was shot twice in one day in the First World War, and his home was bombed twice in the Second. At the age of 78 Cohen recovered from a near-lethal bout of rheumatic fever.

Gus Cohen married his fiancé Hettie, and in their retirement they enjoyed going on cruises. He said once that the cries of the dying are 'never out of my ears.'

Sidney Collett

The theology student was met by his parents in New York; he was the last of his family to emigrate from England. Collett enrolled at Rochester Theological Seminary but was the victim of extreme bullying – his forehead was branded with nitrate of silver by six students. After the incident was investigated by the British embassy, Collett returned home to England. He died in London in 1941.

Harvey, Charlotte and Marjorie Collyer

Harvey's body, if recovered, was never identified. At his home church in Bishopstoke in Hampshire there is a memorial to him in the form of a noticeboard and umbrella stand, with the inscription: 'Sacred to the memory of Harvey Collyer who fell asleep April 15th 1912 Age 31 years. Jesus said "come".'

Charlotte never recovered from the loss of her husband, and died of consumption in 1914. Marjorie was a guest at a special screening for the film *A Night to Remember* along with other survivors. She died in 1965 aged 61.

Harold Cottam

The wireless operator on the *Carpathia* remained at sea until

1922, when he got married and took a job as a salesman. He died in 1982.

Eugene Daly

The Irish piper always believed that it was his overcoat that kept him alive on the lifeboat. It became the lucky coat that he always wore when he travelled. Eugene Daly died in the Bronx in October 1965.

Maggie Daly

Eugene Daly's cousin married widower Bartholomew Griffin in Manhattan in April 1920. She died in April 1939.

Thornton and Orian Davidson

To attract the attention of the *Carpathia*, first-class passenger Orian set fire to her straw hat. She lived to be 94. The body of her husband Thornton, if recovered, was never identified.

Thomas Dillon

The engine room trimmer was pulled out of the sea by lifeboat 4. Dillon said later, 'I would rather die a hundred times than go through such an experience and live.' He made a good recovery and testified before the British inquiry in May 1912.

Washington and Ruth Dodge

Dodge tried to return to his life as a San Francisco politician and banker. But after rumours started that he had escaped in a *Titanic* lifeboat dressed as a woman, he decided to give his account of the sinking at San Francisco's Commonwealth Club in May 1912. The aftermath of a business deal in 1919 in which it was claimed incorrectly that he'd benefited from insider information led to a bout of depression. Dodge went into his garage in June 1919 and shot himself in the head. Ruth Dodge died in New York in July 1950.

Walter and Mahala Douglas

When her lifeboat came alongside the *Carpathia*, Mahala shouted up, distraught with grief: 'The *Titanic* has gone down with everyone on board!' before being told to 'Shut up!' by Fourth Officer Boxhall.

The body of her husband Walter was recovered by the *Mackay-Bennett*.

Sir Cosmo and Lady Lucy Duff Gordon

On the second day on board the *Carpathia*, Sir Cosmo Duff Gordon carried out his promise to the lifeboat's crew to 'give you a fiver each towards getting a new kit'. Laura 'Franks' Francatelli wrote out seven cheques, Sir Cosmo signed them, and a photograph was taken of the event.

When they arrived in New York, rumours began to circulate that the couple had paid the crew not to go back to rescue survivors, because they were afraid of being swamped. Lifeboat 1 became known as 'the money boat'. Sir Cosmo Duff Gordon was forced to defend the payment when he testified before the Board of Trade Inquiry, and denied he had ever insisted they shouldn't go back. His wife later said, 'He never lived down the shame of the charges that were brought against him and from that time he became a changed man... I know that his heart was broken.' Lady Duff Gordon claimed that for her 'the *Titanic* disaster made me and my fortune. When I opened my dress establishments in New York and Chicago, people mobbed the places'.

Sir Cosmo died in 1931, and shortly after Lady Lucy's business collapsed. She died in a nursing home in Putney in April 1935.

Henry Etches

The steward survived the sinking and in later life retired to Worcestershire.

Alfred Evans

Evans worked as a shipyard worker at Southampton docks and then at Harland and Wolff. He died in February 1964.

Cyril Evans

At the US Senate Inquiry, Evans, the *Californian*'s wireless operator, reinforced his shipmate Ernest Gill's statement that distress rockets had been seen from the *Californian*: 'It has been common talk on the ship.' Evans continued to work for Marconi and served in both world wars in army communications. He died of a heart attack in 1959.

Edith Evans

Edith surrendered a place in a lifeboat to her friend Caroline Brown, saying, 'You go first. You have children waiting at home.' Her body, if recovered, was never identified.

Frederick Fleet

Until August 1912, Fleet carried on working for the White Star Line as a seaman on the *Olympic*. But the former lookout was seen as too much of an embarrassment and by some as jinxed. He moved on to work for other shipping lines, and even built ships for Harland and Wolff.

In the 1960s, Fleet ended up selling newspapers on the streets of Southampton, sometimes teased by passers-by shouting, 'Hello, Fred. Seen any icebergs lately?' He hanged himself from his washing line in January 1965, shortly after his wife died. Fleet always maintained that if he'd had a pair of binoculars that night, he would have seen the iceberg in time.

Margaret Fleming

Margaret worked as a secretary for Marian Thayer for the rest of her life, dying in August 1941.

Percy Fletcher

The *Titanic*'s bugler died in the sinking; his body, if recovered, was never identified.

Mary Fortune

Mary's husband Mark and son Charles were lost in the sinking; their bodies, if found, were never identified.

Laura 'Franks' Francatelli

Lucy Duff Gordon's secretary married a Swiss hotel manager and they lived in Manhattan and London. Laura died in Hampstead in June 1967. An account of the sinking that she typed for the Board of Trade Inquiry sold for £20,000 in 2010.

Dr Henry and Clara Frauenthal

The doctor who helped set Renée Harris's broken arm killed himself in 1927 by jumping from the seventh floor of his hospital. Henry left the bulk of his fortune to the hospital. His widow Clara spent the last 16 years of her life in an asylum.

Isaac Frauenthal

Isaac died in New York in November 1932.

Marguerite Frölicher

The perpetually seasick Marguerite married her fiancé Robert J.F. Schwarzenbach in January 1913. The couple lived in Jericho, New York, and had three children.

Her parents returned to Zurich after the wedding, and her father died the following November. Her mother Margaretha died in March 1955 and was buried next to her husband.

Dorothy and Pauline Gibson

The same evening that Dorothy Gibson arrived in New York on the *Carpathia*, her married lover Jules Brulatour gave her a $1000 engagement ring, and told her of his plans for a movie about the disaster. *Saved from the Titanic* was shot mostly on board a derelict freighter in New York harbour, and Dorothy wore the same white evening dress, long sweater and overcoat she had on the night the ship sank.

From then on, few things went right for the actress. In 1913, while driving her precious little grey car, she hit a couple on the sidewalk – the husband was killed and his wife sustained major injuries. Dorothy paid a large sum in compensation. Jules Brulatour divorced his wife and married Dorothy in 1917, but their marriage lasted only a couple of years. Dorothy moved to Paris with her mother Pauline, and lived off the alimony from Brulatour, hosting parties for friends such as H.G. Wells and James Joyce.

Both Dorothy and her mother were trapped in Italy at the outbreak of the Second World War, and in 1944 Dorothy was imprisoned in an internment camp. She died in her suite at the Paris Ritz in February 1946.

James Gibson

The *Californian*'s apprentice officer had a career with the Cunard and Holt shipping lines. He died in 1963.

Victor Giglio

The body of Benjamin Guggenheim's secretary, if recovered, was never identified.

Ernest Gill

The *Californian*'s assistant engineer sold his story about seeing rockets from a large steamer to the *Boston American* newspaper for $500 – more than a year's wages. Questioned by Senator Smith, he stood by his story, and his evidence helped damn Captain Lord in the eyes of the US Senate Inquiry. Lord had not mentioned seeing rockets in the newspaper interviews that he gave. Gill repeated his evidence to the British Board of Trade Inquiry the following month. Little is known of what happened to him after May 1912.

Frank, Emily and Frankie Goldsmith

Emily was one of the first to disembark from the *Carpathia* when it docked at the Cunard pier in New York on 18th April. There was a crowd of over 3000 people and the mounted police had to keep them back. Emily was wearing the wedding ring that Tom Theobold asked her to give to his wife.

Emily died in 1955.

Frankie worked for the US Air Force in Ohio; he could never go to a baseball game as the sound of the crowd reminded him of the screams of the dying.

The Goodwin Family: Frederick, Augusta, Lillian, Charles, William, Jessie, Harold and Sidney

The whole family died on the *Titanic*. One of the first bodies recovered by the *Mackay-Bennett* was a boy estimated to be two years old and thought to be from third class. The sailors who found the body decided to pay for a memorial for the child, and buried him with a copper pendant engraved with 'Our Babe'.

In 2007, DNA samples proved the little boy to be 18-month-old Sidney Goodwin.

Colonel Archibald Gracie

Only once aboard the *Carpathia* did Gracie realise that he'd been hit on the head and legs by wreckage when trying to escape the *Titanic*. He never fully recovered his health and died on 4th December 1912, shortly after writing an account of the disaster.

Margaret Graham and Elizabeth Shutes

When lifeboat 3 came alongside the *Carpathia*, governess Elizabeth Shutes refused to climb a ladder to the deck, and sat in a rope sling instead. A member of the *Carpathia*'s crew shouted as she was hoisted up, 'Careful, boys, she's a light-weight!'

Margaret Graham was not fond of Elizabeth Shutes and she was sacked soon after they arrived in New York.

Elizabeth Shutes died, unmarried, in New York State in October 1949.

Margaret Graham married a lawyer, and died in April 1976.

Charles Groves

The *Californian*'s third officer served in submarines in the First World War. His boat *E-17* ran aground on the Dutch coast and he spent the rest of the war in an internment camp or on parole in England. Groves became the marine superintendent for the Sheaf Line based in Newcastle-upon-Tyne, and worked for the Admiralty investigating maritime disasters. He died in September 1961.

Benjamin Guggenheim

The body of millionaire Benjamin Guggenheim, if recovered, was never identified.

William Gwinn, John March, John Smith, James Williamson, Oscar Woody

All the mail room clerks died in the sinking. Oscar Woody's and John March's bodies were recovered and identified by their possessions; the others, if found, were never identified.

Albert Haines

Boatswain's mate Haines was rescued in lifeboat 9. He was knocked down by a car and killed in June 1933, aged 53.

William Harbeck and Henriette Yrois

Filmmaker Harbeck's body was found clutching the purse of his lover Henriette Yrois. He was identified by his membership card for the Moving Picture and Projecting Machine Operators' Union. When his wife Catherine came to collect his body she was told that she couldn't be Mrs Harbeck as she had drowned with her husband. Catherine didn't buy a headstone for William's grave.

Henriette Yrois' body, if recovered, was never identified.

Henry and Renée Harris

Henry's body, if recovered, was never identified. Renée was convinced that the crew of the *Mackay-Bennett* found the body of her husband and stole the pearls and jewellery that were in his pockets, then buried him at sea. Renée discovered a few weeks after the loss of the *Titanic* that her husband was broke. She tried to follow Henry's example and become a Broadway producer, but with limited success. Renée became friends with the historian Walter Lord and told him that the title of his book should be *A Night to Forget*. Renée died in September 1969.

Benjamin, Esther and Eva Hart

Esther and Eva returned to England on the *Celtic*, and settled again in Essex. Esther died in 1928.

For much of her life, Eva drew 'a complete curtain over the *Titanic* disaster'. To rid herself of her frequent nightmares, she went to sea and locked herself in her cabin until the nightmares went. Eva gave many interviews over the years about the disaster. 'The worst thing I can remember are the screams,' she said in 1983.

The letter her anxious mother wrote in the second-class library on the afternoon of 14th April 1912 was sold at auction in April 2014 for £119,000.

Benjamin's body, if recovered, was never identified.

Wallace Hartley

The violin case of the leader of the *Titanic*'s band was found strapped to his body. In Hartley's pockets were a gold fountain pen, a silver matchbox, a telegram and his tips from the night he died. The White Star Line paid for his body to be shipped home to his family – but not the bodies of the other members of the band that were recovered.

The story of the musicians, who became known as 'the band that played on', and in particular Wallace Hartley, were the focus of British mourning after the sinking. There were 40,000 people at Hartley's funeral in Colne, Lancashire. On the coffin lid were the words: 'Wallace H. Hartley, Died April 15th 1912, aged 33 years. "Nearer, My God, To Thee".' Wallace's fiancée Maria Robinson never married.

In 2013, after two years of tests, it was concluded that a violin with the initials W.H.H. and an inscription 'For Wallace on the occasion of our engagement from Maria' was the instrument that Hartley played the night the *Titanic* sank.

Herbert Harvey

The body of the engineer who fought the rising water in boiler room 5, if recovered, was never identified.

Charles and Clara Hays

The body of the president of the Grand Trunk Railroad was found by the *Minia*, another ship chartered by the White Star Line to retrieve the dead. The Hays travelled on the *Titanic* as guests of Bruce Ismay, paying only £93 10s to cover incidentals. Clara refused to sue the White Star Line for damages: 'When one is a guest, one does not sue one's host.'

Samuel Hemming

Lamp trimmer Hemming died in Southampton in April 1928 aged 59.

James Hesketh

Hesketh escaped from boiler room 6 moments after the iceberg ripped into the hull. He died in the sinking and his body, if recovered, was never identified.

Robert Hichens

In 1933, Hichens, a heavy drinker, attempted to kill a man whom he owed money, and to kill himself, but failed at both. The former quartermaster was released from prison in 1937 and returned to sea, dying on board a cargo ship, the *English Trader*.

Robert Hichens used to say to his family about 'Unsinkable' Molly Brown, 'She could have walked into any lifeboat, why did she have to walk into mine?'

George Hogg

Hogg worked a seaman all his life and died in Southampton in 1946.

Masabumi Hosono

Hosono's survival was considered a national disgrace in Japan. He was criticised in newspapers, fired from his job and used as an example in school textbooks of how to be dishonourable. He died in 1939.

Jock Hume

The violinist's body was found at sea wearing a light raincoat and purple muffler over his bandsman's uniform. On 18th October 1912 his fiancée Mary Costin gave birth to a daughter she named Johann Law Hume Costin.

Walter Hurst

The engine greaser who ruefully looked at lifeboat 1 and thought, 'If they are sending the boats away, they might just as well put some people in them,' managed to clamber on top of the capsized collapsible B.

Walter Hurst died in December 1964.

Joseph Hyman

There is a kosher delicatessen in Cheetham Hill, Manchester called J.A. Hyman (Titanics) Ltd. Its founder, picture framer Joseph Hyman, who travelled to America to visit his brother, survived the sinking. As Joseph was fearful of travelling home by sea, his brother got him drunk before putting him on the boat. Inspired by the stores he'd seen in New York, Joseph opened a delicatessen, which is now run by Richard Hyman, his great-grandson.

Bruce Ismay

Jack Thayer visited Ismay in his cabin on the *Carpathia*. He was 'seated, in his pyjamas and shaking like a leaf when I spoke to him... telling him he had every right to take the last boat, he paid absolutely no attention and continued to look ahead with his fixed stare'. Few others were as understanding.

Ismay was the first witness to stand before the US Senate Committee in a conference room in the Waldorf-Astoria, only the morning after the *Carpathia* docked. Ismay was accused of encouraging Captain Smith to speed towards the ice, and being in charge of a company that cared little for human life – preferring profits to lifeboats. The US papers dubbed him J. 'Brute' Ismay.

Ismay's interest in Marian Thayer that had begun on the voyage continued in the months that followed, and they started corresponding. One letter written while his wife was at church said, 'Oh, how I wish you were here and we could sit out in the garden and help each other...' In another he confessed his many faults: 'I absolutely hate myself. Tell me what I can do to cure myself... What an ending to my life. Perhaps I was too proud of the ships and this is my punishment.' Marian Thayer ended their correspondence in June 1913.

Ismay gave up his presidency of International Mercantile Marine and the chairmanship of the White Star Line that same month. He contributed £10,000 to help the widows of the *Titanic* disaster, and carried out more personal acts of kindness. He gave financial assistance to the family of his secretary William Harrison. Harrison's son wrote back, 'Although our sorrow is still big, we are so relieved that we can live comfortably all together.'

Ismay retired to County Galway and kept out of public life. He died, aged 74, in October 1937.

The White Star Line merged with Cunard in 1934, and for

13 years the flags of both companies flew from their ships. In 1947, Cunard, holding the greater number of shares in Cunard-White Star Ltd, shut White Star down.

Violet Jessop

Violet served as a stewardess on the *Olympic* and the *Titanic*, and then as a nurse on the *Britannic*. When the *Britannic* hit a mine in 1916, Violet got into a lifeboat with a few carefully selected items – a clock, a ring, a prayer book and a toothbrush. She remembered she missed having a toothbrush on the *Carpathia*. In the water, Violet found herself almost alone in the lifeboat as the other occupants had seen what she had not – the *Britannic* was trying to reach shallow water, and their lifeboat was being sucked towards the propellers. Violet jumped into the sea but a giant blade struck her repeatedly on the head. She came to on the surface surrounded by mutilated corpses. Only in later life did Violet discover she's suffered a fractured skull.

Violet retired from the sea in 1950, and died in May 1971 at the age of 83.

Archie Jewell

Jewell survived the sinking of the hospital ship *Britannic*, but a year later, serving as an able seaman on the hospital ship SS *Donegal*, drowned when it was torpedoed by a U-Boat. He was 28.

Thomas Jones

The able seaman who put the Countess of Rothes in charge of his lifeboat later removed the number '8' from the boat and had it framed for her.

Charles Joughin

The ability of the baker to survive in the water for over an hour is a puzzle. Some say that the high level of alcohol in his bloodstream acted like an antifreeze, others that his dry hair meant he had pockets of air as insulation. Joughin died in 1956 in New Jersey, at the age of 78.

Thomas Kelland

The body of the library steward, if recovered, was never identified.

Georges Krins

The body of the violinist, if recovered, was never identified. A memorial to Krins in his home town of Spa in Belgium was shelved after the First World War broke out.

His family unsuccessfully sued the White Star Line for compensation.

Reginald Lee

The lookout who worked alongside Frederick Fleet in the crow's nest died from pneumonia-related symptoms in August 1913 on board the SS *Kenilworth Castle*.

Second Officer Charles Lightoller

A year after the sinking, Lightoller got into a cold bath following a long game of tennis. The water brought back such a rush of terrible memories that he went into a trance and had to be pulled out of the bath by friends.

Lightoller defended Bruce Ismay at both inquiries and

suffered as a result – although he worked for the White Star Line until his retirement in the 1930s, he was never given his own command.

However, during the First World War the Royal Navy, recognising his talents, gave him the command of torpedo boat *HMTB-117*. In July 1916 he attacked a Zeppelin using the ship's guns. For this action he was awarded the Distinguished Service Cross.

In May 1940, Lightoller, with his son, took the family's 60-foot yacht *Sundowner* to assist in the Dunkirk evacuation. The *Sundowner* had carried only a maximum of 21 people before, but 130 were brought home through bombs and machine-gun fire. Charles Lightoller died in December 1952 at the age of 78.

Milton Long

The body of Jack Thayer's friend was found by the *Mackay-Bennett*. He is buried in Springfield, Massachusetts.

Eight days after the sinking, Jack Thayer wrote to Milton's father, giving him an account of the night. He ended by saying: 'Your son was perfectly calm all the time and kept his nerve, even to the very end. I wish I had more to tell you... I am sending you my picture, thinking you might like to see who was with him at the end.'

Captain Stanley Lord

After both the US and British inquiries censured Lord for not going to the assistance of the *Titanic*, his employers, the Leland Line, requested his resignation. Lord had admitted that the *Californian* had stopped in hazardous conditions and that rockets had been sighted and reported to him, and yet he had only told his officers to 'keep on Morseing'. Lord could have woken his wireless operator and asked him to try to contact the ship. There was no reference to the rockets in the ship's log.

Charles Lightoller's wife Sylvia attended the British inquiry and was so furious with Captain Lord for what she saw as his neglect of duty that she agreed to shake hands with him only after her husband said, 'You can't kick a man when he's down.'

In 1913 Lord was given command of a ship owned by the Nitrate Producers' Steam Company Ltd. He retired in 1927 due to ill health and died in 1962, aged 84.

Lord still has supporters – nicknamed 'Lordites' – who claim that the *Californian* was not the ship seen from the *Titanic* and that he wasn't negligent that night.

If the *Californian* had gone to the aid of the *Titanic*, having seen the rockets, she probably would not have arrived in time to save people from freezing to death in the water because she was ten miles away and her top speed was only 14 knots.

Fifth Officer Harold Lowe

Lowe was a star of the US Senate Inquiry, as feisty as he had been on the night of the sinking, often provoking laughter during his exchanges with the chairman, Senator William Smith. Smith asked him if reports were true that he'd been intoxicated on the night of 14th April. '*Me* sir? No, sir! *This...*' – Lowe lifted up a glass of water – 'is the strongest drink I ever take!'

The *Titanic*'s fifth officer told the inquiry that he had to fire his revolver to keep two men out of a lifeboat; about one he said, 'I do not know whether he was an Italian or what, but he was of the Latin races anyhow.' He was forced to apologise to the Italian government, writing in a statement: 'I hereby cancel the word "Italian" and substitute the word "immigrants belonging to the Latin Races".'

Lowe was not rewarded for his action on board the *Titanic* and made only a third officer on the White Star Line's *Medic*. He served as a commander in the Royal Navy during the First World War. Harold Lowe died in Wales in May 1944 at the age of 61.

William Lyons

The able seaman who was pulled from the sea into lifeboat 4, died on the *Carpathia* and was buried at sea. He was 26.

Roberta Maioni

The name of the Countess of Rothes' maid was taken down incorrectly after the sinking, and so it was three weeks before her mother received the following telegram:

> Mrs Maioni, Manor Farm, Surrey
> We are pleased to inform you that amongst the lists of those saved appears the name of Miss Maioni, which is no doubt your daughter, and we congratulate you on the fact of her safety.
> Yours Faithfully. White Star Line

Roberta died in January 1963. For many years she'd suffered from severe arthritis, which she blamed on the freezing night in lifeboat 8. An account she wrote for a short story competition run by the *Daily Express* and the badge she was given by a young steward were auctioned in 1999.

Evelyn Marsden

After the sinking, the *Titanic* stewardess married a White Star Line doctor named William James. They moved to Evelyn's home country, Australia. Evelyn died in August 1938, and William, broken-hearted, died soon after.

Paul Maugé

The maître d' of the à la carte restaurant survived the sinking and worked in Canada. He died in 1971.

Thomas McCawley

The gymnasium steward told one passenger that he wouldn't wear a lifebelt as it would hamper his swimming. His body, if recovered, was never identified.

Chief Purser Herbert McElroy

The *Mackay-Bennett* recovered the body of a man that was hard to identify because it was so badly decomposed. In his pockets were a fountain pen, a set of keys, and some money. Because he was wearing an officer's white dinner jacket, it was decided to investigate further. The crew concluded that it was the body of Herbert McElroy. Because of the decomposition, he was buried at sea on 22nd April 1912, along with 14 others.

Frank Millet

Millet's body was recovered by the *Mackay-Bennett*, and identified by the initials FDM on a gold watch. The close friendship between Millet and Archibald Butt was commemorated with a fountain on Executive Avenue in Washington DC, erected by joint resolution of Congress, and named the Butt-Millet fountain.

Philipp Mock, Emma Schabert

The first-class passenger who helped Edith Rosenbaum into lifeboat 11 went on to have a varied career in banking and piano manufacturing. He died in Florida in June 1951. His sister Emma, who was also in lifeboat 11, died ten years later.

Sixth Officer James Moody

Moody turned down a place in a lifeboat, and Harold Lowe took his space. Moody's body, if recovered, was never identified.

Bertha Mulvihill

Despite broken ribs and what she had witnessed during the sinking, Bertha wrote an extraordinarily cheerful letter to her sister while on the *Carpathia*:

'Dear Maud, I am fine and dandy – never better. What time did you hear of the disaster? I AM SO GLAD I WAS IN IT. I shall never forget it. We are just in New York. Having a jolly time...'

Bertha married her fiancé, and the couple lived on Rhode Island with their five children.

First Officer William Murdoch

Archibald Gracie, who was with Murdoch during the *Titanic*'s last minutes, claimed he would have heard the sound of a bullet if the first officer had killed himself. However, there are enough witness statements describing an officer committing suicide after shooting one or two men to conclude that the man was William Murdoch.

Sahid, Waika and Maria Nackid

One-year-old Maria was the first *Titanic* survivor to lose her life. In July 1912 she contracted meningitis and died. The Lebanese couple settled in Connecticut and went on to have another daughter and four sons.

Michel, Michel and Edmond Navratil (Hoffman)

Michel Navratil was a Roman Catholic, but because his body was found with a ticket bearing the name Hoffman, he was buried in a Jewish cemetery in Halifax, Nova Scotia.

The mystery of the two 'Orphans of the Deep' who spoke no English created newspaper headlines around the world. Marcelle Navratil saw a picture of her sons in a French newspaper and in May 1912 was reunited with them in New York.

After school in France, Edmond became an architect and builder. During the Second World War he was captured by the Germans, but managed to escape. He died aged 43.

His older brother Michel became a professor of psychology. In later life he recalled a patchwork of memories of the voyage. 'I remember looking down the length of the hull – the ship looked splendid. My brother and I were eating eggs in the second-class dining room. The sea was stunning. My feeling was one of total and utter well-being.'

In 1987 he returned to the United States to mark the 75th anniversary of the sinking. Nine years later, Michel crossed the

Atlantic again to visit his father's grave in Canada for the first time. It was on that trip that he remembered his father's last words, whispered to him just before he got in the lifeboat.

Douglas Norman

The Scottish pianist's body was recovered by the *Mackay-Bennett* and buried in Fairview Cemetery in Halifax, Nova Scotia.

Alfred Nourney

The self-styled Baron von Drachstedt irritated Helen Bishop in the lifeboat with his constant pipe-smoking and his refusal to row. On the *Carpathia* he created further animosity by falling asleep on a pile of blankets intended for the survivors. A woman pulled the top blanket from under him, and Nourney fell to the floor to the sound of much applause.

The 'Baron' lost all his money on the *Titanic*. He died in Germany in 1972.

Elizabeth Nye

Elizabeth, a widow, looked after Leah Aks' baby son Frank in lifeboat 11, a bittersweet experience as she had lost a baby of the same age a few years before.

Elizabeth settled in New York and married a Salvation Army colonel called George Darby, and in March 1915 they had a son, also named George.

Alfred Olliver

The quartermaster continued to work for the White Star Line, but traumatised by the loss of the *Titanic*, never returned to sea. He died in Jersey in June 1934.

Dr William O'Loughlin

The body of the ship's surgeon, if recovered, was never identified.

Frank Osman

The able seaman who helped Joseph Boxhall navigate lifeboat 2, went on to serve in other White Star Line and Cunard ships. He died in Southampton in 1938.

Albert Pearcy

The 25-year-old survived the sinking and continued a life at sea as a steward and then as a ship's baker.

Walter Perkis

The quartermaster rejoined his old ship the *Olympic* in June 1912. He died in Southampton in August 1954.

Major Arthur Peuchen

After the sinking, Peuchen was repeatedly criticised for taking a place in a lifeboat. He had asked Charles Lightoller on the *Carpathia* to provide him with a note to prove he had acted honourably. Lightoller wrote: 'Major Arthur Peuchen was ordered into the boat by me, owing to the fact that I required a seaman, which he proved himself to be, as well as a brave man.'

The testimony had little effect, and Peuchen's business and social life suffered. He died a pauper in 1929.

Jack Phillips

Harold Bride never saw Phillips again after they parted on the boat deck. Charles Lightoller said that Phillips was clinging to collapsible B, but as Bride was also on the boat and never saw his friend, it may have been a case of mistaken identity.

Jack Phillips' body, if recovered, was never identified. His home town of Godalming has a permanent display in the local museum dedicated to his memory.

Third Officer Herbert Pitman

On the *Carpathia* Pitman sent a telegram to his family that said simply: 'Safe, Bert'.

After the *Titanic*, Pitman served on White Star's *Oceanic* as third officer and later, because his eyesight was deteriorating, on the *Olympic* as purser. He also served as purser aboard the SS *Mataroa* during the Second World War. In March 1946, just prior to retirement from the Merchant Navy, he was awarded an MBE for 'long and meritorious service at sea and in dangerous waters during the war'. Herbert Pitman died in December 1961 in Pitcombe, Somerset.

John Poingdestre

Having survived the sinking of the *Oceana* and the *Titanic*, able seaman Poingdestre proved to be lucky once again when the merchant ship on which he was serving was torpedoed in the First World War and he survived. Little is known of his life after the war.

Frank Prentice

The storekeeper survived the sinking and went on to serve on the *Olympic*. In the 1960s and 1970s he gave many interviews about his time on the *Titanic*. He died in May 1982, aged 93.

Frederick Ray

Ray left stewarding for poultry farming. He recorded an interview in January 1958 for the BBC about his experiences on the *Titanic*. He died in 1977.

George Rheims

The first-class passenger who stripped down to his underwear during the ship's final moments sent a telegram from the *Carpathia* to a friend saying: 'Meet me dock with two hundred dollars, underwear, cap, big coat – am well but feet slightly frozen. Answer.' Rheims developed gangrene and had to have a toe amputated. He lived in Biarritz, and died there in 1962.

Annie Robinson

In October 1914, the stewardess was on the *Devonian* as it crept into Boston harbour in thick fog, foghorn blasting. Annie became so distressed she jumped overboard. She was not reported missing until the following morning when she failed to appear at breakfast. She was 40 years old.

Edith Rosenbaum/Russell

Edith initially wrote a telegram from the *Carpathia* that said:

'Lost All'. Then, perhaps realising that she was luckier than many of the other survivors on the ship, wrote another that said: 'Safe. Carpathia. Notify Mother.' From the moment she posed for photographs on the *Carpathia* with her lucky pig, Edith enjoyed the publicity and attention the *Titanic* brought her. At a New York preview of the 1953 film *Titanic*, she showed off the pig once more, as well as the dress she wore on the night of the sinking. During the filming of *A Night to Remember* at Pinewood Studios, she made regular visits to the set, raging when she spotted any inaccuracies. Despite this she became good friends with the family of the film's producer, Bill MacQuitty. They described her as having 'a survivor mentality. She was a fighter, an independent woman in an age when that was not the norm'.

Edith Rosenbaum spent her last days living in the Embassy Hotel in London, in a room packed full of newspapers and magazines and visited by pigeons. Edith died in hospital in April 1975, aged 96.

George Rosenshine, Maybelle Thorne

The couple were travelling as Mr and Mrs Thorne to disguise the fact that Maybelle was the ostrich feather importer's mistress. Rosenshine's body was recovered by the *Mackay-Bennett*; Maybelle escaped the *Titanic* on collapsible D.

In 1993, a leather bag was recovered from the wreck site. It was lying in the debris field between the two broken sections of the ship. Inside it were some typewritten letters by Rosenshine that remarkably had survived being under water for almost 100 years. In one legible part of a letter Rosenshine wrote: 'Outlook for next year for ostrich feathers not promising. There is a tendency for shaped hats that do not any (illegible) or French plumes, and what little ostrich will be sold will be in the way of simple little fancy stick-up effects, of which it will be very hard to make a season...'

Captain Arthur Rostron

In 1912, President Taft presented the *Carpathia*'s captain with the Congressional Medal of Honour. In 1915, Rostron was given the command of Cunard's prestigious liner the *Mauretania*. Under Rostron she established a number of speed records. He retired in 1931 and died in November 1940. The *Carpathia* served as a troop ship in the First World War and under the command of Captain William Prothero was torpedoed in July 1918, south of Ireland. All the passengers and crew survived.

Lucy, Countess of Rothes

The countess was met in New York by her husband, who had been to California to visit a fruit farm investment. The story of her taking control of the tiller of lifeboat 8 prompted many flattering newspaper articles. Sand models sculptured on Bournemouth beach to commemorate the *Titanic* included one entitled 'The Plucky Little Countess'.

The countess died in September 1956, aged 77.

Martin Rothschild

The body of the clothes manufacturer, if recovered, was never identified.

Pierre Rousseau

The body of the à la carte restaurant chef, if recovered, was never identified.

George Rowe

Quartermaster Rowe served on the *Oceanic* and the hospital ship *Plassy*. He then worked for the shipbuilder Thorneycroft well into his eighties. Rowe's work included stabilisers for the Cunard liners the *Queen Mary* and the *Queen Elizabeth*. He was awarded the British Empire Medal in 1960. He died aged 91.

Arthur and Emily Ryerson

Arthur Ryerson's body, if recovered, was never identified. Emily Ryerson remarried in December 1927.

Julius Sap

The Belgian was pulled out of the water into lifeboat 11 by his hair. Sap and two other Belgian travelling companions survived and toured America in a travelling show telling their story. They were promised $5 a day, but the show owner, a fellow Belgian, fled with all their earnings.

Joseph Scarrott

The able seaman who saw the iceberg and thought it looked like the Rock of Gibraltar later helped crew Harold Lowe's lifeboat 14. Scarrott remained a seaman and died in Essex in August 1938.

Frederick Seward

Dorothy Gibson's friend and bridge partner survived the sinking and died in New York in 1943.

Imanita Shelley and Lutie Parrish

Even on the *Carpathia*, the mother and dsughter were still complaining about the lack of heating in their cabin on the *Titanic*. They continued to travel the world together after the sinking and settled in Hawaii. Lutie died in August 1930, Imanita in May 1954.

Jonathan Shepherd

The body of the junior assistant engineer who fell and broke his leg in boiler room 5, if recovered, was never identified.

Dr John Simpson

The assistant surgeon died in the sinking. His body, if recovered, was never identified.

Mary Sloan

The stewardess returned home to England on the liner *Lapland*. Her life after that is a mystery.

William Sloper

Sloper was the other bridge player who escaped the *Titanic* with Dorothy Gibson. While recovering in the Waldorf-Astoria, he had a reporter turfed out of his hotel room. In revenge the reporter produced a story claiming that Sloper had 'donned a dress to gain a place in a lifeboat'. This statement dogged Sloper for the rest of his life, but he was persuaded by his father not to sue. He died in 1967, aged 82.

Captain Edward Smith

There are many stories about how Captain Smith died. One has him shouting to the very end, 'Be British, boys, be British!'; another has him rescuing a baby from the water and handing it into lifeboat before swimming away.

A statue was unveiled in July 1914 in Lichfield, financed by wealthy American and British passengers who had sailed with Smith during his long career. The sculptor was Lady Kathleen Scott, the widow of the explorer Robert Falcon Scott, who died at the South Pole just two weeks before the *Titanic* sank. The memorial mentions his bravery and heroic death – but no mention of his last ship.

James Clinch Smith

Archibald Gracie's friend did not survive the sinking. His body, if recovered, was never identified. James Clinch Smith was 56.

William Stead

As far as the British public in 1912 was concerned, Stead was one of the *Titanic*'s most famous victims. One journalist wrote: 'Walking in Oxford Street at midday, when the loss of the *Titanic* was certain, the only name I heard was his.' There are memorials to Stead in Central Park and in London, close to where he had his office.

His body, if recovered, was never identified.

Elizabeth Eustis, Martha Eustis Stephenson

Martha Stephenson, who survived the 1906 San Francisco earthquake as well as the *Titanic*, made a claim against the White Star Line for $1739.75, for the loss of her property. She died in December 1934. Her sister Elizabeth died two years later.

John Stewart

When he got into lifeboat 15, Stewart discovered he still had the steward's key for the Veranda Café in his pocket. His description of Thomas Andrews standing alone in the first-class smoking room, staring at a painting, became one of the most famous *Titanic* stories. John Stewart later became the landlord of the Richmond Inn in Southampton. He died in April 1946.

Herbert Stone

In 1933, the *Californian*'s first officer retired from the sea, and then worked in the Liverpool docks.

For many years after the sinking, there were rumours around the city that, contrary to what he'd said to the Board of Trade Inquiry, he *had* known that what he'd seen were distress rockets. Stone's son John told historian Leslie Reade that his father had confessed to his mother that 'distress rockets were being fired'. It has been suggested that Stone, who had run away to sea from an overbearing father, had inadvertently replaced him with an overbearing captain, whom he was too scared to contradict or, after the sinking, betray.

Herbert Stone was on his way to work at the docks when he had a cerebral haemorrhage and died. He was 72.

Isidor and Ida Straus

Isidor's body was recovered, wearing a fur-lined overcoat, grey trousers, coat and vest, a striped shirt, a pair of brown boots and black silk socks. Ida's body, if recovered, was never identified.

George Symons
Lookout Symons spent his whole life as a seaman. He died in December 1950.

Elmer Taylor, Fletcher Williams,
Taylor, the businessman who invented a paper cup, survived the sinking. His colleague Fletcher Williams, whom he found sitting up in bed casually sipping a highball, did not. His body, if recovered, was never identified. 'Nearer, My God, To Thee' was sung at his memorial service in London.

Percy Taylor
The body of the pianist, if recovered, was never identified. He was the only member of the *Titanic*'s band who was married. His widow Clara remarried in August 1918.

Jack Thayer
Thayer married Lois Cassatt in December 1917 and the following year fought in the First World War as a captain in the 79th 'Liberty' Division. The couple had six children. In 1940, he wrote a short text called *The Sinking of the SS Titanic*, dedicated to his father.

On 18th September 1945, depressed by the death of his son Edward on active service in the Pacific, Jack Thayer slit his wrists and throat while sitting in his wife's sedan. During the two days it took for the police to discover his body, his gold watch and chain were stolen. A few days later, the thief left the gold watch, wrapped in paper, at Thayer's home.

John Thayer

His body, if recovered, was never identified.

Marian Thayer

Marian never claimed for the loss of her husband's life, but did claim for the loss of her luggage. Marian died on the 32nd anniversary of the disaster in April 1944, aged 72.

Alfred Theissinger

Not allowed into lifeboat 15, Theissinger jumped into the water and was rescued by lifeboat 11. He died in 1949.

Robert Wareham

The steward who retrieved Edith Rosenbaum's toy pig died in the sinking. His body was recovered, with a few dollars and a corkscrew in his uniform pocket. He was 37.

Leopold and Mathilde Weisz

Mathilde had enjoyed the hymn singing in the second-class dining saloon a few hours before the collision, while Leopold strolled on deck with $15,000 worth of gold coins sewn into his Astrakhan coat. They were about to start a new life in Quebec.

Mathilde was about to leave Canada destitute when Leopold's body was recovered, along with the coat and the gold. In the spring of 1914, Mathilde married her husband's business partner and settled in Montreal.

Joseph Wheat

The steward who discovered water coming down from E- to F-deck continued working at sea for another decade; he then took a shore job and moved with his wife to Bromley in Kent.

George, Eleanor and Harry Widener

The bodies of George and his son Harry, if recovered, were never identified.

Eleanor Widener donated money to Harvard University for the building of the Harry Elkins Widener Memorial Library, in tribute to her son and his love of books. It is said that Eleanor gave the money on condition that each graduate of Harvard had to pass a swimming test.

Chief Officer Henry Wilde

Wilde's body, if recovered, was never identified. In his home city of Liverpool is an obelisk with the inscription: 'Also Captain [sic] Henry T. Wilde, RNR Acting Chief Officer Who Met His Death in the SS *Titanic* Disaster 15th April 1912 aged 38 years. "One of Britain's Heroes".'

Richard and Charles Williams

The young first-class passenger who found himself swimming in the water with a bulldog survived the sinking. He went on to study at Harvard and to win a number of tennis championships including the Wimbledon Men's Doubles in 1920. Richard Williams always treasured a hip flask his father Charles gave him the night of the sinking. The body of his father, if recovered, was never identified.

John Wesley Woodward

The body of Kate Buss's 'Cello Man', if recovered was never identified. A brass plaque in his memory was installed in the nave of All Saints Church in Headington, Oxford, and in Eastbourne a granite tablet was erected 'to the self-sacrifice and devotion of John Wesley Woodward' close to the bandstand where he used to play.

Hugh Woolner

The smooth-talking Englishman who looked after Michel Navratil in the lifeboat married his rich American, widow Mary Dowson, in 1912. The following year he was accused of exerting undue influence over an elderly lady named Elizabeth Forster, whose property was worth more than £500,000. The case was finally settled in 1917. Woolner died in 1925, aged 58.

Frederick Wright

The body of the *Titanic*'s squash attendant, if recovered, was never identified.

Marion Wright

Marion was reunited with her fiancé Arthur in New York. On 25th April she wrote to her family in Yeovil: 'After all I have gone through I shall be very glad to be in my new home and I don't think I shall ever want to cross the ocean again just yet awhile. It has been sad losing all I had, wedding presents and everything I had worked so hard at, but they are nothing in comparison to all the lives that were lost.'

Together they ran a successful farm, but never returned to England. Marion died in July 1965.

Walter Wynn

One of the more bizarre exchanges at the British inquiry
concerned what quartermaster Wynn took with him aboard lifeboat 9. He was questioned by a lawyer named Thomas Lewis:

Lewis: Did you place your kit bag in the boat?

Wynn: I had two sets of underwear in my bag which I had
never unpacked. I threw it into the first boat I came to
when I was told to get into the boat.

Lewis: That was the boat you left in?

Wynn: Yes.

Lewis: What happened to your kit bag?

Wreck Commissioner: Does it matter what happened to the
kit bag?

Wynn: I never saw it.

Lewis: It would be a good size, would it not – a good long
bag?

Wynn: Not for the two sets of underwear I had.

Little is known of what happened to Wynn after 1912.

Jay Yates

On 20th April 1912, the following story appeared in the *New
York World*:

That Jay Yates, gambler, confidence man and fugitive from
justice, known to the police and in sporting circles as J.M.
Rogers, went down with the *Titanic* after assisting many
women aboard lifeboats, became known today when the
following note, written on a blank page torn from a diary,
was sent to the *New York World*:

'If saved, inform my sister, Mrs. J.F. Adams of Findlay, Ohio. Lost [Signed] J.H. Rogers.'

This note was given by Rogers to a woman he was helping into a lifeboat. The woman, who signed herself 'Survivor', enclosed the note with the following letter addressed to the editor of the *World*:

'You will find note that was handed to me as I was leaving the *Titanic*. Am stranger to this man, but think he was a card player. He helped me aboard a lifeboat and I saw him help others. Before we were lowered I saw him jump into the sea. If picked up, I did not recognize him on the *Carpathia*. I do not think he was registered on the ship under his right name.'

The *World's* correspondent at Findlay today found Rogers' mother, Mrs. Mary A. Yates, an old woman. She broke down when told her son had perished.

'Thank God, I know where he is now,' she sobbed. 'I have not heard from him for two years. The last news I had from him he was in London. I spent nearly a fortune getting him out of trouble some years ago. Then he was charged with forgery.'

In fact, the letter with the accompanying note was sent by 'boat man' and gambler Jay Yates himself, in an attempt to fake his own death. Whether his mother was in on the deception isn't known. Yates was later arrested while using another alias.

Acknowledgements

Titanic: Minute by Minute was originally a three-hour live radio programme for BBC Radio 2, made by TBI Media to mark the centenary of the sinking. When we came off air in the middle of the night, Tim Maltin, one of our experts, turned to me waving my hefty script. 'You should have turned this into a book...' My thanks to Tim for the suggestion that kicked off the Minute by Minute collection.

Thanks also to Rebecca Nicolson, Aurea Carpenter and Paul Bougourd at the mighty Short Books who have championed the format, and to my editor Emma Craigie who knocked the text into shape as wisely as ever.

Despite the best efforts of the media world, Phil Critchlow continues to be one of the good guys – many thanks to him and his team at TBI. Bob Shennan, the controller of Radio 2, and Robert Gallagher, its commissioning editor, continue to be highly valued supporters of this way of bringing history to life.

Finally, an award of some sort should go to my wife Hannah and son Charlie (the only boy who, since the age of five, has known that pictures of the *Titanic* should never have smoke coming out of the fourth funnel) who haven't seen as much of me over the past few months as they, and I, would have liked. If nothing else, writing a book on the sinking of the *Titanic* makes one grateful for one's family.

Bibliography

Booth, John and Coughlan, Sean, *Titanic: Signals of Disaster* (White Star Publications, 1993)

Bryceson, Dave, *The Titanic Disaster* (Patrick Stephens, 1997)

Butler, Daniel Allen, *Unsinkable: The Full Story* (Frontline Books, 2011)

Ballard, Robert D., *The Discovery of the Titanic* (Hodder & Stoughton, 1989)

Barczewski, Stephanie, *Titanic: A Night Remembered* (Hambledon and London, 2004

Barratt, Nick, *Lost Voices from the Titanic* (Arrow, 2009)

Behe, George, *On Board RMS Titanic* (History Press, 2012)

Behe, George, *Titanic Safety, Speed and Sacrifice* (Transportation Trails, 1997)

Davenport-Hines, Richard, *Titanic Lives* (Harper Press, 2012)

Davie , Michael, *Titanic: The Death and Life of a Legend* (Alfred A. Knopf, 1987)

Eaton, John P. and Haas, Charles, *Titanic: A Journey Through Time* (Patrick Stephens, 1999)

Eaton, John P. and Haas, Charles, *Titanic Triumph and Tragedy* (Patrick Stephens, 1995)

Evans, Grace, *Titanic Style* (Moonrise Press, 2011)

Fitch, Tad et al., *On a Sea of Glass* (Amberley, 2012)

Gillespie, John and Gillespie, Vera, *The 'Titanic Man'* (Amereon, 1996)

Gracie, Archibald, *Titanic: A Survivor's Story* (Academy Chicago, 1998)

Halpern, Samuel, *Report into the Loss of the SS Titanic* (History Press, 2011)

Hart, Eva, *The Girl Aboard the Titanic* (Ambeley, 2014)

Holman, Hannah, *Titanic Voices* (Amberley, 2011)

Hyslop, Donald et al., *Titanic Voices* (Sutton, 1994)

Jessop, Violet, *Titanic Survivor* (History Press, 2012)

Lord, Walter, *The Night Lives On* (Penguin, 1986)

Lord, Walter, *A Night to Remember* (Penguin, 2012)

McCluskie, Tom et al., *Titanic and Her Sisters Olympic and Britannic* (Greenwich Editions, 2002)

Maltin, Tim, *101 Things You Thought You Knew About the Titanic* (Beautiful Books, 2010)

Maltin, Tim eds., *Titanic First Accounts* (Penguin, 2012)

Marcus, Geoffrey, *The Maiden Voyage* (Unwin 1988)

Nilsson, Sally, *The Man Who Sank the Titanic* (History Press, 2011)

Paul, Gill, *Titanic Love Stories* (Ivy Press, 2011)

Pellegrino, Charles, *Farewell Titanic* (John Wiley, 2012)

Spignesi, Stephen, *The Titanic for Dummies* (John Wiley, 2012)

Reade, Leslie, *The Ship That Stood Still* (Patrick Stephens, 1993)

Shiel, Inger, *Titanic Valour: The Life of Fifth Officer Harold Lowe* (History Press, 2012)

Strange, Robert J., *Who Sank the Titanic?* (Pen and Sword, 2012)
Tibballs, Geoff eds., *Voices from the Titanic* (Robinson, 2012)
Turner, Steve, *The Band That Played On* (Thomas Nelson, 2011)
Tyler, Sidney F., *A Rainbow, of Time and Space* (Aztex, 1983)
Wade, Wyn Craig, *The Titanic: End of a Dream* (Penguin, 1986)
Ward, Christopher, *And the Band Played On* (Hodder and Stoughton, 2011)
Wilson, Andrew, *Shadow of the Titanic* (Simon & Schuster, 2011)
Wilson, Frances, *How To Survive the Titanic or The Sinking of Bruce Ismay* (Bloomsbury, 2012)
Welshman, John, *The Last Night of a Small Town* (Oxford University Press, 2012)
Winocour, Jack eds., *The Story of the Titanic as Told By Its Survivors* (Dover, 1960)

Other sources:

BBC interview: Joseph Boxhall, 22nd November 1962
BBC interview: Harold Cottam, First Hand, 27th November 1956
BBC interview: Frederick Dent Ray, 6th January 1958
BBC interview: Charles Lightoller, I Was There, 1st November 1938
BBC interview: Edith Russell, Line Up, 14th April 1970

http://www.encyclopedia-titanica.org
http://titanicpiano.blogspot.ca
http://oceanservice.noaa.gov/facts/iceberg.html
http://postalmuseum.si.edu/titanic/index.html
http://www.charlespellegrino.com
http://www.titanicinquiry.org
http://www.jackbinns.org

http://query.nytimes.com

Index

331

I Was a **Bottom-Tier**
Bureaucrat for **1,500 Years**,
and the **Demon King** Made Me a **Minister**

Kisetsu Morita   Illustration by **Benio**

"Aaaaaaaaahhh

the water is s

©Benio

Contents

Story by Kisetsu Morita   Illustration by Benio

I Was a Bottom-Tier Bureaucrat for 1,500 Years, and the Demon King Made Me a Minister

©Benio

I Was a Bottom-Tier Bureaucrat for 1,500 Years, and the Demon King Made Me a Minister

Kisetsu Morita

Illustration by Benio

YEN
ON

NEW YORK

I was a Bottom-Tier Bureaucrat for 1,500 Years, and the Demon King Made Me a Minister

KISETSU MORITA

Translation by Jasmine Bernhardt and Sarah Neufeld
Cover art by Benio

SLIME TAOSHITE SANBYAKUNEN, SHIRANAIUCHINI LEVEL MAX NI NATTEMASHITA SPIN-OFF HIRAYAKUNIN YATTE SENGOHYAKUNEN, MAO NO CHIKARADE DAIJIN NI SARECHAIMASHITA
Copyright © 2019 Kisetsu Morita
Illustrations copyright © 2019 Benio
All rights reserved.
Original Japanese edition published in 2019 by SB Creative Corp.

This English edition is published by arrangement with SB Creative Corp., Tokyo in care of Tuttle-Mori Agency, Inc., Tokyo.

English translation © 2021 by Yen Press, LLC

Yen On
150 West 30th Street, 19th Floor
New York, NY 10001

Visit us at yenpress.com • facebook.com/yenpress • twitter.com/yenpress • yenpress.tumblr.com • instagram.com/yenpress

First Yen On Edition: March 2021

Yen On is an imprint of Yen Press, LLC.
The Yen On name and logo are trademarks of Yen Press, LLC.

Library of Congress Cataloging-in-Publication Data
Names: Morita, Kisetsu, author. | Benio, illustrator. | Bernhardt, Jasmine, translator.
Title: I was a bottom-tier bureaucrat for 1,500 years, and the demon king made me a minister / Kisetsu Morita ; illustration by Benio ; translation by Jasmine Bernhardt and Sarah Neufeld.
Other titles: Hirayakunin yatte sengohyakunen, mao no chikarade daijin ni sarechaimashita. English
Description: First Yen On edition. | New York : Yen On, 2021–
Identifiers: LCCN 2020057456 | ISBN 9781975318291 (v. 1 ; trade paperback)
Subjects: CYAC: Fantasy. | Demonology—Fiction. | Humorous stories.
Classification: LCC PZ7.1.M6725 Is 2021 | DDC [Fic]—dc23
LC record available at https://lccn.loc.gov/2020057456

ISBNs: 978-1-9753-1829-1 (paperback)
978-1-9753-1830-7 (ebook)

1 3 5 7 9 10 8 6 4 2

LSC-C

Printed in the United States of America

I Was a Bottom-Tier Bureaucrat for 1,500 Years, and the Demon King Made Me a Minister

BEELZEBUB

Main character.
A lowly, plain
pencil pusher in the
demon realm who
lived a comfortable,
lazy life…until she
caught the eye of
the demon king.
Shenanigans
ensued.

PECORA
(PROVATO PECORA ARIÉS)

The demon king.
A girl with a devilish
temperament who
loves to use
her power and
influence to bewilder
her subordinates.

BOSS, THERE ARE TIMES WHEN A DEMON MUST FIGHT.

VANIA

The younger leviathan sister. Right after Beelzebub was made minister, she was assigned to be her secretary (and supervisor). A klutz.

FATLA

The older leviathan sister. Right after Beelzebub was made minister, she was assigned to be her secretary (and supervisor). Levelheaded.

LADY BEELZE-BUB, I AM TRULY GLAD YOU ARE OUR MINISTER.

I Was Promoted from Bottom-Tier to Minister

My name is Beelzebub.

My name makes me sound important, but really, it's too important a name for me. It once belonged to a great demon of the past, and I was given that name, common as I am, so I may one day reach those same heights.

For the past 1,500 years, I've been quietly, plainly, and simply working as a public servant for the demon government.

The post I took was in the Agricultural Policy Organization, the lower branch of the Department of Agriculture.

To put it simply, it was the place that created projects and produced data for the country's agricultural administration. For 1,500 years, I was a clerk there—basically the lowest of the lowliest bureaucrats. You might believe my record was awful or that my attitude at work was terrible, but that wasn't true. I had stopped there intentionally.

Personnel prodded me, occasionally suggesting I become a manager at least, but I turned down every offer. I told them I didn't have those skills.

According to the rules governing public servants, if the person in question refuses a promotion, they are able to stay in their position. I could never be fired, because I was a government official!

I was going to live on lazily as a rank-and-file employee with no responsibilities!

Some people are suited for life in the fast lane, and some aren't. I was the latter. I didn't feel like summoning the drive to climb the bureaucratic ladder all the way to the top, nor did I feel like having a passionate affair.

It was far too much trouble, so I didn't have the confidence to establish a household, either.

And so I concentrated on working as the least important clerk—or, as they say, "the bottom tier."

I didn't even have the caliber to stand before people, much less to stand above them. I knew that best of all.

I wore clothes that were a little uglier than average, and my hair was pulled back only because it'd grown out and was bothering me. And although my eyesight was perfectly fine, I wore glasses to make me stand out even less.

I was just someone in the office. I was never a topic of workplace gossip, and if I disappeared, very little would change. Of course, the men I worked with would never even consider me as an object of romantic interest.

I'd managed to preserve my lifestyle of living in the shadows, undetected, for 1,500 years. It was my way of protecting myself.

My only miscalculation was that my coworkers always casually came to ask me for help because I was so plain, but I just endured it as an inevitable hardship.

You see, the frightening and domineering ladies stuck in middle management would never ask for help from the female employees beneath them. And a man always hesitated when it came to asking things from a beautiful, unmarried coworker. Someone else might be suspicious that he was interested in her. In that respect, I had no relation to office politics, and I was outside the fight for success.

Not only that, but with my nonexistent fashion sense, I appeared to have thrown away my femininity entirely.

Both men and women alike saw me as androgynous and approached me without hesitation.

And as a result, I turned into the one people came to when they were in trouble.

On my right, I would have an employee who didn't know where the file room was, so I'd go with them to show them where it was; on my left, I would have someone frazzled by their boss's very peculiar style requirements for any documents submitted, so I'd use my 1,500 years of career experience to help them.

I usually just got a piece of candy as thanks. For bigger jobs, I'd often get a drink at the bar.

I mean, that was fine. I was totally okay with that, if the alternative was moving up in the ranks and being saddled with more responsibility.

And for that, I think I was pretty well-liked within the office.

My unrefined lifestyle would get even worse when I returned to my single apartment.

When I got home, I would immediately change into my roomy pajamas!

Then I'd lie on the floor!

And my shoes were dirty, so I'd take them off. "No shoes" was the rule in my house.

On the table would be empty bottles and cups of alcohol and nuts to snack on. The pile of books in the corner of my room was collapsing, but I hadn't put them back.

If a lady friend came, she'd retreat immediately, but honestly, I didn't have the courage to invite anyone here in the first place. I didn't even want to invite my family over.

But this tepid lifestyle suited me. My personality was perfect for these lazy, unchanging days.

©Benio

I wasn't wrong. If I could live my long life with ease like this, I would consider it a victory. Perhaps one could call it my "win condition."

And wasn't it nice to just get drunk at home without anyone scolding you?

On the morning of my day off, the light streaming in through my run-down apartment woke me up. But—

"I stayed too long yesterday helping people. Maybe I should sleep a little more…"

That morning I fell back asleep, then finally woke up for real with bed head.

"What shall I do today? First I'll go to the restaurant with spicy hell pasta for brunch."

That place offered large portions and allowed us to add extra spice for free during lunchtime.

"Then I'll pick something out from the bookstore—it looks like it's going to rain tonight, so I'll come back early, and I can just have the hell-pot and bread I made yesterday… I suppose I'm fine as long as I'm eating spicy food."

Savoring the little things was a good way to live, in my opinion.

Sometimes I felt like the little things were too little, but big dreams would only leave me exhausted.

I was born as a daughter to greengrocers and spent some time helping with the store, and after I reached a suitable age for a long-lived demon, I took a test and became a civil servant. I was indifferent to the promotion ladder at that point. To be honest, I lacked any interest in moving up in the world, or in becoming important.

I yawned as I milled about Vanzeld Castle town.

As I walked along a market road, I saw a flyer:

CORONATION OF THE NEW DEMON KING ON THE XTH DAY OF THE XTH MONTH

*   *   *

Ah, indeed. It was finally time for the succession.

Now that the war with the humans had reached a cease-fire and the aftermath was mostly over, the demon king was apparently putting his daughter on the throne.

Her name is Provato Pecora Ariés, I believe.

I'd heard she was young and reform-oriented. Because of that, the people at the top of the organization were apprehensive that she might interfere with the status quo for the civil servants based on her whims.

When a new demon king was crowned, they often put the scalpel to the bureaucracy in order to freshen it up. The agricultural minister at the top of the department would probably change, but, well, that had nothing to do with me. I'd just go about my business quietly. There was no fight for power at the bottom. I didn't have any power to begin with.

I wolfed down my extra-large and extra-spicy pasta at my usual place.

A demon couple walked hand in hand in front of the bookstore. They were too lovey-dovey; they'd probably break up in six months. They should take more care so as not to deepen the inevitable wounds.

I sighed as I stored my warning away in my heart.

Some people out there just had brilliant lives.

And so coronation day for the new demon king came.

Us civil servants all attended to give praise to our new ruler up on the stage.

She *was* young. Far younger than I had imagined.

The new demon king had a pair of sheeplike horns growing from the sides of her head and wore a black dress for the ceremony. She struck me as a well-raised girl, but she looked so much like a child that I heard voices of concern around me.

I understood their opinion; things could prove difficult if the demon king wasn't an already battle-hardened individual, even if we weren't currently at war with the humans.

"I am the new demon king, Provato Pecora Ariés. I hope to work together with everyone to create an even better nation."

Her plain, generic general policy speech came to an end.

Still, if she could follow a template like that, she could at least keep the status quo. From the perspective of all the civil servants, that would be the most ideal—

And then.

The new demon king suddenly locked eyes with me.

I was standing way, way, way behind the agricultural minister, and yet it felt like she was looking directly at me. No, I had to be imagining things. The new demon king would never look at a low-level grunt like me. Our eyes had just happened to meet when she was scanning the audience.

"And now, I would like to announce each new cabinet minister~ I believe our new personnel will be more youthful than ever."

What she said was also something all too common.

The words meant she was breaking up the old ways, but it was normal to promote the powerful members of some faction somewhere.

If they had any interest, the minister would be selected from the same faction that supported the previous demon king, or possibly a different faction.

According to the rules, even someone of low standing could climb up to a higher position, but there was nothing but lip service to the idea. Every position at the top was and always had belonged to the privileged class. A noble title was necessary to be a minister, especially.

"First, our foreign minister shall be Nastas. Next, the home minister shall be Velts; the economic minister shall be Vector..."

She read names one after the other. It seemed the designated demons had no idea of this announcement beforehand, so a few of them made victorious poses upon hearing their name.

Everyone seemed strong. If the war with the humans were still in progress, then they'd probably be dispatched to towers here and there as bosses.

The new demon king offered simple explanations for why she selected these first few people as ministers.

I paid no attention to it as I thought about who came from what faction.

She was appointing ministers from all different factions. Maybe that meant the new demon king's authority was weak.

"Now, I shall return to the personnel. The labor minister shall be Chanoir; the health minister shall be Mix…"

The rank-and-file workers weren't interested at all. Many people around me started yawning. None of it affected us personally, after all.

"…The agricultural minister shall be Beelzebub…"

At first, I didn't really understand what she said.

Actually, it might be more apt to say that I ignored it. This couldn't have to do with me.

Beelzebub was the name of a great demon from the past, so it wouldn't have been strange to hear of other civil servants with the same name. It was probably someone else, someone important in the agricultural department.

But all my coworkers standing in front of me turned around to look at me with blatant disbelief.

"Wait, can she do that?"

"How many ranks are you going up?"

Everyone was thinking I was going to be the agricultural minister…

"Wait, wait! This has to be a mistake! I've always been at the bottom; I can't be the minister!" I cried with conviction.

Such a personnel shift was unthinkable!

But the new demon king continued with her explanation.

"Beelzebub has worked dependably for one thousand, five hundred years in agricultural policy. She has also helped many of her coworkers and is extraordinarily popular. In the past, we received many comments in the suggestion box requesting she be placed in an important post. And yet, she herself never boasted about it, working for years as an unsung hero. I believe the time has finally come to raise her into a position of authority."

The new demon king replied with a lengthy and unbelievable explanation. Perhaps she was just trying to catch everyone by surprise with a sensational cabinet selection because she was young, but I wouldn't be part of this!

Once I took on the position of minister, a colossal amount of work would be waiting for me. I certainly wouldn't be able to continue the easy life I had now. My humble delights would crumble to dust...

I would not stand for this.

I leaped out of my row.

"I am Beelzebub! Your Majesty, I don't think this assignment will be possible!"

It was a rude thing to do to the demon king, but desperate times called for desperate measures, and no one was coming to stop me.

The new demon king looked down at me playfully from the stage. I could see on her face that she had predicted this very reaction.

Which meant I hadn't been imagining it when I thought our eyes met...

"It seems you are not satisfied with the situation," the new demon king said to me, blatantly ignoring our difference in status.

I wanted to applaud her for her frank tone, but my promotion was what was at stake here.

"Of course I'm not! The minister's post is for a person who is already important! Someone fourth or fifth in the pecking order may end up becoming a minister, but there's no precedent for bottom-tier trash like me to take the position!"

I hadn't been working for 1,500 years for show. I *knew* this was unprecedented.

"I see. What you say is correct. So I will answer your question." It wasn't like the new demon king was using any kind of voice-enhancing magic, but it still carried really well. "You've been serving for one thousand, five hundred years; is that correct?"

"Yes. I was originally helping out with my parents' greengrocery, so I only took and passed the civil service exam after I turned one thousand. And for the fifteen hundred years since then, I've been working where I am now."

I wondered why I had to give my life story in front of everyone, but if this was going to create a scandal and make it clear that I shouldn't be promoted that far up, then that was reasonable to me.

"So you've been working for the current public Agricultural Policy Organization for fifteen hundred years, Beelzebub. In that case, it should've been impossible for you to remain at an entry-level position this whole time. Yet there's no record of you having been promoted."

"I've turned down every offer of promotion because it would be beyond my abilities."

My job was just to complete the tasks that came down to me from the top, no thought required. I'd always be in a position for others to use me, but I wouldn't have to take on any heavy responsibility.

I could hear my colleagues: "Someone's been at the bottom for fifteen hundred years?" and "I guess that's not a post that comes with a fixed term."

It was true; the way I worked was not a common trick.

This might've been difficult to pull off if I were human, but demons were long-lived, and with my youthful looks, my low position wouldn't seem strange.

"Indeed, and so I've calculated to see what would've happened if you had been continually promoted with your grades. Please look at this."

A plan written on a large poster unfurled next to the new demon king—she must've had this ready beforehand.

"Taking into account your service record, service history, and reputation among your bosses and colleagues, you have accumulated results that prove there would be no problem if you became minister. Congratulations!"

"Wh-wh-wha…?"

I wanted to believe it was a dream and softly pinched my left arm.

Ow.

Around me, I could hear comments:

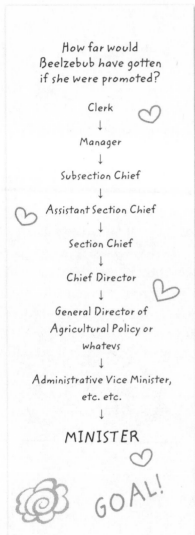

How far would
Beelzebub have gotten
if she were promoted?

Clerk
↓
Manager
↓
Subsection Chief
↓
Assistant Section Chief
↓
Section Chief
↓
Chief Director
↓
General Director of
Agricultural Policy or
whatevs
↓
Administrative Vice Minister,
etc. etc.
↓
MINISTER

GOAL!

"I see. Making a big jump after raising your reputation by working hard for a very long time on the bottom is one way to do it."

"Maybe it's like trying to become the strongest by only killing slimes."

Wait, wait, wait—why are they okay with this...?

The new demon king placed her right hand against her right cheek and sighed theatrically.

"*Sigh~* I also thought of a more orthodox personnel selection, but we discovered corruption as well as embezzlement from both the vice minister and employees in similar posts, so we asked them to resign~ I was truly lost as to who I should make the minister of agriculture~"

The new demon king eyed me again, chuckling softly.

Oh, so she's a prankster...

This was just a big experiment using me, a low-ranking employee...

Give me a break! I don't want to be your guinea pig!

"Then I thought that perhaps this was our chance to use someone who'd spent their career at the bottom and yet maintained an excellent reputation."

After she said that, the other bureaucrats around me offered more comments.

"Ohhh, I get it now."

"That's one way of going about it."

Why are you okay with this?!

Calm down; calm down. I'll be doing just what the new demon king wants if I get worked up here.

I was still a civil servant, so I should calmly refuse the offer as was afforded in the rules.

"Your Majesty, in this instance, I would respectfully recommend that I remain a low-level employee."

I bowed my head politely and folded my wings. They had spread in my excitement, and it'd be rude to keep them out.

"Oh, no. It's normal to appoint people who've shown great achievements."

"However, I'm the daughter of a humble greengrocer in the country-side. What I want to say is, I don't have any noble status or any similar rank. It has been the long-standing practice that those of noble standing take the position of minister. I am completely undeserving of this post, and I am terribly sorry to say that I can't accept it."

Despite how quickly the bureaucratic organization had developed in the past two thousand years, there were still slight traces of a class system among the demons.

Depending on the era, minister-level demons would sometimes command their subordinates to carry out massive wars against the humans, so it required someone with a rank worthy of such responsibility.

"I see now. What a pickle~"

"Yes, so if you would kindly choose someone else to—"

"Then I will give you an empty manor belonging to a former noble family. And I will also give you a title. You may introduce yourself as Lady Beelzebub. Problem solved."

"......What?"

She decided on that far too easily...

Then the new demon king stepped down from the stage and, for some reason, started walking toward me.

The civil servants on either side of her naturally parted the way for her. I also courteously knelt before her.

"Beelzebub, this may seem unreasonable to you, but had you climbed up through the ranks normally, you would truly be a talent on par with the minister after working so hard for fifteen hundred years. The score that the personnel department gave you was unnaturally high. In reality, plenty of other posts requested you, but agricultural policy stopped them all."

"Th-that's because a clerk's work is easy, so it probably just looked like I was working hard…"

"Raise your head, Beelzebub."

I had to obey when she commanded me. There stood the new demon king, smiling with royal dignity.

She then plopped her hand on my shoulder.

"It was the previous demon king who settled the war with the humans. But there are a heap of problems yet, and the agricultural department is full of them. Right now, we require new forces without prior obligations tying them down. This is a request from me, Demon King Provato Pecora Ariés."

The new demon king graciously bowed her head to me.

All my options for excuses were gone. I'd shame her if I turned her down now.

Not only would I not be able to keep my easy low-level job, I wouldn't even be able to live in Vanzeld Castle town.

"I—I humbly accept the appointment…"

And so I, Beelzebub, suddenly went from entry-level clerk to the minister of agriculture.

I had to bid farewell to my run-down apartment and its proximity to the market, which was really the only good thing about it. It was a sudden good-bye.

I was moving to a stout three-story building outside of the Vanzeld Castle moat. It reminded me of the main branch of a bank. The yard in front of the manor was even big enough to play sports on. There was a garden with a large pond in the back, and I'd heard that rocs sometime came to drink the water. Behind it was a whole forest, like a sea of trees.

When I stood before the building, I stared at it in blank amazement.

"If there was a coup tomorrow, I'd probably be one of the first to die…"

I checked every single one of the large, abundant rooms. One room was already bigger than my old apartment. There was even a ballroom.

I'd have to employ some kind of help in the future. Otherwise, I'd have to take off every day to clean if I wanted to keep up. Or I could just use the minimum amount of rooms needed for my day-to-day life…

Then I saw something in the enormous mirror in the changing room before the chalky-white bathroom.

I was terrified.

Standing there was a woman with no hope of getting ahead, with no prospects for entering society, with no money—with nothing, because she'd thrown it all away.

It wasn't a ghost, of course. Demons weren't scared of ghosts.

The only thing in the mirror was my own face.

Indeed—standing out wouldn't do anything for a low-level employee, so I'd had no qualms about it. I'd treated my appearance as a good way to keep as many people on my side as possible.

But now I was a noble and a minister.

Someone in those positions couldn't look this plain. I wouldn't be mistaken for a minister's secretary, much less a full-blown minister.

Even if the new demon king acknowledged me, that didn't mean the other ministers from real houses wouldn't snicker behind my back. And my staff would undeniably laugh at me, too…

I made up my mind.

It's time I change my character.

*　　*　　*

I placed as many gold and silver coins into a bag as I could fit and went out onto the main avenue.

I bought everything that caught my eye at a women's clothing shop and returned to the manor. Then I carefully tried on each item before the mirror.

It would have been nice if I had had friends for a time like this, but I didn't have any. Seriously, zero.

In reality, after working at a low-level position for 1,500 years, I had watched all the people I'd joined with go to higher ranks, and there was no one in the workplace I got along well with. It was all my own doing.

Glasses didn't fit my character, so I took them off. I didn't have bad eyesight in the first place, so it was no problem.

I chose my outfit. It was a little revealing, but ministers were like dungeon bosses, so I figured this was fine.

Next up was my style of speech. I couldn't stay as a bottom-ranking employee—I had to master an appropriate style of speech. Your word choice clearly changed depending on your status, so I had to learn how to speak like a minister.

I underwent a strange, intensive training.

I practiced all through the night until the sun rose, and I established my form.

"Ha-ha-ha! My name is Beelzebub! I am the great Lord of the Flies! Prepare yourself, for I will make you painfully aware of what agriculture should be!" I recited, striking a pose in front of the mirror.

No—I *introduced* myself, taking my stance before the mirror.

"I am Beelzebub, demon noble and minister of agriculture. Adequate results will not be enough for those of you beneath me. Oh, talking like this might end up putting pressure on my subordinates, so I'll have to be careful… Oh shoot, now I'm talking like I used to…"

I'd been practicing my transformation this entire time.

Ten out of ten people might think I was joking around, but—

I wasn't joking around at all! I was super-serious!

Without these drastic changes, I didn't have confidence that I could carry out my work from now on...

And I wasn't *the* great Beelzebub, Lord of the Flies, of course. I could use magic that could turn me into a fly, and I did sometimes eat the bruised fruit at my parents' greengrocery back when I was working there. Actually, they were tastiest just before or just as they were beginning to rot.

Oh, no, no... I mean... Oh dear. Sheesh. I have to keep my inner voice consistent with my character.

I stared at myself in the mirror.

My clothes left my shoulders bare, and my hair was straightened to give me a more powerful image.

All I needed to do was show confidence on my face and hold myself high.

"I am Beelzebub, minister of agriculture. I am Beelzebub, minister of agriculture. I am Beelzebub, minister of agriculture, and so I shall act as of today. My inconspicuous self is a thing of the past."

And so I went to work at the Agricultural Policy Organization for the first time as the new Beelzebub.

'Twas my debut as the minister of agriculture!

"Good morning. How fare my underlings?!"

My coworkers stared at me blankly.

Surely they were surprised by my noble carriage! Perhaps they thought I was a pure-blooded noble!

A lowly woman who was once my coworker slowly raised her hand and said—

"Beelzebub, you're the minister of agriculture; I don't think this is where you're supposed to work..."

"......Indeed. Old habits die hard."

I left the room, my face bright red...

"I should not have left my comfort zone..."

MY NAME IS
AGRICULTURAL
THE DEMON

I Was a Bottom-Tier Bureaucrat for 1,500 Years, and the Demon King Made Me a Minister

BEELZEBUB, MINISTER OF REALM!

©Benio

Communicating with My _____ Underlings Is a Pain

There was a huge sign that said MINISTRY OF AGRICULTURE, and I stood before the building where it hung.

"So this is my workplace…" I looked up at it and recoiled. "I am suddenly working at the main office, and as the minister herself, no less…"

I'd been told that working in the ministry building was much harder than working at the related organizations, and I had been planning on consistently working not here but at the Agricultural Policy Organization.

It was once my path to victory…

"I can no longer go back… I cannot quit after two or three days; I have no choice but to work as the minister of agriculture…"

Bureaucratic officials busily came and went around me like ants hard at work.

It was now a new era with a new demon king, and that probably brought with it plenty of paperwork.

I watched it all for a while.

I had changed my image from a plain-glasses character to a high-ranking demon, and not only that, but no one recognized me as the minister because I barely knew anyone. That made it easy.

But on the other hand, when I entered the building, people stared at me, wondering who I was.

"...I should have come through the back door..."

I went up the floors by a staircase that wasn't being used.

The minister's office was a big room on the top floor. *Whew, I managed to get this far in secret.*

Then, when I slipped into the office—

I found a whole line of officials.

Everyone was gathered already!

I saw all sorts of different horns, as demons had. I even saw a minotaur and a Cyclops among them.

They all turned to face me at once, noticing my arrival.

This was bad for my heart. They were wondering why such a low-ranking worker was promoted to minister and thinking of how incompetent I was, I was sure...

Then a woman with unique horns took a step forward.

"Pardon me. I don't recognize you, so you must be Minister Beelzebub, yes?"

"I-indeed... It is I, Beelzebub..."

"Then I ask that you make a few remarks as you assume your post now. Oh, pardon me—I am Fatla the leviathan, secretary here at the Department of Agriculture," she said, unsmiling.

Leviathans were high-ranking demons in their own right.

At the moment, she resembled a human, but I'd heard that a leviathan's original form was like an airborne battleship that could carry hundreds of people.

So she must be a career civil servant...

I knew what she was thinking: *What a terrible joke, making a small fry like this into a minister.*

My stomach started hurting. My body wouldn't be absorbing anything I ate now.

"Some initial remarks, you say. Very well. I don't want to cause you any trouble, so I'll finish it quick...er, I shall finish this promptly, so stay there."

It was hard to play my supercilious character before officials who were *actually* important. But it would be awful if I made a fool of myself at first contact.

I stood before the officials. Walking just those few steps to reach my spot was spiritually exhausting, like walking through a deadly poisonous bog.

"Erm... I am Beelzebub, and I am the minister of agriculture as of today... In all honesty, I am powerless and unable to do much of importance, but I believe that together, we may overcome this...so..."

Was that okay?

But I was calling myself powerless; was I just making a fool of myself? Wouldn't that just tempt them to underestimate me?

I thought I heard someone snickering.

It was probably just paranoia, but I definitely thought I heard someone! *I have no choice but to toot my own horn now!*

I spread out my wings in a snap.

"'Twas but a joke! I have been chosen to take this place by the omniscient and omnipotent demon king! As such, I possess a great power that will guide you! So, so...er... Should there be anything you do not know or any problem you may have, you come to me!! I shall brilliantly solve all your problems as your superior!"

""Yeah!!!""""

The officers raised their voices in admiration.

That was the right answer. I got through it without acting servile.

I heard whispers:

"She looks like she has it together."

"Maybe she really is from a high-ranking family."

My first impression wasn't bad.

"Perhaps she really is a policy expert."

"Maybe she was, like, a right-hand man for the previous demon king."

"You can keep an eye on a lot if you stay down at the lower levels."

"She must be the reason all the high-ranking officials' scandals were exposed at the same time!"

Mmm... Now I suspect they are overestimating me!

"I was wondering what we'd do with a shabby entry-level worker, but that isn't the case at all."

"She's a secret bigwig."

"With her, we could even win our disputes with the finance ministry."

"She must have the next hundred, two hundred years planned out for the demon race."

"Long live the new minister!"

Their hopeful looks hurt more this time...

I'm not a policy expert, not even in a worst-case scenario...

I was just someone from a tiny, distant corner of the agricultural ministry. I was only ever confident in my abilities to do miscellaneous chores... I wasn't even thinking about what was going to happen in a month. The most I ever thought about was whether I was going to drink at home or at a bar on the weekends.

I thought I had to start showing results fit for a minister right away, otherwise things would be bad...

"Then you are dismissed... Get to it now..."

The officials poured out of the minister's office.

Phew, that was stressful. I was finally free...

But there were still two left in the room.

One was the earlier leviathan, Fatla. The other was another leviathan who looked a lot like her.

"Well done, Lady Beelzebub. Allow me to introduce myself again. I am Fatla, the secretary. It is my job to assist the minister of agriculture. It's a pleasure to meet you."

Right, she did say she was a secretary earlier, too.

Oh man, I already had someone so square and straitlaced attached to me. I wouldn't be able to relax like this...

©Benio

"Yes. A pleasure. And who's that beside you?"

The second girl flung her hand into the air. "Hello! I'm Vania the leviathan. I'm the assistant secretary and Fatla's little sister! It's nice to meet you!"

I see. It was the sisters who were assisting me. Their personalities were exact opposites.

"Right, right. Well, it's—'tis lovely to meet both of you."

I stuck my hand out toward Fatla. A handshake was a general way to show respect.

Fatla grasped my hand, still not smiling. Maybe that was her default.

Asking her to smile didn't seem like the right way to go about this, though.

"By the way, Lady Beelzebub?"

"What?"

"You've made quite the transformation. Is this your attempt at a debut as a minister?"

She hit me right where it hurt. The attack was surprisingly close to home.

"I don't...do not understand what you mean."

"That manner of speech of yours is a mere facade, and I can see your faults surfacing. You clearly rushed to create this whole charade after being forced into the position of minister, correct? You were planning on living your whole life as a lazy low-level clerk, weren't you?"

This conversation was draining my magic dry...

"Q-quite the opposite... Now that I am a minister, I'm able to be myself, and, you know, it's like the persona I've hidden all this time is rising to the surface..."

"Is that so? I see. I see now."

This leviathan woman didn't smile at all, so it was hard to tell what she was thinking. But from the circumstantial evidence, I was undoubtedly being cornered...

"My only duty is to make sure that the new minister is comfortable doing her work. Let me know if there's anything I may help you with."

"Yeah... All right."

Our hands were still clasped together, but Fatla wasn't letting me go.

I was above her in status, but I was from a family of scruffy demons, so I was nervous in front of a leviathan.

"However—"

Oh no. That "however" told me straightaway that what she just said wasn't how she really felt!

"I'm not working because you're paying my salary, Lady Beelzebub. I am at most a bureaucrat working to support our country. If you are not fit for the office of minister and I judge that agricultural policy has regressed, then I will be taking the appropriate measures."

"So you're kicking me out if I don't do a good job..."

It wasn't hot at all, but I was starting to sweat.

This is scary! The bureaucratic world is terrifying! I wanna go back to the bottom!

"I don't appreciate the term *kick out*. I will simply take the proper steps to deal with the situation as a public servant," Fatla continued in a monotonous voice. "In the event of any major mistakes, I will suggest that you make it public instead of attempting a cover-up; I will question you if I see any dishonest accounting; I will suggest you quit if you find yourself unable to bear the weight of your duties as minister because you are unwell—and any other such measures I deem necessary."

Ahhh! She's totally gonna kick me out!

"And so I would be perfectly fine if you considered me as a regular secretary."

This is intimidation! What am I supposed to do if my own secretary is my enemy?! This is like putting the demon king in the hero's party! I wanna quit!

But if I quit, then the demon king would be responsible for appointing someone new, and I suspected I'd be erased from existence for the crime of besmirching the demon king's name. There was no real assurance that I would be safe if I quit.

There was no way out...

"I got it. I've spent fifteen hundred years at the bottom of the ministry, after all. I am not a complete amateur. I will do everything in my power!" I told her sharply.

But she was still stern with me.

"Very well. I sincerely hope you are right." Fatla finally let me go.

These leviathan sisters weren't my assistants. They were monitoring me.

Once my handshake with the elder sister was finished, the younger sister, Vania, immediately skipped over to me and shook my hand.

"Can't wait to get started, boss!"

"Yes, of course."

I had to keep my guard up—she could be acting like a sunny, cheerful girl when she was actually the mastermind behind it all.

In the action novels I read in the past, the more a character smiled, the stronger they were, and they wouldn't bat an eye when it came to killing others.

"All right, then, boss. There's something I need for you to pick."

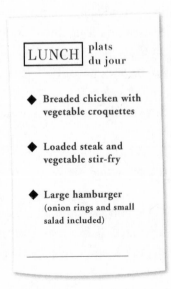

LUNCH plats du jour

◆ Breaded chicken with vegetable croquettes

◆ Loaded steak and vegetable stir-fry

◆ Large hamburger (onion rings and small salad included)

"And what might that be…?"

I didn't know if I was being tested or anything, so I was extremely uneasy.

Vania produced a piece of paper.

"We need to contact the traders who deliver lunch soon. Which one do you want, boss?"

These choices had nothing to do with work!

"Vania, you can leave this for later…"

Fatla, the elder sister, looked at her with annoyance, silently asking her not to ruin the mood.

"Whaaat? Picking what to have for lunch is so important, though! It helps give you another push in the morning."

The younger sister had the energy of an entry-level worker. There sure were all sorts of people on the career ladder…

"Then…I suppose I shall have the loaded steak-and-vegetable stir-fry…"

"Okay! I will put in that order right away! Oh, and by the way, I'm very good at cooking, so as long as you let me know beforehand, I can make lunch for you about once a week."

"That's not secretary work!"

The big sister, Fatla, was angry again.

Maybe they had been appointed together as secretaries because they canceled each other out and worked well together as a pair?

My work as the minister of agriculture started that day.

My main job was signing things.

The signing itself took only a fraction of a second to do, but when it came to matters that needed the approval of the minister, the matters themselves had to have some weight, and occasionally they involved the movement of astronomical sums of money. I couldn't just scribble on these and call it a day.

Having said that, if I vetoed all the things that had been considered okay up until this point just because I was at the top, I'd be a tyrant.

And so I had to sign things while also carefully checking the contents.

Luckily, I had a very knowledgeable secretary with me, so that made it easy.

Fatla was the perfect bureaucrat.

The new demon king must have had a say in these personnel appointments beforehand, so maybe she put the sisters here as my personal support, regardless of what Fatla herself thought.

"This farm should not pose any problems, yes? I believe they could produce this more cheaply, though."

"You may check anything concerning the budget in the attached document."

"Can I ask you some things about this application for authorization?"

"Certainly. There isn't much time to ruminate on it, however, so do make up your mind quickly."

In a word, I'd say I was doing pretty well. But I wasn't exactly enthusiastic about it all; I was just desperate. There was no room for me to slack off and do sloppy work.

For the first three months, I dedicated a lot of time to getting a grasp on the current state of the agricultural administration.

I had lunch with people beneath me who were responsible for relevant matters as much as I could, and then I examined each department's own problems and what they perceived to be problems.

I could do only what I could, so that was what I did.

I put everything I learned down into my notes.

It was a lot of trouble, but I ended up creating volume after volume of notes. This was my strategy for dealing with things, one that I had cultivated when I was a low-level employee.

Write and remember. Write and arrange.

When things felt difficult and confusing, they could be conquered in this manner. Learn a strategy to deal with it and understand the precedents!

Six months went by in a flash.

"You are quite the stickler for notes, Lady Beelzebub," Fatla said to me as she was checking documents on the desk beside mine.

She was making her little sister, Vania, do mostly menial tasks, like disposing of or retrieving documents.

It wasn't too odd for her position, since she was a lower-ranked secretary, and she personally enjoyed moving around.

"'Tis much harder for me to forget things when I write them down with my own hand like this. No matter how many documents I collect, I have such trouble remembering the government's style. If I make a little list of all the things in the library, I can find them immediately; I wouldn't be able to find them without one, no? It's the same idea."

I'd even gotten quite used to my grandiloquent minister speech after six months.

At the moment, I hadn't made any big mistakes. I hadn't been impeached yet, at least, so I supposed that meant it was going quite well.

I didn't have any opportunities to do anything untoward, so I wasn't involved in corruption at all. Well, I didn't even belong to any faction, so I suppose there was little to be gained by abusing my power...

"I see. You are a different breed from all the past ministers, Lady Beelzebub." Fatla finished her checks and placed the documents on my desk. "They all have been eager to be political—or should I say, eager to wield the power they'd accumulated. Perhaps it's a given, considering this is the highest position they may reach without the blood of a demon king, but in exchange, they tended to neglect the fundamental work."

"That's because I started from the bottom—well, more like I leaped from the bottom straight to the top. Of course my perspective is different."

Recently, I started to be able to pinpoint where the main point of a document was amid the complicated language. Practice was everything. I determined that there were no problems and gave my signature.

"To be honest, I said some brash things to you when we first met, but now I realize that my comments were unwarranted," Fatla said suddenly. She stood to face me, then bowed her head. "Please forgive me for testing you."

I turned my gaze right back to the documents. It was nothing to apologize for.

"'Tis only natural to worry that an unknown was suddenly the minister of agriculture. While they were not as open about it as you were, others were certainly thinking the same way. If a newbie is angry at being called a newbie, then a cow might as well be angry at being called a cow."

"Thank you." Fatla bowed.

I thought I saw a little smile on her face, but I couldn't really tell because I was focused on paperwork.

"There's no reason to give your thanks. Now get back to work. After you do a bit more, you should take some time off and spend it with your little sister. I can keep things moving without a secretary for a day, at least. I have most things memorized now."

"Very well. I will strive to match your clerical prowess, Lady Beelzebub."

"I doubt there is much difference between our skills."

"No, you are truly the most capable of all the recent ministers of agriculture, Lady Beelzebub."

That was probably because I didn't conspire with other high-up officers.

The role of a worker at the bottom was just doing clerical tasks as the situation called for it. When someone climbed up from such a position, people would start one-upping each other with what sort of projects they did in their time.

I was still merely a clerk at heart. I acted all high-and-mighty for show, but I hadn't changed the way I lived.

"That being said, it's always around the six-month mark after beginning a new post that people tend to let their guard down and make bigger mistakes, so do be careful."

"Yes, of course. I understand. I am still not relaxed enough to let my guard down yet."

Now, next was some work relating to the construction of a seed nursery center. Many people were going to be removed from the land as part of that process, so I had a large number of valuable documents asking for consent to remove the residents there.

"Mmm? All the documents that should have been here are gone."

The things I had placed next to Vania's spot on my left were missing.

Vania was up from her seat, burning documents we didn't need anymore in the furnace.

"Vania, the set of seed nursery center documents is gone. Where is it?"

"Huh? I thought you didn't need those anymore? You always put the documents you don't need anymore to your left, right?"

"No, I placed them to the open spot on my left because it would take time to check them."

Vania's face went white. "I—I—I—I—I—I burned them..."

"You did *whaaaaaaaaaaaaaaaaaat*?????????"

The one who let her guard down six months after taking the post wasn't me but my secretary!!!!!

Vania fell to her knees, and Fatla pulled her up with a blank expression. There was no emotion on her face, but I could tell she was furious.

"You were supposed to double-check every single document you take from this room before destroying it. Did you do that?"

"I-I'm sorry... I thought they were in a discard pile..."

"This is a huge question of liability. You will most certainly be demoted, and according to precedent, we might have you resign at your own convenience."

"Wait, I'm fired? Am I going to be fired...?"

"Those papers included documents asking for the consent to remove over fifty civilian households, as well as those of various other related parties. It would take an immense amount of time to go around and ask each and every one of these people to write them all over again, please and thanks. In the worst-case scenario, this would delay construction by one or two months..." Fatla's voice was growing louder and louder. "Quitting is the least you could do!"

Fatla's hand slowly wrapped around Vania's neck.

That was a leviathan hand, so her grip was probably insanely strong.

"E-erm... Isn't there any way we can find an amicable compromise, Big Sis...?"

"You will have to bear the blame. Otherwise, the responsibility rests on Lady Beelzebub's shoulders! Secretaries have disappeared after taking the fall for such incidents! Although I suppose the secretary really was at fault this time..."

Fatla's hands were shaking.

It was definitely hard for her to say such things to her sister.

But it was also true that we needed a scapegoat in this incident. It wouldn't resolve itself.

Oh well.

I slowly stood.

We'll just have a scapegoat, then.

"Fatla, rearrange the schedule. Once we've estimated how long this will delay the project, we will go apologize to each party. Most people will have no choice but to forgive us if I apologize. If the minister herself goes, I doubt anyone will lose face."

"B-but you have absolutely no fault in this matter, Lady Beelzebub...," Fatla said hesitantly.

It was her own relative who made the mistake, so it was probably especially difficult to stick up for her.

"Don't be a fool. 'Tis the boss's job to take responsibility for her subordinates. I had many bosses bow in my stead when I was a low-level clerk. Now I must be the one to apologize. If all I do is offer my apology, then there is nothing more you need to do!"

We just needed to get this nonsense done and out of the way.

"Now, Fatla, create the necessary documents. The quicker we apologize, the lesser the damages. And while we are at it, we shall also create preventative measures to ensure this does not happen again. There should be no more problems if we only place documents for destruction on a separate desk."

"Y-yes!" Fatla tensed her shoulders and responded with a high, strained voice.

"But first, take a deep breath. That is all."

Fatla inhaled deeply as she was commanded, then gave a very long exhale.

"Understood. I will devise remedial measures right away."

Afterward, Vania and I paid each party concerned a visit, apologized for the loss of the documents, and spent almost the whole time with our heads bowed to the floor.

The minister herself appearing for the incident had a tremendous effect, and it was understood that we would be re-creating the documents internally at the ministry.

Thus, we went on our apology pilgrimage, and thanks to Fatla's efficient schedule, there wasn't much damage done in terms of time.

It was times like these that I was thankful we could fly on the leviathans' enormous forms.

But I couldn't go too fast, so I clung to Vania when we went to certain places.

We were finally done apologizing and re-creating documents after about two weeks, and we somehow managed to settle the matter without any delays to construction.

"Phew, that's finally over!"

After I had carefully gone over every re-created form, I stretched my body and wings.

Fatla was stretching at her own seat as well.

"There is no need for you to bow your head anymore, Vania! How many times do you think you've bowed in total this time?" I said, intending to make a joke—

But it fell completely flat.

"I...I am truly sorry, so very sorry..."

When Vania had gone out with me to apologize, she had been frightened and jumpy the whole time, like a frog before a snake.

I wouldn't approve if she'd been laughing the whole time we were out apologizing, but the constant doom and gloom made things difficult, too.

This was one of those times I had to act like a boss. I patted Vania on the shoulder and said, "Are you free today? I would like to have a drink with you—how about it?"

"A-all right…" Vania's face went even paler.

Wait, don't tell me—maybe bosses aren't supposed to invite their subordinates to drink in this day and age…?

I didn't take Vania to a loud tavern but instead to a fancy bar.

I'd heard from my officers that this place had a decent reputation.

"Order what you like. The food here is quite good."

But even after I'd brought her all the way here, Vania was stiffer than before. I almost mistook her for a gargoyle instead of a leviathan.

"Relax. You're quite important yourself—take up as much space as you need."

"I—I can't…"

Hmm? This was strange. I read in a how-to book that the boss treated everyone jovially at times like these, but this was feeling more like a funeral…

Was she afraid I would boast on and on about the past or force her to split the bill at such an expensive restaurant?

I was paying for everything. And since I had been a bottom-tier worker, there was nothing for me to brag about. From the way she was acting, I had a feeling she was afraid of something else.

What else could there be?

Maybe she'd made an even bigger mistake…? If she had, then I wasn't sure how much more I could cover for her…

"If there is something that troubles you, speak up. That is why we've come here. My lips are sealed. I am your boss, after all."

I had subordinates now. I would act like the boss I was supposed to be!

"A-a-all right... Then let me ask you bluntly..."

"O-okay..."

"Um... You're demoting me, aren't you...?"

I almost fell from my barstool. "What do you mean, 'aren't you'? When did I ever mention demoting you?"

"I mean, I've smeared your name with this whole incident... I thought some form of retaliation was inevitable..."

"Wait, wait, wait! That makes no sense! Why do you think I went to apologize with you?!"

What a shock! I wasn't telling her to be thankful for everything I did for her; I just wanted her to be glad that she wasn't being punished!

"That's what I thought at first, but...then you invited me alone to such an expensive restaurant, so I thought, 'Oh, she must be announcing the end of my clerical life...'"

That's how she interpreted this?!

"And then I started imagining all sorts of things, like how I'd be put in a windowless room to count the number of rejected papers..."

"There is no such job."

"I spent this whole time thinking, 'Maybe it's fine because I'll still get paid; maybe it's better than quitting; no wait, maybe I should just quit anyway...'"

Didn't that go against her obligation to give her undivided attention to her duty?

I patted her on the shoulder.

"Ahhh...the fabled shoulder tap... I knew I was being demoted! I'm going to be flown out to the far, uninhabited reaches of the north and placed at a counter where no one will ever come!"

"You need to let this go already." I gulped down some of the expensive alcohol. "Look, I invited you out to drink today because you have been looking down. Drink as much as you want to forget your troubles. That is all I wanted to say."

"Th-then…you're not demoting me…?"

"Of course not. Drink and forget the pain of the past. Order freely: I shall pay for it all!"

"…Boss…are you a god?!"

"Not at all. I am a demon." I grinned like a high-ranking demon.

That was the first time in my life I treated someone as a proper boss would.

I was maturing, too.

I didn't mind the bottom-tier life, but perhaps the minister life wouldn't be so bad after all.

—Two hours later.

I walked through the city with a drunk Vania on my back. "I never expected she'd be causing me problems in this way…"

"Eh-he-he-he… Booze, booze…"

Vania was completely gone, so I had to take her home myself. I did such things when I was a lowly clerk and my bosses drank themselves into a stupor, but to think I'd do this as the minister of agriculture…

I wanted to fly her home, but I was drunk, too. Causing an accident while flying under the influence was a grave offense…

I somehow managed to reach the residential district, and there was Fatla, standing at the corner.

"I am so sorry, Lady Beelzebub. My sister is so irresponsible…" She bowed to me with a tired look.

"You've been putting in quite a lot of work as well, haven't you? But I clearly see why you were chosen to be my secretary."

"What do you mean?" She looked at me quizzically.

"Your hands are quite full taking care of your little sister. That is why they deemed you capable of handling a minister who did not know her right from her left."

Fatla's mouth opened in surprise.

She had treated me rather gruffly at first but was still a solid assistant for me after all that. She worked hard, exactly as she needed to as a good secretary.

Otherwise, my efforts on my own were insignificant; my work as minister wouldn't be very effective.

Had Fatla not created countermeasures for Vania's mistake this time, things would have been more complicated for much longer. And if that happened, I would probably have had to drop the problematic secretary after all.

"Fatla, do you think I can become a minister good enough for you to serve?"

"As of now, you're about seventy-five percent there."

I wanted eighty, but that was still a passing grade.

"Now do something about your sister." I handed over Vania.

"Lady Beelzebub, I am truly glad you are our minister." Fatla gave me a gentle, natural smile.

"And I'll take you to a good spot next time, too."

The night breeze on my way home felt perfect.

I think I'm starting to enjoy my work as the minister of agriculture.

"Oh, I see nothing else for me to sign."

"Lady Beelzebub, that one was the last for today. Well done," Fatla said, straightening out the stack of paper by tapping it against the desk.

That was high praise coming from Fatla. One might not notice at first, but she rarely openly complimented me. Though I suppose it would be strange if my own employee came up to me, patted me on the head, and called me a good girl.

Ah yes. I suppose I can rest a little now.

These lulls in the deluge of paperwork weren't so bad—when things started getting down to the wire, my hands could get so full that I couldn't afford to stand up and stretch.

"Boss, you've gotten a lot faster at work!" Vania cheered. Praise from both ends of the spectrum. But of course—

"Vania, please do something about that desk of yours..."

—there were still mountains of paperwork waiting on Vania.

"Boy, I'd planned on finishing a while ago, but then I was dreaming about a school trip from years and years back..."

"You were sleeping?! Do your job!"

I had to help her anyway. Alas, my poor break. Still, work was far easier now than it once was; there was no doubt about that. Recently, I could even afford to pamper myself on my days off.

Although, to be more specific, I had far too many rooms in my house to use well, so I simply sequestered myself in the few rooms I lived in and slept until noon...

My standard of living had not changed much. Actively improving my living situation required far too much effort.

"Oh right. I forgot to check if any of the afternoon mail is for you!" Vania rushed out of the room.

"That girl forgets too much... Why can't she do things properly...?" Fatla rubbed her temples.

Her life must have been quite an ordeal, looking after her sister for so long. This was Fatla's career, yes, but her time in it would not have been purely smooth sailing. All lives had their ups and downs.

Or perhaps that was the natural consequence for those who didn't put as much effort as I did into maintaining an uneventful, predictable life. Even the fields that seem flat from far away are full of ridges and stones once you walk through them.

But right now, the demon king's schemes had me working as the minister of agriculture, so I hadn't exactly succeeded in my endeavor...

If I'd known this would happen, perhaps I should have taken over my family's grocery store in the countryside? No, running a shop would bring its own challenges. I would be in debt in the worst-case scenario. That wasn't for me. I made the right choice in coming to Vanzeld.

A little while later, Vania returned with a basket full of mail.

"Here's your afternoon letter drop, boss!"

"Mmm, well done. Just put them there."

I would sort through it myself. Few letters came to the minister directly.

As usual, more than half of what I received were farming magazines. Several departments within the ministry were subscribed to them.

"*Demon Farmers Monthly, Demon Farming Tools Monthly, Farming Artifacts Monthly, Wheat Cultivation Monthly, Double-Cropping*

Monthly, Cyclops & Lumber Monthly, Pests Monthly... There are too many magazines."

"It is what it is. Telling them we want to unsubscribe will only hurt the image of the Ministry of Agriculture. Even if you do not read a single page, we must purchase them as a perfunctory measure," Fatla said breezily.

Some of these magazines were very strange, and I knew little about the corporations that created them. I wasn't so sure about using tax money to purchase these. But it wasn't my own money, so it was all right.

"I love the columns in *Cyclops & Lumber Monthly*. They don't hold back; it's so refreshing. Hardly anyone reads it, so they can be as aggressive as they want!"

"Oh, so you have time to read *these*, do you...?"

I wish she would show off some of that diligence when it came to work.

Among the magazines, there was a small envelope addressed to me that caught my eye.

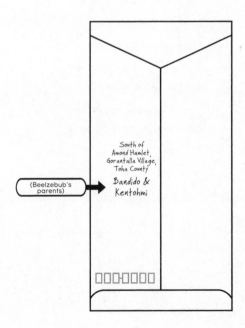

"Oh, a personal letter? I was under the impression that I shouldn't be able to receive things like this."

There were plenty of troublemakers who wanted to tell me, the head of the ministry, their personal opinions on things.

There would truly be no end to their complaints if the minister were to read them all, so there was a different department that checked the contents of these letters. That meant this envelope had already been opened.

"Who is this from?" I flipped the envelope over.

"Bufuh—" I'm not sure how to categorize the sound I made, but I suppose it was closest to a sob.

An envelope from my parents!

I checked inside and found a note.

"Bfffff..."

I made another noise, louder this time.

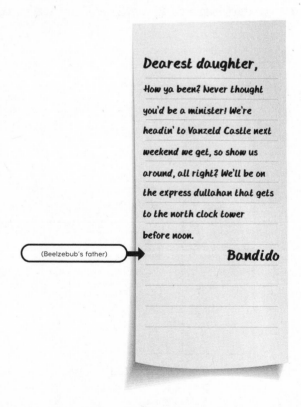

Dearest daughter,

How ya been? Never thought you'd be a minister! We're headin' to Vanzeld Castle next weekend we get, so show us around, all right? We'll be on the express dullahan that gets to the north clock tower before noon.

(Beelzebub's father) →

Bandido

They're coming! This is way too sudden!

I couldn't use work as an excuse if they were coming on a weekend, so I had to show them around… It was as if I'd been surprised with a weekend shift… Please release me…

I hadn't been home in the past several years; there was nothing enjoyable for me there.

But I had not accounted for the possibility that they might visit me.

"Lady Beelzebub, what's the matter? You're making some odd noises," Fatla pointed out. *So even they can tell…*

I couldn't have them knowing about this.

"'Tis nothing…"

"I doubt anyone would react this way over nothing."

"Oh, no, I simply have something in my windpipe."

"If that's true, then please go to the doctor."

If anyone saw my parents, the humiliation would be unimaginable. This was too difficult.

Vania never had much to do on the weekends as far as I could tell. If she found out that my parents were coming, then she might stake out some famous sightseeing spots.

You may think my terror is an overreaction; after all, it's only a visit from my parents. Perhaps some of you might even be thinking about how *I* was before my makeover.

You know nothing.

"It was a fan letter for me from a civilian. Even we bureaucrats have our supporters. I must concentrate and continue to do my best."

I wrapped up that conversation neatly and forcefully, then immediately stuffed the letter into my bag.

Once I had written down where we were to meet, I would burn it…

That weekend, I stood before the north clock tower. This was a transportation hub for all different means of transit from many different regions.

The express dullahan carriages were one of those. My parents could fly, but long distances were exhausting, so they'd chosen to take the overnight express.

Finally, an express dullahan from my home region came to a stop at the parking area.

The driver opened the door to the carriage, and out came my parents, both of them wearing straw hats that were too wide. They were so big, they nearly got caught on the door. Where in the world do they sell hats like those…?

"Woooo, Beelzebub, lookitchu! I'll be a nettle on a bee, you barely look like my girl!"

My father, Bandido, stepped forward. (The expression about nettles and bees meant he was surprised.)

My mother, Kentohmi, then exited the carriage.

"Sure's sugar! Whatta right flar yuwar now, Beelzebub!"

My mother's accent was so strong, I doubted anyone who wasn't local would be able to understand her.

Also, what she just said was *Indeed! You've become quite lovely, Beelzebub!*

"I wish you would've given me more advance notice… It may be a day off for me, but I do sometimes have to make inspections for the ministry, you see…"

My parents looked at each other and burst out laughing. And so loudly, too! *People are staring!*

"Ah-ha-ha-ha-ha-ha-ha! Beelzebub, why're you talkin' all hoity-toity? I'm a right thicket *full* o' bees!"

"Why y'gotta go talkin' fromma high horse? Nettle my bees, I'm rightan my reer now!"

"Oh, it's all right! You understand me, don't you?! And the way you talk, Ma, it's like code only locals can understand!"

Also, my mother said, *You're speaking with such authority. What is the meaning of this? I find it so bizarre that my legs nearly collapsed beneath me, truly!*

And yes, I call my parents Ma and Pa. That's typical where I come from. But soon after moving to Vanzeld, I stopped using those terms of address after discovering it was a very rural way of speaking.

"Wow, ben me-yup, Beelzebub, with'r city talk and city look!"

"Ma, please at least make an effort to use the standard dialect. I don't mind if you speak to me like that, but people in the shops most definitely won't be able to understand a word you say..."

I could hear passersby behind us conversing: "What language is that?" "Dunno. Human speech is easier to understand than that." "I saw a study that said Human and Demon languages are rapidly getting more and more similar now that the war's over."

No one caught a word. Of course they didn't. Even I was having some trouble after spending so long away from home.

"Well. You're here to sightsee, then?"

"We wanna see the Topallar Temple Ruins!"

"Pa, even if we left now, we wouldn't get there until nightfall..."

"Huh? Ain't it right 'round here?"

That was when I knew they had come with no plans.

But perhaps that would be more convenient for me. If we stuck to the main sightseeing areas, then it was unlikely someone I knew would find us. I doubted even Vania would be wandering around the most touristy areas.

"Then I shall lead the way. Be thankful."

"Scuzy ratawn, then, ya mawn-pa'r seenasitty!"

I'm not entirely sure what my mother said, unfortunately.

"Here, this is the Hundredth Triumphal Arch! Just as the name suggests, this one was the one hundredth triumphal arch built, so it was named thusly!"

"Hoo-wee... It's massive..."

"Shoo'nup lakachree!"

The first speaker was my father, and the second was my mother voicing her thoughts, which meant *How tall!*

Yes, going around to see the usual sights would entertain them enough, so I doubted this would be too exhausting—

"All right, Beelzebub. What's next?"

"Already?! That was fast!"

It had only been a minute since we came.

"See, we've gotta go around to all the places we can, or we'll waste our day. We're using profits from the shop t'day."

"Very well… Then next, I shall take you to the Abyssal Springs…"

After five seconds at the spring, my father said, "Awright! What's next?"

"Er, would you mind sitting with your thoughts on the spring for a little while longer…?"

"It's a monster spittin' black water. Got no other thoughts."

That was the truth, so I could not fault him for it.

My mother said something, too, but I could no longer understand a single word out of her. As mother and daughter, perhaps we could simply sense each other's feelings. Yes, it was fine.

Afterward, I introduced them to many, many spots all over.

To be honest, I was rather tired. My throat, especially.

Not only did I have to take them to these places, but I also had to explain what was special about each of them.

And since my parents were visiting many more of them than a typical tourist would, I was doing an astronomical amount of work…

"Umm, this is a lake with a legend where…a demon king, many generations ago, received a spear from a, uh…fiend."

"Beelzebub, your explanations are gettin' all *bower*."

Bower was a regional term for "sloppy."

"Oh, give it a rest. They say throwing a coin into the lake will make your wishes come true, but it's advised that you not pollute the water. I am exhausted… I'd say you two are rather energetic for such a trip… And at your age…"

Even among the long-lived demons, my parents were starting to look middle-aged. That could apparently be fixed with antiaging magic, though.

"Used to it at the store, y'see. We sell heavy barrels of real nice-quality water. And wheat's pretty heavy. And carryin' used horse carts and whatnot can wear ya out, too. And the big sheep…"

What?

Something wasn't right…

"Aren't you grocers?! Why are you selling used carts and sheep?!"

"No other shop to sell 'em at. So we trade it all."

I suppose that happened in the countryside… I started to doubt whether they even carried groceries anymore.

My mother then said, "Where's'a mu'n, Beelzebub?"

"Indeed. I'm getting hungry, so I suppose we should eat."

I wanted to rest a little bit as well, so it was perfect timing.

I took my parents to a somewhat modern restaurant, one that wasn't too trendy for a middle-aged couple.

In my personal opinion, restaurants marketing to young people looking for the next dining revolution didn't always have good food. Famous establishments with a long history generally had a much higher standard.

"That hits the spot~" "Woo, scrum!"

"Right? I doubt you can find anything as good as this in the countryside~"

Oh…

That was when I realized something. I'd gone native.

The town around the castle was practically my home now…

I hadn't cooked the food in this establishment, of course, but the compliment still did wonders for my confidence.

Then my eyes met my father's.

"Beelzebub, it is such a relief to see you like this."

My father, who had worn an expression of feigned ignorance, now looked at me seriously. My mother was the same.

"What do you mean, Pa?"

I was never quite certain how to handle their parental side.

"When we heard you was a minister, yer ma and I thought there musta been some kinda mistake. We didn't even brag t' the neighbors till we were sure it was real."

Wait, that meant they waited a month to start going around boasting? C'mon.

"Ma said ain't no way you woulda got that promotion. Started worryin' you'd run back home with yer tail between yer legs!"

My mother laughed, scratching her head with embarrassment

"But I see we shouldn'a worried. Ya look great livin' it up here, city girl!"

I suppose that meant my parents were recognizing my accomplishments.

At that moment, I wasn't quite sure how to react to that.

Do I simply reply, Thanks? *But I don't think I've earned it with the life I've been living. I haven't changed* that *much.*

"When you said you were sick o' country life and ran off to the city, I thought it'd be too much for you."

My father stared up at the ceiling.

For a little while after that, no one spoke.

He wasn't entirely wrong. I'd nearly fled from the town around the castle more than once during my most impulsive phase.

Eventually, I'd chosen to strive for a life without much adventure, but had I wished for no adventure at all, I never would have come to the city in the first place.

"But this whole time, you were workin' in the government. Your ma and I were thinkin' 'bout how we failed you. Our girl had all this potential, and her parents never noticed 'cause she came from the boonies."

"I was simply a pencil pusher. 'Tis not much to be proud of…"

My appetite was nearly gone now.

"You might not be proud of it, but someone thought you had the chops to be a minister."

Who could that "someone" be? Had it really been the demon king herself? Or was it someone *else* who made the suggestion?

Either way, the truth was that my life had made a dramatic turn because of this someone.

"Keep yer nose to the grindstone and remember yer ma and pa are always thinkin' of you back home. We'll manage the store on our own. I ain't gonna ask you anything farrem like taking over the shop."

Farrem—that meant "killjoy" or "boring."

I guess he couldn't ask the nation's agricultural minister to take care of their local shop.

No matter one's age, a blessing from one's parents is always a welcome thing. "I appreciate that. I had no intention of taking over the store to begin with."

"We have five branches now, and we've got great managers lookin' over 'em."

What?!

That was some unusual news.

"Hey! When did you open branches?! I didn't know about this!"

"We got real popular after we started expanding our stock. And we don't have too much in the way of competition since we're out in the country. We bought up dead stores, remodeled 'em, and set up shop there."

Honestly...? I hadn't the faintest clue that my parents were so business savvy, but I had assumed they were putting in at least some effort if their grocery store hadn't gone under yet...

"No need to worry about us. And you keep ministerin', y'hear?!"

My mother was nodding enthusiastically, too. In the end, they were encouraging me.

"You don't need to tell me to work!" I joked.

Then I felt a chill.

"Oh yes, the level at this restaurant is so high~ It will really help me improve my own cooking."

Vania entered the restaurant!

I most certainly did not want to introduce my parents to her. If she heard their accent, then it would be clear as day that my manner of speech was entirely artificial. I had a feeling she might know already, but the true distance between our levels of refinement was rather intimidating.

"And it's great for a girl to eat alone. I can order anything I want—the way it should be!"

I slowly stood from my seat. "Apologies, but I must go wash my hands. If I am not back soon, then please take your time finishing your meal. We will be leaving once I return."

I shut myself inside the bathroom stall for a little while to make absolutely sure that I did not encounter Vania.

My apologies to the establishment, but some problems required sacrifice!

I returned to the table with utter nonchalance.

"All right, it seems you have both finished eating. Now, shall we depart? Yes!"

And thus, I gracefully avoided all contact with Vania.

When we left, it was already nighttime. We'd finished sightseeing, too.

"We had lots of fun today."

"Whadda mendical tahm, Beelzebub."

"I'm glad to hear it."

I wasn't exactly sure what my mother just said, but from context, I could tell she had enjoyed herself.

"We'll be in the city for the next few days, but your ma and I will be sightseeing alone together. Work hard."

"Of course. I shall do my utmost."

I would have to visit them next time.

My day off was not relaxing at all, but I suppose that was all right every once in a while.

"I shall take you to your hotel tonight, then. Where are you staying?"

"Venalleg inyer'an, Beelzebub!"

"Ma, could you please speak closer to the standard language...?"

"Ma said, *We don't have an inn. We'll be staying at your house for the next few days. Spending hotel money would be a waste. Please lend us one of your empty rooms, and we'll manage on our own. Where's your house?"*

How did her dialect compress so much information into such a little phrase...?

But that did not matter.

They were planning on staying at *my* house!!

My palatial residence was rotten with rooms, yes. Not literally rotting—although there were many rooms that were quite dusty since I never cleaned them.

But...I could not *abide* being in the same building as them! I would never know a moment's peace. And they would come and peek into my room... If not when I was at home, then certainly while I was at work...

"I shall reserve a place for you at one of the finest hotels! Are you not glad your daughter is a minister now?! Ha-ha-ha-ha-ha-ha-ha!"

Now was not the time to be stingy! I had money, and I definitely planned to flex a little!

After shoving my parents into a hotel that looked no less like a palace than my own house, I went home.

Once I walked through the door, I realized something.

"I had no idea today had exhausted me so... My shoulders are so stiff..."

I flopped onto my bed.

"Good morning, ma'am!"

When I arrived at the ministry for work, the others employed in the building greeted me.

"Aye, good morning. Do your best today."

I gracefully entered my office. Inside, the two leviathan secretaries were already at work.

"Good morning, Lady Beelzebub."

"Morning, boss!"

"Now that the holiday is over, let's get back to work."

Yes, this was my home battlefield. The unique challenges presented by my parents' sudden visit over the weekend had worn me down, but that was over and done with. I hoped they did all the sightseeing they wanted before returning to the countryside.

But two hours later—

Knock, knock, kno-knock, knock.

How uncouth. Who would knock on the door like an amateur percussionist?

—the door then flung open.

"Heya, Beelzebub! How ya doin'?"

"Dag'n a vier, Beelzebub!"

My parents walked in!

And I knew despair.

"Why are you here?! Leave right now!"

But they ignored me and started talking to my secretaries.

"Thanks for always lookin' out for our Beelzebub. I'm Bandido, her pa. This here's my wife, Kentohmi. Here, have some of our local sweets and a few of our finest vegetables."

For a moment, Fatla turned to the side.

"Pfft..."

She most certainly turned away to laugh just now, didn't she?

But Fatla's recovery was impressive. Afterward, she treated my parents with her usual matter-of-fact expression.

"Thank you. I am Fatla, a leviathan, secretary to the minister of agriculture."

"I am also Vania, a leviathan. Wow, I can barely understand you. Where are you from?"

Don't say it outright!

"Aww, shucks. You think I've got an accent, just wait'll ya hear my wife! Your ministry buildin' sure is tall! We went round givin' out sweets and vegetables at every floor, so we're plumb wore out!"

Now I knew true despair.

They said hello to everyone at every floor...?

I believe it was a historian who once wrote, *There is no greater enemy than one's closest relatives*, and I now knew that meaning well. To be honest, I wish I didn't.

"Begone, the both of you, now! I do not want to commit parricide! Go, go, go, go home!" I screamed.

For a little while after that, Vania took to greeting me with "Mornin', ma'am!"

"Vania, every time you say that to me, the hatred toward you within me grows. I hope you are prepared for the consequences..."

But Fatla's surreptitious chuckling was even more infuriating!

"One, two, one, two, one, two!"

Lately, I'd been running around the castle's inner moat before reporting in to work, putting my morning to good use.

A passerby who was walking his hellhound early in the morning (the general public is allowed as far as the outer side of the inner moat) said, "Oh-ho! Trying to lose weight, are you?"

Nope. I was exerting myself for a completely different reason.

When I'd finished my usual two laps around the moat and was resting in the shade of the trees, someone came over in front of me.

"You're out working hard very early, Miss Beelzebub, minister of agriculture."

It was the very one responsible for my position: Her Majesty the demon king, Provato Pecora Ariés. She was by herself today, under a parasol.

They said she hardly ever went around with attendants and that she popped up randomly all over the castle. In fact, I'd run into her several times myself, so I knew that was true.

"Oh, fancy meeting you here, Your Majesty." I started to get up, but she put out a hand, stopping me.

"You're training yourself physically to build the strength not to embarrass yourself as a minister, aren't you?"

"...Was it that obvious?"

"I have an *excellent* eye for my subordinates." Her Majesty sat down beside me.

She was mischievous, but she tended not to act all high-and-mighty. When she first ascended the throne, some demons were uneasy about that, but lately, she'd acquired a fine reputation as a demon king who did what it took.

"I'm a minister, whether I'm suited to the position or not... It would be embarrassing if I couldn't defeat my own subordinates."

In the demon world, even among bureaucrats, we tended to lionize strong fighters. Maybe it was a holdover from when we fought humans long ago.

When you're at minister level, some more conservative types believe you're doing something wrong if you can't nonchalantly plunge humans into terror.

Even now, people from noble stock who tended to end up at minister level were put through the mill from a young age, and they were pretty formidable, both physically and magically.

Here in the demon world, we didn't have pampered young nobles. Most of ours were tough.

"And not only do I hit harder, I believe I've managed to beef up my Ice and Snow spell quite a bit lately, too. I'll have to keep developing it—well, enough to let me defeat my two leviathan secretaries without trouble, at least..."

There was a deep-rooted stereotype among demons that masters must be stronger than their subordinates.

If the master was that strong, you'd think the subordinates wouldn't have joined battles, but when you were taking on an enemy, the subordinates had to go up against it first. You might have seen many examples of that in war chronicles and novels.

In addition, even among demons, leviathans were a pretty big deal. People said they were a match for ten thousand human soldiers each.

"If you keep putting in so much effort, I'm sure you'll make progress. I believe in you."

The demon king smiled at me, then left me to my devices.

"Effort... I hope the day comes when my efforts are rewarded, but I dunno..."

$$\diamond$$

When I made the rounds of my sections, I could feel the tension rise slightly.

Hmm. I must have more of a presence now.

It had been about eight months since I became minister of agriculture, and as far as I could tell, I had started to gain recognition in the ministry for the way I worked.

If I keep this up, I may be able to get away with taking a day of paid vacation next week. Or maybe I'll say I caught a cold and spend a day or so just lazing around.

The only problem with that plan was that my mansion was too big, which made it hard to just take it easy. Lazing around in a studio apartment felt more authentic. In a mansion, it might just feel pointless...

"Lady Beelzebub."

As I was thinking about stuff that didn't mean much, I realized Fatla was right in front of me, waiting. "Wh-what is it...?"

"An urgent job has come in for next week."

"Urgent, hmm? Well, that's fine. After all, I'm pretty familiar with almost everything in the ministry by now!"

"No, this is a business trip."

Ugh... I still wasn't completely used to business trips. Back when I was a bottom-tier bureaucrat, my job had hardly ever required them.

"It's an audit. An on-site audit of a fruit farm run by the relative of a

Ministry of Agriculture executive who fell from power. The farm and the executive may be colluding with each other."

"Can't somebody else handle this?"

"It's necessary for the head of the Ministry of Agriculture to go in order to show the people that the ministry itself was not a party to the relationship. It is also an order from the demon king."

Vania came up beside us. "We really should go, boss! Let's go!"

"Why do you look like you're having so much fun? Do you plan to sample all the local gourmet cuisine during this business trip? Is it a hobby of yours or something?"

"It's a fruit farm! We can eat all the fruit we want!"

"You're treating this too much like an ordinary trip! Besides, there's no way we'd be able to eat at a place we're auditing!"

"You might be surprised. You never know until you try!"

Why was she getting all worked up over this...?

Fatla gave Vania a proper scolding later, if you were wondering.

My two secretaries and I headed for the Bellgundeal Fruit Farm.

Fatla had transformed into her true form as a leviathan, an ultra-large flying beast, to carry us there.

"Hell's bells, this really is a flying ship."

I was sneaking peeks at the scenery from way up in the sky while I looked over the documents I'd brought along. Vania was helping me.

There were several buildings lined up on top of the leviathan, and we were inside one of them.

"This is the true charm of leviathans, after all. Long ago, we flew freely through the skies, but since there's a risk of bumping into dragons and other creatures, we have to get permission first now."

"Life is hard as a leviathan, isn't it?"

I could never beat something like this. I sighed inwardly.

I'd have to do some absolutely ludicrous training, or it would never work… No, even if I did, there's no way one person could beat a battleship.

"That's why my big sister became a bureaucrat, and I followed her lead and took the test. Once I was out of cooking school, I could have just become a chef, but my sister told me not to. She said I'm not suited to that type of management."

"You went to a cooking school? I see I still know next to nothing about my subordinates."

Just then, something like a shipboard announcement came on.

"Vania, you're only talking about personal matters, and your hands aren't moving. Do your job."

I see… So Fatla was keeping an eye on us even when we were riding on top of her.

"This farm is suspected of aggressively marketing low-quality fruit as high quality and yielding considerable profits. Potential tax evasion has also been indicated."

"That's terrible in several different ways, huh…"

"There were doubts in the past as well, and audits have been conducted twice, but they found no problems on either occasion."

"Doesn't that mean they're innocent, then?"

"You see, there are rumors that the individual who was a Ministry of Agriculture executive at the time interfered, or that someone under the influence of that executive was sent to conduct the audit. This is why you—a former commoner who is not hampered by any of those things—are looking into the matter."

Being called a commoner irritated me a little, but it was the truth.

"Well, I'll take a real thorough look for you, then."

Still, it sounded like the company was under suspicion for quite a few things. *They aren't going to just up and attack us, are they…? Quite a few members of demonkind are still pretty hotheaded. We can't get careless.*

"If it comes down to it, Vania and I swear to protect you, so have no fear."

I guess I'm still weak enough to need protecting.

"Thank you very much for your visit! I am Bellgundeal, proprietor of Bellgundeal Fruit Farm!"

No sooner had we arrived than a one-eyed evil eye demon met us with a smile. There were even employees holding a WELCOME! banner behind him.

"Well, this isn't quite what I was expecting…"

"I'm a little taken aback myself." Even Fatla, who was always cool and collected, was blinking rapidly.

Next to her, Vania was waving cheerfully and saying, "Thank *you* very much!"

"You must be tired after that long journey. Come make yourselves comfortable in the office first. While you do, we'll prepare the documents for the audit!"

We were escorted right to the office.

"Say, Fatla, is this how audits generally go? Aren't they usually more solemn? This is nothing like what I'm familiar with…"

For audits at the Agricultural Policy Organization, we'd only had to go to another institute in the same organization, so there hadn't been any issues with finding a compromise. But I'd expected a very different experience from an external audit.

"I'm very sorry; I don't have much experience with audits myself."

In other words, we were all total amateurs at auditing. Was this really going to be okay?

That said, if nothing turned up, then so much the better.

The important thing was the fact that an audit had taken place.

"This is the office, honored inspectors!"

The space we'd been shown into looked like a glass-walled café with a view into a hothouse garden. The tables and pillars were pure white, and the space was very bright and cheerful. If rooms could be poseurs, this one fit the bill.

"Ooh! This is fascinating! And there are colorful exotic birds in the garden!"

Vania was already in full-blown tourist mode. *Granted, this might be the first time I've seen tropical birds. Are these related to parrots?*

"Is this really an office?"

"Yes, we designed it based on data that shows that providing a good environment raises efficiency at work!"

When we dubiously sat down in a seating area that looked suspiciously like a café, another staff member came up and served us fruit juice. "Your beverages."

"This is fresh-squeezed juice made exclusively from fruit grown at this farm. It isn't too sweet, and it's an extremely effective beauty tonic," Bellgundeal the proprietor said, smiling.

"I—I see... Well, I suppose being offered drinks isn't that odd..." When I tried a little, it was refreshing, and the straightforward sweetness tickled my nose.

This was exquisite.

Fatla and I looked at each other.

"Lady Beelzebub, this juice is the real thing."

"My thoughts exactly."

Vania had already drained her glass and requested a refill.

"You should probably learn to hold back a little at times like this..."

"Well, I mean, it's good for your looks, you know?! I want to drink it while I've got the chance!"

She's completely forgotten that we're here for work, I thought, even as I ordered seconds myself. I wish my neighborhood market carried stuff this good.

"W-well, all right... We'll just have to conduct that audit thoroughly..." I dabbed at my mouth with a napkin. No particular problems here.

Just then, the documents for the audit arrived. Most of them were accounting records and the like.

And they came accompanied by an assorted fruitcake set.

"B-Bellgundeal, what on earth...?"

This place actually is a café, isn't it?

"You see, on an audit, you have to look at all those fiddly little numbers one by one, don't you? There's nothing better than sweets for tired minds. If you clear your heads with my company's fruit, I'm sure your work will go more smoothly."

"I—I see. Now that you mention it, perhaps…"

For a second, I thought I heard a voice say, "Talk about easy."

"Did you say something, Bellgundeal?"

"No, nothing, nothing. Good luck with your work."

With my eyes on the documents, I started on the fruitcake.

The first bite was shockingly delicious!

"The pleasant acidity of the oranges harmonizes perfectly with the sweet cake!" I cried.

"The slight dusting of sugar looks like powdery snow!" Vania added.

"Ahhh! Even in the castle town, quality like this isn't available anywhere! I'm so glad I came along on this trip!"

"Lady Beelzebub, Vania, we aren't here to eat cake, you know. Th-this is wonderful… Sinfully delicious…"

All smiles, we somehow managed to get through the first stage of our job, the audit.

We didn't find anything particularly problematic.

When our work reached a stopping point, the evil eye proprietor came back and said, "Would you like to take a tour of the farm as a little diversion?"

"But if that delays the audit, won't it cause trouble for your company as well?"

"No, I thought that having you see for yourselves that our humble establishment grows fruit of good quality could serve as part of the audit. I'd like you to confirm that we do not grow anything low quality!"

"I—I see… You do have a point."

"Yaaaay! A factory tour! It's a field trip for grown-ups!"

"Vania, curb your enthusiasm. Still…it is intriguing, isn't it?"

Fatla might say otherwise, and it didn't show in her expression, but it was clear that she was enjoying herself, too.

I got the feeling the proprietor said "Seriously easy," but I might have been hearing things.

They ushered us into the hothouse.

"Demon territory is located in the frigid north, so we provide a variety of fruits from southern climes by building greenhouses like this one," the proprietor explained.

The colorful fruits were indeed unmistakably tropical.

"Sister, Sister! A big bird landed on my back!"

"Be a little quieter, would you? But...put it on my back later, please."

So you're letting it ride on you anyway, huh? This seemed to have turned into a sisters' trip. *Bureaucrats are busy, so maybe it's all for the best.*

No... No, that's wrong; this isn't a trip.

"Bellgundeal, I think we'd better be getting back to the audit."

"Yes, I understand. In that case, shall we return to the office?"

This time, we were given a very fancy mixed juice, and we checked into their accounting records.

No money was flowing in any particularly opaque directions.

"Even if we are taking breaks, my eyes are getting more and more tired."

Earnest Fatla was the type who focused and worked intently for a short burst. However, not only was the amount of work too great for that this time around, we were currently on a business trip, so her pacing was off.

"I've started to get sleepy..."

"Vania, you are a real piece of work. No sleeping. I mean, fatigue is inevitable for a task like this, and I do understand how you feel, but..."

I nearly yawned, too, but I fought the urge desperately. As a bottom-tier employee, I'd spent a long time doing dull work, so I still had a tolerance for it. That said, whether I could handle it or not and whether it was interesting or not were completely different things.

Even so, if I fell asleep during an audit, it would embarrass the entire Ministry of Agriculture.

C'mon, tough it out, tough it out...

That was when Bellgundeal the evil eye came by again.

"You seem fatigued. Our company has female staff members who give beauty treatments. Would you like one?"

For a moment, I almost broke into a smile, but I managed to bite it back. "Hrm... A kind offer indeed, but wouldn't that count as entertaining us?"

"It wouldn't do to have your concentration lapse and cause you to overlook something. I believe it would be best to clear your bodies of any metabolic waste, then begin your work again in a refreshed state of mind."

Hmm. I'm beginning to feel as if I'm being cleverly manipulated. If I don't shut this down now, we may not be able to go back...

"That's a valid way of looking at it. May we take you up on that offer?"

Fatla nodded. She should have been more hard-nosed than that!

No, let's look at this from another angle. If Fatla's saying it's okay, doesn't that mean there's no problem?

"All right. In that case, yes, please let us try this beauty treatment of yours."

I got the feeling the proprietor smirked, but that was probably also my imagination.

The beauty treatment was, in a word, heaven.

It's a bit weird for a demon to be talking about heaven, but it really felt that good. A piping-hot towel was placed over my eyes, and I dozed through the whole treatment.

My body definitely felt lighter, and my face seemed more delicate than before.

"Boss, you look incredibly cute now!"

"Vania, flattery will get you nowhere. But I will admit your skin looks younger as well."

"If it weren't for work fatigue, would I be more attractive...?"

In the end, all three of us were satisfied in three different ways.

Back when I was a bottom-tier bureaucrat, beauty treatments like this one were barely even an option. Although that was because I'd use that money to buy cheap liquor and beer snacks, then drink at home. I never knew such happiness existed...

While we were checking documents again, feeling rejuvenated, night fell.

"Nnnnnn! I think that's it for work today! We'll get through the rest tomorrow morning!" Vania stretched.

Yes, it was about time to call it a day.

"All right, let's get something to eat," I said. "We obviously can't let the group we're auditing invite us out, so we'll go somewhere else."

There weren't many places around, and we went into a slightly trendy restaurant.

If you let the group you're auditing entertain you too warmly, the audit doesn't work. We might have gotten a little too cozy today. *I'll let those regrets remind me to keep a clear head tomorrow...*

However, even there, something peculiar happened.

We kept receiving dishes that were clearly more luxurious than what we'd asked for.

"How odd... Did we order a full-course meal like this?"

"If it was not you, Vania, we must not have." I thought it was strange, and I asked a staff member if there'd been some mistake.

"Oh... As a matter of fact, it just so happens that you're our five-thousandth party of customers, so we're serving you a special full-course meal for no additional charge," the staff member said, averting his eyes awkwardly.

The hallmark of a guilty conscience.

I was positive.

No matter how you looked at it, this was weird.

Meanwhile, Vania was pleasantly drunk, and Fatla had eaten too much and was holding her stomach in pain.

These two won't be any more use today...

◇

That evening, after the three of us had checked into the inn, I went back to the farm by myself and grilled the employees who were there working overtime.

"Is the proprietor still here?"

"No, I believe he's already gone home... If you need him, please try again tomorrow."

I grinned.

Yes—when the proprietor isn't here, the place is vulnerable.

"No matter if he's not here. Earlier, they brought the documents for the audit to us; could you show me to the vault where those documents were originally?"

"Huh?! You mean right now?!"

"There's no rule that says audits can't be conducted at night. Hurry up and open it. It's nothing important; I only have the urge to check the ones that weren't there earlier. A personal interest, you understand. That is why I'm here by myself."

With no other options, the employee opened the vault.

I carefully checked through the accounting records for the period that I'd wondered about, working by the light of a small hand lantern.

We'd been entertained far too well.

There had to be something to find.

And after about fifteen minutes—

I pinpointed a stream of capital that was clearly anomalous.

"The company's positively gushing money, and I can't tell what it was used on, either."

Just then, a figure appeared in the vault.

It was Bellgundeal, the evil eye proprietor.

"Minister of Agriculture. How dedicated you are to be working at an hour like this. With your status, you shouldn't need to do such a dull task."

I sensed a hint of sarcasm.

"Hmph! I am a new noble who got promoted all of a sudden. I spent forever doing accounting. I've gone over the same books again and again because they were off by less than the cost of a meal. When something's fishy somewhere, I can feel it."

"And did you?"

"We'll still have to do a detailed investigation, but it's almost certain that you've been conducting financial transactions under the table with that Ministry of Agriculture relative of yours and having them grease some wheels for you. You may also have been falsifying production areas and using goods that are past their sell-by dates, but everything from here on out is a job for the lot from the audit bureau and the police."

"So you've finally tracked it down, have you?"

Bellgundeal was holding something. A blunt instrument? Was he planning to strike me down here?

I tensed up. *I may not look it, but I'm still a demon minister. I'd never lose to a mere evil eye!*

However, while the object could have been used as a bludgeon, that wasn't what Bellgundeal did with it.

"I don't suppose we could settle the matter with this?"

What Bellgundeal the evil eye held out to me was—

A pyramid-shaped stack of gold ingots!

"Mistress Beelzebub— Ah, forgive me. As you are a noble, perhaps I should call you Lady Beelzebub. You have only just been elevated to the nobility. You have no economic foundation whatsoever. This farm can create that foundation for you."

"Do you intend to bribe me with this?" I glared at the evil eye.

"To be honest, you have my sympathies. With no backer to support you, even if you've been given a position as minister of agriculture, there are any number of opposing forces, and should you prove inconvenient, you might be cut off at any time. You could conceivably be hounded out of your current rank next year, or the year after that. Should you not at least have savings to use in your retirement?"

"On its own, that's a sound argument. I'm like an insignificant little fly."

Slowly, I approached the pile of ingots.

"That's right. Come, prosper along with this farm!"

And then—

I swept my right hand through those gold ingots and sent them flying.

"But don't take me for a fool! While I love fruit that's nearly rotten, I have no intention of fraternizing with such rotten characters! What you just said is so filthy that I want to wash out my ears; go get me some cold water!"

The evil eye's expression abruptly hardened. His hand tightened around a gold ingot.

"I'll teach you to push your luck, you upstart commoner! You'll die here!"

The evil eye brandished the ingot—which I suppose *could* serve as a bludgeon!

Not good! My Ice and Snow spell wasn't going to make it in time!

I managed to dodge the first attack somehow, but this really wasn't a good environment for fighting.

"It's too cramped in here! I can't even draw a magic circle!"

"Exactly! All right. Now suffer!" Slowly, the evil eye closed in on me.

What do I do? Should I take a risk and close the distance? No, I'll get hit before I can manage it... There's no room to take flight...

However, before he could slam that gold ingot into me—

The man slowly tipped forward and collapsed.

Behind him were the two leviathan sisters.

"Lady Beelzebub, we really can't have you going off on your own like this."

"My, that was a close one, wasn't it?! Still, all's well that ends well, huh!"

"Fatla? Vania?!"

Vania nodded happily. "When your serious-minded boss disappears, work is the first place you look."

The relief made my legs give out on me, and I sat down right where I was.

Fatla picked me up and put my arm around her shoulders.

After the wave of relief passed, I started feeling pathetic. *Even though I'm a demon minister, I'm seriously weak.*

"I'm sorry… For a demon, I'm still not that powerful. I really am no match for you two leviathans. I'm not living up to the Beelzebub name…"

"Don't get the wrong idea, please." Fatla sounded a little sniffy. "I serve the Lady Beelzebub who devotes herself to her official business as minister of agriculture. I am not groveling because of your strength."

"We'll support you when you can't manage on your own, Lady Beelzebub!"

"You have my gratitude, both of you. Thank you…"

Uncharacteristically, I was crying.

As a result of the audit, quite a few arrests were made. I can't say this on the record, but it served them all right. Demonkind may last forever, but evil will always fail.

Several months later—

"Hah! Hiyah!"

—I was sparring with Fatla and Vania.

We were starting with special training to boost the power of my punches and kicks.

I'm the minister of agriculture, and I'm going to get to midlevel boss-class strength if it's the last thing I do!

"You're doing well, Lady Beelzebub." Fatla, who was receiving my attacks, encouraged me with compliments. "At this point, you have power on the level of a Ministry of Agriculture section chief."

"I'm still at section chief level, huh? This is going to take a while." I got close to feeling discouraged, but I didn't give up. As if I'd ever give up.

"No—no, boss, you're strong! If there were three of you, I'd lose."

"That prerequisite makes no sense! I don't turn up in groups of three!" Vania's method of praising me was a little strange.

"But remember that nasty evil eye from earlier?" Vania continued. "You could beat him easily now."

I stopped attacking. "Is that the truth?"

"I'll swear to it as well. You really are stronger, Lady Beelzebub." Since Fatla had said it, it probably was true.

Great. I'm going to keep on getting stronger. I'll become an outstanding minister of agriculture. I won't lose to anybody.

Huh...? When had I set my sights on that particular goal? As a bottom-tier bureaucrat, I'm pretty sure I was an idler...

At that point, the demon king passed by under her parasol again.

We stopped practicing and saluted briskly.

"A very good morning to you, ma'am, Your Majesty," I said.

Smiling, the demon king came up to me. I got the feeling she was plotting something again.

"Miss Beelzebub, this is an order. Would you bow your head there for a moment?" she said, still smiling. Did she mean I was acting too proud? Either way, it was an order, so I couldn't refuse.

"...All right, ma'am, Your Majesty." I bent forward, inclining my upper body.

"Very well done. ♪"

The demon king stretched out a hand—

And patted me on the head.

"Your Majesty...?"

"Yes, very good. If you keep putting in that kind of effort, I'm sure you'll make progress. After all, Miss Beelzebub, I've placed my confidence in

you." The demon king giggled, smiling impishly despite her status. "I need you to get stronger and become my right-hand demon."

Then she shifted the angle of her parasol slightly and departed.

It didn't make much sense to me, and I cocked my head.

"Lady Beelzebub, has the demon king taken a liking to you?" Fatla asked.

"Frankly, it's a mystery. I don't know her all that well."

"She may have recognized your potential from the very beginning."

Potential, huh?

It would be nice to have, but even if I don't, it won't change what I'm doing.

"All right, let's keep going! I'll be as strong as a chief director by the end of the month!"

The town surrounding Vanzeld Castle and the area around the town did not get much rain. When it did get rain, it was little more than a mist.

But the misty rain clung to me when I went out for a jog, relieving the heat of exercise at the most perfect rate.

"How comfortable~ I feel like I'm going a little faster than usual~"

I had added a morning run to my daily routine, so I was not tired.

I would be an exemplary demon; no one would dare mock me!

Then I caught sight of the demon king going for a walk. She did not have her typical parasol, but a normal umbrella.

I dropped to my knees before her; it would be inexcusable to ignore her.

"Oh my; the road is all wet. There is no need to do that~"

Her Majesty reached out to hold the umbrella over me.

"No, I cannot allow myself to neglect my manners."

"Oh, you are much too formal, Miss Beelzebub. Well, I suppose that is one of the things I like about you."

Her Majesty was smiling as she always was, but to be honest, I was not exactly sure what she was thinking. I had learned that those who smile the most are often the most terrifying within. I mustn't let my guard down.

Fewer and fewer demons had dared to scorn her as of late. Even other ministers were rather nervous around her.

For me, making light of her had never been an option. I had no faction backing me. While other ministers had entire armies at their disposal, I was alone. At best, I had Fatla and Vania with me.

That was why, when I met the demon king, I erred on the side of caution...

We often crossed paths, so perhaps it was still a little easier compared with when I first became minister, though.

"I would have been powerless had you not pulled me up, Your Majesty. I have no choice but to obey you. Thank you for all you have done for me."

I suppose that's enough.

"Oh-ho, you have no choice but to obey me? I see~ ♪"

Her Majesty chuckled, and the smile she wore now was not the same as the one from before.

Oh dear, I may have made a slip of the tongue...

"Then why don't you accompany me all day today? I was just searching for someone knowledgeable in the agricultural sector."

"Well, I must be heading to work at—"

"And the demon king's orders have now canceled your work. ♪ I will give Miss Fatla the power to make final decisions in your place~ ♪"

She was taking this much further than I'd expected!

I should have been more careful in my choice of expression... Of course she would take advantage of my pledge to obey her...

But what I'd said was true; I *did* have no choice. She was the demon king, after all.

"Then I will make arrangements to give you the day off, Miss Beelzebub." She pointed to a gazebo not too far from us. "Take shelter from the rain there. I'll be right back. ♪"

"Ah, but I don't know what—"

"You don't need to know anything. ♪"

Her Majesty had already started skipping off toward the castle.

I did not know what exactly was going to happen, but I knew for a fact that it would be trouble.

◇

As I sat staring off into space in the gazebo, the demon king returned.

"I am sorry to keep you waiting. Now, let us be off!" With a dramatic flourish, Her Majesty raised her right hand.

"Be off to where? No, first, I'd like to know the reason behind all this."

I had been given almost no information beforehand, so I was nervous.

"You know there is an herb garden on castle grounds, don't you? I'm searching for a plant to cultivate there."

Her reason was more respectable than I'd imagined.

The herb garden was beside the castle's regular garden, which was a facility some would call a botanical garden with a farm added to it.

The castle was large, so if we ever found ourselves in a siege, we would need food. The plants growing in the herb garden were vegetables we could harvest during a crisis.

In addition, there were also plants that proved to be good poisons, should the need ever arise for that.

Of course, many of us simply saw it as a botanical garden, so most of the demons who worked in the castle treated it that way.

Now, since the herb garden fell under the Ministry of Agriculture's jurisdiction, I had no choice but to go. It made sense.

However, everything in the castle itself belonged to the demon king, so anything she wanted to plant would be prioritized. The normal garden was more like something she managed as a hobby.

"If I may ask, what sort of plant are you looking for?"

"Before I answer thaaaat... Pop quiz!"

Was this a test for her vassal...?

"Please name as many plants growing in the herb garden as possible! Ready, go!"

"What? Demon carrot, demon onion, northern thick-shell beans, tundra wheat, tundra barley, demon capsicum, monster capsicum, demon eggplant—"

I was surprised by the suddenness of it, but I listed one plant name after another. I omitted many of the finer subvarieties, such as the large, small, red, and other types of demon eggplant we bred, because otherwise, I would never finish.

Of course, the poisonous herbs were not used in cooking, so I knew little more than the names of those.

After a while, the demon king started to clap.

"Amazing! You know so many! I thought you might even be a researcher working in the herb garden!"

"When I became the minister of agriculture, I made sure to memorize what I would need to know, you see."

I did not mind the compliment—though, of course, I was not a plant enthusiast. I didn't even pay attention to what sort of capsicums or spices they used in the hell spaghetti at the restaurant I frequented.

By the way, I've heard that the demon lands used to be too cold for capsicums to grow. They were brought from another faraway land, modified, then grown here.

Though I was the daughter of greengrocers, there were quite a few vegetables in the herb garden that I had never seen before. It was a bit of a shock.

But since I was now at the top of the Ministry of Agriculture, there was much I needed to know. That was why I had memorized every plant in the herb garden.

At the time, the task had felt rather pointless, considering they would not appear on a test or anything…so I never thought I would *actually* be tested on them. One never knows how fortune might favor them.

"Yes, you're such a hard worker, Miss Beelzebub. You truly deserve praise for your efforts. I do love that about you. ♪"

I didn't know what to make of that last bit, but if she was praising me, then I suppose it was all right to be happy about it.

"Now that I know how skilled you are, let us be off. ♪"

Her Majesty turned to face the gazebo exit and opened her umbrella.

"Wait, Your Majesty, where are we going?"

I knew all the places we could get to from Vanzeld Castle. There were scarcely more than farms in the outskirts of the city, but that would be a bit of a journey.

"You'll find out if you follow me."

The demon king grabbed my hand.

I reminded myself I had no choice but to obey her.

The demon king brought me to…

…a corridor in the castle's fifth-floor basement. I scarcely ever came down here, as I rarely had any reason to.

"It is so spacious under the castle…"

The corridor stretched forward, and at regular intervals along the walls sat candles, as though someone had been taking care of the place.

That said, it was eerie.

"Yes. Those working in the ministry and the government office buildings don't appear to be aware of this area's existence. Even if they were, it seems hardly anyone knows the proper routes down here."

The demon king was still grasping my hand. I had a feeling our positions should be reversed, but as this was my first time seeing this place, I could not act as the escort here.

"This castle was built only to prevent an enemy attack, after all~ It's one big maze!"

"I see… Ah yes, the castle is a dungeon, isn't it…?"

I was astonished. How long had it taken to build such a large structure? How much did it cost?

Uh-oh… Perhaps it would be best if I did not think of the budget right now.

My job may have made me far too conscious of money issues…

"One of the previous demon kings was a little crazy for architecture~

The design of this place is so complicated, one might easily lose their way!"

"Indeed, I no longer know where I am anymore... Hmm?"

I realized there was a fundamental question I should have been asking.

"We can wander about underground, but no plants grow down here, do they? Unless there is some especially valuable mold you're after?"

"You're right; they don't grow down here~ ♪"

I could see the question mark in my mind.

Then where is she taking me...?

But the answer practically leaped out at me.

"Um, I believe it was around here~" Her Majesty opened a door, and I saw a glittering light on the other side.

A magic circle drawn on the ground was glowing.

"...I suppose this is for transportation...?"

"How perceptive of you! Yes, we will be warping! Here we go!"

Her Majesty tugged on my hand even harder, pulling me into the magic circle.

When we arrived, a forest of tall pine trees spread as far as the eye could see, and the ground was covered in a thin frost.

"Augh! It's so cold... I should have worn a coat...!"

I hugged myself instinctively. The temperature was so much colder here compared with the town around the castle!

"Oh, come now~ Don't let go of my hand. I believe you can endure the cold and stay linked with me at the same time." I gave my hand back to her. Ah, it had been so cold, I'd let go...

"Still, to think we could reach this place from the castle... I had no idea..."

"It is top secret, after all. In fact, we've secured routes to all sorts of locations~"

This was highly classified information—but I was a minister, so it wasn't bad for me to know.

"Look at the base of the pines. See the mushrooms growing there, breaking through the ice and living out here in the cold? Those are what I'm here to collect."

Just as she said, there were mushrooms and other grasses peeking out from the ice, clinging fast to the tree. Her Majesty plucked them and put them in the cloth bag she had brought with her.

"Ahhh, now this feels like agricultural work."

"Of course. This is proper work, you know. We're not here to play."

I honestly thought this was another one of Her Majesty's jokes, but she was taking it surprisingly seriously.

That said, it was still much too cold...

And then came a freezing gust of wind! *There's frost in my hair...*

"I can stand this no longer! Let us return!"

"What? But this is nothing." Her Majesty seemed entirely unaffected. She did not even seem to be putting on a brave front.

So this was Her Majesty's true power... It was an odd way to discover how outmatched I was.

"You seem to be in pain, so I suppose we can move on to the next area."

"The next area?" I had a terrible feeling about this.

"Yes! ♪ Let's return to the castle via magic circle, then we'll warp to another place with a different teleportation circle."

"What is the next place like...?" I had to ask before I could feel better about it.

"It's not cold at all! I can guarantee that!"

Then, after leaping into a magic circle in a creepy and deep part of the castle underground—

—we came to a thick, dense forest.

The trees were not all that tall, and all of them had ivy wrapped tightly around them.

"'Tis not cold at all, no. But it is a damp, uncomfortable heat…"

"We might find delicious nuts here, no? Let us get to looking!"

Compared with that horridly frigid place, it might be worth searching around here.

Planting them as is in the castle's herb garden might cause them to die due to the difference in climate, but we could manage through selective breeding.

Her Majesty dragged me deeper and deeper into the forest. Her initiative was impressive, and this was much better than staying cooped up in the castle.

But I felt some pressure on my stomach.

I looked down and saw that a snake as thick as a rope was coiling around me.

"Your Majesty, stop, stop! We have a big snake problem!"

"Oh~ That one isn't venomous, so there's no need to panic. It's simply trying to suffocate you."

"Then I have every reason to panic! I cannot… Hrgh—!"

Pain coursed through my body.

"Relax, Miss Beelzebub."

"If I relax, I'll die!"

"I doubt you're weaker than a little snake. Can't you simply pull it off you?"

I snapped back to reality when she said that. Indeed—I had been training. It would take more than a snake to defeat me!

"Rrrrrrgh!"

I grabbed the snake and pulled!

"Rrrrgrah! Do not underestimate a demon! You're nothing but a common reptile!"

All of a sudden, just as I could feel its grip on me loosening, the snake let go and began to wriggle. It seemed to recognize that it would be in danger if it didn't.

"Now don't cause any more trouble." I tossed it to the ground, and the snake escaped into the brush.

"Yes, yes! Of course you wouldn't lose to a snake! ♪ Let us con-tinue~ ♪" Her Majesty pulled on my hand again.

"Understood... I shall follow you anywhere..."

"Music to my ears."

Oh...

Another slip of the tongue. *I keep creating opportunities for her like this. Or perhaps this is a sign that I still have much to learn?*

We encountered more snakes later, but I kicked them all to the side. Literally. I kicked them, and they squirmed away. They knew I was not to be their prey.

Every single time, the demon king complimented me ("What good form on that kick~ ♪"), so I suppose it wasn't so bad.

"By the way, Your Majesty, I have not seen any snakes attack you yet; are you wearing snake repellent or something?"

If so, then she should have told me. I would have to protect her if she got attacked, but if such a convenient item existed, I wanted to use it, too.

"Ah~ For some reason, the snakes are avoiding me~"

Ah, the theory that animals instinctively know who is most powerful!

That meant the snakes were approaching me because they felt there was a chance they could defeat me. The idea upset me a little, so I decided to proactively attack a snake whenever I saw one.

"Where are you, where are you?! I will rip you in half, fry you, and eat you! I hear snakes taste delicious, and I'm *dying* to try one!"

"That's a bit much, Miss Beelzebub. Please mind yourself."

Her Majesty had been unusually serious on this outing.

"Y-yes, ma'am..."

I wasn't entirely sure of why, but something I did must have offended her.

"Do you understand? You serve me, but you are also older than me. I want you to follow me faithfully as a minister while maintaining the image of an elder sister. You are my escort, so please do not forget to act like one."

"I see what you are saying, but you have been the one pulling my hand, Your Majesty, so when it comes to the question of who is escorting whom—"

"You absolutely must think more of yourself as my elder sister, as older than me! You need heart, I say!"

Her Majesty placed her hand atop her heart. It seemed everyone had their line in the sand.

We managed to collect all sorts of plants from the thick forest, so it was apt to say the trip was a success, but—

"My whole body itches..."

"I see the mosquitoes have made a feast of you~"

I had been the prey of a horrible number of mosquitoes.

"Are you all right, Your Majesty?"

"Strangely enough, they haven't come to me at all~ ♪"

Even the mosquitoes knew she was powerful!

Afterward, we used the teleportation circle again and arrived in a strange land.

The third location was a small piece of flat land atop a cliff.

"Argh! I'm so tense; how terrifying!"

"Oh, you can fly, so no need to worry. In fact, I'd say this view alone is well worth the trip~"

Her Majesty was calm and relaxed, perhaps because she always knew where we were going to warp to.

"I see that, but why have we come here...? Are you sure there are any plants—?"

"There's a legendary flower here! It can only save one's gravely ill childhood friend!"

"Why is it limited to saving childhood friends?"

I relaxed when I spotted the few pretty, blooming yellow flowers, however—and then I saw a hand reach up over the cliff's edge!

But the answer to that mystery came quickly. A young human man had climbed all the way up here.

Which meant we were in the human lands.

"Oh, what a coincidence it is to see someone else here~ Hello~"

Her Majesty greeted the man as though they were passing each other in the street as she pulled up the yellow flowers, root and all. She was going to plant them in the herb garden.

There were only a few flowers, and now they were all gone.

"Aaah! Now I won't be able to save my gravely ill childhood friend!"

What a dramatic plot twist!

"Aww~ But I believe this is finders keepers, as they say~ There are other cliffs, so why don't you go and climb those~?"

"Give it to him, Your Majesty! It wouldn't hurt to give him one!"

I had a feeling that we were in the wrong here!

"Then why don't we do this? If this man can defeat me in a fight, then I shall give him—"

"You're only pretending to give him a chance; that's even worse!"

There was no human who could defeat the demon king!

I negotiated and managed to secure one flower for the human man.

"Thank you very much, angels. Now I will be able to save my childhood friend, my love!" The man thanked us.

"We are not angels, but...w-well, I suppose we are similar..."

"They say no one returns alive from climbing this cliff, but because of your help, I should be able to take this flower back! Thank you so much!"

The man, touched, climbed down the cliff with tears streaming down his face, an endeavor which was quite unsafe.

"Your Majesty, he said any human who came here never returned. Could that mean...?"

I dropped my gaze to the magic circle.

"Ah~ Some humans stepped into the magic circle and exited into the castle underground. We were at war with them before, and I hear we did not let them go home back then."

From a human point of view, it was essentially a one-way portal...

The next place we came to was a desert. The sand was hot underfoot.

"If the magic circle gets covered in sand, then we'll simply come out on top of it~"

There was a mound of sand beneath our feet, so the magic circle was likely below it all.

"I see. Unlike the previous locations, I cannot see the magic circle at all."

"Miss Beelzebub, will you please clear away the sand so we can get home?"

"This is pure pain!"

It was awful... No matter how much sand I dug up, more would simply flow in from the sides...

"I will be at this forever... Forever..."

"Oh, you can do it~ Do it for your younger sister~ ♪"

"I may be doing this for the demon king, but it is still painful..."

I let my mind wander, and eventually, I had dug up the sand-covered magic circle.

The demon king had vanished, but she did return with all sorts of plants. I did not know where she could possibly have acquired them.

Again, the demon king and I stood before a magic circle within the castle.

It was deep, deep underground.

We had walked down so many flights of stairs that I no longer remembered what floor we were on.

"This will be our last one today~"

"Finally, the end..." I lightly smacked my cheeks to perk myself up.

I could get through this so long as I remembered that this was the last place. No matter where we ended up, it was unlikely that we would die. It would simply be an inconvenience.

Once again, Her Majesty held my hand, and we hopped into the teleportation circle.

We moved in an instant—

—and my lungs filled with water!

I began to choke.

We were under the sea! I could see light filtering through the water, so we weren't terribly deep, but this was grueling torture!

On the other hand, Her Majesty floated beside me, leisurely picking marine plants.

Oh no! Those will not grow if you plant them in the herb garden!

"Mlab Beelbebeub, blobelbulubulelbueubueb?"

She said something to me with a smile, but I could not hear what she said.

Then I sensed bloodthirst.

A shark was approaching us!

Ha, so what?! I would never lose to a shark!

I aimed a punch toward its head.

Thunk.

Oh no. We were in the water, so my punch didn't pack much of a... well, punch.

Our situation had taken a turn for the worse...

The shark opened its jaws.

I moved to swim away—and I would have succeeded, if it weren't for the demon king's hand still grasping mine!

"Blorowub Abababwuebee, bwaaaabababababublbb!"

Your Majesty, shark! was what I meant to say, but I doubted she understood... She was still plucking marine plants!

What should I do? Should I risk my life to save Her Majesty?

...I had no choice.

It was a retainer's job, and I had said it myself anyway.

I would obey the demon king. I must take responsibility for my own words. A minister could do no less.

I came to float before the shark.

Come on, bite me! I doubt I taste very good! If you get food poisoning, you're on your own!

The shark widened its maw.

But at that very moment—

—something that looked like a black mist swirled around the shark, and it simply turned up its belly and began to float away.

Her Majesty had cast a spell, and her face seemed quite satisfied.

The first thing I did upon returning to the castle was take a deep breath. Air had never tasted so good…

"I cast a spell on the shark that sapped its strength. It didn't stand a chance."

"That tells me that being underwater is nothing to you, Your Majesty."

I was once again reminded of the demon king's incredible power.

"That may be true, but I am so happy."

The demon king approached me and embraced me, lightly patting me on the back.

She and I had just returned from the ocean, so we were both soaking wet, but she felt much warmer than me.

"You put my safety above yours."

"Well… I am your vassal…"

"You pass," she said and let go of me.

"I pass? Pass what?"

"Miss Beelzebub, I have high hopes for you. I hope to bring out more of your best in the future. ♪" Her Majesty smiled, avoiding my question. "But through our activities today, your weaknesses have come to light. I hope you work on correcting those."

At some point, this had turned into a performance review.

"When you say 'weaknesses,' are you referring to when we were underwater?"

I hadn't known how to face the shark. The castle and the town didn't give me many opportunities to fight them, after all.

"Miss Beelzebub, have you ever gone sightseeing before?"

"Rarely," I answered instantly.

I had lived for a long time in the town around Vanzeld Castle, but I spent my weekends exclusively lying around.

"I thought so~ You strike me as rather narrow-minded." Her Majesty gave a dramatic sigh. "That is why I wanted you to see and experience many different places personally. You must develop that part of yourself in order to be a minister, after all~"

I was startled.

"A minister cannot simply be strong..."

One needed strong intuition and farsightedness. Someone who only ever looked at documents in her office, only ever jogged around the castle moat, and never left the city during her days off was hardly suited to be the minister of agriculture. A solid grasp on the nature and climate of places all around the world was essential to the job.

I suppose that was what Her Majesty was trying to teach me.

"Thank you very much, Your Majesty! My eyes have been opened!"

"Aww, Miss Beelzebub, teasing you is so worth it~"

"What do you mean by that?!" I could not let that one slip by!

"Exactly what I said. You take everything at face value, so I'm always amused by our interactions."

I wonder if she had simply been toying with me the whole day...

"Well, I hope for more good things in the future. ♪"

The demon king smiled gleefully. She seemed more delighted than I thought she would be.

Perhaps a minister should also take care not to be tricked by something that only sounds believable...

In the days that followed, I diligently went jogging.

Also, to the surprise of no one, the marine plants that the demon king had procured from the ocean now sat brittle and dry in the dirt.

The reason I knew that was because I'd changed my jogging course to go *through the herb garden.*

I was the minister of agriculture, so it would be a good idea to check on the growing plants as part of my morning routine.

There was also something else that caught my eye.

The flower said only to grow at the top of cliffs, the one that could save one's gravely ill childhood friend—it was flourishing in the herb garden!

"It does not just grow atop cliffs! The climate simply did not agree with it elsewhere!"

Eventually, the flower might become a widely used medicinal herb in the demon lands.

"—And that concludes my report as minister of agriculture," I said with a triumphant look, then sat down.

I was right in the middle of a ministers' meeting in the presence of Her Majesty. You could call this the very heart of demon politics.

The other ministers were whispering among themselves.

"What an admirable response."

"You'd never think she was self-made now."

Good, good, gimme more of that.

I'd been minister of agriculture for several years at that point, and it felt like I was completely used to my rank.

"Thank you, Miss Beelzebub. I wouldn't be ashamed to introduce you as my minister anywhere now." Beaming, the demon king complimented me as well.

"No, no, it's all because your virtues cover the whole of the demon world, Your Majesty."

It was a standard expression, but I praised the demon king right back.

Right now, I was shining more brightly than I ever had in my life. I was performing my duties brilliantly, and I'd been blessed with good subordinates.

Vania bungled things pretty frequently, but we handled it.

I was actually even interviewed by a girls' magazine the other day for a feature titled "Five Demon Women Who Are Flying High."

They sent me a sample copy, but I personally bought about ten of 'em and gave copies to Fatla and Vania, too. Fatla told me, "It's far too obvious that you're boasting," but I don't think that's really a problem.

The demon king was in that same magazine, in fact. She's still young, and she's governing demonkind with a steady hand. Of course she'd get into print.

"My virtues, hmm? Unfortunately, there's one place where that isn't necessarily the case." The demon king gave an affected-sounding sigh.

On the whole, she tended to ham it up, but the demon kings have had a penchant for drama for generations. Maybe it ran in her blood.

"You know, when I engage in politics, people and factions gain my support, which means that no matter what I do, someone's rights, interests, and power must suffer. Inevitably, there are complaints from those quarters."

"Outrageous! We cannot let them get away with opposing you, Your Majesty."

I could give socially acceptable responses quickly now, too. I was not nervous like I was back when I first took up my post.

The other ministers followed suit.

"Precisely."

"Let us show those demons hell."

"Thank you, all of you. As it happens, I'm having difficulties with a certain area that has fallen behind on its tax payments. The lord of that territory says this is unavoidable due to a poor harvest, but I strongly suspect it may be a gesture of defiance against me."

Saying you couldn't pay your taxes because your harvest was bad, and that you just wouldn't be able to manage unless you got a discount, was the oldest trick in the book.

"What do you think, Miss Beelzebub?"

"They must pay! If they say the harvest was poor, then I'd recommend dispatching a supervisor and seeing what things are actually like over there."

"Yes, you're right."

Then the demon king smiled.
For some reason, a chill ran through me.
"The area that hasn't paid its taxes is the domain of Lord Nastoya the alraune."
Hmm? I feel like I've heard that name somewhere before...
"He once held power in the Ministry of Agriculture and was favored to be its next minister, but he lost his position due to graft."
Curses! This had everything to do with me!
"Since it just happens to be an issue with a formerly influential person in the Ministry of Agriculture, Miss Beelzebub, can I ask you to go?"
At this point, I suppose I can't refuse.
"Yes, ma'am, Your Majesty..."
All I could do was nod my head.

"Lady Beelzebub, this is a terribly alarming situation."
When I returned to my minister's chamber, I was met by Fatla's reproachful eyes.
"Lord Nastoya the alraune is the great noble who was expected to become minister of agriculture upon the ascension of the new demon king, but he was instead cross-examined regarding corruption and ended up retreating into his domain. And now the new minister of agriculture will walk in. He will take it as spite... *Sigh.*"
"Oh, so this really is headed in an unpleasant direction?"
"You may not come back alive. I mean it. Even if he is an alraune, Lord Nastoya is an ultra-high-level demon."
If you were wondering what an alraune is, they are a sort of plant

spirit. Strictly speaking, you can't call them demons, but demons are extremely lax when it comes to drawing lines like that. We may have wings, or horns, or tails, or one eye, or maybe three—there are too many differences when it comes to those things, so we don't sweat the small stuff.

Vania was shaking harder than I was. "No! I don't want to! The food in alraune territory isn't even good! It's all just weeds!"

"Why are you worried about *that*?!"

"People who live in territories with bad food are peculiarly stoic and narrow-minded! Lord Nastoya and his hangers-on were so unpleasant to be around. They were extremely picky about little things, too!"

*The views expressed here are those of the characters. Well, just Vania, really.

"Still, if an executive from the Ministry of Agriculture is causing trouble back in his territory, as the current head of the ministry, I expect I'm the one who should go and resolve it."

"There are tax collectors, aren't there?" Vania protested. "I'm pretty sure the group was made up of top necromancers and things. Let's ask them to handle it, okay?"

"Apparently, the tax collectors all oh-so-conveniently caught the flu, and they can't go."

"In other words, a conspiracy. They're trying to shove an unpleasant job off onto you!"

"Now, calm down; just settle down. Even alraunes won't grab you and eat you. They're demons, too."

"That's why I'm worried! If they were humans and they attacked, we'd be able to take them out instead, but demons are scary! I mean it!"

She's a leviathan; why is she this jumpy?

"Anyway, we're going. It's a simple job. We'll just tell him to pay his taxes, and that'll be the end of it. We'll leave next week."

"You know, that just happens to be the day my stomach always hurts, so I won't be able to g—"

"Do you take me for a fool?" I hit the side of Vania's head with a noogie attack.

"Hey! This is assault! This is blatant workplace violence!"

"So says Vania. What say you, Fatla?"

"I see nothing. It just happens to be the day when I can't see my little sister." Fatla summarily took my side.

Apparently, my loyal secretary would choose to side with her boss rather than her sister.

"I'll go... I'll go, so please stopppp!"

And so we ended up going to see Lord Nastoya the alraune.

Vania assumed her true, enormous leviathan shape, and we rode on her back to alraune territory.

In a way, it was a job that showed off her abilities as a leviathan, something that could boost her reputation.

However, there was a rather sizable problem.

"There's too much rocking going on..."

The cup I'd been about to drink from flew toward the wall of the room, along with the table, as Vania tilted again.

"I'm sorry. My sister is a bad pilot."

Fatla was standing there as if it was nothing. *She must be used to this,* I thought, until I saw that she was holding on to a ring that hung from the ceiling.

"What's that thing you've got there?"

"This is a strap for stability. If you grab it quickly when she leans or rocks, you can maintain your balance."

"Riding leviathans sure is rough..."

"I'm sorry! Every time I remember we're going to alraune territory, the stress interferes with my piloting."

An announcement from Vania echoed through the room. She had the same sort of method for that as her sister, Fatla.

"Just deal with it. You are a leviathan, so even if they do pick a fight, you can certainly win it," I said.

"*Alraunes are treacherous. They might use some sort of cheap trick...*"

"You never know; they might welcome us warmly, the way that farm did several years back."

"*You say that because you don't really know alraunes, boss. They'd never be generous.*"

How much does she hate alraunes anyway? If she said things like that in public, they'd call her a racist and run her right out of town.

"On that point, my sister's view may be the correct one," Fatla said. She was still hanging on to the strap. "Alraunes are vicious at heart. You really mustn't let your guard down. And family lineage is extremely important to them, so I expect their hatred of you is murderous, Lady Beelzebub."

"Oh, come on. Don't threaten me too much."

"It isn't a threat. That said, you're far stronger now than you were when you first became minister of agriculture, so I doubt it's anything you can't handle."

She just takes it for granted that we'll be fighting, huh? I thought, grabbing one of the ceiling straps myself as Vania rolled to the side again.

Hell's bells, I'd fare better flying with my own wings...

And so we went to see Lord Nastoya.

We told the alraune gatekeeper why we were there. His feet looked like plant roots, which was typical for an alraune.

"Understood. My master will be here before long, so if you'd be so kind as to wait..."

As we'd been told, we waited outside the gate.

Let us in first, would you? I thought, but it wouldn't do to get hostile right off the bat. We'd wait.

Fifteen minutes went by.

"Excuse me, is he going to be much longer?" Fatla asked the gatekeeper.

They'd kept us standing there the whole time, so I could understand why she was irritated. Fatla always looked irritated, but I was positive she was genuinely annoyed now.

"Ah, my apologies. I'm sure he's having trouble deciding what to wear." After that, we had no choice but to wait.

Thirty minutes went by.

"Really, what is the meaning of this? Hurry and summon your master, if you would," Fatla pressed the gatekeeper.

However, the gatekeeper only said, "I don't understand it myself."

Fatla turned my way with a really scary expression on her face. I thought she was going to yell at me for a second, and I flinched.

"He already got us. He's harassing us by making us wait forever."

"That…seems extremely likely." Something was obviously amiss.

Vania had sat down in front of the mansion and was taking a nap.

"That's disgraceful! Wake up!" Fatla scolded and promptly shook her, but…

One hour later.

"Thank you for coming, plebian Minister of Agriculture."

Finally, Lord Nastoya turned up, walking on root feet that looked like octopus tentacles. One look at his face was enough to tell he was of noble blood.

"Plebian? I am a proper noble now, mind you. Well, that doesn't matter. I'm tired after all this standing. Show us to a room with chairs."

My rank was currently higher than his, so I went with the arrogant approach. I was getting used to acting more pompous, too.

"Yes, of course, do follow me. Plebian Minister of Agriculture."

They did have chairs waiting for us—ratty, rickety chairs that looked ready to collapse the moment we sat on them. They were warped and leaning; a stiff breeze might knock them apart. Saying they were collections of boards in the shape of chairs would have been more accurate.

"Oh-ho, is this an attempt at living green or something...?" My temples were starting to twitch.

Fatla was glaring steadily at the man.

"These are the only chairs I can provide you with. I'm terribly sorry."

He really did have a nasty personality. I hadn't expected him to be such a lowlife.

Vania whispered in my ear. "Boss, please don't take a swing at him, okay? He's trying to get you to start a fight. He's planning to make it so that we attack them, and then they can thrash us in self-defense."

I couldn't entirely write that off as Vania's delusion. They were out for blood.

"Let's get down to business, Lord Nastoya. I'm told your territory hasn't sent in even the slightest bit of tax money, so I came to look into it. Would you show us to your farmland?"

"Before we get to that, I imagine you're tired. Please have a drink."

They brought us a purple mystery beverage that was very obviously sinister. No matter how careless you were, nobody would just gulp this down without asking questions.

Or so I thought, but Vania was about to drink it until I covered her mouth with my hand.

"Mrgl, mrgl...!"

"You make it too easy." Fatla slowly took something that looked like pink stationery labels out of her jacket. "This paper tests for poisons. If mild poison is present, the pink paper will turn brown; for strong poison, it will turn black."

She put some on.

It turned jet black.

"Yes, that's lethal poison. We must not drink this under any circumstances." Fatla turned a menacing glare on Lord Nastoya.

We couldn't start that fight, so she was threatening him with her eyes.

"My, my, I'm sorry about that. I must have added poison completely by accident."

Nothing was beneath this guy when it came to mocking us... That was a crime, not an accident. Couldn't we put together a case?

"Now then, I'll show you to the farmland. Be sure to check the harvest numbers."

This time, they took us to a farm that was a short distance from the manor.

They grew wheat here, and we were going to take a look at how well it was growing.

While we were on the move, we never let our guard down and kept an eye on the situation at all times.

Lord Nastoya was in the carriage with us until we were close to the farmland, and the man might very well attack us himself. Everyone here except us was the enemy.

In the end, we got to the wheat field without incident.

"To be perfectly frank, it's an excellent crop." Fatla sounded annoyed.

I nodded.

"It looks delicious, doesn't it? The ears are hanging low. I bet you could bake good bread with this." Vania was missing the point a little, but she meant the same thing.

This was not a poor crop. As a matter of fact, it was a bumper crop.

So his failure to pay taxes really had been a kind of sabotage.

"Lord Nastoya, I really don't think you could ever consider this a bad crop—"

I turned to look at the lord—

And he was gone! Even though we'd gotten out of the carriage together!

Instead, alraunes armed with bows and arrows were bearing down on us!

They were most definitely planning to kill us.

"Why you little…! You tricked us!"

"I knew it! Alraunes are the worst! We should never have come here!"

We ran for it. If we didn't run, we'd get shot!

Ah, if this is how it's going to be, should I have followed my instincts and just kept pushing my pencil as a bottom-tier bureaucrat? At the very least, there wouldn't have been any attempts on my life…

I considered striking back with magic, but there were mage types stealthily lurking in the field, too. They were probably there to get in the way if we tried to cast spells. Since casting spells would make us more vulnerable, it would actually be a fatal error…

However, it wasn't as if we'd made no plans of our own. We weren't grunt-level demons.

"Lady Beelzebub, distance yourself from me a little, please," Fatla said, moving to stand in front of me. "This is a field, so I have room. Leave it to me."

"All right. Don't you dare get hurt, though."

I took Vania's hand and put some distance between us and Fatla. We appeared to be abandoning her, but that wasn't the case at all.

As Fatla stood there by herself, they prepared to launch their arrows at her. Just then, she transformed into her enormous leviathan shape!

The arrows bounced off her hard skin like little toys.

"Sh-she's way too huge!"

"We can't fight that!"

At the sight of the leviathan, the alraunes ran away with their tails between their legs.

…Not that alraunes have tails.

"We seem to have made it out alive…"

For the moment, Vania and I decided to hole up in a building on top of Fatla.

"Honestly, what they're doing is beyond unacceptable. Let's go back to the demon king immediately and report them!" Vania was already on the verge of tears, and I completely sympathized. However—

"If we go home when things are like this, it will cause trouble for them, too. Their boss will probably come out to explain it."

Sure enough, from our vantage point up on top of Fatla, we spotted Lord Nastoya emerge.

I had Fatla turn back into her human shape, then confronted the lord.

"I'm terribly sorry, plebian Minister of Agriculture. The fact that there was hunting here today slipped my mind. That was a bit of a blunder. Ha! Ha! Ha!"

I see. So he's going to keep playing innocent, huh?

"Well, everybody makes mistakes. I'll forgive you," I told him, smiling proudly.

Lord Nastoya's smirk crumbled, probably because I was being excessively nonchalant.

"You see, I don't trouble myself with trivial matters. As you well know, I'm the minister of agriculture. If I got caught up in the details and neglected the big picture, I'd never make it as the minister of agriculture. Indeed, I am from common stock, but the minister of agriculture is the minister of agriculture. ♪ Because she is, after all, the minister of agriculture... ♪"

Lord Nastoya's expression froze over.

I knew it.

This man had one heck of a complex over not getting to be the minister of agriculture.

"And so, Lord Nastoya, I'd like to ensure the big picture is clear. From the looks of it, there are no problems at all with your harvest, and I want you to pay your taxes properly. Understand? That's all I came to accomplish as the minister of agriculture, so you do your job as a backcountry lord, would you?"

"S-silence, whelp!" Lord Nastoya roared, finally showing his true colors. "What 'minister of agriculture'?! A nobody from nowhere becoming a minister—the world's gone mad! By all rights, I should have been minister of agriculture!"

"What you think doesn't matter. The fact is, right now, the head of the

Ministry of Agriculture is me, and you are just a retired noble has-been. Pay your taxes, would you? You can talk nasty about me all you want, just pay your taxes! Pay up, pay up, pay up!"

"Hmph! Making a pathetic wench like this the minister of agriculture... That little girl of a demon king is a benighted fool!"

That was crossing a line.

"Hey! Insulting the demon king is an inexcusable crime—one you might pay for in blood!"

I couldn't care less what people said about me. I'm sure if I listened to every uninformed opinion about me, my whole life wouldn't be enough time to hear all of it.

I was a minister who made an unprecedented rise to power from the bottom of the heap. I must have blackmailed somebody, right? I was some high-ranking official's lover, right? I'm sure somebody was saying it. If I let that get under my skin, I'd never survive.

But I couldn't let insults directed at the demon king slide.

"The leviathans who serve you are just as foolish. They must be completely devoid of pride to obey such a low-class demon!"

Why, that little—! Fatla and Vania, even!

"Lord Nastoya, I challenge you to a duel. If I win, first you will apologize to both my secretaries, and then you will present yourself to the demon king and apolo— Bwuff!"

Fatla had come up behind me and caught me in a nelson hold.

"What are you saying?! You were coolly backing him into a corner, so why bring up dueling?!"

"Lemme go, Fatla! Insulting me is one thing, but I cannot let him get away with insults to the demon king and my subordinates! Otherwise, I am a failure as minister of agriculture!"

Vania came to help Fatla out. She was almost crying. "Boss, in a duel, you might get killed, you know?! Please take it back!"

Right. Depending on the situation, people sometimes die in duels.

Lord Nastoya was licking his chops. He probably expected this to go his way.

©Benio

"In that case, if I win the duel, may I respectfully request your resignation as minister of agriculture? Can we agree to those terms?"

"Yeah! I'd be happy to! And your attempts at politeness now are completely pointless." I didn't back down one little bit.

"I am of noble birth, after all, and my family's status reaches back for generations. Low-level demon though you may be, I acknowledge the fire that makes you stand your ground so firmly."

$$\diamond$$

We chose to duel in the mansion's garden.

Lord Nastoya had a sword. Alraunes could attack with vines that extended from their bodies, too, so that blade was probably a weapon meant to take my life.

I was empty-handed. As a rule, I didn't carry weapons around with me.

The spectators all had ties to my opponent's house, so this was an "away" game for our team.

That said, I didn't intend to excuse myself by saying, *I lost because our cheering sections were different sizes.*

"Lady Beelzebub… If you feel you're in danger, please forfeit…"

"Boss, even if you get fired, we'll support you at the leviathan house for life!"

My two secretaries were cheering for me, and that was enough… *Wait, is that cheering? They might actually be worrying…*

"Hrrmmm. *Siiiigh…* My blood's begun running rather hot over these past few years."

It was almost hard to believe I'd ever plugged away processing accounts.

I wonder what sort of rank-and-file bureaucrat is doing my job at this point. I made a manual and left it for my replacement, so if they read it properly, they should be able to do the work by now…

"I'll crush this low-born demon and make my return to the Ministry of Agriculture! Your resignation should change the winds of fate!"

Yeah, sure, talk all you want. The only way to drain the pus with this type is to crush it completely.

I understood why I'd been sent here, too. It was to fan the flames of jealousy for someone I'd personally bumped off the ladder of success.

In that case, let's have him burn himself to ashes.

I drew a deep breath. *Always take deep breaths before the important things.*

That wasn't something anyone had taught me. Actually, it was something I'd said to Fatla back when Vania had burned some important documents. Even calm Fatla had turned so red in the face, I'd had to remind her to breathe.

"After all, if this were another era, I'd be an executive of the demon king, blocking the humans' advance. If I can't put down one country-bumpkin noble, I'll never get anywhere."

"Hold your tongue, lowly commoner!" Lord Nastoya ran at me on those root legs of his.

I spread my wings and charged at the enemy.

Don't underestimate the Lord of the Flies!

I slipped through the enemy's vine whips, and—

"Who are you calling a commoner?! I'm a proud noble!"

—I decked him in the face.

Whuddd!

"You insolent oaf!" I cried.

I'd knocked the enemy off balance, so I hit him again.

Krakk!

"And you even insulted the demon king! That's a grave crime!"

This time, I kicked up from the lower left.

Whomp!

Then I clasped both hands and brought them down on his head like a hammer.

Boooooooom!

Okay, now for the next attack, I started to think, but Lord Nastoya had already blacked out.

"Hmm...? Is it over? Was that good enough?"

I'd expected the fighting to get fiercer, but my opponent didn't even look like he was going to move, and not even a noble as rotten as this one would play dead and watch for an opportunity.

I kicked him one more time, just in case, but he only dribbled something like drool from his mouth. Sap, I guess?

When I looked at my secretaries, they weren't jumping around and cheering at all. They just looked stunned.

"What...? Did I break the rules somehow? I'm rather concerned by your reactions..."

"Boss! You're so strong, it's almost creepy! Actually, it *is* creepy! It's creepy!"

"Hey, Vania! If you say any more than that, I'll dock your pay!"

You could hardly even call that a compliment!

"Lady Beelzebub, you did keep diligently working all this time to get stronger... However, I never dreamed it would be so... You're top class, even for a demon..." Apparently, Fatla couldn't believe it, either, but before long, a smile bloomed on her face. "Congratulations, Lady Beelzebub."

That brief comment made even my eyes get a little moist.

"I feel as if I'm your boss for real now."

I walked over to the sisters and pulled them both into a hug.

"—And that concludes my explanation of the plan to distribute the territory under Lord Nastoya's control."

I wrapped up my report in the demon king's chambers.

There was no point in telling the other executives about this, so it was just the two of us.

For a variety of reasons, including his crime of neglecting to pay his taxes without a legitimate reason and the crime of insulting the demon king, Lord Nastoya had been exiled.

"Yes, Miss Beelzebub, well done." The demon king came up to me and patted me on the shoulder. "You're rapidly growing into a demon after my own heart. It makes me happy."

"Your Majesty, you sent me because you knew it would turn out this way, didn't you?"

Send in the person most likely to irritate a fallen noble and goad him into picking a fight—both Lord Nastoya and yours truly had been neatly manipulated by our king.

"Oh, that's so complicated; I'm not sure I understand." The demon king feigned ignorance with a smile.

After that reaction, I can't even pursue the issue.

"However, I do have an ideal—an image of an ideal elder sister."

"H-huh…"

What the heck is she talking about?

"Somebody everyone loves, even idolizes—who exudes an air of nobility despite her common birth, who has earned all of it with hard work. Splendid, don't you think?"

One thing's for sure—she's talking about me.

"And that big sister's sworn little sister is a girl born into the most noble of noble families. Don't you think that's a marvelous gap?"

This time, the demon king put her hands on my shoulders.

Her eyes look dead serious…

"I feel as if I've finally managed to mold you into my ideal elder sister, Miss Beelzebub. Hee-hee-hee-hee…"

I sensed that I was in danger.

Yes, it was true I couldn't come close to matching the demon king's true power, but this fear was based in something else entirely.

"W-well, I still have work to do as the minister of agriculture, so I'll be going!"

I backed away from the demon king, then got out of the room fast.

©Benio

From behind me, I heard a voice say, "Wait! Please don't run away, my elder sister candidate!" but I ignored it.

I thought I'd crushed an enemy and finally managed to act as a minister of agriculture should—

But I got the feeling another awkward problem had reared its head.

"I am truly sorry, boss!"

As I entered the ministerial office early that morning, Vania suddenly apologized to me.

"Ah yes. Let me know once you've finished writing your apology. And be sure to include what you plan to do to make sure this does not happen again," I said, using my folding fan to cool my face.

I gracefully took my seat at my desk.

If I were to get angry at every mistake Vania made, I would be upset for the rest of my life. I had to maintain a forgiving mindset.

"Oh, no, this won't require a letter of apology, boss."

"Oh? Then what sort of mistake have you made?"

"Aren't you being a little too casual about this…? Can't you sound a bit more interested?"

She was starting to sound like a pushy girlfriend…

"Just say it. I shall decide whether or not to be interested once I hear about it."

"Here!" Vania presented to me a piece of paper.

"Ahhh, our lunch provider is closed today."

"I'm sorry! I completely forgot! Which is why I didn't have any time to
make lunch for myself... I have nothing to eat today!"

Vania seemed overly guilty about this, but—

"It's all right. No need to apologize so much."

"What? It's really okay? But lunch is the greatest source of working
energy!"

"I care not for your unique definition of lunch."

She would only ever think about lunch before noon.

Fatla ignored our conversation entirely and was already checking
some documents.

There was no question that she cared even less for this than I did. I was
surprised that sisters could have such opposing personalities.

"Then we shall eat lunch at a restaurant somewhere in town. 'Tis a bit
far, but that cannot be helped."

A good majority of the offices for each ministry sat in the district
between the outer moat and inner moat of the castle. So by some definitions, our office was within castle grounds.

One could not cross the bridge on the outer moat and find oneself in a shopping district, so there was a bit of distance before one came to a street with proper restaurants.

"Ten minutes one way means it would be twenty minutes there and back, and having to wait in line could pose a problem. However, no customers at lunchtime is surely a sign that the establishment is no good... Hmm, this is distressing..."

"Exactly! You need real tactics when it comes to lunch in town! Now you understand!" Vania seemed to be enjoying this. "Depending on whether you discover a hidden gem or a dud, the place you go to can dictate your working energy for the rest of the day! You can't make thoughtless judgments when it comes to work!"

"Even if you end up in a restaurant that might not be so good, you must still do your work," I interjected.

And do you not make mistakes even on days when you loudly proclaim the virtues of your lunch? I doubt it affects the quality of your work.

"If that does not give you enough time, then why not use the cafeteria here in the building?" Fatla suggested, her eyes still trained on the documents.

This was not worth it to her to stop working, and I thought the same. Still, she was listening.

"The cafeteria, hmm. Ah yes, that is on the first floor, no?"

Most offices had a cafeteria, and that included the Ministry of Agriculture.

The one Fatla mentioned was also open to regular citizens, not just employees, so anyone could walk in and use it.

I doubted any regular citizens would come all this way to have lunch at a ministry cafeteria, but 'twas likely for the many visitors we had from various companies.

"I have never used it before. I worked in the Agricultural Policy Organization previously, and that is in a different building. After I became minister, I've only ever had the Darkness lunch box."

And the lunches Vania would sometimes make for us.

While I did pay her properly, she had said it was simply a hobby of hers. A hobby she was excellent at, given she had graduated from culinary school.

"Then let's go to the cafeteria on the first floor! I haven't eaten there in a long time, so I'm thrilled to try it!" Vania was getting excited.

Her motivation was truly and deeply tied to food.

"What?" I said. "You both work in the main building; haven't you had plenty of opportunities to eat there?"

Her reaction made it seem like she knew nothing about the cafeteria.

"It is a bit of a pain to go all the way down to the first floor, so I always had Vania order Darkness lunch boxes for us," Fatla replied, still working.

You will do anything to keep working, won't you?

"The career bureaucrats start working on the upper floors right after joining the ministry, after all. It was too much trouble to go down."

"Hrrm… What a hierarchical society… But 'twould be a bit unsatisfying to have someone of high status on a lower floor…"

There was a consensus among us that the more powerful, more important people should be stationed on the upper floors. I suppose that came from when we were at war with the humans, and the bosses would often wait on the higher floors.

"And when you're on the wrong floor, the elevator rarely comes. All the important people would get on from the upper floors, so it would often fill up before it got to the lower floors. On the other hand, we did not want to take the stairs."

An "elevator" was a box that moved up and down. There was someone to pull the ropes (an employee from a private company, not a staff member of the ministry) that would bring it to the different floors. The cost of the labor tended to run up very high, so they could only be found in tall buildings like the ministries.

"I see… I suppose that is a thing that happens here in the office…"

"I also agree we should try the cafeteria."

"Very well. Then we shall do so."

"However, I believe it will be terribly crowded if we go during lunch-time, since all the employees will head there at once," said Fatla. "Why don't we work for an extra hour before heading down? I believe that will smooth out our lunch plans."

"You are the definition of detail-oriented, Fatla…," I mused.

Vania was pouting a bit at the prospect of her morning work hours being one hour longer as a result, but I ignored her. She wouldn't be putting in any overtime, after all.

And then the clock struck one.

"Yes! It's lunchtime! Lunch! Lunch! Lunch!"

"Vania, how enthusiastic can you be?!"

She was yelling like a cuckoo clock.

"Lunch is later than usual! So I'm extra hungry, and extra excited to eat at the cafeteria, and twice as enthusiastic as I usually am!"

"If I could find as much joy in food as you do, my life would be pure bliss…," I commented.

The leviathan sisters and I headed down to the first floor, where the cafeteria was.

Ah, the cafeteria. Now that I thought about it, I rarely ever passed this corner of the building. I wondered what it was like.

Perhaps it would be surprisingly modern and stylish. I wondered if they had a fluffy-omelet lunch set or anything similar.

When we arrived at the entrance, I first noticed that it was dark.

There was a gauche sign that read MINISTRY OF AGRICULTURE CAF-ETERIA. There was no door, so we could see all the tables inside before going in, but I felt as hesitant to enter this place as I would an eccentric little hole-in-the-wall bar.

There was no one else inside, perhaps because we had come an hour later. It was too quiet.

I suppose that was one reason why I felt so hesitant to go in. An empty cafeteria is never a good sign.

There was a panel next to the entrance:

Meal-Ticket System

Tell the staff member to the right of the entrance what your order is, then retrieve a ticket. Once your food is ready, the chef will call for you, and you can hand in your ticket.

Water is self-serve.

This system felt quite old-fashioned.

"Hmm, this is very retro…" Vania seemed somewhat uncomfortable.

"We are not going to be attacked. Come now, let's go in. Oh, I suppose we must choose what we want first."

The menu contained things like Lunch Set A, Lunch Set B, Lunch Set C, and curreh.

Also, in terms of noodles, they had ra-ment and spaghetti.

Lunch Set C was the most generous, so I went with that one. As an added bonus, it did not cost very much.

I turned right from the entrance and said, "One Set C."

Once I'd paid the money, a middle-aged demon lady rushed over and handed me a tag that read *SET C—5*.

And I would hand this off to the chef once my number was called to receive my food.

After I waited a little while, at a corner labeled PICK-UP WINDOW, the cook came over and called, "Set C!"

I placed the tag on the counter and received the tray with my food.

The main dish of the Set C was fried meat—what kind of meat it was, I was not sure. It also came with an unidentifiable soup and some bread. And finally, a small bowl of salad.

The place was empty, so I sat at a four-person table.

Vania and Fatla soon joined me, carrying a Set B and ra-ment respectively.

"Now let's dig in!" Vania placed her set tray before her, her excitement back in full force.

"Aye, let's." I brought a spoonful of soup to my mouth, while Vania took a sip of hers.

Ugh!

I was frightfully close to yelling aloud.

That was how bad it was. I suppose *bad* was not quite the right word—*flavorless* would be more accurate.

What is this? Lukewarm water?

"...This soup is quite bad, isn't it?"

I had not seen Vania scowl like that before. So my reaction was not wrong.

I next took a bite of the mystery-meat cutlet. This meat was dry and unpleasant, and the seasoning was scant. Even after munching on it for a bit, I still had no idea what sort of meat it was.

"This cannot be edible without any sort of sauce... But there is no sauce on the table..."

The only seasoning stand was in front of the counter, so I had no choice but to go and get it.

After I drowned the meal in sauce, I somehow managed to stomach it. Any flavor it pretended to have was utterly eclipsed by the taste of the added sauce.

Vania wore a look of displeasure as she ate her odd stir-fry that came with the Set B.

"The heat hasn't been well distributed, and the vegetables are all mushy. The texture has been entirely rendered into nothing. There was no effort; the chef believed that it was okay to fry everything so long as it was all cooked through. They may not be able to use expensive ingredients, but first and foremost, the problem lies with the skills of the one who prepared this food."

"You have so much to say about cooking."

This was the most serious I had ever seen Vania.

In the meantime, Fatla was quietly slurping on her ra-ment, which sat in an amber soup.

"What does that taste like, Fatla?" I asked.

"Perhaps very low-quality ra-ment that would be served at a cheap, run-down restaurant in the countryside. Or the kind served at food halls in a carriage station's waiting rooms."

"Mmm... So when one has no other choice..."

"It tastes exactly the same."

A damning assessment.

"Not much can be done about the noodles, considering they aren't handmade, but I would like it if they took a little more care. This is the sort of thing I would eat if I simply needed something in my stomach."

After eating about 70 percent of the noodles, Fatla put her fork down. A small gesture to show that this establishment was no good.

I looked around the cafeteria again.

We were here past the peak, yes, but it was still much too empty.

"Well, I suppose we can go search for a place in the town around the castle next time. We will call this a defeat for now. There are some things we will never know without trying them, after all." Vania looked so unbelievably discontent that it scared me. I wondered if she would be able to get any work done in the afternoon.

This awful lunch would put a damper on the rest of our day. *Perhaps I should take these two to a nice restaurant in the evening... Perhaps there, we could complain about the cafeteria...*

*   *   *

But contrary to my expectations, Vania worked at a nice, brisk pace in the afternoon.

She was checking all sorts of papers, and she even left the office several times to fetch relevant documents from other departments.

At the very least, she seemed to be going above and beyond expectations.

But when it came time for work to be done—

"Vania, why don't we go and eat together, all three of us? You must want to complain about that cafeteria, no?"

"My apologies, but I'm busy assembling some materials, so please feel free to go with my sister," she replied.

"Are you all right? Your personality has changed. Have you been brainwashed by a spell?"

Fatla patted me on the back. "Lady Beelzebub, Vania is a public official, so she does have the requisite skill to do her job. She simply never has the motivation for it."

"I see... Well, if she's finally taking her work seriously, then we shall leave her be..."

I did wish this would happen more often, however.

The next day, Vania handed me a very thick stack of documents.

"Please take a look at this, boss!"

"Let's see, *Proposal for the Renovation of the Ministry of Agriculture Cafeteria*?"

"I cannot stand to see such an unmotivated eatery! I will spearhead the cafeteria's rebirth!"

She was oddly enthusiastic about this!

I looked through the contents.

She had collected detailed data. As a result of the current tab system, the cafeteria was ordering food from the cheapest provider, which meant those who used it were not at all satisfied with the experience.

"I believe you'll see this when you look through the data, but more than seventy percent of the people working in the ministry do not use the cafeteria. Everyone knows the food is terrible. And when employees who do regularly use it were asked about their degree of satisfaction, only twenty percent responded either 'very good' or 'good.' Over sixty percent said it was 'bad' or 'infuriatingly terrible'!"

"When did you collect this data?"

"I conducted a survey after lunch yesterday."

What unbelievable enthusiasm...

"By having the cafeteria serve better food, our employees will be more eager to work! And if everyone eats at the cafeteria, then we will not have to get lunch all the way out in the town around the castle! Think of the convenience! Let's do this! We must do this!"

Vania leaned in toward me hungrily, supplicating.

"Very well... I understand how you feel... Due to the contract, we cannot immediately change our supplier, but we can change the furnishings and the menu... However, that is quite a major project, so someone will need to take charge—"

"I'll do it!" Vania yelled. "Lunch will be the core of my work! Neglecting our food is the same as neglecting our work! The same as neglecting the whole Ministry of Agriculture!"

"Those things are not equal."

"Yes they are! No demon can live without eating! Equipping the office with a bad cafeteria is like trying to kill our employees!"

I had no idea this side of Vania existed...

Her logical progression was a bit of a mess, but she'd convinced me.

I glanced over to Fatla, but she naturally carried on with her assigned work with an air of nonchalance.

I do wish she would help her minister when I am being cornered.

Well, if Vania herself said she would do it, then I suppose I would leave it in her hands.

To be honest, if there were any parts of this project that she couldn't handle, I was sure Fatla and I could easily fill in the gaps.

On the signature line, I wrote, *Approved—Minister Beelzebub.*

"Go on, then. Do as you please."

"Thank you so much! I have taken the very first step on the path of the cafeteria's rebirth! The gears of change have begun turning and will usher in a new era!"

"Calm down, Vania."

But since she had gone through all the trouble, it was time to watch and see how much potential Vania really had.

Starting that day, I couldn't say for sure if the gears of change were turning or not, but what was certain was that Vania was now working. And working hard.

For a while after that day, she was often away from the ministerial office.

"I have a meeting with a contractor regarding the cafeteria renovation now!"

"I will be helping with the lunch lady's culinary training!"

"I am going on a business trip to a rural farm to procure ingredients!"

And so on, for days on end.

To be honest, I'd scolded her when she said she would be taking a business trip far away—"*Write a business-trip request form! Do not go without my permission!*"—but I mostly left everything in her hands.

One day when she was gone on a trip, I quietly murmured in Fatla's direction, in a tone that suggested I was musing to myself and required no response:

"I thought I knew everything about Vania, but I was entirely mistaken."

"There are those across the world who have no passion at all, but my sister is particularly passionate about cooking." Fatla sounded rather proud of her—or at least, not annoyed. "In fact, I would say she is so uncompromising because she is not working as a professional in the field."

I thought back on my time living in the countryside. "I am a tad jealous."

Back when I was helping with my parents' greengrocery, my life felt somewhat unsatisfying.

I had blamed the rural environment and fled to the castle town, but in the end, I had only continued my simple life. I had chosen not to put my all into anything for a long time, and that was my own fault.

After a moment of silence, Fatla responded, "You are rather passionate about your work as the agricultural minister now, Lady Beelzebub, so I suppose you're all right."

I could see the demon king's face in my mind's eye.

I suppose she had changed my life. For better or for worse, there was no doubt that it had changed.

How can I ever repay you, Your Majesty?

Ever since Vania jumped into the cafeteria renewal project, I, too, started to pass by the cafeteria more frequently.

Though, I still did not use it; I only did so to check on the renovations.

One day, I found a paper that read *WE WILL BE OPENING AFTER REFURBISHMENT SOON* plastered in front of the old-fashioned cafeteria.

And one week after that, it was temporarily closed for renovation.

The establishment had not been very popular to begin with, so no one seemed especially inconvenienced. I was unsure how to feel about that, though…

One day, I could hear Vania's voice coming from inside.

"Just fifteen seconds should be enough! You'll ruin the texture if you leave it on the heat any longer than that! Be careful!"

She was instructing the cafeteria lady, apparently.

"Now here's the old vegetable stir-fry, and here's the one you just made. Compare them! Totally different, wouldn't you say? You can use this technique for your own recipes, too, so please take this knowledge home with you!"

What was her real job again...?

And then another week later.

The exterior of the cafeteria had transformed into a stylish café! It seemed the inside was still under construction, and there was no doubt they were making drastic renovations.

There was a sign outside that listed the date they were planning to reopen.

Under Vania's watchful eye, the place would be completely revived soon...

Finally, it was opening day.

Surprisingly, I found Vania working in the minister's office bright and early that morning.

"Oh, are you sure you don't need to be in the cafeteria?"

"What are you talking about? I'm a secretary. I'm supposed to be in the minister's office."

"I apologize for being sarcastic. But you have been spending much more time in the cafeteria as of late."

Plus, it was odd to complain about her working, so I chose to take my own seat for the day.

A little before eleven, Vania came to stand before my desk. "Boss, there's a task the minister needs to do."

"I am doing plenty of them right now."

"No, I mean the first customer at the renovated cafeteria should be the one at the top of the ministry."

Ah, so eleven was the opening hour.

"Very well. Then I suppose I shall be eating lunch a little earlier than normal." I stood.

"Just to be sure, you haven't ordered the Darkness lunch box today, have you?" Vania asked.

"You haven't asked me about the order today, so it's all right."

I had indeed planned to pop by the renovated cafeteria on its opening day.

"Fatla, you—"

—*Should come, too* is what I was going to say, but she was already standing up.

"I will see my sister's project through to completion." It seemed Fatla was curious to see what her sister had been up to, as well.

We went down to the first floor and walked over to the cafeteria.

I had seen the modern exterior before, but not the brand-new menu.

"There are considerably more sweets on the menu now. And there are tea-set options, too."

"Exactly. You can now come down for a quick visit for your three o'clock snack. Also, would you mind if we stepped outside for a moment?"

We did, and there we found terrace seating! The outer moat was nearby, too, so it felt a bit like dining by the riverside.

"We've planned this out so that outside customers can use it as a café. Of course, you can also hold meetings here. I'm certain some tea will help with efficiency!"

"I'm not so sure about that, but you have entirely transformed the whole area, that's for certain."

Now—for the inside.

We went back into the building and made our way toward the cafeteria entrance.

"Welcome!" A young female demon greeted us.

"Mmm... I see you've fired the old-lady staffers and hired younger ones... That might have been a step too far for just renovating the cafeteria..."

"No need to worry about that. They're only under a Glamour spell right now; they're actually all the same employees!"

"You have made quite the change!"

"I have one granddaughter!" one of the employees said, shining with Glamour-induced youth.

If you can get a seemingly lazy person to invest in an activity, they can do it quite thoroughly, and this was a perfect example. It was similar to a person who rarely ever cleaned picking one day out of the year to get it all done.

"What will you have, boss? My treat!"

Well, it wasn't as though the cafeteria cost very much.

"Hmm, I suppose I'll order the three-salad lunch plate..."

"I will have ra-ment."

Is Fatla secretly a big fan of ra-ment?

"It will be hard to tell the difference if I do not order the same," she explained.

"I see... Fastidious as ever..."

The windows were open, and a breeze came in from the terrace.

The inside had been repainted a refreshing white, and the tables and chairs were the kind one would find in a stylish establishment (I did not frequent fancy restaurants, so I am well aware that I lack the vocabulary for this... I never had the courage to go alone... And nothing like this existed in my hometown).

"These tables and chairs must have cost quite a bit, no? Are you sure you're still within budget?"

"Oh, I bought all the tables and chairs from a scrap-renovation company. They were actually very cheap."

Vania wore an expression that read, *I'm glad you asked!*

You're the star today, Vania. Shine as bright as you want.

"And all the things on the menu are about twenty percent more expensive now. The five-hundred-koinne lunch sets have been replaced with six-hundred-eighty-koinne lunch plates and whatnot."

It sounded like she was planning on running a successful business by raising the prices.

"Ah yes, I see that all those uninspiring names like 'Lunch Set B' are gone... But do you think customers will come after you raise the prices so?"

"Hardly any customers were coming before, so we didn't have much to lose!"

"Indeed!"

Before, everyone believed it was cheap because it was bad...

"And the truly trendy establishments in the town around the castle ask for even more money. Paying more makes the customers feel rich. That is the concept for this cafeteria!"

"Please keep your voice down—you'll ruin the effect..."

Then a young-looking staff lady called out, "Three-salad lunch plate!" from the counter.

"Vania, is she also—?"

"That is the kitchen lady. The one who has been here for ages."

The Glamour spell was working well.

But everything I'd seen so far was simply superficial. The real question was how the food tasted.

I stabbed my fork into the vegetables on my lunch plate and carefully brought it to my mouth, making sure not to spill any of the dressing.

The tangy dressing, the fresh, sweet, leafy greens...!

"This tastes like something from a fancy restaurant!"

"Doesn't it?!" Vania cackled with the confidence of a boss monster. "Our staffers will feel themselves leveling up eating here! It will bring out the best in them! And it doesn't hurt the wallet at all! Here they can recharge their energy, then tackle their afternoon work undaunted!"

"Oh, Vania... I am so sorry for having doubted you thus far..." A tear rolled down my cheek.

Vania looked even more distinguished than she usually did, and I doubted any Glamour magic was involved.

"I honestly thought you were exaggerating when you said the quality of one's lunch could change one's motivation for work... But this food does boost my morale, certainly more than the lunch set from some run-down cafeteria..."

It might not be an exaggeration to say a revolution had occurred within the Ministry of Agriculture.

Many more people would start using the cafeteria. I was sure of it.

"Thank you so much for understanding. This is what I hoped to achieve with the Improving-Work-Through-Food Project!"

"What an ambitious task you've been working on..."

"Oh, no, I thought up the name just a moment ago."

Some things never change, including Vania's impulsiveness.

As Vania and I spoke, Fatla quietly slurped her ra-ment and even drank all the broth. That is bad for you, Fatla!

"I see how it changed."

Fatla showed no sign of satisfaction, so it was hard to tell what she was thinking.

So did it pass? Or fail?

"I can see the noodles are now made at a proper noodle-making factory. And I can tell that you are using the fat from the chicken as a key ingredient. The addition of heavy spice gives it even more character. This cafeteria has a wide array of offerings, so it can never truly compete with specialty establishments that boil their own broth for hours. So in order to make up for that—to *hide* that, though I apologize for the word choice—you've chosen to embrace the spiciness of the broth and make it especially strong. I would not say this is the best way to increase customer satisfaction without raising costs too high, but it is certainly a better way."

Her answer was over one hundred words.

"Fatla, you certainly love ra-ment, don't you? I had no idea, since you never said anything."

"No, that is not so."

She was also stone-faced when she replied to my question, so I was uncertain if she was answering honestly, making a high-level joke, or trying to brush me off.

"Why don't you take me to a ra-ment place you like sometime in the future, hmm?"

"I will have to think it over." She dodged that one quite easily. "Ra-ment is not the type of food to chat over noisily with a group."

Oh, she is a fan...

All of a sudden, I started hearing lively voices.

"Whoa! It's so nice-looking now!"

"We can start showing off to the other ministries!"

"Let's eat outside on the terrace!"

Though it was still a little before noon, employees were starting to arrive, and the seats were filling up.

"It seems we have more customers than the noontime rush, and it's not even noon. While I'm sure the renovations are the reason so many more people are coming by, it's still a good way to start anew!" Vania said, looking around the cafeteria.

She was like a mother proudly watching after her child.

"Aye, you did well, Vania."

Thanks to our abysmally awful cafeteria, I got to see one of my underlings come into her own. One can never tell where they might find a silver lining.

One week later...

When I entered the minister's office, the leviathan sisters were arguing over something.

"Stop this at once!"

"Leave me alone, Sis!"

"I cannot let you do this—you know that!"

"This isn't a phase!"

Though the two had vastly different personalities, they did get along. The way they were fighting now was not normal.

"What is going on here?"

"Boss, I have a favor to ask of you!"

Vania's energy reminded me of when she asked my opinion on the cafeteria renovation. Perhaps she was thinking about renovating another ministry's cafeteria, too?

"This is for you!"

The paper she gave me read:

LETTER OF RESIGNATION

"……What?"

"When I was working on the cafeteria renovations, I started thinking that it was time I open my own restaurant! I want to resign and become a great chef! Thank you for all you've done for me over the years!"

This was something I could not accept, and I told her exactly how I felt as her boss.

"No, hold on, hold on!" I cried. "Calm down and think a little before you make this decision!"

"Yes, exactly!" Fatla agreed. "You'll never be able to run an establishment on your own! You can't use taxpayer money for your own restaurant!"

"It's fine! I'll just take out a loan of five million koinne from the bank and start it up that way!"

"Then wait until you have earned enough money to start a business before you quit!" Fatla cried. "Just thinking about you borrowing money is a terrifying prospect!"

"Indeed! Keep cooking as your hobby! I'm afraid you might do something terrible if you get caught between your dreams and reality, so please don't do this!"

The fuss over Vania's resignation subsided about three days later.

I suppose wanting the talents of one's underlings to blossom wasn't always a good thing…

All the wingless bureaucrats rolled into the corner of the building.

"Ahhh!" "Can you drive a little safer?!" "Ow, my back!"

As her passengers cried in agony, Vania, in her leviathan form, flew smoothly toward her destination. People knew her speed because she was like a warship.

We had quite a few passengers this time—sixty-five, to be precise. A lucky number for us demons, as it was a multiple of thirteen.

"I knew we should have taken Fatla..."

I was flapping my own wings, staying afloat within the building. Hovering would tire me eventually, so I planned to grab hold of something later.

Beside me, Fatla sat bound to her seat with some contraption she called a "seat belt." It had apparently been newly installed for Vania's shaky flights. A stability device did seem to be a safer option.

"The hard-and-fast rule of bureaucracy is to do the worst things first," she said. "It would be best to experience our panic going outward first, then have my safe flying on the return trip. Especially since many will be very relaxed on the way back."

"Mmm… But our whole department vacation will be for naught if people are injured before we even arrive."

"None of us are so weak that we would be injured from this, so I wouldn't worry." Fatla was reading a book while she sat in her chair. I thought she might get motion sickness, but she seemed fine. "Besides, this is a business trip coupled with a training excursion. This is not a pleasure jaunt. This is work; please do not get these mixed up," Fatla mentioned, reminding me of the surface reason we were going on this business trip.

"Oh, erm, yes… Indeed. We will have a good, thorough training session in the hot springs! We will learn of agriculture!"

Then I heard a voice. *"Ding-dong!"*

It was Vania's sign that she was going to talk about something. She always said it before some sort of announcement or warning. Perhaps it was a kind of spell.

"My apologies for the turbulence. It is dusty up here in the atmosphere today, and my nose is all itchy. There might be even bigger bumps and shakes when I sneeze and whatnot, so please be careful~ You might fall off if you stand out on the deck, so those who cannot fly—please refrain from going outside~"

Vania's carefree announcement echoed inside, and I heard our participants complaining soon after.

"Don't take us on board if it's going to be this dangerous!"

"At this point, I'd be safer clinging onto a drunken roc bird!"

Their criticisms were apt, but there was little we could do about her.

We had to save money on our trip. If the costs went too high, then we risked a reprimand for simply going off gallivanting…

"I'm sure it will turn out all right… Even if someone gets hurt, we are still on training. Our workers' comp should apply…"

This whole incident began with a comment from Vania.

"I want to go to a hot spring."

"The Purgatory Baths are in town. They are open quite late, so you can head there before you go home."

The Purgatory Baths were a nice public-bathing area, but one had to be sure not to stay too long (or worse, fall asleep) and melt in the demonic spring waters.

"No, no, not a cozy little public bath, a bona fide hot spring. The kind you stay over at."

"Hmm." I gave a noncommittal response as I read my documents.

"You're not listening, are you, boss?"

There was a hint of disappointment in Vania's voice, though I was too busy reading to see her face.

"And you're not working. You are on the clock, you know." From my right, Fatla gave a sound argument.

Vania was on my left, ensuring I was properly flanked by my secretaries. This formation was apparently a holdover from when bosses fought with humans.

"Oh right, boss, you don't have a lot of hobbies, do you? I don't hear about you going out and stuff on your days off at all," Vania commented.

It was rude, but it was the truth, so it was hard to argue.

"I relax in my manor on my days off. Is there anything else to do?"

"Obviously! Make food, go sightseeing—lots of stuff!"

"Why am I not allowed to relax, even when I don't have to work? They're called days *off*, so why shouldn't I be off?"

Ever since my days at the bottom of the ladder, I'd been without any hobbies. If I had to pick one, I'd say lazing around and drinking was mine. I lived my life doing nothing, especially since I had no dreams or goals.

However, the hundred years since I became a minister had passed so quickly.

Yes—over a century. It almost felt like it had been barely two weeks since I crushed those pompous alraunes, but in human terms, it had been almost four generations.

I had once heard that time flew by when one did the same sort of work for a long time, and that was true. Now that I had grown accustomed to my work as minister, the years after the first ten or so flew by in an instant. Perhaps it was time to do something different.

"Fine. We will go to a hot spring," I said as I scrawled my signature on the document. Then I looked at Vania. "You decide the itinerary. You're the one who wanted to go to this hot spring, so you must have a good place in mind, no?"

"Wait, really? Are you sure?" Vania was overjoyed. As her boss, I was happy to see it. "Are you really going to pay for everything? You're so generous, boss!"

"Hey! I said nothing about paying!"

This wasn't a drink or two at the bar; how much was she planning on make me pay?

"Aw, what? After all the hard work I've done as your secretary these years, I really thought you'd do at least that much for me..."

"Shall I carefully list every single incident in which I've had to clean up after you?"

Vania made mistakes on a regular basis. The problem lay in her personality, and if a century hadn't been enough to fix it, I doubted anything would.

In the meantime, Fatla was working silently. If we chatted for another three minutes, we ran the risk of angering her, so I had to speak while keeping our limits in mind.

"*Sigh*, I want to go to the hot spring on the boss's money~ This is a part of the service and benefits program, too~"

Just as I thought about how shameless she was—

Those words stuck in my ears: *service and benefits program.*

"Now that you mention it, the Ministry of Agriculture has not gone on a company trip yet, have we?"

"We have so many employees that we have never quite been able to hold one." Fatla had been listening to the entire conversation.

"I see, I see. Well, if we have no precedent, then we may as well make one, no?" I stood and took a book down from the bookshelf in the room.

It was one that had a collection of newspaper-article clippings relating to farming. "I feel as though I saw a good one about six months ago."

I flipped through and finally caught sight of this headline.

BEAN SPROUTS IN HOT SPRINGS GROW QUICKLY!
QUICK SHIPPING, MANY VARIETIES

I chuckled to myself. We could do this. "Vania, Fatla, we're going on a training excursion." Vania frowned when she heard the word *training*, so I added a bit of extra information.

"We're going to a hot spring."

Things moved quickly after that.

In order to make sure this was a real training excursion, we got approval for things that needed approval, and made our sixty-five-person trip—I mean, training excursion—a reality.

Even though the volcano with the hot spring was in human territory, it was deep in the mountains where only dragons lived. We didn't expect any trouble; dragons didn't fear demons.

It wouldn't feel like much of a trip if we didn't go very far, and if it was close enough for a day trip, then we would not be granted any lodging expenses.

Additionally, by having all of us take the leviathans, we made sure to cut out all transportation expenses. If we paid for everyone's traveling expenses with taxes, that would be difficult to excuse. We managed to keep our costs low by just asking for lodging for sixty-five people.

And so our trip...I mean, training excursion brilliantly took form!

Vania's flying was unbelievably rough, but we arrived at the foot of Mount Rokko right on time.

"She knows what she's doing with this trip," I said to Fatla.

"I think my sister simply wants to relax for a long time," she replied.

"This is nothing more than a training excursion, you see."

"Indeed, nothing more. I know. Let us enjoy it to the fullest."

I thought about how she was so good at separating her internal and external thoughts.

A fire-breathing species called the red dragons lived in Mount Rokko.

Dragons had all sorts of temperaments—the red dragons were honest and good-natured, but I had also heard they were rather prideful. Well, I was sure there must be some more subservient among them.

A man with horns growing out of his head was standing where we landed. Dragons had horns when they took on their human forms, so it was easy to tell them apart. He wasn't a normal human, at least.

"We have been waiting for you, demons."

"Greetings, I am Beelzebub, minister of agriculture. Could you take us to the hot spring...that is being used as a cultivating field for vegetables?"

Thanks to the volcano, there were hot springs bubbling up in the area.

"Yes. I will take you there—right this way."

I followed him, while the rest of the group followed me. The dragons looked on in curiosity since there were so many of us.

"We received a very enthusiastic offer from Vania the leviathan. We did everything we could to make sure you all have a wonderful time here."

"Yes, Vania is always on the ball when it comes to these things."

I glanced over at her, and Vania was smiling with satisfaction. She popped her right thumb up at me.

"I am envious that you have such skilled subordinates."

I was sure what he said was just lip service, but a compliment toward my subordinates was not unwelcome.

"She has a lot of potential, but it only ever shines through in times like these..." I wished she would be so enthusiastic about her regular work...

As we chatted, we arrived at our destination.

First, we came to a facility that was growing bean sprouts in the hot spring.

"The bean sprouts grow best here. The yield is high, too."

"Hmm, I can almost tell by looking that they have a nice, crisp texture."

This was work for the agricultural minister, but it reminded me a bit of a field trip. It was rather nice.

Vania tapped me on the shoulder. "Boss, I got them to prepare samples for us today. I really bargained with them!"

"You spared no effort, did you…?"

I was given a plate of bean sprouts with a drizzle of dressing on it.

"Mmm, these are—"

"SOOOOO GOOOOOOD!!"

Vania shouted from beside me.

"What, what?! Why are you so loud?!"

"These are nothing like anything I've had before! They're resilient and not grassy and just a little sweet—I've never had bean sprouts that were so proud to be bean sprouts!"

"You are much too excited about bean sprouts!"

"This is how impressed I am! See, the producers are happy, too!"

The dragon farmers certainly seemed happy to have grown them.

Next, we went to the carrots that also used hot spring water and received some cooked samples. It seemed like we would be trying them at every turn.

"Yes, the flavor is—"

"Sooooo gooooooood!! I cannot believe how sweet this is! It's almost like a fruit! It's warm and delicious, like a completely different vegetable than the carrots I know! This is excellent! I'm seeing carrots in a whole new light!"

Fatla slid right up next to me. "My apologies, my sister gets incredibly excited about these things… She goes so over-the-top that it might even seem fake, but she is not exaggerating. I believe this will continue all day long, so please just endure it…"

"Very well… I will just accept that this is how it is…"

After that, Vania sampled all sorts of food with the same energy.

Garlic

"Sooooo gooooooood!! I can feel my stamina rising! When I eat one, it feels like I could fight for an entire week! A+! I could fly to the ends of the earth!"

Onions

"Sooooo gooooooood!! It's so sweet! Onions usually have a bit of a bite, no? But there's none of that here. It's like all the nutrients from the hot spring and the soil have gone right into the vegetables! It's almost like a fruit!"

"Hey! Your report on the onions is starting to sound like the one on the carrots! You just think you can call everything 'like a fruit'!" I had decided I would stay silent, but in the end, I couldn't keep it in. "And you open every evaluation with a loud 'Sooooo gooooooood!!', tricking us with your enthusiastic reaction! It's unfair!"

"Wh-why…? I'm just saying it's good, and it is…"

"I can see how excited you are about this. It sticks in my mind—and gets on my nerves…"

Then Vania popped up her thumb on her right hand again.

"What are you doing with your finger? Is this a joke I'm not understanding?"

"Next, we will be receiving a drink and some food that will go with it. Let's have a good round of drinks for lunch!"

My resolve began to falter at that. "Ooh... A drink at lunch... I suppose it's all right, since this is a training excursion..."

We were served pork fried with onions and a generous amount of garlic, along with a nice, cool glass of alcohol. I could feel my mouth watering at an alarming rate.

"This would certainly go well with the drink—perhaps this dish was chosen to complement it."

"Hee-hee-hee, your body knows what it wants, boss."

"Don't be crass. Listen. This is a training excursion. We are not here to play," I said. We took a few bites of our lunch and washed them down with the drink.

""Ahhhh! Sooooo goooooood!!""

Vania and I cried at the same time.

We made a toast, enthusiastically clinking our glasses together.

"Well done, you! You pass!"

"I want a raise, please!"

"That is a different conversation."

"Why are you suddenly so calm?!"

Fatla seemed a little exasperated at our antics, but she ate her food and drank, and her cheeks flushed red. She was probably having fun at the end of the day. I knew her well enough after all these years together to tell.

"Well, now that our training is finished, I suppose it's time for us to head to the inn."

Then the dragon-man who had shown us around approached us, slightly hesitant. "Pardon me, Lady Beelzebub. My daughter has mentioned she would like to have a brief spar with you..."

I had heard that dragons tended to be fond of battle—although, in the case of red dragons, it might be better to say they had a warrior's spirit.

©Benio

"My daughter has taken a great interest in you since you are known for your power, Lady Beelzebub…"

Since becoming minister of agriculture, I had certainly worked very hard in my training until I was a rather formidable member of my race. No demon would disparage me for being powerless now.

"Very well. I take no responsibility for any injuries, however."

When I gave the okay, a young girl with horns came over to me. "My name is Laika. I am striving to become the strongest among the red dragons—no, among all dragonkind. Please spar with me!"

Her clear eyes reminded me of mine, back when I was struggling to get even stronger.

I folded my arms and nodded. "Take me to a place where you can breathe fire freely. You dragons cannot use your full power unless you are in your dragon form, no?"

I never thought I would be fighting on a trip.

Even though we currently lived in an era of peace, violence hadn't been completely eradicated.

We moved to a vast, empty area, and Laika the dragon-girl changed into her dragon form.

"Yes, you seem quite strong. And tense."

"Here I come!"

"I'm ready!"

We then engaged in a rather intense battle.

In the end—

It was my overwhelming victory.

I knew this would happen. I hadn't trained myself so little that I would lose to the likes of a dragon.

After five minutes, Laika returned to her human form and lay on the ground. Her shoulders were heaving; she'd yielded.

"You still have much to learn. It was like you were attacking me with a rusted weapon."

"Where did I fall short?" she asked me candidly.

There was no doubt that she was trying to grow stronger. I could sense that she was not so much vexed with herself, but that she felt the need to grow.

"You are too intense."

"Should I not be...?"

It didn't seem like she understood what I said.

"To be hardworking is good. You are simply not giving yourself room to breathe, however. That is why you see nothing but what is right in front of you, and you leave so many openings in your stance. A taut thread is much easier to cut."

I thought back on the past, and I almost laughed remembering how much my two leviathan secretaries had built me up. Before that, I had run laps around the castle moat. I couldn't sit still unless I was doing something.

"Well, I am sure you'll break out of your shell soon enough. Discard your rust. Well sharpened, the same weapon will be much mightier. Life is long. You may understand if you continue with as much intensity as you have now. But if you still don't understand, then..."

I looked to my two secretaries, who stood a short distance away from us.

"Then perhaps it would be best to find a teacher who is nothing like me."

Laika stood and bowed politely. "Thank you very much!"

"I hope we see each other again somewhere, though I can't guarantee I'll remember after such a short bout together."

After that good round of exercise, we headed to the hot spring inn in Mount Rokko.

I was staying in a three-person room with my two secretaries. As the minister of agriculture, I got to stay in a higher-grade room with fewer people.

There was still time before dinner, so we decided to take a quick soak in the private outdoor bath connected to our room.

"Aaaaaaaaaaaaaaaaaaaaaaaaaaahhh, the water is so niiiiiiiiiiiiiiiiiiiiiiiiiice."

"Vania, no need to draw out your words quite so much."

"It's fiiiiiiiiiiiiiiiiiiiiiiiiiiiiiiiiiiiine."

"Oh, I'm beginning to sweat." Fatla's expression was slightly relaxed. It must be the hot spring taking effect.

"It is nice to relax like this every once in a while."

"This is still a training excursion, however."

"You're a tough one, Fatla." I ruffled Fatla's hair.

"Ugh! Don't you tease me, too, Lady Beelzebub!"

"What? It'll dry out. Heh, I was much too frightened to try anything like that when I first became minister."

It was foolhardy for a low-level demon to prank a leviathan, but I finally felt like I had grown into my shoes as agricultural minister.

I was almost worthy of the legacy of my name, too.

"I am glad you are our minister of agriculture, Lady Beelzebub," Fatla said quietly. "Things started to change in the demon world once the previous demon king ended the war with the humans. Many things had to change in order to keep up with the times. We needed new people like you, Lady Beelzebub, in order to make that happen. I think the current demon king had a keen insight when it came to that."

Being naked together—or rather, being in the hot spring together—made it easier to put some things into words.

But to me, it seemed too early for such a confession. "I will not say thank you just yet. You will have to wait a little for that."

"Of course. Please pretend I was talking to myself."

"By the way…what's my score as the minister now?"

After a moment of thought, Fatla responded. "Ninety-three."

Much higher than seventy-five, which was what I had gotten last time.

"That's an unusual number."

"Minus two points for messing with my hair."

"I should have asked before I did that!"

"And the other five points I've left open, because you might rise to even greater heights, Lady Beelzebub."

For now, I would be satisfied with a passing grade as the minister of agriculture.

Or perhaps her grading scale was a little generous because of the hot spring?

$$\diamond$$

Everyone gathered in the great hall of the inn so we could all eat dinner together.

On our tables were some of the vegetables that we sampled earlier that day, accompanied by the copious portions of meat typical of a dragon establishment.

I could see quite a few appetites had been whetted, but they would have to sit tight for a little bit.

I took my glass and slowly made my way to the front of the room. My job was to give the toast.

The chatter naturally died down, proving I had won their trust.

"Has everyone enjoyed themselves today? There's no harm in having days like this every once in a while."

It was a little embarrassing, but I had to say it at times like this.

"We've been working together for quite some time now—thank you all." I bowed my head as though I was talking to close friends. "I used to spend my empty days idly, with no dreams or hopes for the future. I did not understand why I had been made minister of agriculture at first, and I even cursed Her Majesty for foisting such a troublesome job onto me. Oh, no actual curses; don't worry."

This was where they were supposed to laugh, but no one did.

Surprisingly, they were listening to me earnestly.

"Of course, I knew I could not carry on as I had, so I worked hard in my own way. I have no intentions of denying my hard work. But if it were not for your support, nothing would have happened. It is all thanks to every one of you..."

As I spoke, tears started pooling in my eyes, but I knew not to worry. No one was going to laugh at me for crying in front of them now.

"Thank you... I really hope to have your support from here on out. I believe I can do my job without causing you as much trouble as I have in the past. That's because I want you to think of me...as the best minister in history..."

"Hooray for Lady Beelzebub!"

Someone suddenly shouted, and I realized Vania had stood up with tears streaming down her face.

"Hooray for Lady Beelzebub! Hooray for Lady Beelzebub! I'm not going to call you boss or minister right now! You are a noble, so you're Lady Beelzebub! Hooray for Lady Beelzebub!"

Hooray for Lady Beelzebub.

That chant finally spread throughout the entire room, and it kept on going for a while.

I was incredibly glad I had decided to go on this training excursion. Everyone in the Ministry of Agriculture was now connected by a tight bond!

"You are all the best! Hooray for the Ministry of Agriculture!"

Almost four hours later...

"Will you cut it out already?!" I yelled, walking among the rooms and down the hallway.

A pillow flew at high speed and slammed into the back of my head.

I whirled around to find one of the directors watching me with regret.

"How long will you all keep up this child's play?! What is this pillow war?!"

It was something very small that started it all.

Some of the people in one room started throwing pillows at one another, mostly in jest. A few of them then decided to take their pillows and "attack" their good friends in another room.

Those in the second room decided to carry out their "revenge" as a joke. Which was met with more "revenge." Meanwhile, the "conflict" grew larger and larger—

And it was now on an unprecedented scale, with the rooms allying together to form an eastern and a western army...

If these were children playing, I wouldn't mind, but more than half of the people here were high-ranking demon officials. The force of the pillows alone was terrifying enough. I even received a report that some of the rooms were already damaged.

Perhaps this was how wars started. No one wanted it to happen, but before you knew it, the conflict had escalated.

No, this was not the time for me to think quietly to myself.

This pillow war was unfolding in the present continuous tense...

"You understand what will happen if you embarrass me any further, don't you? It is absolutely, unconditionally unforgiveable! All of you, take a bath and go to sleep!"

And so as I proceeded along the hallway, shouting cease-fire instructions—

I discovered Vania looking out on the situation from the landing on the stairs.

"Heh-heh-heh. The enemy will never know I'm here."

"Well, *I* do."

"Ugh! Boss!"

I was the one who wanted to grunt in frustration upon discovering my secretary participating in this.

"I *will* cut your pay... Are you ready for that? Stop this at once and go back to the room... And please tell me I am wrong when I ask you if you were the one to break the wall there."

For some reason, she wore a bandanna (?) on her head that said VICTORY, too. Where did she buy that?

"Boss, there are times when a demon must fight. This is one of those times."

I was impressed she said that with such a straight face—not a trace of mirth.

"Very well. I will not force you to stop, then."

"Thank you! You *are* the best minister of agriculture! Hooray for Lady Beelzebub!"

"—But I cannot speak for your sister."

Fatla gave Vania a good whack on the head from behind.

"Gaaah! When did you get there?!"

"Stop with this silly nonsense and go back to the room. If you do not listen to me, then I will tie your feet together and drop you from the stairs."

"O-okay..."

Afterward, it took almost an hour for the fighting to stop, and as the minister of agriculture, I was obliged to offer my deepest, repeated apologies to the innkeeper. We did break a wall.

Maybe I should resign...

But it was because of the training excursion that I found a new hobby.

Now, when I had a day off, I would go travel, and I was slowly starting to visit more and more places in the human lands.

Perhaps now that I had occupied my current position for over a hundred years, I had the time to expand my horizons.

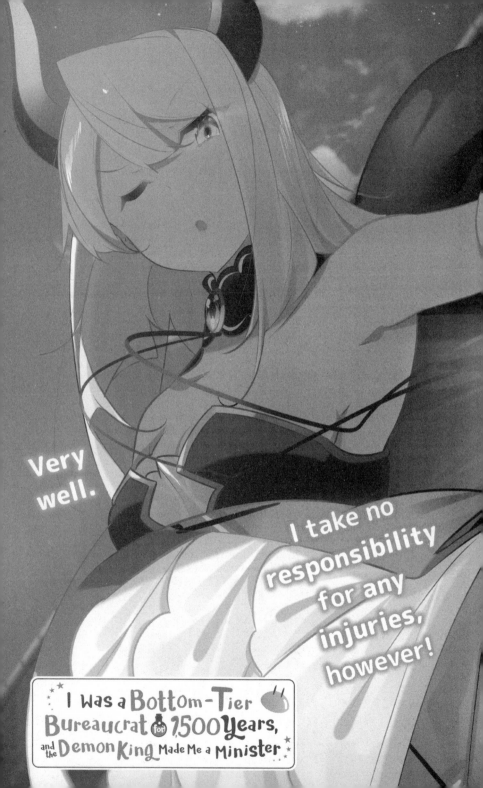

"Ahhh~ There's nothing to do~ I'm so thankful~"

"Vania, do not invite bad luck! If you must make such comments, do so inside your head!"

Vania's sentiment was an odd thing to say during working hours, so I cautioned her.

"Whaaat? Maybe it would be bad if I said there was nothing to do and started wandering around the building, but it's not a problem if I'm just sitting in the office, right? And the autumn harvest is over now. We're going to have less work moving forward anyway."

It did not seem Vania was happy with my response. Fatla would understand what I was trying to say.

Moreover, Fatla was concentrating on her work on the opposite side of the room. I sensed her conscious refusal to participate in this conversation, though I knew she was listening to all of it.

"I know we do get periods of relative free time throughout the year, but there is work that must be done every day. That is why I am working now. And it would be unlucky to repeat what you just said."

"I'm not cursed or anything! Do you get ghosts in this room? I can't actually see ghosts."

"No! It is not a good thing to remark on how idle you are! You are simply inviting more headaches!"

It was a strange thing; once we became aware of how idle or calm everything was, then an unbelievable amount of work would start coming our way.

I was aware that it was not a rule, but such situations often occurred.

When it came to things like this, it was much easier when I was at the bottom of the ladder. The breadth of my responsibilities back then was quite narrow.

Odd jobs that suddenly bubbled up or fell out of nowhere were usually not for the lowliest of the low to take care of, after all. They were for the most important people.

So now that I was the minister of agriculture, I was always alert, keeping an eye out for sudden showers of work.

"You're a worrywart, boss. Fine, if we get a terrible job in the next three days, then I'll treat you to a mea—"

The door suddenly flew open, and one of the department directors, a Cyclops, burst in.

"Miss Minister, this is an emergency! A dragon has made landfall on a farm to the east of the town around Vanzeld Castle! We need you there immediately!"

I clapped my hand onto Vania's back.

"I'm looking forward to that meal," I told her with a brilliant smile.

"Wait, no, that happened before I was done saying what I was going to say, so it's technically invalid—"

"You had essentially finished speaking, so it was a valid declaration. I am holding you to it."

Even if she did treat me to a nice meal, we still had an obnoxious job to take care of now...

The leviathan sisters and I made our way toward the eastern farmland.

It was just far enough for us to consider flying on one of them, but there was no space for them to take off or land, so we decided to fly on the back of a midsize wyvern. This was even faster.

Many people lived in the town around Vanzeld Castle, which shouldn't come as a surprise. It was the biggest demon city, after all. That meant we had to procure enough food to provide for the entire population.

It would be much too ineffective to import it from far away, which was why we had farmland right near the city.

This apparently was not exclusive to demons; I had read in some essay that there were pastoral regions around the outskirts of cities in the human world, too.

The location we were headed to was one of those farming regions.

"The weather is a bit cold today, but otherwise calm. I don't see how a dragon would have been downed in this."

On top of the wyvern, Fatla was flipping through some documents that she would be submitting soon.

"Dragons can fight fiercely over even the pettiest differences. 'Tis quite possible that a battle of sorts broke out somewhere, and they fled all the way here."

Though most dragons lived in human territory, there were some who lived in the demon lands. For the faster fliers, distance was not a problem at all.

"I don't really want to fight a dragon..." Vania had gone pale. What she ought to be worried about was the meal she owed me.

"You need not worry too much about that. Though dragons are often on bad terms with one another, they rarely cause fights with nondragons. According to the first report I received, 'twas only one who landed. They are not here to start a war."

"You are quite calm about this. You truly have the presence of a minister." The sudden compliment from Fatla was a little embarrassing

"There has been a lot of trouble, so I am used to it..."

As I thought about how little trouble a dragon would be, we spotted the eastern farms in the distance.

Right in the middle of it, I could see that a giant someone had skidded right through the farm, leaving a gash in the earth along the way.

"The leafy vegetables have been hit hard…"

We landed at the scene of the incident.

It was easy to see where our destination was—the dragon sat on the ground in their original form. Had they been in their human form, the inspection might have been more difficult.

The case worker on the ground led us to the drowsy-looking dragon. Dirt was caked on their chest, indicating they must have landed on their front.

"I am Beelzebub, agricultural minister. I take it the damage to this field came from you?"

"*Yaaaaaaaaaaaawn.*"

They opened their mouth wide with exhaustion…which irritated me, to be honest.

"Yep. I, the great Flatorte of the blue dragons, am responsible. *Yaaaaaaawn.*"

"Flatorte, you say? I hear blue dragons are particularly belligerent; were you fighting with another dragon? Did you fly all the way here?"

"No." The dragon shook their head. "I'm behaving right now. I'm actually so bored that I sometimes end up sleeping all day."

Now my hackles were up. *'Tis all your fault that I have more work now…*

"Then why have you done this? I would like to hear your side of the story."

"*Paaah~*"

The dragon exhaled, and their breath reached our noses.

"Ugh! This dragon reeks of alcohol! They were flying under the influence!" Vania pinched her nose. Their breath alone was enough to make me tipsy.

"I had *nothing* to do, so I just drank and drank. I started in the late afternoon, but I stopped before it got really late at night. After that, I decided to go flying to sober up, then I fell. *Yaaawn...*"

The dragon's explanation was rather curious. There was a possibility that they were lying, so I had to listen carefully.

I did wish I could hand this beast over to the army and be done with it all... Why did they have to fall on a farm...?!

"I doubt a dragon can get drunk in the short period of time between 'late afternoon' and 'before it got really late.' Tell me the truth."

"I'm not lying. Everyone knows Flatorte never lies! I'm just stupid!"

I did not see why the dragon would belittle themself like this...

"Then were you downing drinks in one go for an extended period of time?"

"I started drinking in the late afternoon four days ago, and I stopped last night."

"That is *too* long of a drinking binge!"

Everyone who was listening was astonished. This was on another level.

"I mean, what else am I gonna do? Everyone's so bored, there really isn't much else to do but drink. Almost none of us blue dragons have jobs, y'see. And we don't really do fussy stuff like labor 'cause we're big."

Why did this unemployed dragon sound so haughty...?

"Flatorte, do you acknowledge that you are the one who caused damage to this farm?"

"Yeah. Not many could accomplish something so impressive. My rivals, the red dragons, could never do something like this."

As I said, there is no need to be so haughty.

Fatla whispered to me, "She was right about being honest and stupid."

I thought the same. "So you acknowledge your crime. Then if you are able, transform into your human form. 'Tis not easy to speak to one so big."

"*Yaaawn.* Fine."

The dragon changed into a human form—a girl with horns and a tail. She also wasn't wearing anything at all.

"Hey! Why are you naked?!" I yelled.

"What?! You saw me naked?! You're shameless!"

"Oh, give me a break! One typically wears clothing when going outside!"

"I think I took off my clothes while I was drinking 'cause it got too hot."

Fatla whispered to me again, "She is an idiot."

We all knew that; she did not need to tell me every time.

The dragon had covered her most private parts at first, but she quickly stopped caring and now arrogantly had her arms folded.

If she wanted to move to the demon lands, I would simply make up a reason to deny her... She could go bother the humans in the mountains...

"Someone fetch some undergarments and work clothes... And you there, bare-assed fool, you will have to pay compensation for the damage you have caused."

"I don't have any money. Blue dragons aren't a bunch of gold-hoarding misers like the rest. That's 'cause we use any money we get right away! *Savings are for the weak,* as we say!"

If she and her people were not such a hardy species, they would have died out ages ago...

"Hmm... Then you can work off the damages on the farm."

"Is it 'cause I ruined it? When I felt myself falling, I thought it was perfect that there was such soft-looking ground beneath me, too..."

She deliberately aimed for the fields! Could she get any worse?!

"No matter how much you hate labor, I will put you to work until you have paid back the damages. I hope you are ready for that."

"Leave it to me, the great Flatorte. Actually, I picked fights with about fifty-five other blue dragons while I was drunk, so I was hoping to lie low somewhere until that blew over. Perfect timing."

"Why so many?!"

I never knew how dangerous a blue dragon on a bender could be until now!

"Anyway, put together a work program suitable for this nincompoop," I ordered Fatla. "That will be the end to our work here, then."

"Understood. She's a dragon, so she should survive a bit of harsh treatment."

What a terrifying thing to say with a straight face...

"And if she loses control again, there will be more damage. It does not seem the blue dragons have any form of government or unions, so our only choice is to have her work and repay us. Put together a program that is just tough enough, but still one that will give her a sense of accomplishment."

I did not know what Fatla was truly thinking, but—

"I will start on this immediately."

—she replied just as a staffer of mine should.

"Then let's return to the ministry," I said.

"I'm glad it didn't turn out to be that much extra work~"

I gripped Vania's hand with a smile. "I haven't forgotten about that meal."

No matter what she thought, I was going to make sure she kept her word.

"O-okay... I'll manage something! I take pride in my cooking!"

I wished she could take pride in her office work, too.

Over the weekend, I paid my first visit to the leviathan sisters' house.

Fatla came to pick me up and take me there, and I learned they lived much closer to the office than I'd thought.

"A lovely home, but a bit smaller than a leviathan's original size."

"It is only the two of us here. The rest of our family lives in our hometown."

"I see. I suppose you selected this more for an easy commute than for size."

"And leviathans are much too big naturally, so a smaller house feels more secure and puts us at ease."

"I cannot tell if that is true for all leviathans, or if that is just particular to you..."

When the door opened, Vania emerged wearing a white outfit that looked similar to a chef's uniform.

Indeed—when Vania had said she would treat me, she had not once mentioned going to a restaurant. She would be showing off the cooking skills she was so proud of.

"Welcome to our fine establishment today. I am Vania, head chef of our restaurant, Sea-Drinking Whale."

"Head chef? You are the only one cooking here."

"You must be Beelzebub with the reservation, yes? I see you have ordered the Chef's Surprise Lunch for one today."

It seemed she was going to stick with the restaurant story through and through. I did not mind, but—

"*Surprise* lunch?! Wouldn't *select* lunch be better?! It sounds as if your meal could either be fantastic or a total flop! This isn't a gambling den!"

"No need to worry. We have prepared all our ingredients ahead of time, and we will only be serving dishes we know will be excellent."

So this wasn't a "select" lunch or a "surprise" lunch... Ah, no matter. All this complaining ultimately felt rather pointless

I was brought to the dining room and served dish after dish—

—and they were all absolutely perfect, both in taste and appearance! The vegetables in my salad were even stacked in a three-dimensional pattern; I could scarcely believe that the airheaded Vania could have made such a thing.

"Today's theme is *towers falling*. We used seasonal vegetables to create the image of an old, crumbling tower. Please enjoy!"

"I cannot say this is a particularly auspicious theme... But the level of skill exhibited in each of these dishes is magnificent."

Now that I was the minister of agriculture, I often had dinner meetings at fancy restaurants, so I could say her food was on par with those establishments.

The meat was perfectly grilled, and she did not cut corners when it came to the side vegetables, either.

"It's rather odd that you haven't opened your own restaurant...," I began, but then I hesitated.

I would be sad if she said with confidence, *Then I will quit my job and go off on my own.*

"Ah-ha-ha. I could never run a restaurant~" But Vania loosely waved her hand.

I was surprised that she would refuse so easily. "Hmm? Are the hurdles you set for yourself that high when it comes to running your own establishment? Are you unwilling to be anything less than the best of the best?"

"Oh, no. If I opened a restaurant, then I'd need the skills to run the business side, too~ No way could I do that. I'd close in a year~"

"I suppose you do have some semblance of self-awareness. But are you certain?!"

"My sis always tried to discourage me. So one day, I got so mad that I bought a book on starting a restaurant."

Ah yes, after Vania worked on renovating the cafeteria a little while ago, she had wanted to quit, but Fatla had stopped her by saying she would never succeed.

"I fell asleep reading the foreword."

"You break down much too quickly! I am certain the author is disappointed!"

I had a feeling that the business side of things would turn out all right if Fatla joined her as an adviser, but then both of them would resign... I chose to say nothing.

"It is perfect for my sister to cook only when she wants to, Lady Beelzebub," Fatla said, sitting across from me. "I am certain if she made it her job, her hobby would soon lose the joy it gives her. I believe our current situation suits her best."

Vania was nodding, too. The older sister knew her younger sister well—keeping hobbies as hobbies was a valid approach to life.

"And sometimes, if you work at a restaurant, then you'll have to work really late, right? But people from fancier restaurants still need to wake up early to beat the rush and get their hands on good ingredients. Such long hours would only cause me to make lots of mistakes~"

"Ah yes… I suppose you are better off not doing that."

I could see her restaurant becoming infamous for serving customers the wrong dishes…

That aside…I got to visit my underlings' house, so perhaps this dragon business wasn't all so bad after all.

One month later, I was at the eastern farms.

Parts of the field were still a mess, but the places that had been truly ruined were now reborn as new fields.

"Well? Whatcha think? I worked pretty hard, huh?"

The blue dragon stood in her work clothes with an expression of pride, waiting for us to compliment her.

"Did you plough this all on your own?" I was shocked by how much ground she had covered.

Though I knew dragons were strong, I had not imagined she would do this much.

"Obviously. With demons and other outsiders around, you end up joining in the ploughing, too. The ground was kind of hard, but it made the work feel worth it. When I started thinking about it as exercise instead of labor, all the pain went away."

Ah—whether a task is viewed as work or not would make a big difference.

It was similar to Vania's case, where her cooking hobby would no longer be fun if she were to make it her job.

The most likely explanation was that while the blue dragons hated being forced into a job, they would enthusiastically take on things that they enjoyed. I believed that was how money came about for them, too. Doing nothing would lead to a most boring life.

"Hey, demon, what about all the damages payments?"

"Ah...yes. I believe it has been compensated." My reply came a little late since I had been thinking. "I might have to pay you a salary instead."

"I don't need that. I had fun. Maybe I'll come hang out here in the demon lands sometimes." The blue dragon cackled. "Honest yet stupid" indeed.

"Vanzeld will always welcome you whenever you would like to visit."

"Maybe I'll fall around here again."

"Do *not* do that!"

We could not afford to have a dragon constantly falling in the town around the castle!

After the dragon had a quick meal in the farm shed, she assumed her dragon form and took off into the sky. She did not even really say good-bye. I suppose that was simply how dragons were.

"Dragons are rather unusual characters, aren't they?" I murmured, looking up at her as she vanished into the sky.

Then I found something on the ground near the house.

"Oh, this—"

I picked up the dirtied article and immediately knew what it was.

"—is the work uniform she was wearing..."

The dragon had gone home without any clothes on.

"So she went home naked... I suppose she is in her dragon form, though..."

She would not be able to enter her house in her dragon form, so I could imagine her nakedness creating trouble. Still, she would manage, I'm sure.

The central demon conference was a meeting where the royal family, all the ministers, and other demons of great influence came together in the same hall.

This conference took place once every three years and, by some definitions, was the single most important event in demon politics.

It was here that the demons' future and goals would be decided.

Furthermore, the Ministry of Agriculture had proposed a project that would transform a vast wasteland into arable land. As expensive as it was, it would need the permission of this conference in order to proceed.

As the leader of the Ministry of Agriculture, I watched the conference with enthusiasm.

This project was inevitable for the demons' agricultural policy!

I would have it approved, no matter what!

In the end—

"In regard to the Ministry of Agriculture's proposal, I think it's fine. I doubt there are any objections, hmm~? ♪"

—with an easygoing tone, Her Majesty let it pass like a breeze.

Fatla leaned over and whispered to me, "Many people think of you as Her Majesty's favorite, Lady Beelzebub. No one will go out of their way to say no."

"I believe I am more of a favorite *toy*..."

Though I would still be grateful for the demon king lending me her power, even if indirectly.

The conference proceeded smoothly afterward. Eventually, it became time to talk about the events Her Majesty would be involved in. Whether it was in public or private, everything she did held great meaning.

"I would like to carry out a few royal visitations. It's been ever so long, ♪" she said.

To put it simply, a royal visitation was when Her Majesty would come to the homes of important political figures and have them entertain her.

Though the hosts did need to spend money, a visitation had been considered a great honor throughout demon history.

And since only the most powerful nobles with money, land, and pedigree ever hosted, the visit would not create any economic burden.

Well, I was certain such an honor would never fall upon an upstart noble such as—

"This time, I would like to stay at Miss Beelzebub's house~ ♪"

Everyone present at the meeting turned to look at me.

"Whaaaaat?!"

This felt...exactly the same as when I was made minister...

The powerful nobles started protesting immediately.

"Your Majesty, if I may, the houses that are generally made a part of the royal visitation have been established through a long tradition..."

"Oh, it's all right~ Precedent is meant to be overturned~ ♪"

"No, I *also* think that this is impossible!"

I turned her down as well. I did not want to get swallowed up in another one of her schemes.

And my manor...was a mess.

It was not as though the rooms I typically used were full of garbage, no. I had grown a bit since I was at the bottom of the ladder.

But I did not even enter rooms that fell outside my living space, so they were all filled with dust…

What else should I have done? I did not have a single servant to my name, so I had no use for this mansion I had been given. If I were to use every space on my own, then I would end up cleaning all day, every day. So I decided to live within a limited number of rooms on the first floor.

Of course, I had done nothing to care for the massive garden, either. I could not even begin to name what sorts of plants and animals were living there now. From my window, all I could see was a dense forest.

A royal visitation was a proper event; it would not be over with a quick five-minute chat at the front door. Manners dictated that the host guide the demon king through the manor, prepare a meal, and even show her around the garden.

I could never do such a thing!

And so I would not let her settle on this.

"Your Majesty, my abode is an embarrassment compared with the noble houses of old. I appreciate the offer, but I must decline…"

"Hmm, I see. I suppose it's your prerogative."

Oh, that was easier than I thought.

"By the way, I've realized there might be a problem with the Ministry of Agriculture's project after all, so I may have to reconsider it~"

She was taking the ministry project hostage!

Her Majesty was grinning.

Oh. Once she decided something was going to happen, she was going to make it happen at any cost. I knew my fate.

"Y-yes, Your Majesty…," I said weakly.

Countless staff members of the Ministry of Agriculture had ceded so much of their time for this project. If I had to sacrifice myself to save it, then so be it!

Once the conference was over, Fatla tapped me on the shoulder to encourage me.

"Lady Beelzebub, you made a wise decision."

"Decisions begin and end quickly. What happens next is the problem…"

Even when the date for the royal visitation was set, I felt no motivation to make any preparations. They meant nothing at this point.

The cleaning, I could manage. But the rest of the hosting duties required manpower, and that I did not have. I could not hire amateur extras, either. I needed a whole roster of people knowledgeable in etiquette; otherwise, they could not even participate.

But the people I was considering were all employed by the pedigreed nobles, and I would never be allowed to borrow them.

And so my only choice was to wait for Her Majesty, empty-handed…

It would be an embarrassment, but it was not a sin. I would accept the shame.

Almost three weeks until my moment of disgrace…

Fate, however, was on my side. About ten days before the visitation, something happened.

"Boss, boss! This is bad!"

Vania, who had gone to deliver some documents to other departments, came running back into the office.

"Must you make so much noise?"

"Her Majesty is sick with the stubborn demon cold!"

The stubborn demon cold was a mild but irritating illness whose symptoms lasted for a whole month.

"All the events on her calendar for the next month have been canceled!"

"Yesss!"

There was nothing more disrespectful than cheering for the demon king being sick, but that was how I honestly felt. Even the demon king could fall ill, and how grateful I was for that!

"Now the visitation will be called off!"

"But you know how Her Majesty is, Lady Beelzebub. She may come to visit once she's better."

Fatla reminded me the world was not as kind as I thought it was. I had already considered that, of course.

"She has already given us permission for our wasteland-to-farmland project! She may be a royal, but she cannot go back in time and retract her approval! We have no hostage to worry about anymore!"

It was as though a test one did not study for was suddenly canceled.

When Her Majesty was feeling better, I would accompany her shopping or something similar.

◇

On the day the visit was originally scheduled for, I went to work as normal and returned home as normal.

I entered my room and splayed out over the bed, stretching my arms and legs.

"Ahhh, what a wonderful thing to keep all the work I am spearheading."

Perhaps I would laze about for the rest of the day, take a bath, and go to sleep. It felt like receiving paid time off. If the visitation were to have happened today, I could have easily spent another twenty hours cleaning on top of my office work.

However, when I was in bed and reading a book—

Klang, klang.

—the bell rang to signify a guest had arrived, echoing especially loud in the night.

I glanced at the clock to see it was nine.

"Who could it be...? Solicitations at night are illegal."

Dubiously, I went out to the gate, and—

"Why are you here, Your Majesty?!"

—the visitor was unmistakably the demon king, though she was hiding her identity with a hood.

"*Cough, cough...* Today is the day of the visita—I mean, of our sleepover, though..."

©Benio

"Your cold has not gotten any better at all!"

Her Majesty tried to force herself to smile, but she was too unwell; the smile came out strained.

"Oh, I know I'm…*cough*…sick…"

In the end, I brought Her Majesty to my bedroom.

I had no other rooms with a bed. Strictly speaking, there were other rooms within the manor that did count as guest rooms, but there was enough dust in them to make a healthy person sick.

I laid her down in the bed. She was sweating, but I had a feeling that the best way to go about this was to warm her up and let her sweat it out. I pulled up the covers as well.

"I feel all dizzy just coming this way~"

"Of course you do. 'Tis what happens when you walk around outside while ill."

I placed the wet towel I had prepared over her forehead.

"But I believe this could be an opportunity on its own…" Exhausted, the demon king smiled.

"For what? An opportunity to worsen your cold, perhaps."

"My candidate for the role of my elder sister will be taking care of me, that's what~ Eh-heh-heh…"

Then I realized why I had been chosen for the visitation.

"The little-sister figure sleeping over at the big-sister figure's house—so that's what you wanted to do."

"Yes, yes. I see you know well~"

I was appalled. *I cannot believe I was so anxious over something so insignificant.*

"Allow me to confirm just one thing, Your Majesty, but do the people at the castle know about this? You have not simply left of your own accord, have you?"

"They do. I made an excuse that I had to run an errand~"

So her errand was coming here to rest, was it?

She was always so meticulous with her jokes.

"What you are doing is quite reckless, but I suppose I appreciate your enthusiasm." I wiped away the sweat at the nape of Her Majesty's neck. "Very well. I shall stay up to look after you, so get some rest."

"Thank you very much, Elder Sister." The demon king smiled in delight. "Despite all your complaints, you would do everything you could for your little sister~ You do have the makings of an elder sister."

"Even if you were not my 'little sister,' any vassal would do the same if the demon king showed up sick at their doorstep."

"So cruel, Elder Sister."

"I am not your elder sister," I shot back.

The towel quickly grew warm, so I swapped it out with a cold one.

"Ah, it's so nice and cool."

"You should keep your eyes closed. You'll fall asleep soon enough if you do."

"Aww, but this is our sleepover. I want to chat with you~ What a waste it would be if I slept all our time away~"

"Your cold will only get worse, so you must—"

No, this sort of conversation would go on forever. I might tell her to sleep, but of course, she would not listen. In fact, it might instead give her the energy to be even more stubborn.

It was quite embarrassing, but...I suppose it was time to try acting as an older sister. If I satisfied Her Majesty that way, she might fall asleep.

I leaned in close to her ear.

"Get some rest now, Pecora," I said in my smoothest voice.

Her Majesty's ears went bright-red, and her smile disappeared. It seems I gave her a shock.

And 'twas a good thing, too—if she'd had a comeback, I had no other tricks up my sleeve.

"A-all right... I shall do as you say, Elder Sister..."

"Yes, good girl. Don't make me worry."

Even saying it was rather embarrassing... But I would persevere.

Now, how about that?! That was my plan. Perhaps she would listen to orders if they were coming from her older sister...

Her Majesty closed her eyes and spoke no more. A little while later, I started to hear her soft snores.

Yes, my plan was perfect. I did not wish to do such a thing a second time...

I placed both my hands on the wall to support myself, panting.

"That was painful... What punishment is this...? I suppose it was exactly what she wanted to hear..."

All that was left was for me to watch over her the whole night. It was not going to be easy, but it was nothing compared with the line I had to deliver earlier.

I went to fetch water for the wet towels.

"Perhaps I should wash my own face, too..." It was burning up, after all.

Her Majesty awoke early the next morning. I suppose it was because she had fallen asleep so early the night before.

"Good morning, Miss Beelzebub—no, Elder Sister."

She was in a good mood from the moment she opened her eyes.

"Good morning, Your Majesty." I gave her the vassal's bow beside the bed.

"What? Aren't you going to call me Pecora?"

"I do not know of what you speak. You must have had some strange dreams due to your cold."

I had decided to blatantly dodge the topic. There was no proof of what had happened anyway.

"What? What?! That is not true! You called me Pecora right before I went to sleep! You said, *Good night, my dear Pecora!*"

That was even worse than what I actually said!

"I said no such thing!"

I decided to dig in my heels and feign complete ignorance.

There would be a great deal of trouble if Her Majesty remained away from the castle, so I took her back. I carried her the whole way, too, so that she wouldn't collapse on me.

"Oh, bridal style~"

"I would appreciate it if you would not use such phrases."

"You did call me Pecora yesterday, didn't you, Elder Sister?"

"I cannot recall doing such a thing, no. Your symptoms seem to be quite severe. Please take care of yourself."

The castle guards seemed shocked when they saw Her Majesty and me, but—

"I just made sure to carry out the visitation as scheduled, ♪" Her Majesty said, and they appeared to accept that answer. They seemed accustomed to her unreasonable behavior.

One way or another, I managed to return her to her own room.

That was quite a long journey...

"Thank you so much for escorting me all the way back, Miss Beelzebub. ♪" Her Majesty offered her thanks just outside her room.

"Oh, think nothing of it. I am delighted to see that your cough is less noticeable than yesterday," I responded with a smile. It was a relief knowing my job was done.

"Please feel free to call me Pecora again—"

"You are quite insistent about that, aren't you? I haven't the slightest clue what you are talking about." I rebuffed her flatly, so she pouted like a child.

"You are so rigid!"

"You simply rely too much on shortcuts."

It seemed that at this point, she understood she was not going to get her way. A firm attitude is crucial to dealing with these things.

"Well, I suppose that's all right. It is like you to never do entirely what I want, after all."

Rrrgh... She would always turn things to her favor, wouldn't she...?

"Now then, I have work to attend to at the ministry, so I must be off." I bowed, turned away, proceeded down the corridor—

—and suddenly started to cough.

"Cough, cough, cough, cough! Cough!"

Now that I thought about it, I felt rather hot. And my head was heavy. Was it the all-nighter…?

My face has been hot since yesterday…

I had just experienced a triple whammy—the possibility that I'd caught Her Majesty's cold after being with her all night, the weakness of being awake for so long, and the immense relaxation once the burden of returning Her Majesty to the castle had been lifted from my shoulders…

That day, I went to the ministry, applied for paid time off due to how unwell I felt, and went home.

I Want a Bit of Decoration in My Office

Skrtch skrtch, skrtch.

Fatla was writing something in pen, and the sound resonated through the minister's office. The noise was quiet, but this room was so echoey for some reason. Why did they build it like this?

I doubted I would be able to hear the pen if Vania and I were talking, but Vania was presently working in silence. I felt no need to speak, either, so the room was utterly quiet.

In a way, we were spending our time at the office properly.

Yet on the other hand, the pen sounded rather loud in the silence. In fact, the silence was so intense that I could not concentrate.

I once thought that phrase was a way of avoiding responsibility, but it felt a bit too on the nose right now. It weighed on my mind.

But when I looked around the room again—

It's quite bleak in here, isn't it?

There were desks for work and shelves of documents—a given, considering this was an office. I was not about to complain. On the other hand, there was nothing else. Perhaps the door, windows, and curtains counted as exceptions, but essentially, there was nothing but the bare minimum required for work.

Of course, it did not hinder my work, but it was much too simple, no? This was not a factory where suits of armor and dolls that moved by magical means were working. This was an office used by three high-ranking demons.

Oh, just thinking about it was extremely irritating... And the sound of that damned pen seemed much louder now! Once I noticed it, I could not get it out of my mind!

Wham! I slammed my hands on my desk and stood.

"Fatla, Vania, I have a query for you!"

"What is it, Lady Beelzebub?"

"Are you growing into a cranky old lady, boss?"

No, I was not.

"Don't you think this room is a little too bland? There is nothing here, nothing at all to say what sort of people work in this office, no? Yes, they should know a minister works here, but why don't we add a bit of our own personal touch?"

"I suppose one could surmise that the demons who work here have no hobbies," Fatla paused from her work to say, but—

"Does that not make you sad?" I asked.

"A bit."

—she also seemed to acknowledge the joke at her own expense.

"I know only the three of us use this room on normal workdays, but plenty of other demons from other departments come to consult you here in this room. I doubt we will be able to bring in anything that is clearly not meant for work," said Fatla.

"I am not saying we will be putting in games. But there is nothing in here that shows character, not even a desktop calendar of cute little animals."

That seemed like something Vania would do, but there was practically nothing feminine about her desk. There was nothing on it but messy piles of paper.

"Is this not the room for the head of the Ministry of Agriculture? Why do we not have at least something related to agriculture in here? At minimum, should we not put up a painting of a farming scene? Or posters of fruits and vegetables?"

"I understand the sentiment. However, I am against the posters. I believe that will cheapen the atmosphere of this room and make it feel less like what it is, which is our office," Fatla replied with a rather powerful criticism.

"I—I suppose you're right..."

It was hard to tell by looks alone, but Fatla was the most feminine of the three of us. Especially compared with me and Vania.

That was one reason why this room was so bleak.

"Placing one or two paintings in this room will not change its mood very much. I have heard that other ministerial offices have paintings, but I do not think that is what makes their offices so beautiful. They barely bring any color."

"A-aye... I suppose you're right... There are paintings by the first-floor entrance, but it still feels like a normal office..."

If we put one here, it might only emphasize how much it was an office.

"But I understand what you're trying to say, boss~ There's no green in here. A decorative plant might be nice to have~"

"Yes indeed!"

That was a good idea, Vania!

"A decorative plant! We will add green to this room that way! I hear indoor plants help one relax, and it will not harm the image of the ministerial office!"

But there was still a problem.

Vania pulled out a catalog for equipment and supplies, then flipped to the indoor-plants page. "Oh wow, they're expensive~"

I peered at the page as well, and they all cost so much that I was tempted to drop the idea and go with something else.

"They all cost this much...? Just for one...? A single lonely plant in the corner hardly seems like enough... Mmm, are there more pages for plants near the front? 'Tis cheaper over there."

Vania had opened to the pages displaying midpriced plants, apparently.

"But the minister's office shouldn't have a cheap plant~ We need a big one."

"You are right on that account..."

It was not just my femininity but also my dignity as minister that I had to protect.

Our plan to get a nice indoor plant quickly ran aground.

"Oh well. I suppose I shall give up on decorating and bringing color into this room. We are demons anyway; perhaps the bleak decor is more appropriate for us."

But then—

"*Sigh...*"

The sound was borderline contemptuous, and it came from Fatla.

"If you do not mind my personal articles, I believe I will be able to transform this space into one befitting the Ministry of Agriculture. I am rather knowledgeable about plants, you see."

"Are you now?! Perhaps I will ask you to do so, then!"

Fatla's own personal items would not cost us money, so it was two birds with one stone.

But Vania seemed worried, which in turn worried me a tinge.

Well, this is Fatla taking the helm; it could not be too big of a failure.

The weekend was over. I went to work at the ministry as I always did and pushed against the door to the minister's office.

This door always felt a bit heavier at the start of the week. I knew it was a mental thing, but it had not changed in the years I'd worked here.

It was a little different today, however.

"Hrm... 'Tis truly heavy today..."

I pushed with both hands, but it still did not open. Was someone pushing on the other side?

"Oy, Vania! You've done something again, haven't you?! You don't want me to see, so you're pressing against the door, aren't you?!"

"No! Please, please don't blame me for this! I haven't taken part in this at all!" Vania was pleading false charges.

"Then why does this door not open?!"

"Oh, I'm sorry. It's caught on a shelf."

A shelf? Did we have a shelf in front of the door?

"I moved it, so it's all right now. Come in."

I once again pushed against the door, and it opened easily this time.

But this was not the office I recognized—there were several shelves placed throughout the room. On each separate area sat little glass containers.

Plenty had dirt or rocks in them, so I wondered if they were sets for raising insects. None were lidded, so it must have been for something else.

"What is this, Fatla? Hell's bells, what on earth...?"

I rarely found myself so completely clueless. What was she putting on display?

"Decorative indoor plants," Fatla said, as though I should not have even asked.

"What? What about these things are plants...? All these containers are very cute, but they are full of dirt and stones..."

"Can't you see? They all contain moss."

When she said that, I finally understood the purpose of the containers.

There was moss!

Moss in the dirt!

Moss on the rocks!

Moss in the artificial beach in the container!

"Wait, wait! This isn't it... This is moss, not decorative—"

"Do you mean to say moss is not an indoor plant? I am afraid you are incorrect," Fatla replied with unusual firmness. She was not spoiling for a fight, but she was upset that I disapproved of her moss.

Then I recalled how uneasy Vania had looked last week.

"Um, boss... Sis likes to collect and cultivate moss...," Vania said, exhausted.

I see she had been forced to help with the shelves.

In the meantime, Fatla pointed to the container of moss right in front of me.

"Lady Beelzebub, please look inside. Moss is so small, but upon closer inspection, you can see it has leaves. Cute, is it not? It's like a miniature. Each individual glass container is its own pocket garden."

"Well, cuteness is in the eye of the beholder..."

I could say there was something fashionably modern about putting dirt or rocks into a little container and growing moss in it. And a little feminine, I suppose.

If I were to place one on my desk, the simple decorative pocket garden might even relieve some of my tension.

However—

"There are too many of them! The whole space at the front of the room is filled with shelves! What is this, a moss shop?!"

"We would need at least this many to bring life to this dreary room."

Fatla was holding something—was that a mist bottle?

With a quick spritz, she watered the moss in the container.

The green of the shriveled moss appeared to brighten up.

"Oh! You gave it a little more life, didn't you?"

"Indeed. The moss waits patiently until it receives water. And then once it does, it flourishes. Are you not proud of them? Are they not adorable?"

"Everything comes back to the cuteness factor..."

Fatla retrieved something else that looked like a round piece of glass.

"You can see the moss up close with this. You'll be fascinated by what you can observe. Here, Lady Beelzebub. Give it a go."

I didn't exactly have the option to refuse, so I examined the moss with it.

"Oh! Up close, I can see the tiny leaves. 'Tis indeed a plant!"

"Of course. A world too small for us to know is still filled with life.

©Benio

Within this little garden, there might even be nations inhabited by the tiniest creatures. Does it not fill your heart with wonder?"

Fatla's eyes were full of life, too, gleaming even brighter than the freshly misted moss.

She took this very seriously...

Fatla was the type to rarely speak of her own hobbies, but now I knew what she liked. I saw a new side to one of my staff today. One will always make new discoveries.

"But do you not think this much moss would get in the way of—?"

"With all due respect, we cannot say that for sure."

The look on Fatla's face told me that she would firmly fight me on this.

"...Indeed. Our desks are not being overwhelmed, so I suppose it will be fine like this."

"Thank you." Fatla bowed politely.

She certainly was stubborn when it came to moss. I suppose everyone has a "thing"...

◇

And so the minister's office had been reborn into a green environment.

It did not take long for others around the building to start secretly calling us the moss office.

Hrm, well, I suppose I don't mind... There was enough greenery around us that it was almost off-putting, but seeing it every day did start to give me a greater sense of attachment.

Now and again, Fatla would spritz the moss with her mist bottle, but it did not hinder her work.

The one problem was that the only space to walk was between the shelves; reaching the corridor from my desk was rather troublesome, but it was not so bad that I could not bear with it.

"Boss, I decided to raise some moss myself!" After a little while, Vania decided to put a little moss garden on her desk as well.

"Aye, 'tis not a bad thing to raise another creature yourself. It will not immediately perish if you forget to feed it, so I feel it is perfectly suited for you."

"You're making fun of me, aren't you?"

"I would not dream of it."

Even I started to consider raising some moss myself.

After several days of rain, I arrived at work feeling as though the room had been rearranged. The shelves of moss were between the desk and door as they always had been; nothing in particular had changed.

I doubt I would notice if all the little containers were flipped around; I did not think it was such a small change as that.

"Fatla. The room feels somewhat different than usual today. Have you done anything to it?"

"No, I haven't touched anything."

Fatla was not the type to lie, and if she had added another container of moss after all this time, she had no reason to hide it.

"Oh, I thought something was a little different today, too. I don't know—I feel way more relaxed than I usually am." It seemed Vania thought the same.

"Are you certain you are not simply being influenced by my comments?"

"Of course not! I thought of it myself! There is definitely something new about the room today!" she said with confidence.

"Then why is it you feel something is new about it?"

"I don't know!"

Why do you sound so confident?

But it was true, then, that the room had changed. I could feel it in my bones. Then again, we had not changed the carpet, nor had we painted the walls.

And then there was another thing to add to the list of oddities.

"I am working at such a terrible pace today..."

I had been working as normal, but I was much less efficient about it.

"You too, Lady Beelzebub? My work is going quite slow as well." Fatla seemed a bit troubled. "I feel far more relaxed than I am willing to be—suddenly, I come to my senses and realize I've been resting. I am having trouble buckling down to work."

"How strange. Hmm, wait a moment..." A terrible possibility came to mind. "Is any of the moss in this room poisonous?"

"Impossible," Fatla replied readily. "Some may be harmful to eat, but cultivating moss will never create poisonous gases. And I have heard that a good majority of the moss are too unappetizing to eat. You never hear about them being used in cooking, do you?"

"Now that you mention it..."

Perhaps I was overthinking it? Still, there *was* something wrong with this room.

Broadly speaking, it felt like it was almost too bright in here. So much brighter and more colorful than the green of the moss.

Due to Fatla's and my malaise, Vania's desk was piled high with documents. It almost resembled what our desks looked like after a vacation.

"Come now, Vania, get it together."

"Boss, I'm way less effective today, too... Whenever I try to work, I lose all my motivation."

"Are you sure you are not simply being careless?!"

Right at that moment, something fell onto Vania's documents.

"Vania, your papers... They're emerald-green!"

Yes, there was something fuzzy on them, a truly beautiful and brilliant green.

"Hmm? I've never seen moss like this before~ Sis, what kind is this?" Vania showed the paper to Fatla.

At that moment, a look of panic spread across Fatla's face. A rare sight indeed.

She opened her mouth, and her voice quavered.

"That is not moss. That's mold!"

Oh no...

I slowly turned my gaze up toward the ceiling.

The whole surface was covered in emerald-green fuzz!

Then I heard the sound of the rain drizzling outside.

"The humidity! Not only have we saturated this room for the moss, but the rain dampened the area even more! 'Twas perfect for mold!"

"…I may be mistaken, but I believe this is the laziness-and-lethargy mold. Its spores affect a creature's mental capacity and takes away their desire to work. We should not be breathing in this air…"

I pressed my hand against my mouth and stood up.

"Everyone, out of this room immediately! Before you lose all motivation!"

But Vania had already planted her face onto her desk and was snoring soundly. She had put her face too close to the paper when the clump of mold fell on it!

I pinched Vania's face.

"Stay awake! If you fall asleep, you may never wake up again!"

"Mmmm… Don't wanna work…"

"Lady Beelzebub, let us leave Vania for now and get out of here! We can save her later!"

But when we made our way to the door, Fatla made such a ruckus as she walked. "I can hardly move. These shelves are in the way!"

Never block the passageway to the exit—you'll regret it in an emergency!

"Who put these here?!" she cried.

"You did! You clearly did!"

In the end, we were forbidden from using the minister's office until the mold was cleared away—and all the moss shelves had been removed from the revitalized room.

As I gazed at the refreshingly dreary room, I murmured, "Safety over decorations…"

I would make sure we did not place anything that blocked the evacuation route…

"Indeed. I will settle for just one thing on my desk."

One of Fatla's proud moss pocket-gardens sat on her desk. Perhaps that was the perfect amount of decor for a room like this.

It was one of my days off.

Holding hands, Her Majesty and I walked through a human village.

The market was especially interesting; what the humans had on sale was completely different from what we sold in the demon lands. That difference was partially due to culture, yes, but also the climate. The indigenous plants and animals were nothing like what I knew.

But I didn't mind that so much—at least, not compared with my holding hands with a certain someone.

"Ah, Your Majesty?" I whispered.

I didn't want others to hear she was royalty, much less the demon king. There were more and more demons visiting the human lands recently, so the humans wouldn't be as terrified as they would have been back when I first became the minister of agriculture. Yet the name of the demon king still had a lot of impact.

I doubted any humans would even believe she was the demon king.

"Yes, what is it, Miss Beelzebub?"

"Is it all right if we let go of our hands now?"

"Awww, of course not. You can't have me getting swept away in the crowd," said the demon king, wearing a hood to hide her horns.

I was also wearing a hood as my basic disguise. My horns were so long that the hood was sticking up in a decidedly unnatural fashion, but it was better than nothing.

"Still, I am off duty today, so strictly speaking, it is not within my realm of responsibility to look after you, Your Majesty. If you are worried about getting lost, then you may as well stay in the castle."

But I couldn't just leave the demon king alone, so my protests were ultimately empty.

"Gosh! Don't say things like that!" Her Majesty tugged on my hand, dragging me in a different direction.

"Fine, fine. There was a nice café over that way, so let's go there. Do be a proper escort, please."

"I still have things I would like to see."

"Please allow the young girl's opinion to take priority."

"I am biologically female as well, might I remind you."

She answered with an especially insistent tug not even I could resist, and we escaped the flow of people.

"*Sigh*, you still have no idea of the proper way to treat me, Miss Beelzebub. On a scale of one to ten, you'd be a three," Her Majesty complained over tea.

"But conversely, this means you trust me enough to give your honest opinion of me. This is the highest honor."

"My, but how eloquent you are. You really have grown into your position as a minister."

She was looking at me reproachfully, but this was no different from usual. It would be even more worrying if she never felt like she could say anything.

"You've been there nearly two full centuries now, alas. You are getting strangely good at it. It was much more interesting when you were new."

"Yes. We've been in office for the same amount of time, Your Majesty. Your general reputation is that you've gotten rather good at your job, too."

We drank tea as we conversed.

Human tea was rather weak. Personally, I would prefer something just a tad spicier, but one of the rules of a seasoned traveler was to accept the flavors of the destination.

"I had planned to mold you into the absolutely perfect elder sister for me after holding the position of agricultural minister for so long. I failed in your training."

I brought the teacup to my mouth, feigning ignorance.

We'd had this conversation dozens of times now, perhaps even hundreds.

"I would rather not take on a leadership role relative to you. I know that your goal with someone like that is to have them wrapped around your finger."

"That's not it at all~ And I mean it! You can't refuse because you would find it a nuisance if you were at my whims! An elder sister must be on her feet at all times caring for her little sister, but also strict when circumstances call for it. And the little sister is to be inspired by her elder sister. Doesn't a spiritual pseudosistership like that sound lovely?!"

"I believe I've told you this many times now, but I don't understand it at all. I am simply thankful that you brought me up into the position of agricultural minister. You also gained another close adviser, so I believe this is a win-win."

"You wouldn't know romance if it bit you on the nose, would you, Miss Beelzebub?"

"Indeed. One who spends her holidays drinking and lazing about alone hardly has the chance to become familiar with the concept."

I had started gaining much more out of life once I'd become minister, compared with my stint as a bottom-tier bureaucrat.

I had established my power as the agricultural minister, and the demon king was the same. It would not be an exaggeration to say this was the most the demon world had developed in history. We were much more advanced than any human nation.

And if I didn't end up at the beck and call of my ruler, even better...

"I planned to use as my close adviser someone who wasn't on the career track, like you are, and I succeeded—but your individual development has gone way beyond what I was expecting. I cannot have my way."

"Cannot have your way? Well, neither can I, since I've had to make time for you on one of my few days off. Traveling is one of my hobbies, and I would love to have the chance to fully enjoy it."

"I cannot have this anymore." Her Majesty abruptly stood from her chair.

Then she finished the rest of the tea in her cup before slowly placing it back on the table.

"Today, you will be acting entirely as my escort! First, you will accompany me on my shopping!"

I placed my elbows on the table, knowing full well it was rude. "Shopping, Your Majesty? You don't have anything you want, do you?"

"So what if I don't? I specifically mean the act of shopping itself. You have no feminine sensibilities when it comes to these things, my dear Beelzebub."

"That is what I'm saying—if you want someone to act as your elder sister and indulge these interests of yours, then please look elsewhere. Or more precisely—" I stared hard at Her Majesty's face. "You would hate it if I were inclined to stick so closely to you, no?"

"Yes," Her Majesty said, grinning. "There is no point if she doesn't disobey me. I look at people who do nothing but follow me all the time, every day!"

Which meant she wanted to have someone like that wrapped around her finger.

This is complicated... Much too complicated...

I stood wearily. "Then why don't we cool down in a different town?"

"Indeed. There are too many people here."

Her Majesty leisurely left the shop. I, obviously, paid the bill.

Afterward, we entered a forest we did not know the name of.

I did wonder why we had taken this route, but Her Majesty said there were beautiful flowers growing in the area, so we went.

Once we had grown tired of walking, we found a small mountain hut nearby, so we decided to rest there for a little.

Living there were two twin girls, young enough to be considered toddlers.

The older of the two was bright and cheery, and the younger one spent all her time reading books.

Their personalities were so different; were they faring all right?

"Do you not have parents? It must be rough on your own."

"Hmm, I guess you could say we do have a mommy...," the cheerier of the two girls answered hesitantly.

Perhaps I asked a question I shouldn't have?

"I will defeat Mother... Our mortal enemy...," growled the bookworm.

Their home environment was much more complicated than I had thought it was...

"What are you two walking around in the forest for?"

That was a reasonable question. Only hunters ever had business out here.

"A date," joked Her Majesty. "We're on a date."

I made sure I didn't give her a reaction. "This girl is important, but she has been clinging to me for some time now. This is my day off, yet she's assigned me to a big job."

The girls didn't really ask any more than that. My explanation wasn't too detailed for the children, so it was perfect.

"I thought we should take a detour and walk somewhere quiet."

"In that case," the girl who was reading suddenly spoke up, "if you keep going straight for a while, you'll find a highland. I think it's a nice spot, but there's a terrible, evil entity that controls everything from the shadows."

An evil entity controlling everything? That's an interesting thing to say to the demon king.

But Her Majesty seemed to like that. "Thank you. Then we will visit the highlands."

We thanked the two girls, then headed off.

"It sounds rather far. How are we going to get there?"

"Pull me up and fly, Miss Beelzebub. Can you do that?"

"...I would get tired, but it's not impossible."

I braced myself for a future backache as I grabbed Her Majesty and flew off.

The towns and villages dotting the highlands had much cleaner air than Vanzeld Castle.

And perhaps because of the dry climate, my skin wasn't sticky. The buildings formed neat, aesthetically pleasing rows, too.

Her Majesty did no shopping in the end and instead gleefully walked along the streets.

When we were holding hands, I often felt like I was dragging Her Majesty along with my longer strides, but she apparently didn't find much fault with it. I didn't understand her values.

On the other hand, she was disappointed with something else.

"There's too little entertainment around here."

Her Majesty sat on a low wall, her head tilted.

There weren't a lot of people in this village, so they only had the minimum shops needed for survival.

Minstrels would never step foot in a place like this. I doubted there would be any evil entities here to begin with—only bored adventurers.

"I suppose this is how it is with a low population. The town around the castle is densely populated, and because of that, we have plenty of different kinds of shops."

"Hmm, so our hometown is ultimately the best. I'm a little sad to think that's the lesson we've learned..."

Then a crowd started gathering before us. Maybe some kind of celebrity had come by.

In the middle of the crowd was a young girl wearing a black pointed hat. But despite her age, she had a dignity, a sophistication about her that suggested she was more than she appeared.

"Ah, she's the same type of person as us," Her Majesty said.

The villagers were calling her "the great Witch of the Highlands."

"I see. A long-lived witch has made this her territory. Perhaps she is our mysterious 'evil entity.'"

A small handful of witches had gained methods for immortality and lived for a long time; this witch must have been one of them.

Some witches were not so trustworthy; calling them *evil* wasn't entirely off the mark.

In that case, I understood why villagers who looked much older than her treated her with reverence.

The witch was selling medicine to the villagers, as her kind often did.

There likely weren't any thick woods in the highlands, so it seemed somewhat inconvenient to specialize in making medicine, but she must have her reasons.

Finally, the villagers who were talking to the witch left.

Once there were fewer people around, the witch turned to face us. Of course she noticed two strangers in the small village, especially since we weren't wandering adventurers.

"Are you two travelers? There's nothing to see here, but it's not a bad place to stay. Feel free to relax here."

"Indeed. That is exactly what we were doing. We are of a long-lived race, so we can live a hundred human lifetimes within our own."

It wasn't *exactly* a hundred, but I just decided to give a simple answer.

"I see. I've been alive for a little over two hundred and fifty years, too. I sell medicine, but I get most of my money by killing slimes."

"You live a rather idle lifestyle if you get money from killing slimes..."

I'd never really heard of such a laid-back witch.

"My past is a little complicated. I died after working too hard, so now I'm just doing what I can at my own pace. But maybe it wouldn't be bad to go traveling around like you two once in a while." The witch approached us. "Especially you—you look so small, but you're out here traveling! Good for you. If only I had a little sister like you, I think she'd make a great addition to my laid-back life."

The witch placed her hand on Her Majesty's hood.

"Good girl."

In that moment, with incredible force, Her Majesty stepped away to put distance between them.

"Wh-what is it?!"

I looked at Her Majesty to find her expression frozen and tense, as if she had just met someone she wasn't supposed to meet.

"Is it true she is the evil entity...?" Her Majesty's attitude wasn't normal.

Yet the witch seemed entirely relaxed; she didn't seem interested in harming us.

"What's wrong? Don't tell me that touching your head is an insult or anything? I'm sorry if it was."

"No, nothing like that..."

"Oh phew. I'm glad~" The girl placed her hand in my hood to pat my head. "You have long horns, don't you? Are you a kind of beast-person?"

I could feel every hair on my body standing on end, and I immediately stepped back to create distance.

"Who *are* you...? I felt something terrible..."

This woman had strength she wasn't fully able to hide—the kind that only high-level demons had!

I wasn't entirely sure of the reason, but after Her Majesty's reaction, I could tell this wasn't trivial!

"Huh? What? I don't have any hidden power or anything—I just make my living killing slimes! I'm just a witch who's lived a long time!"

I couldn't detect any dishonesty in her words, but she was powerful enough to do anything she wanted.

We could not afford to let our guard down.

"Witch, if there is nothing evil about you, then we will be leaving this village now, so don't pursue us, all right? With that, I would like to verify you have no ill intent about you."

"O-oh... That's fine... I have no reason to chase you... I don't know—something feels off here, but I won't go after you. I get the sense my laid-back life might become a thing of the past if I get too involved with you. I try to live life avoiding trouble anyway."

"I see. Well, that way of thinking isn't wrong."

Her Majesty was staring unnervingly at the witch the entire time.

Her Majesty was still frightened, but I took her by the hand and led her out of the village. Her instinctive wariness eventually disappeared.

"Are you all right, Your Majesty?"

"Yes, I'm calm now."

Once we came to the center of the wide-open highland, Her Majesty plopped down on the grass and placed her own hand on her head.

"When she patted me, I felt so strange. I was actually shivering with terror... But my heart is still beating fast, even though the trembling is gone..."

"Oh, someone patting you on the head is unthinkable, Your Majesty. You must have been surprised by such an unfamiliar experience."

"Hmm, I don't think that's quite it, but it's hard to put into words." She was speaking calmly, but her behavior wasn't normal. She was typically smiling in most situations, but she was not smiling now.

At that moment, I sensed several hostile people around us. Our guards were already up after encountering that witch, but this time, we noticed a number of demons flying ahead. We called them hawk-men or bird-people.

There were five in all.

I didn't see the witch anywhere. But although there were five of them, I didn't expect them to pose much of a threat.

"Demon King Provato Pecora Ariés! Your life is ours!"

They were holding swords and spears. I guess they had been watching us from above.

"Let me ask you, you wicked fiends, is there a witch among your ranks?!" I cried.

It was apparently an unexpected question, because one of the hawk-men wrinkled his nose. "What? No! We are only demons! We will change the current demon king's lenient policy!"

"I see, I see. That is a relief."

I promptly cast a spell, and two of the ones in front of me froze over.

By the time I was finished, Her Majesty had already buried the other three into the earth.

I didn't exactly see what had happened, but I was sure the enemy didn't, either.

"Well, that's that."

Her Majesty clapped her hands together.

"And so my strategy to lure out the assassins has been a success. ♪ Thank you, Miss Beelzebub."

"There would not have been any problem to begin with had you stayed protected inside the castle," I said, exasperated. "Even if it did mean you couldn't lure them out."

That being said, my mind was at ease. After all, in the time that I had defeated two of them, Her Majesty had taken care of three. Her Majesty wasn't so weak that she needed my protection.

"I'm sure I've told you it's terribly boring to stay inside the castle all the time. That is why I decided to go with you on your travels. We can also lure out assassins like this, so it's two birds with one stone."

"And it turns my holidays into more workdays."

Her Majesty threaded her arm through mine. "But you get to be with me. Please consider it a bonus instead."

When I saw Her Majesty smiling in high spirits, a part of me gave up—she would be toying with me a lot from here on out, wouldn't she?

"I don't think I would go so far to think of it as a bonus, but I will consider it evened out."

"Fantastic. I will allow that, then."

I had fun working as agricultural minister, but I could do with fewer threats on my life.

"I see there are plenty of those who don't like my way of doing things, but I think it's about time we annihilate them all."

"I am not sure if that perception of them is the right approach. But the first fifty years of your rule had the most assassination attempts, with the next fifty only having a third of that, and now it is relatively peaceful."

Her Majesty stood before me and grasped my hand. "Even if you can't act as my elder sister, I would hope that you continue to support me as a political partner."

"Yes. Beelzebub is your greatest servant, Your Majesty," I replied to the one who decided my fate.

"Um, is there something on my face…?"

Laika was looking at me dubiously.

Of course she was; I was staring at her quite intensely.

"Oh, it just came back to me—I feel like I sparred with you once a long time ago. I often went to the hot springs at Mount Rokko, and I wonder if we didn't…"

"I have been training since I was little, but my memories from back then are not so clear."

Laika seemed to have trouble remembering, but little would change if she did.

"Perhaps you might learn if you ask your parents about the demon pillow-war incident. Although...I would rather leave that incident buried, actually, so on second thought, there's no need..."

I got a sound beating from the ministerial meeting after that... I shall just let it lie...

"I can't even remember what I ate three days ago~," Vania offered.

"That is a problem," Fatla snapped back at her.

Today, I had brought my two subordinates to eat at the house in the highlands.

Azusa said we were pushing it, but holidays like these weren't all that bad. We typically worked hard, you see.

"Miss Beelzebub, thank you for buying me another book." Shalsha bowed politely to me.

Falfa followed suit. "The math book was really interesting!" she said with a smile.

"Of course, I have plenty more books at home if you want to visit. I am a high-level demon, after all. I have lots of space in my manor~"

"Hey, hey, hey! You can't just adopt my girls!" Azusa put her foot down.

My strategy to adopt them amid the confusion never seems to succeed.

"To be honest, I suspect I may have I met the two of them before you did. I feel as though I once visited a small hut in a forest."

"You have no proof of that, and there's nothing stopping you from making up whatever story you want. Honestly, they're from a completely unremarkable and ordinary forest. There's no reason to go there."

"But fate has a way of bringing people together. Actually, I do believe our paths crossed once, as well. It might have been thirty-five years ago—no, perhaps even longer..."

"You mean we ran into each other? I don't remember anything. Word hadn't gotten around back then that I was strong."

It did not seem that Azusa remembered anything.

I was much the same. I only had a faint inkling that we'd met. "I remember that I once came to Flatta, but I have traveled round the entire country, so I cannot say exactly when that was."

"Hmm. I know you like traveling, but why would anyone come to Flatta…? Well, we'll never know what happened in the past, so we should concentrate more on the present and the future."

"Those clear-cut solutions are much like you." Impressed, I took a sip of my drink.

"Yes. The future is much more important than the past," Fatla agreed. "Personally, so long as you take your duties as agricultural minister seriously, Lady Beelzebub, I am perfectly fine with that."

She was alluding to how I didn't do my job properly long ago.

"But Beelzebub, you've had that high-and-mighty attitude ever since you were a baby, right? You were born a noble and lived your whole life with that incredible ego, didn't you?"

I wanted to tell Azusa to let go of her assumptions, but I decided not to say anything.

"Vania, at least, has been scatterbrained since the day she was born."

"What?! Why is that a reason to insult *me*?!" Vania protested her older sister's surprise attack.

"Your first word was *whoops*."

"No, that can't be! Don't make these things up! I've never heard about this!"

"I cannot verify Fatla's story," I said, "but Vania's scattered brain is undeniably true."

"Please give me a break, Boss!"

Here, as her boss, I had to help cover Fatla.

"*Sigh*, you sure are close. Especially for a boss and people working under her," Azusa said with a hint of envy. "I wish I'd had an understanding boss, too. That's the past, too, but I just can't help thinking about it, you know?"

"Indeed. If the boss herself has a desire to improve, her subordinates also change the way they are." Fatla glanced briefly at me. "It's all right if she's incompetent to begin with. But once she becomes aware of her shortcomings, that is when she can begin to grow and improve. Life is long, after all."

"You sure are talkative today, Fatla."

"I have no ulterior motives. I am simply speaking generally." A ghost of a smile crossed Fatla's face.

Silently and to myself, I said to her, *Thank you.*

There have been a lot of detours, and I had been bumped up to a position I never imagined I would have...

But on the whole? I'm happy.

"Oh, whoops," Vania blurted out.

"All right, Vania, tell me what it is. I'll get mad."

"Wait, aren't you supposed to say you *won't* get mad...?"

"Just say it..."

"I forgot to turn in the documents that were due yesterday..."

I stood up and gave Vania a noogie to the side of her head.

"Ow, ouch! This is workplace violence!"

"No need to worry. We are not in the workplace!"

My road ahead as the agricultural minister wasn't going to be a smooth one, it seemed...

THE END

©Benio

Hello, nice to meet you. I'm Kisetsu Morita!

—But I suppose there will be a lot of you whom I'm not meeting for the first time. If you're not a first-timer, then long time no see—this is Morita.

This book, *Bottom-Tier Bureaucrat* (which is my name for it because the title is so long), is a spin-off of *I've Been Killing Slimes* (which also has a long name, so I keep it short). The original novel series, *I've Been Killing Slimes*, has ten total volumes so far released by GA Bunko, and the comic adaptation, drawn by Yusuke Shiba, has five volumes on sale from Square Enix! For those who want to know what'll happen next, you can check it out on Shousetsuka ni Narou, so please take a look!

Now then, as you may have been able to tell from the cover, this book is about the demon minister of agriculture, Beelzebub, who appears in *I've Been Killing Slimes*.

Bottom-Tier Bureaucrat was originally serialized in *GanGan GA*, and thankfully, many people read it. Not only have I been able to add a great many new chapters to her story, but we have now been able to publish an entire stand-alone novel! I truly, truly thank you all!

Among the new chapters, we have Beelzebub's parents appearing, and Beelzebub has some intimate moments with Pecora. Beelzebub's parents, especially, are a type of character that have never shown up in the original *I've Been Killing Slimes*, so they were a lot of fun to write!

There are also a great many new illustrations added by Benio, so please enjoy them all together!

Also, Volume 1 of the comic adaptation of *Bottom-Tier Bureaucrat* by Meishi Murakami will go on sale at the same time this book comes out! Please check that out, too!

Murakami has beautifully portrayed Vania's spacey moments, that look on demon king Pecora's face when she's plotting something, and other things I couldn't fully describe in words in this adaptation. I honestly recommend it!

Also, Volume 5 of the comic version of *I've Been Killing Slimes* will be going on sale at the same time, too! Beelzebub is also on the cover of that one, so it's a whole Beelzebub party out there!

Which means three total volumes related to the *I've Been Killing Slimes* series will be coming out this month. Nothing would make me happier as the author than if the world of this series grows bigger and bigger. Just like how slimes multiply.

Well, since I have the space, I may as well talk about why I ended up writing a Beelzebub spin-off in the first place.

First, *GanGan GA*, which is serializing the comic adaptation, asked me if I would write some sort of short story for the same world. So then I decided to write a story about Beelzebub, since she is my favorite character in *I've Been Killing Slimes* (I know this started off sounding like it would be a long story, but it really wasn't).

One other reason was that Beelzebub was the only one of the main cast who lived apart from the rest of the group, so I thought it might be easier to write about her. But the biggest reason was definitely that I like Beelzebub.

*   *   *

Also, there are other spin-offs, like the Halkara side story, "Food for an Elf," and the Laika side story, "The Red-Dragon Academy for Girls."

For some reason (since they're short stories), both are available to read on the smartphone manga app Manga UP! Also, the Halkara side stories are included in Volumes 8 to 10 of the original series, with two chapters in each.

I hope you keep an eye out for more spin-offs!

I also hope to see you in Volume 11 of *I've Been Killing Slimes*. That will be hitting shelves in December!

Finally, my thank-yous. Thank you so much to Benio, who has done the illustrations for this and *I've Been Killing Slimes*! I am so happy we got to see new sides of not just Beelzebub but of the leviathan sisters, too!

Additionally, I want to thank all of you who have supported both the spin-off and the original series! It's because of your support that we've gotten to publish a stand-alone novel! Please keep reading the main series and the spin-offs!

An addendum:

Starting on the next page is a bonus chapter. I hope you enjoy it.

The last chapter of this spin-off novel takes place mostly in the past from the perspective of Azusa, the main character of *I've Been Killing Slimes*, but the bonus chapter occurs in the present.

I hope to see you somewhere again soon!

The guy who orders at the only fancy ramen shop by the local station only to find it's Jiro-style,

Kisetsu Morita

When I arrived at work, Vania was looking at something with great joy.

It was a large book. I knew Fatla was a reader, but I rarely ever saw Vania very interested in them.

At the moment, though, Fatla was staring lovingly at her little moss garden. That was unusual enough already, but there was no need for me to disparage others' hobbies.

Was Vania studying? Oh, it did not seem to be a very serious book. She was smiling too much for it to be serious.

"What in the world are you reading, Vania? —No, I suppose you are simply looking at something, hmm?"

I peeked at it from the side to see the pages filled with pictures. It appeared to be some sort of art collection.

"This is so fascinating! I suppose everyone has a history, don't they~?"

"What is it, then? Show me."

But Vania slammed the book shut. "Uh, I don't think it's a good idea for you to look, boss…"

"You worry too much! And after that reaction, I could hardly pretend I never saw it!"

"No, no, this is for your own sake! I might lie sometimes, but I'm being serious right now!" Vania insisted as she pressed the book against her chest.

She would refuse to show me, no matter what.

"I see, I see, so this is for my sake, hmm? I am happy to hear that."

"I'm really glad you understa—"

I snatched the book from her.

"Hey! You tricked me!"

"You just said that you lie, even when you are telling the truth! I can no longer trust you! I will be checking for myself!"

I doubted it would be all that horrible. Not even Vania would open a book of such serious content in this room, nor would she look at it with such glee.

I opened it, and—

—there was a portrait of me when I was a bottom-tier bureaucrat.

My expression was so pathetic. I seemed bored, perhaps because of how little pressure there was in my position. And then there were those glasses I wore back then. The image screamed *low-level civil servant*.

"Rrrgh…"

"O-ohhh… Boss is so shocked and angry that she doesn't know how to react!"

Indeed—I had no idea how to respond to this.

"What an idiot you are, Vania. Did I not tell you to make sure that stayed hidden? I am keeping out of this."

Fatla's tone suggested this was all on Vania, but what she said told me that she most certainly knew something.

I flipped to another page and found several lackluster portraits of me from when I lived in the countryside.

Why was this book full to bursting with my disgrace?!

I immediately put the screws on Vania.

"Tell me where you got this. Tell me now, and I'll go easy on you."

"You're scaring me, boss, you're scaring me…!"

There was no question that this book was appalling, but it was still strange that Vania had something like this.

My answer then came from Fatla behind me. "The original came from your parents."

"Aha! Of course, it had to be them! I cannot believe them!"

My parents had paid an artist for all these commemorative portraits.

The further I went back, the older the portraits got, and some had notes written by them like *First Day of School*.

However, I looked bored in every image... Did my past self truly live in ennui for such a long time...?

"I see the gist of it. My parents made copies of all my past portraits, put them into a book, and sent them here... The nerve!"

They must have hoped to give their daughter a nice little surprise, but I wished they could see things from my perspective.

But there was something else that angered me on a different level.

"This should have been addressed to me. You may be my secretaries, but it is not something for you to open and look at first."

Mail addressed to the minister of agriculture directly could be a petition or a threatening letter, but there was a specific person within the ministry who was responsible for checking for that. Of course, that job fell within their normal scope of duty.

However, things addressed to me were still for me to open and read first if they did indeed make it all the way to our office. The secretaries should not read them first—this was not a question of hierarchical relationships within the workplace. It was a moral question of opening someone else's mail without their permission.

"This is an obvious thing, Vania—can you not even do that? I am disappointed, to be honest. This will affect your assessments."

"Wait, please! Please don't tell me you're disappointed without hearing what happened first! We would never look at any mail addressed to you without permission!"

So she was going to make excuses, was she? She had better give a good reason.

"Oh? So then why were you looking at these horrid records?"

My parents had sent letters to the ministry before, so that was the only connection I could make.

But then the door clicked open.

"Greetings, everyone. ♪" The demon king walked in without knocking.

Argh!

It was the one person I did *not* want to see right now.

She would most certainly laugh at me if she saw such a dangerous item from the past! Actually—if all she did was laugh, I should count myself lucky. She would use this against me!

I immediately threw the portrait collection of my dark past into a drawer.

"Your Majesty, why have you come all the way to our ministry yourself...?"

I had to make sure she never found out, no matter what.

"Hmm~ I think it's best if you don't hear this, Miss Beelzebub~" she said with an innocent smile (and clearly malevolent intentions).

"I have no choice but to listen if you put it like that!"

"But it's about your old portraits."

"You already knew?!"

Of course she would... Someone of my caliber could not keep something like that hidden from her...

"I don't just know; *I* was the one who requested a copy of your portraits from your parents in the first place~ ♪" The demon king beamed.

And that was when all the mystery was dispelled. Vania was not lying.

Meaning Her Majesty had negotiated with my parents to obtain the book in the first place...

"You parents so kindly and willingly agreed~ ♪"

I stood frozen in place, not sure how to let off my anger...

I would have destroyed them if they were not my parents...

What have they done?!

My quick temper would only harm me, however. Right now, I had to remedy this situation.

If I did not quickly throw the portrait book in a fire, the demon king would use it for even further evil.

If she showed it to Azusa and the others at the house in the highlands, I would never recover. The image I had so carefully cultivated would crumble! I could never let that happen!

"Uh, um~ Your Majesty, it has been quite a long time since I got to indulge in my memories, so would you mind if I borrowed it for a little longer...? I'd love to reminisce next to a warm fire."

"Of course~ Indulge away! ♪"

Yes, here was my chance. She may be the demon king, but they were still pictures of *me*. I doubt she could ask for them back right away.

"Oh, I requested ten books, since I was having them made anyway. I'm happy to give you one."

She was one step ahead!

Things were looking bad for me, so once I was done with work that day, I went to visit the demon king.

I knew what I was going to ask.

As soon as I was admitted, I flung myself to the ground. "Please burn all the books!"

"Aww, but I was thinking about taking them to the highlands and looking at the pictures with Elder Sister Azusa and the others~" Her Majesty, sitting on one of her guest couches, was really hamming this up.

That was exactly what I was afraid of!

"No, please, anything but that... They know not how I was in the past..."

"It just means you've grown since your promotion. Wonderful, isn't it? I want them to see how far you've come~"

"I know you are spinning it in a positive light, but what you are trying to do is expose my dark past!"

Think, Beelzebub, think!

Pleading wholeheartedly would do nothing. I had to convince her that my past didn't matter.

"See, Your Majesty—is Azusa, the Witch of the Highlands, not your current candidate for older sister?"

Her Majesty tapped her finger on her lips, thinking for a moment before responding, "Yes, that would make her Elder Sister Azusa."

"Then that means I have graduated from being your elder sister! You no longer need ways to toy with me anymore!"

Indeed, I no longer had to play big sister to the demon king anymore.

That was now Azusa's job. She had taken on the very sisterly role of defeating the demon king when they fought, and she even scolded her when it was necessary.

But then an impish smile crossed Her Majesty's face, she shot up from her chair...

...and placed one hand on my shoulder.

"Elder Sister."

"No, I am no longer your—"

"One can have multiple elder sisters."

So that was her angle!

"I hope you keep up your good work as my second sister, Miss Beelzebub. ♪"

I nodded weakly. "A-all right..."

I was doomed to remain in the demon king's evil clutches in the end...

"Well, since you won't be able to quit your role as my sister, I suppose I won't take this book to the house in the highlands."

My despair turned to joy.

"R-really?!"

"Yes. I would rather not betray my elder sister too much."

That meant she would only betray me sometimes, but I would trust that everything would work out for the best.

After having tea in Her Majesty's room, I excused myself, relieved that she would not spread word of my embarrassing past around.

She was truly a kind person deep down.

......

....

I stopped in my tracks.

"Wait... This means she will always have a card to threaten me with..."

Now that I thought more about it, I had solved nothing!

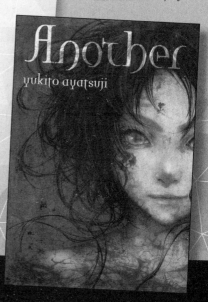